Hispanic Hagiography in the Critical Context of the Reformation

HAGIOLOGIA

Études sur la sainteté et l'hagiographie – Studies on Sanctity and Hagiography

Volume 19

Comité de Rédaction – Editorial Board

HAGIOLOGIA

Anne-Marie Helvétius   Gordon Blennemann   Philippe Castagnetti
Stefanos Efthymiadis   Stéphane Gioanni

BREPOLS PUBLISHERS

2022

Hispanic Hagiography in the Critical Context of the Reformation

Edited by
Fernando Baños Vallejo

BREPOLS

The studies of this book have been developed within the framework of the research project *La hagiografía hispánica ante la Reforma protestante* (FFI2017-86248-P) funded by the Government of Spain.

© 2022, Brepols Publishers n. v., Turnhout, Belgium.

All rights reserved. No part of this publication may be reproduced, stored in a retrieval system, or transmitted, in any form or by any means, electronic, mechanical, photocopying, recording, or otherwise without the prior permission of the publisher.

D/2022/0095/231
ISBN 978-2-503-60212-7
E-ISBN 978-2-503-60213-4
ISSN 1378-1006
E-ISSN 2565-9553
DOI 10.1484/M.HAG-EB.5.131280

Printed in the EU on acid-free paper.

Table of Contents

Fernando BAÑOS VALLEJO, Introduction 7

María José VEGA, Mediator Unus: The Intercession of Saints in the Expurgated Bibles of the *Censura Generalis* (1554) 21

Fernando BAÑOS VALLEJO, Villegas' Deviation in the Compositional Criteria of his *Flos sanctorum* 49

José ARAGÜÉS ALDAZ, Holy Folly and *Simplicitas* during the Counter-Reformation: A Context for Lope de Vega's *El rústico del cielo* 75

Natalia FERNÁNDEZ RODRÍGUEZ, Hagiographical Theater and Counter-Reformation: Between Baroque Aesthetics and *Arte Nuevo* 101

Alicia MAYER, *Delendus est Lutherus*: The Triumph of the Saints and the Virgin Mary over Heresy in New Spain's Imagery 127

Marcos CORTÉS GUADARRAMA, The Evolution of the Figure of St Michael the Archangel: From Medieval *Flos sanctorum* to New Spain's Hagiography (*c.* 1480–1692) 163

Carme ARRONIS LLOPIS, Catalan Lives of Saints after Trent (1575–1602) 189

Cristina SOBRAL, *Nota, pio leitor...*: The Hagiographical Critical Discourse in 1567 215

Abstracts 251

Index 257

Introduction

Fernando Baños Vallejo

The sixteenth century was a time of great religious upheaval in Europe, in which tensions caused by criticisms within the Catholic Church reached a breaking point and led to a schism and the consequent persecutions and wars between Protestants and Catholics, a conflict of such magnitude that it defines the Modern Age. Part of the controversy was related to the cult of saints, given that from 1523 onwards Luther rejected the mediating role of the saints and repudiated what he considered to be excessive devotion towards them. As a theological issue, the polemic regarding the cult of saints may be considered less important than other substantial issues, such as those related to justification by works or by faith, grace, free will, papal authority or the sacraments, but the truth is that, in social terms, the saints and the Virgin Mary framed the devotional practices of the faithful, for whom reading the lives of the saints was a common and daily practice. After the break within the Church, Catholic prelates and writers refuted Protestant ideas and reaffirmed their commitment to the cult of the saints in reaction to attacks from adversaries, although they also became aware of the need to prevent superstition and excesses regarding relics, images and miracles.

Hagiographic literature also continued to be an instrument for channelling popular devotion and heavily influencing the reading habits of Catholics. The lives of saints were presented in the three literary genres: laudatory poems, prose narrations and hagiographic theater. The *comedias de santos* came to characterise the Spanish Golden Age and had considerable impact through live performances of the adventures of the saints and even of certain supernatural episodes, whether heavenly or diabolical. However, even more so than the theater, the most far-reaching genre consisted of the *flores sanctorum*, which offered a compilation of the lives of the saints, so that, among other possibilities, the faithful could read about the life of each saint on their feast day each year. Moreover, the importance of hagiography was not limited to the Golden Age, but rather continues to be felt down to the present, to the extent that this style of narration has left traces that still remain in our collective imagination and that, if we pay attention to them, can also help us better understand certain key aspects of some current beliefs.

In relation to all this, the studies presented in this volume are part of a line of research that seeks to fill a void by examining the impact of the religious reformation on Hispanic hagiography, the history of which has largely ignored this polemic. It analyses how theological positions and controversy were projected onto literature and how they were incorporated, explicitly or implicitly. It is clear that the Catholic Church tried to reassert itself through the hagiographic tradition, but what we try to clarify is to what extent hagiographic literature, specifically Hispanic literature, was also affected by reformist approaches. This book therefore deals with less evident and hitherto neglected issues, such as the fact that the Hispanic Catholic authorities and authors, influenced by complaints about the excesses surrounding the cult of saints and hagiographic fables, and in line with Catholic reform prior to Luther, declared that the apocryphal episodes in the lives of saints must be expunged. In practice, they encountered difficulties in applying theoretical criteria to such an extensive subject as the lives of the saints, and ended up falling into certain contradictions between such criteria and their commitment to the hagiographic tradition, which they wanted to expand and update. All this is illustrated by the studies gathered in the present book on hagiographic prose in Catalan, Portuguese and Spanish, in the Iberian Peninsula and in America, and on the theatrical works that were intended to spread the legends of saints.

The year 2017 marked the 500th anniversary of the beginning of the Lutheran Reformation, and to analyse its repercussions in the social, economic and cultural spheres, many in the academic community published important studies. It was therefore also a propitious occasion to start the present project, in which we intend to analyse and critically review these contributions and incorporate them into the study of the evolution of devout literature.

In the same vein, in recent decades many historians have reviewed how the reformist ideas that spread throughout Europe after 1517 were received in the Iberian Peninsula. Many studies have qualified some widespread beliefs from the twentieth century, such as the origins of certain trends considered to be heretical, the real impact of Erasmus, the activities of the Inquisition, the emergence of the Counter-Reformation, even the term Counter-Reformation itself, etc., but these new historical investigations have not covered the way in which a subject so sensitive to these phenomena, such as hagiographic literary production, reflected those ideas or was conditioned by them, nor have they examined how these changes were received by readers. This is what we want to offer in this book.

The researchers involved in this project have devoted themselves to studying medieval and Renaissance Hispanic hagiographic literature, and have attempted to compensate for the disregard in which this abundant body of literature was held almost up to the end of the twentieth century, despite the fact that in its time it was one of the most, if not the most, widespread genres. That has now changed and nowadays Hispanic hagiography receives a lot of attention, with a number of works approaching the subject from different perspectives and thus reviving interest among researchers and educated readers, who find in these stories an attractive fusion of the historical and fabulous elements and of the everyday and supernatural dimensions. The researchers gathered in the present volume have laid the foundations of knowledge of medieval and Renaissance Hispanic hagiography, in particular regarding the issues of literary genre, tradition and textual affiliation, editing, interpretation in relation to the historical context, etc. They have consequently produced a book that offers contributions that advance all areas of the current line of research, which, among other things, seeks to establish a list of representative works of hagiographic literature in the various Iberian languages, to analyse the aspects that best show the reaction to the Reformation, to assess the scope of censorship, and to establish to what extent all this marks the evolution of the genre and the way it was received.

The articles brought together in this miscellany all seek to increase our understanding of the aforementioned issues through different and complementary studies. The authors employ analyses that differ not only in linguistic or geographical terms (two chapters address America, specifically the Viceroyalty of New Spain), but also in their approach and scope, given that some focus on a specific work or part of a work; others deal more with hagiographic genres; one takes a panoramic approach; one looks at theological aspects, and, finally, some relate the texts to iconography.

Most of the articles deal with hagiographic literature and its connections to iconography, and study the presentation of specific models of holiness, an issue related more to moral theology than to dogma. In contrast, the first article complements these by dealing with a theological-dogmatic question: the controversy surrounding the intercession of the saints. Nevertheless, the belief in the capacity of the saints to mediate goes beyond the realm of theologians to form also the basis of popular devotion, and is reflected in hagiographic literature, not so much in the descriptions of the saints' lives and behaviour, but rather in their miracles, which they frequently bring about for the benefit of the faithful.

Specifically, María José Vega (Universitat Autònoma de Barcelona) discusses the controversy surrounding the intercession of the saints in the first half of the sixteenth century (1517–1554) and, above all, its impact on the reading of the Bible and on the interpretation of the Scriptures. She thus deals with the theological foundations of worship, which sustain and legitimize both Catholic social practices and hagiographic discourse, and examines the paradoxes and contradictions found in treatises in defence of the saints. To do so, she reviews the terms of the so-called *quaestio de sanctis* that was central to the first Catholic controversialism (Clichtove, Eck, Cochlaeus) and, especially, its role in Hispanic culture, both as part of the "new" heresiology of the School of Salamanca and through the censorious activities of the Holy Office. Catholic polemicists and heresiologists shared the common purpose of building a repository of biblical passages related to the saints in order to counter the Reformers' powerful *ex silentio Scriptura* argument and to manage the possible interpretations given to a series of New Testament passages that explicitly identified Christ as the only mediator between God and men. The article first examines the cumulative construction of this new (Catholic) pathway for reading the Bible, and describes the coincidences and nuances between European and Spanish Catholic theologians, notably Alfonso de Castro. All of them defend the legitimacy of the cult of the saints, but Castro fails to address specific Protestant arguments, unlike Clichtove and Eck. Vega then analyses censorship by the Inquisition of printed Bibles (*Censura generalis*, 1554) to eliminate any dissident or Lutheran interpretations regarding saintly mediation that can be found in summaries and margins. The analysis highlights both the parallels in the censorship decreed by the Universities of Louvain, Paris, Salamanca and Alcalá and the differences in its severity, in particular between the (prohibitive) Parisian censorship, which entirely condemned heterodox Bibles (such as that of Estienne), and Hispanic censorship, which allowed the circulation of such Bibles albeit with expurgations. Vega's study concludes with an invitation to examine the paradoxes of the Catholic discourse on the intervention of the saints prior to the pronouncement of the Council of Trent, to assess the weight of Latin Bibles as a locus of conflict in confessional controversies, and to research the various forms of vigilance and control of dissent over sanctity.

Fernando Baños Vallejo (Universitat d'Alacant) examines the consistency of the criteria adopted by the author considered the most representative "counter-reformist" hagiographer in the Spanish language, Alonso de Villegas. In 1578, he published the first part of his *Flos sanctorum*, which he dedicates to none other than King Philip II and describes as "reformed", that is, carried out "according to the Catholic reform". From the outset, the first volume showed certain contradictions, but to fully illustrate the extent of Villegas' deviation from his own initial criteria, Baños compares his preliminary statements in the First part of the *Flos sanctorum* to those in the Third part (1588), and examines the most atypical cases of the latter, which is divided into two sections: the main one features extravagant saints, that is to say, those not present in the Roman Breviary, thus contradicting Villegas' claim in 1578 that his book of saints "conformed to the Roman Breviary". What is truly shocking and contrary to most canonical criteria is that the third part contains an extra section listing characters who are not canonized, but who, according to Villegas, are "illustrious in virtue" and who therefore are presumably in Heaven.

His justification for producing a list that diverges so far from the strictest criteria is that so do his sources, namely the works of Luigi Lippomano and Laurentius Surius. But the truth is that Villegas also allows in characters that are not in his sources; for example, some are taken from the chronicles of religious orders and others from various individual stories. The most striking case is that he presents the assassin of the Prince of Orange, a soldier named Balthasar Gérard, as "illustrious in virtue" and as a new martyr. Villegas praises his commitment to the Catholic cause by risking his life to eliminate the leader of the Protestant rebellion in Flanders, and describes his patience and strength during the torments prior to his execution and during the very cruel execution itself, with features close to the supernatural and with evident analogies to the passions of the martyrs or of Christ himself.

Baños also considers seven other lay characters who were not canonized at that time and who therefore are not eligible for official classification as saints. Moreover, they also diverge from the most common model of holiness (in the absence of martyrdom), which is that the individual must have led a religious life. Some of them are very famous and were canonized much later, for example, Saint Joan of Arc or Saint Thomas More. Also included are Saint Juan de Dios (one of the fools for Christ's sake) and Gonzalo Ruiz de Toledo, the subject of El Greco's painting "The Burial of the Lord of Orgaz". At the other extreme are humble characters, such as the three married women, two of whom nevertheless maintain their virginity.

Villegas' digression from the canonical is also marked by the fact that he includes a story that would be expurgated the following year by the Inquisition, that of a supposedly "living saint", María de la Visitación, a nun from

Lisbon who professed to bear wounds that, despite convincing Villegas and many others, including the Pope, turned out to be fraudulent.

Despite Villegas' deviation from his initial criteria, he maintains the basic principle that unites all his work and that characterizes the Catholic position as opposed to the Protestant one, namely that all the lives described are examples that salvation is earned through good works and constant struggle.

The character of Juan de Dios, one of the "fools for Christ's sake", is mentioned in the contribution by José Aragüés Aldaz (Universidad de Zaragoza), which examines a work by Lope de Vega, regarded for many reasons as the most prominent Spanish playwright of the time and the most prominent to write about the subject of holy folly, which appears in several of his plays, including one about Juan de Dios. In the case of Aragüés' article, however, the play studied is *El rústico del cielo*, whose protagonist is the discalced Carmelite Fr. Francisco del Niño Jesús. Aragüés analyses this work in the context of other similar writings by the playwright and the general context of the theme of holy folly and sacred simplicity in the Counter-Reformation, during which the concepts of humility and obedience acquired new connotations due to the religious controversies. Certain extravagant saints from the desert and from Eastern monasteries are found to have a literary and archaeological appeal that makes them a good starting point for rescuing an ideal of Christian perfection based on some principles that were held up as being central to the Catholic faith (in contrast to Protestantism), namely extreme humility, submission to ecclesiastical authority and firm acceptance of the deepest mysteries of faith.

Aragüés begins by observing that the tradition of the holy fools and holy simpletons is wide and varied, and is more prevalent in the Eastern Church than in the Western one. The mental condition of such saints can range from intellectual limitation or extreme naivety to insanity, and can also be real, feigned, or merely imputed by a hostile environment. The common denominator is that the holy fools willingly decide to become an object of mockery and humiliation, but that their words and gestures reveal (paradoxically and sometimes with humour) a truth of a higher order. Aragüés also reviews Biblical references to the subject, notably Saint Paul (1 Corinthians 1), who asserts that the "wisdom of God" is superior to the "wisdom of this world", and that the "message of the cross" can be perceived as "foolishness". Next, the brief but rich outline that Aragüés gives of the Eastern and Western traditions relating to holy folly leads him to the idea that holy folly is a Catholic sign in opposition to Calvinism, which condemns the simulation of madness to feign holiness. Aragüés also takes care to clarify that the notion of sacred simplicity is different from that of holy folly, although both are associated with each other in these religious traditions.

Finally, he studies the aforementioned work of Lope de Vega. After reviewing the texts that the playwright dedicates to holy fools and holy simpletons, he delves into the most significant features of *El rústico del cielo*, which concern the plot and the characterization of the protagonist, whom Lope met personally. Lope accentuates the rusticity of the character and opposes it to the vanity of wisdom, represented by the university students of Alcalá and the allegorical characters of Pride and the Demon. The reading that Aragüés offers us, and its connection with other works on the same subject, shows that such texts are a counter-reformist promotion of the virtues of obedience, self-denial and self-humiliation, and the acceptance of the mysteries of faith, that is, a reaffirmation of a tradition that goes back to the story of the Passion and Paul's own reflections on the "folly of the cross".

The study by Natalia Fernández Rodríguez (Universität Bern when she wrote it, currently at the Universidad de Sevilla) also deals with theater, but takes a broader approach. She analyses the combination of components in the *comedia nueva* with elements that are in line with the counter-reformist ideology. She uses a comparative method whereby in order to assess the presence of post-Tridentine religious ideas in Castilian hagiographic theater, she compares three works dedicated to Saint Jerome, Saint Augustine and Saint Anthony of Padua from the last third of the sixteenth century to six more works from the following century, which were also dedicated to these saints and which by then formed part of the *comedia nueva* sub-genre, the *comedia de santos*. In doing so, Fernández produces a fully consistent comparison, in which she selects three anonymous works featuring the aforementioned saints from manuscript 14767 of the Biblioteca Nacional de España, which is a representative corpus of post-Tridentine hagiographic theater and is notable for containing defences of Catholic positions on the cult of saints, justification and the Eucharist; she then compares the substantial elements of these three works to six new comedies, two about each of the saints, written by Lope de Vega, Francisco González de Bustos, Pedro Lanini Sagredo and Antonio Fajardo y Acevedo, and one attributed to Juan Pérez de Montalbán.

One of the aspects common to the works from both centuries is the iconic representation of the saints. The cult of the saints, reaffirmed at Trent, had acquired during the Middle Ages a sensory dimension, in particular through images, whose veneration was also reaffirmed at the council. The projection of this connection in the theater of the Modern Age, which uses the plot as a mechanism to show how man becomes a venerable image, can be considered a unifying element in the otherwise diverse body of hagiographic dramaturgy. The combination of word and image (both of which were materialized in the staging) was based on the connection between the hagiographic and iconographic traditions, and enhanced the impact on the audience, an effect that the *comedia nueva* would use staging and literary resources to produce at the highest levels.

The other issue that Fernández studies comparatively is the addition of profane elements that do not come from hagiographic sources but which are added to satisfy the tastes of the spectators, namely plots involving gallantry and love, humour, conflicts of jealousy and honour, etc., which created the mixture of the sacred and the profane that is so characteristic of hagiographic theater. And the *comedias de santos* remain this way from their origin until their prohibition in the eighteenth century. What Fernández finds is that the works of both centuries differ in the way that they include such profane components: those from the sixteenth century present the pious and supernatural elements first before inserting the specifically profane scenes, which nevertheless remain separate, with no attempt to resolve the heterogeneous nature of the composition. The works from the seventeenth century, on the other hand, especially the second half, start with the profane and then gradually integrate pious elements, so that the configuration of the saint is not isolated from the elements of the *comedia nueva*, and, furthermore, these profane ingredients, such as plots involving love and honour, end up becoming moralizing devices in themselves.

In short, Castilian hagiographic theater can be considered to offer an aesthetic modelling of the cult of the saints that was reaffirmed at Trent, and shows an uninterrupted commitment to that ideology, although the compositional mechanisms vary.

The following two articles continue in the linguistic ambit of Spanish, but study vestiges of the controversy between Catholics and Protestants on the American continent, specifically in the viceroyalty of New Spain. Alicia Mayer (Universidad Nacional Autónoma de México), who has previously researched how Luther was viewed in that distant territory (*Lutero en el paraíso*, 2008), turns her attention here to the Mexico of the Modern Age and the connections between the popular devotions to the saints and the Virgin Mary, on one hand, and the configuration of an image of Luther that represents, emblematically, heresy, error and evil, on the other. On this occasion, Mayer takes texts from the sixteenth to eighteenth centuries that allude to Luther, sometimes in opposition to the saints and the Virgin, and relates these texts to paintings on the same theme and the so-called "Triumphs of the Church", which follow European models. The study contains reproductions of iconographies, which readers can fully understand thanks to Mayer's comments and her comprehensive explanation of the representation of saints and the virgin Mary as protectors against heresy, both in painting and written discourse, in particular sermons.

INTRODUCTION

To introduce the subject, she takes the examples of a donation of relics in Mexico City in 1579, which led to the staging of a play entitled *Tragedia del triunfo de los Santos* featuring Martin Luther as the antagonist; and the funeral of King Philip II in 1599, in which the king is praised because of his struggle against heresy, and Luther is defined as the worst heresiarch who ever existed. Such mentions are striking given the reality that Lutheranism was scarcely present in the viceroyalty, leading Mayer to explain why the figure of Luther was so profusely and so negatively used in imagery and discourse. Mayer therefore reviews how anti-Protestant propaganda arose in Spain before analysing the textual and iconographic pieces.

In pictorial and sculptural representations, heretics, and specifically Luther, like Jews and Moors before them, become a symbol of dissent over which the Church triumphs, as is shown in the abundant paintings of the Triumphs of the Church, which were standardized images that proliferated in the Middle Ages and were re-defined in the Early Modern Age in Germany, Flanders, Spain, and, following these models, in Hispanic America from the seventeenth century. In some of these paintings Luther's image is used as a representation of the defeat of evil and heresy.

Other iconographies of the power of Catholicism over its enemies are the images of Saint Ignatius of Loyola and the Society of Jesus, the Carmelite Order (including the figures of the reformers Saint Teresa de Jesús and Saint John of the Cross), and medieval saints such as Saint Thomas Aquinas and Saint Nicholas of Bari. All of these follow European models but are adapted to the American context; in contrast, a synthesis of attributes from Mary and the woman of the Apocalypse, combined with native American elements, led to the image of the Virgin of Guadalupe, who also came to be praised in sermons as the guardian of Mexico against Protestant infection and whose images, quite deliberately, associate her with the protector Archangel Michael.

Regarding the Archangel Michael specifically, the article by Marcos Cortés Guadarrama (Universidad Veracruzana de México) deals with his hagiographic representation and with his evolution from the medieval *flos sanctorum* to the hagiography of New Spain. He studies the characterization of this figure in different sources ranging from the late fifteenth century to the late seventeenth century. There are two pre-Tridentine Castilian *flores sanctorum*, another two post-Tridentine ones (by Villegas and Pedro de Ribadeneira), and six religious texts written and / or published in Mexico, including two that specifically deal with the Archangel Michael, as cited below. Another of the texts that best show the connection with indigenous culture is the *Diálogo de doctrina christiana* (1559), by Maturino Gilberti, a Franciscan of French origin who writes in an indigenous language, Purepecha or

Tarascan, with a section on the Archangel Michael that also contains one of the first engravings printed in New Spain of his image. Cortés offers reproductions of engravings that illustrate the other texts that he studies, so that we can know the iconographic singularities and the narratives.

Cortés' article also shows that in the Middle Ages, in addition to Archangel Michael's role as messenger of God or guardian of souls ascending to Heaven, he is depicted as a warrior, thus symbolizing the struggle between good and evil, and, specifically, the triumph over the devil. It can be sensed that in the context of the division of the Church and the Council of Trent, Archangel Michael also becomes the protector of Catholicism against the Protestant threat. This is echoed in the territories of the Spanish Crown, such as New Spain, that are so far away from the Protestant presence, hence, for example, the publication in Mexico of the ideas of the Jesuit Juan Eusebio Nieremberg (*De la devoción y patrocinio de san Miguel*, Madrid, 1643). However, in America the primary purpose behind the defence of Catholicism was to do away with and replace the pre-Hispanic religions. A significant example is the official nature given to the local cult of Saint Miguel del Milagro, the most complete account of whom can be found in the *Narración de la maravillosa aparición que hizo el arcángel san Miguel a Diego Lázaro de San Francisco* (Seville, 1692), by the Creole Jesuit Francisco de Florencia. According to this account, Archangel Michael appeared before a virtuous indigenous person, a fact that connects this narrative with the apparitions of the Virgen de Guadalupe and the Virgen de los Remedios, the most important Marian invocations in Mexico. Furthermore, the fact that the apparition happens on May 8 and is commemorated on that date, in times of drought, turns that devotion into a Christianizing superimposition over the rite of the pre-Hispanic god Tezcatlipoca, who was invoked at times when water was scarce, hence the archangel's revelation of a miraculous source of water with healing powers.

In short, if in Europe the times of the Counter-Reformation led to the Archangel Michael being seen as a defender against the Protestants, in New Spain, a place largely free from such a threat, his role was increasingly diluted, and he was instead appropriated through local miracles, just like the Virgin Mary.

The last two studies in the volume take us back to the Iberian Peninsula, but this time to discuss the impact of the Reformation on hagiography written in other languages, namely Catalan and Portuguese. As regards Catalan, until now its hagiography has not been studied in terms of post-Tridentine transformations, nor has the relationship between the changes that occur in Catalan works of this genre and those that take place in Hispanic and European hagiography. This gap is finally addressed in the work of Carme Arronis

Llopis (Universitat d'Alacant), who examines the first hagiographic samples to emerge in Catalan after Trent and tries to elucidate what specific changes were applied to the stories, and what were the intentions of the compilers of the new books of saints. She reviews three texts: the latest edition of the *Flos sanctorum romançat* (1575), a translation of the *Legenda aurea* by Voragine, and the first two compilations of reformed hagiography, namely the handwritten notes of the Jesuit Pere Gil, known as *Vides de sants de Catalunya*; and the compilation by the Dominican Antoni Vicenç Domènec, *Historia general de los santos y varones ilustres en santidad del Principado de Cataluña* (1602).

The last edition of the *Flos sanctorum romançat*, in Catalan, was announced as having been revised by the doctor of theology Pere Coll, prior of the Dominican convent of Santa Catalina in Barcelona. From the analysis, Arronis concludes that strategies aimed at adapting the book of saints to post-Tridentine sensitivities have been applied to the text, and include a prologue to the reader that aligns the compilation with the new religious instructions, and in which the need to do good works to achieve salvation is emphasized; some precautions in relation to passages of apocryphal origin, which are either omitted or marked as apocryphal; and an improved doctrinal exposition of some chapters, for example by simplifying the syntax, or by reinforcing the authority of the doctrine. In spite of these measures, the review was neither systematic nor exhaustive, and it did not meet the standards required for hagiography in the Counter-Reformation and so was never published again.

More than two decades pass until the first initiatives of reformed hagiography appear in the Catalan context, and both are limited to their own territory. Until now, the works of Gil and Domènec had only been studied as exponents of patriotic Catalan hagiography, and had not been related to the general movements in the Counter-Reformation aimed at extolling the martyrs of each Catholic territory, nor had it been noticed that both hagiographers explicitly argue in the preliminaries that they created their compilations to refute heretical attacks on the cult of the saints. Gil's notes also include an interesting chapter that sets out the critical method to be followed when reviewing hagiographic matter, based on criteria of authority and historicity, in accordance with the principles of reformed European hagiography. Domènec's compilation reinforces the legitimacy of the devotions with the publication of documentary news dug up from archives throughout the territory. Both authors encountered similar obstacles: contradictory information, scarce and incomplete news, lack of documentation about certain devotions, etc. The way in which they faced such inconveniences allows us to appreciate the discursive efforts of the first post-Tridentine hagiographers to legitimize local devotions, trying to fit them in with the demands of authority and historicity that characterized the Church of the Counter-Reformation in such a way that these devotions would help to refute Protestant criticism.

Finally, Cristina Sobral (Universidade de Lisboa) devotes her study to the main example of post-Tridentine Portuguese hagiography, the *Historia das vidas e feitos heróicos e obras insignes dos sanctos* (1567), written by the Dominican Diogo do Rosário and commissioned by the archbishop of Braga Bartolomeu dos Mártires, who was also a Dominican and participated in the Council of Trent. It is the first Iberian reformed book of saints, that is to say, it is derived from Tridentine stipulations and is thus ruled by a new moral and historical accuracy and claimed to be purged of any kind of falsehood such as those denounced by Protestantism.

Sobral's article is a continuation of her previous studies on the post-Tridentine orientation of this work and on this occasion she analyses the points at which the author suspends the narrative to address the reader with critical considerations about the apocryphal nature of the subject matter, or to discuss the divergence of sources that sometimes leads the author to justify his choices, or to use a form of certification to support the authenticity of certain miracles that could be considered fantastical. In relation to the apocryphal passages, Sobral offers examples of Rosário's restrictive approach when he eliminates episodes that are found in other sources. In such cases, Rosário complies with the Tridentine injunction to expurgate apocryphal material. On the other hand, the researcher also observes that the hagiographer is not systematic, since he admits some episodes that had been described as apocryphal.

Sobral analyses textual examples of each of the types of critical notes, and compares these passages with their sources to assess their degree of innovation and modernity. In this way, she also seeks to verify whether that critical discourse is a continuation of the procedures of Dominican hagiographic criticism dating back to the thirteenth century, or if it is a consequence of the Council of Trent instead. She finds that medieval Dominican hagiographers, such as Jean de Mailly, Bartholomew of Trent, Vincent of Beauvais, Jacobus de Voragine, Bernard Gui and Antoninus of Florence, were conscious of the problem of apocryphal material, and were committed to truth as a feature of a hagiographic programme that produced short accounts of the lives of the saints, initially as a tool for preaching. However, the concept of veracity for them had more to do with the authority of the sources accepted in the Dominican Order and with the narratives included in liturgical books, and less with empirical data, which explains why they showed different positions in relation to the inclusion of apocryphal elements. For his compilation,

Rosário uses different sources, but follows Lippomano's hagiological model which contained the first Latin reformed legendary, predating that of Surius in 1570. When compared to medieval Iberian books of saints, Rosário's is characterized by the rewriting of some narratives to emphasize the saints' pastoral qualities and exemplary virtues for the faithful. Like the other post-Tridentine hagiographers, Rosário also differs from the medieval ones in his very explicit statement of the theoretical principle of eliminating the apocryphal, although in practice, leaving to one side his specific expurgations, we will not find in him nor in the other Counter-Reformation hagiographers an in-depth critical analysis of the veracity of the stories. In any case, his work is a balance, on one hand, between rhetorical strategies that seek credibility and imply erudition and, on the other, an accessible text in the vernacular that serves the pastoral objective of presenting models of holiness to the faithful.

To conclude, during the Reformation the Hispanic world produced a body of hagiography that revealed the impact of Protestant criticisms of the fabulous and even ridiculous extremes of the medieval tradition. Despite certain explicit and acrimonious attacks on Protestants, the impact of the criticisms levelled by Protestantism is clear, as is shown by the fact that the hagiographers, in line with the criteria declared by Lippomano and Surius, assert their adherence to the theoretical principle of purging the apocryphal, in any of its variants; that is, not only what is openly false, but also what is of doubtful veracity and what is of uncertain origin. In practice, however, throughout the Catholic world, despite the fact that there were expurgations, post-Tridentine hagiographic activity ends up becoming above all, according to Lippomano and Surius, a massive compilation of lives of saints that reaffirms the Catholic tradition. True critical treatment of the hagiographic tradition only began in the middle of the seventeenth century with Jean Bolland and the *Acta sanctorum*, but it was a very different approach that no longer consisted of rewriting, but rather on the recovery of ancient texts, editing them faithfully and applying philological criteria, whilst complementing them with studies that evaluate the historicity of the saint, of the events narrated and the reliability of the textual chain itself.

Mediator Unus

The Intercession of Saints in the Expurgated Bibles of the *Censura Generalis* (1554)

María José VEGA
(Universidad Autónoma de Barcelona, Spain)

Introduction

The Catholic Church made no explicit pronouncement about the intercession of saints until December 1563, when it approved the Tridentine decree *De invocatione, veneratione et reliquiis sanctorum, et de sacris imaginibus* (sessio xxv). This came at the culmination of a long period of theological controversy across Europe.[1] Consequently, when Luther and other Reformers in the early

---

[1] The Latin text of the decree is in Pierre-Antoine FABRE, *Décréter l'image? La XXVe session du Concile de Trente*, Paris: Belles Lettres, 2013. It was one of the decrees developed by *via compendiosa*, since, until November of 1563, the Conciliar fathers had still not decided important issues like intercession, images, indulgences, or Purgatory. The decree was begun and concluded in the space of a very few days, at the urging of the French theologians. A large part of the Spanish delegation lamented the haste and lack of reflection that characterised its writing and approval. On the circumstances under which the decree was developed and, in particular, the debate surrounding images, see Hubert JEDIN, "Genesi e portata del decreto tridentino sulla venerazione delle immagini", in *Chiesa della fede, chiesa della storia*, Brescia: Morcelliana, 1972, pp. 340–90; FABRE, *Decreter l'image?, op. cit.*, pp. 83–99, and "Une théorie en mouvement: Laínez et les images entre Paris et Trente (1562–1563)", in *The Council of Trent: Reform and Controversy in Europe and Beyond (1545–1700)*, ed. by Wim François and Violet Soen, Göttingen: Vanderhoeck und Ruprecht, 2018, III, pp. 9–30. On the decree's impact, see only Simon DICHTFIELD, "Tridentine worship and the cult of saints", in *Reform and Expansion, 1500–1660*, ed. by R. Po-Chia Hsia, Cambridge University Press, 2007, pp. 201–24. Eliseo SERRANO MARTÍN, "La santidad en la Edad Moderna: límites, normativa

1520s denied saints' ability to intercede for humans before God, they were not opposing a Catholic truth (*veritas Catholica*) but rather a collection of convictions of lesser rank (theologically speaking)—though indeed approved by the Fathers, tradition, custom, and the *consensus theologorum*. The 1563 decree gave bishops the power and responsibility to restrain festive and cultic excesses, curb profanation and idolatrous features, keep watch regarding images and the authenticity of relics, and to be extremely wary of "new" objects of veneration. Paradoxically, the decree itself shows a clear uneasiness with cultic "abuses", expending more effort restricting and correcting Catholic practices than combatting Protestant theses. It affirms the saints' mediatorial function—their ability to act on behalf of humans before God, and the usefulness of invoking them—and goes on to qualify as impious those who believe that devotion to the saints detracts from the honour of Christ or of God himself.[2]

Thus, a period of forty years separated the earliest Reformation writings opposing the intercession of saints from the Council's pronouncement. Given this fact, we ought to be careful not to treat the *quaestio de sanctis* anachronistically. Rather, account must be taken of undefined issues during the first half of the sixteenth century to which one can apply, at least partially, Joseph Lortz's thesis regarding the many areas of dogmatic imprecision that encouraged religious polemic in the first decades of the Reformation.[3]

The Tridentine decree on the intercession of the saints was a late intervention (written without a great deal of prior reflection on the Council's part) in a dispute that had stretched over four decades, that had left in its wake a large number of polemical writings, and that had been debated in several religious colloquies during the 1530s and early 40s.[4] One part of the

---

y modelos para la sociedad", *Historia Social*, 91 (2018), 149–66 and Antoine MARUZEK, "Réforme tridentine et culte des saints en Espagne: liturgie romaine et saints ibériques", in *The Council of Trent: Reform and Controversy in Europe and Beyond (1545–1700)*, pp. 221-48 give special attention to Spain. Fernando BAÑOS, ("Paratextos, ilustración y autoridad en los *flores sanctorum* castellanos del siglo XVI", *Versants*, 65.3 (2018), 33–61; "Lutero sobre la hagiografía y los hagiógrafos sobre Lutero", *Studia aurea*, 13 (2019), 7–40) analysed the traces of the polemic about saints and the Tridentine decree in the paratexts and statements of authors of the most important *flores sanctorum* published in Spain in the sixteenth century.
[2] *Sacrosancti et Oecumenici Concilii Tridentini sub Paulo III, Julio III, Paulo IV Pontificibus Maximis celebrati Canones et Decreta*, Matriti: ex Typographia Hilarii Santos Alonso, 1781, pp. 301–02.
[3] Classic German historiography on the Reformation had advanced the thesis of *Unklarkeit* (Joseph Lortz) and of doctrinal confusion or unsettlement, *doktrinären Verwirrung* (Hubert Jedin), for referring to the fact that, during the first decades of the sixteenth century, many doctrines were hazier than our present conception of them, simply because they were refined after the *tempestas haereticorum* and the Council's "clarification". Indirectly, then, Lutheranism is seen as a force for theological definition within the bosom of Catholicism.
[4] As John O'Malley recalls, the Council had a narrow agenda: in doctrinal matters, it treated the major and most controversial doctrines (like those related to the sacraments) and

Catholic reaction to Reformation theses—the one that interests us in these pages—had been fought on the field of Scriptural interpretation, through scrutinising the passages used to support Reformers' arguments and, above all, through searching for a "deposit" of Biblical passages that could be wielded as counter-arguments in favour of the invocation of the saints. The Council's decree gave more attention to images and relics—that is, to the material culture around the saint—than to the foundational principles of the cult of saints; it was therefore aimed more at regulating practice than at settling theological debate.[5] Paradoxically, therefore, the cult of saints—essential to understanding the intellectual and religious history of Europe—was a minor theme of the Council, and was decided upon with a last-minute sense of urgency and using few supporting arguments.[6]

Historians who have studied the Catholic reaction to the *quaestio de sanctis* have concentrated mainly on Germany and Italy, paying scant attention to the lands of the Spanish Crown in Europe and America.[7] The polemic

---

sidelined many doctrinal and pastoral issues, like indulgences, fasts, priestly celibacy, the veneration of saints, and images. These were precisely the doctrines that most affected the daily life of religious and lay people and which caused the most social upheaval. O'Malley affirms that the Council's limited focus of interest also left to one side many of sixteenth-century Catholicism's most dynamic aspects, such as the great missionary enterprise in America. See John O'MALLEY, "What happened and did not happen ar the Council of Trent", in *The Council of Trent: Reform and Controversy in Europe and Beyond (1545–1700)*, vol. I, pp. 50–51. On terminological vagueness and the (deliberate) imprecision of many of Trent's doctrinal conclusions, see also Günther WASSILOWSKY, "The Myths of the Council of Trent and the Construction of Catholic Confessional Culture", in *The Council of Trent: Reform and Controversy in Europe and Beyond (1545–1700)*, vol. I, pp. 78–79. In 1588, Sixtus V created the Congregation of Rites, charged with canonisations. The first of these, in 1589, put an end to a period of 65 years without any proposals of canonisation in the Roman Church.

[5] The decree was primarily pastoral. According to Pabel, "an official dogmatic treatment of the cult of the saints... would have to wait for four hundred years", until the Second Vatican Council (Hilmar M. PABEL, "Critique, Reform and Defence of Prayers to the Saints", in *Conversing with God. Prayer in Erasmus' Pastoral Writings*, Toronto: Toronto University Press, 1997, p. 95).

[6] The Council's response seems to answer the most pressing and perhaps most destructive of the Reformation positions, after several cycles of iconoclastic violence. Italy, Spain, and Portugal escaped iconoclasm during this period. Because these were the best-represented territories at the Council, O'MALLEY ("What happened and did not happen at the Council of Trent", *art. cit.*, p. 63) thinks that this explains why the veneration of sacred images "was a non-issue at Trent until the arrival of the French delegation" during the Council's last period. The decree's consequences for material and artistic culture were incalculable, despite the text's lack of theological precision. In fact, the most important regions for the production of religious art were in Catholic territory (Flanders, Spain, and Italy).

[7] An exception is the research project, *La hagiografía hispánica ante la Reforma protestante* (FFI2017-86248-P), under the direction of Carmen Arronis and Fernando Baños, which aims to analyse the Reformation's impact on Spanish collections of legends and hagiographical writing of the Counter-Reformation.

surrounding images, acts of iconoclasm, relics, pilgrimages, and hagiographical writings has sparked more interest than the theological debates regarding the saints' mediation or the use of Scripture in controversial writings and censorial projects. These are the focus of the following pages. My purpose is to examine the Catholic response in Spain to the Reformers' positions on the intercession or mediation of the saints, and to analyse the controversy's impact on Scriptural interpretation during the middle years of the sixteenth century.[8] To this end I shall analyse the *Censura Generalis*, the 1554 censure of Bibles which the Spanish Inquisition entrusted to the theologians of Salamanca and Alcalá, whose purpose was to expurgate the summaries, marginal notes, and glosses that accompanied the sacred text in Latin Bibles published from 1528. I shall give particular attention to the (paratextual) passages referring to the saints which were suppressed in these printed Bibles, and to the theological qualifications or *notes* applied to these *propositiones*. The *Censura* provides a privileged standpoint from which to view the Spanish Catholic reaction to the polemic regarding saints, and sheds light on the structure of doctrinal power in the Habsburg Empire, a structure that rested essentially on the work of the theological faculties of Louvain, Salamanca, and Alcalá. This study also allows for a reconsideration of the dynamics of editorial confessionalisation and censorial dis- or re-confessionalisation of the Biblical text during the first half of the sixteenth century.

The reading policies of the *Censura Generalis* are linked to the discourse of controversialists and heresiologists as well as to that of the Louvain Theological Faculty's indices of prohibited books. For this reason, I shall first review the chronology of the Protestant denial of the intercession of the saints and the texts that are foundational to this denial, for the purpose of more fully evaluating the uses of Scripture in the Catholic responses. These contrasting pathways of reading Scripture lead us to the *Censura generalis*, the analysis of which will be the focus of this study's final section.

Mediator Unus: The Polemic Surrounding the Mediation of the Saints

All the key arguments in the Reformation controversy regarding the saints were well defined theologically in the 1520s. Between 1522 and 1523, Luther had taken a stand in sermons and letters: he had denounced the excesses of the cult of saints and its approximation to idolatry; he had criticised hagiographical writing, pointed out the absence of Biblical support for the

---

[8] I leave aside the discussion of the meaning of the Credal expression *communio Sanctorum*.

veneration of saints, and had denied, in the final analysis, the ability of a saint to intercede for human beings before God.[9] These last two arguments were especially relevant since they, unlike critiques of abuses or of wasteful spending on devotional practices, involved theologically essential areas, invalidating acts of devotion, pilgrimages, offerings, prayers, entreaties, and promises directed to the saints. On the one hand, the argument *ex silentio Scripturae* deprived the cult of saints of the status of revealed truth (the highest level of certainty for the Christian). At the same time, the critique of intercession was itself based on Scriptural passages, using them to undo the main function attributed to the saints: their ability to act as mediators before God, to obtain gifts and material or spiritual benefits for the devotee, and to secure protection or aid. A particular passage from the epistle to Timothy (1 Tim. 2:5) acquired a key function in this argument. Here, St Paul affirms that, just as there is one God, there is one mediator between God and man, which is Christ: *unus enim Deus, unus et mediator Dei et hominum homo Christus*.

These words, often shortened to the formula *mediator unus*, gave support that was at least highly relevant, if not in fact foundational, to the Reformers' position, and became for Catholic controversialists an uncomfortable passage that proved difficult to manage. The Pauline text summarises in memorable fashion the core of the controversy; it had a polar function for reading

---

[9] David V. N. BAGCHI (*Luther's Earliest Opponents: Catholic Controversialists, 1518–1525*, Minneapolis: Fortress, 1991, pp. 153–54) identified, as the most relevant critical texts, the *Sermon von der Geburt Mariae* (September 1522, with at least eleven exempt reprints in two years) and the *Sermon von der Heiltumen* (14 September 1522, with five reprints before 1524) in D. Martin Luthers Werke Kritische Gesamtausgabe, Weimar: Böhlau, 1883–1983 (= WA), 10/3: 312–31 and 332–41. The most aggressive writing was perhaps the one criticising the canonisation of Benno, former bishop of Meissen, an action which Luther interpreted as Romanist propaganda showing the political use of canonisation by the Papacy (*Widder den newen Abgott und alten Teuffel der zu Meyssen soll erhaben werden*, 1524, with no less than five reprints in the following two years). On these, see also Stefano CAVALLOTTO, *Santi nella Riforma. Da Erasmo a Lutero*, Roma: Viella, 2009, p. 96: Heidrun RIEHM, *Sternbilder des Glaubens oder Abgötter? Martin Luthers Stellung zur Verehrung der Heiligen*, Marburg: Tectum, 2010, pp. 98–103; BAÑOS, "Lutero sobre la hagiografía…", *art. cit.*, pp. 22–23. The sermons denounced the excessive expense and sumptuousness of the cult of saints, and aimed to redirect the external practices of veneration of saints, places, and relics toward a form of spiritual practice that would give first place to Christian charity. On the Benno case, see also Robert SCRIBNER, *Popular culture and popular movements in reformation Germany*, London-Ronceverte: Hambledon Press, 1987, pp. 74–75, and Robert BARLETT, *Why can the dead do such great things? Saints and Worshippers from the Martyrs to the Reformation*, Princeton University Press: 2013, pp. 85 ff. In texts earlier than 1522 there is some criticism of hagiography, pilgrimages, and the abuses of the cult: Cavallotto has identified several sermons from 1514–1517 that denounce or criticise books of legends. BAÑOS points especially to an analysis of texts prior to 1522. See also RIEHM (*Sternbilder des Glaubens oder Abgötter?*, *op. cit.*, pp. 49–96).

(that is, it determined how other Scriptural passages were interpreted), and it had in addition an iconographic counterpart in Protestant propaganda.[10] It allowed the dispersed or "dilapidated" worship, directed at myriad human mediators, to be reoriented towards Christ. The passage was so significant that Luther, Zwingli, and Calvin used it, along with its supporting passages (e.g., Mat. 4:10, Jo. 16:24), as the starting point for developing the theological aspect of the *quaestio de sanctis*.[11] In fact, the formula *mediator unus* referred back to this cluster of texts. In the *Epistel oder Unterricht von den Heiligen* (1522), Luther invalidated the cult of "the dead" on the basis of Christ as *only mediator* ("an dem *eyningen mitteler* Jeshu Christo helt");[12] he further elaborated the idea of *unus mediator* in *Vom Abendmahl Christi* (1528), included it in the 1529 Catechism, and explained it in detail in the Coburg letter of 1530, which contains one of his most fiery critiques of intercession.[13] As it happens, these were also the years in which Erasmus wrote his colloquies *Naufragium* and *Peregrinatio religionis ergo*, which portray, in the guise of fiction, the invocation of saints as foolish and laughable.[14]

---

[10] It is so recognisable that it rose to the level of a title in Sebald Heyden's treatise, *Unum Christum mediatorem esse* (*Unum Christum mediatorem esse, et advocatum nostrum apud patrem, non matrem eius, neque divos*, Parisiis: s.t., 1525), translated into French and printed at Paris in 1526 and at Geneva in 1538, with several later editions, such as *D'un seul mediateur entre Dieu et les hommes* or *D'un seul mediateur, advocat et intercesseur entre Dieu et les hommes* (Genève: Jean Girard, 1538). This little tract refers not so much to the saints as to the mediation of the Virgin Mary, and its rewrote, amongst other things, the Salve Regina as a Salve Iesu, in which, for example, the words *advocata nostra* become *mediator noster*. The tract was included on the Paris indices of prohibited books of 1544 and 1556 and on the Louvain indices from 1546 (Jesús MARTÍNEZ DE BUJANDA, ed., *Index des Livres Interdits* (= ILI), Genève: Droz, 1985-2002, see ILI, vol. I, n° 453 and 458). The Spanish indices inherited this entry from Louvain (such as Valdés, 1559: ILI, V, n° 682, p. 578). On the various French editions between 1526 and 1564, see PETTEGREE et al., *French Vernacular Books. Books published in the French Language before 1601. Livres vernaculaires français. Livres imprimiés en français avant 1601*, Leiden-Boston: Brill, 2007, vol. I, p. 159.

[11] I pass over the position of Karlstadt on the saints, directed primarily at images, which he formalised in January of 1522 in his treatise on abolition (*Von Abtuhung der Bilder*). On the relationship between Karlstadt, Luther, Zwingli, and Calvin on the matter of images, see Carlos EIRE, *War against the Idols. The Reformation of Worship from Erasmus to Calvin*, Cambridge University Press, 1986, pp. 55-72, and Sergiusz MICHALSKI, "The Iconophobes: Karlstadt, Zwingli and Calvin", in *The Reformation and the visual arts: The Protestant image question in Western and Eastern Europe*, London: Routledge, 2011, pp. 43-74.

[12] WA 10, II, 164-68. Cavallotto indicates that the 1523 letter to the canons of Wittenberg makes the idea of *unus mediator* foundational to the Christian life: "Sic extinctus et sublatus unus mediator hominum Christus in locus suum accepit sylvas et arenas istas mediatorum et intercessorum" (in CAVALLOTTO, *Santi nella Riforma, op. cit.*, p. 97, n. 10).

[13] *Ein Sendbrief*, WA 30, II, pp. 632-43. See CAVALLOTTO, *Santi nella Riforma, op. cit.*, pp. 68, 97-98; RIEHM, *Sternbilder des Glaubens oder Abgötter?, op. cit.*, pp. 148-54.

[14] There is analysis of Erasmus's critique of hagiography and the invocation of the saints, in relation to Reformation positions, in EIRE, *War against the Idols, op. cit.*, pp. 28-53; PABEL,

In the works of Zwingli, Bucer, and Calvin published between 1523 and 1539, St Paul's authority continues to be central to the denial of the intercession of saints.[15] Ulrich Zwingli dedicated Article XIX of the *Usslegen und Grund* (1523) to the topic of Christ as sole mediator, giving the article that very title: "Das Christus *ein einiger mittler ist* zwischend gott und uns".[16] The issue reappears in *De canone Missae*, where he denies all efficacy to the saints, saying that their veneration is based on a false idea that the merits acquired by them in life are in some way "transferable" after death; to which he opposes free grace and, above all, the *uniqueness* of Christ's mediation.[17] In 1523, a little polemical tract authored by Johannes Lonicer or Lonicerus was published in Strasbourg against the parish priest of Esslingen, with the title *De sanctorum cultu et invocatione*.[18] The text took that same passage as its starting point: the work's *propositio* that prefaces the polemic interprets the Pauline passage using that same idea: "Solus Christus est mediator dei et hominum, idemque unus intercessor et interpellator noster, nullus Sanctorum, quantum vis magnus praedicetur".[19] Calvin's *Christiana religionis institutio* (1535-1536) also reminds readers that Christ is humanity's *only* advocate, and it deems the mediation of saints to be an erroneous idea; this section grew with each

---

"Critique, Reform and Defence of Prayers to the Saints", *art. cit.*, pp. 69-109, and CAVALLOTTO, *Santi nella Riforma, op. cit.*, pp. 17-64.

[15] On Bucer and the saints, see EIRE, *War against the Idols, op. cit.*, pp. 89-93, and especially CAVALLOTTO *Santi nella Riforma, op. cit.*, pp. 84-94, who refers both to the thesis in *Grund und Ursach* (1524) and to the project for cultic reform in 1543-1544.

[16] Ulrich ZWINGLI, *Ußlegen und gründ der schlußreden oder Artickeln* (= *Usslegung*) Zürick: Gedruckt durch Christophorum Froschauer, 1523, Artickel xix, z iii.

[17] Pamela BIEL ("Personal Conviction and Pastoral Care: Zwingli and the Cult of Saints", *Zwingliana*, 16.1 (1985), 443-69) identifies and comments on passages from Zwingli's writings directed against saints, images, and relics. According to Biel, "Zwingli attacked the role of the saints as mediators or intercessors. This constituted the primary theological objection to the cult [...] Owing to the Christological emphasis in his theology, a trait fostered by his reading of Paul, it is the saints as intercessors which disturbed Zwingli most of all". On Zwingli and the saints, see also CAVALLOTTO, *Santi nella Riforma, op. cit.*, pp. 86-88, and Bruce GORDON, "Polity and Worship in the Swiss Reformed Churches", in *A Companion to the Swiss Reformation*, Leiden: Brill, 2016, pp. 489-519.

[18] This is the second of two treatises that were printed together, in German (with the generic title *Berichtbuchlein...*) and in Latin. It is directed against the preaching (favouring the saints) of Balthassar Sattlers, parish priest of Esslingen, where Lonicer resided after receiving his Wittenberg doctorate. The essence of the work is a confutation, argument by argument, of his adversary's thesis, which we know only from Lonicer's relation of it. He gives one of the purposes of the work as: "Deinde scripturam, quae Christum Ihesum probet mediatorem et intercessorem, Sanctosque nec mediatores nec intercessores esse monstrabo" (Johann LONICER, *Catechesis de bona Dei voluntate, erga quemvis Christianum. Deque sanctorum cultu et invocatione*, s.l., s.t., 1523, diij).

[19] *Catechesis... et de Sanctorum cultu*, s.p.

subsequent edition and was largely constructed upon the foundation of St Paul.[20] Christ's sole mediation also finds a place in the *Confessio Augustana* (1530), specifically in the declaration of Protestant convictions ("Sed Scriptura non docet invocare santos, seu petere auxilium a sanctis, *quia unum Christum nobis proponit mediatorem*"); it reappears in the Articles of Schmalkald, and the discussion of this topic becomes, in the final analysis, a regular part of the agenda of religious colloquies in the 1530s and early 1540s.[21]

The 1520s were therefore the decade when the principal arguments that make up the so-called *quaestio de sanctis* were formulated. During these years, the foundations were laid for reconfiguring what a saint was in the Reformation churches, and for constructing a new hagiography and a new model of exemplarity. A critical discourse was fashioned that confronted luxuriousness, profligate spending, and external rituality with legitimate forms of devotion directed toward God and Christ, and that likened the cult of the saints and its external practices to idolatry and to a paganism that acknowledged local gods and guardians. Finally, this period saw the formation of central theological arguments that were aimed against the very foundations of traditional practices: namely, that the cult of the saints was a merely human invention without Scriptural support, a way of detracting from the

---

[20] Denial of intercession is addressed in a section of chapter XV, on prayer; this section is expanded in all later editions until 1559. The emphasis on Christ's unique mediation was already included in the indices of notable topics in the 1545 edition: *Mediator et intercessor unicus est Christus* (*Institutio Christianae Religionis*, Argentorati: per Wendelinum Rihelium, 1545, s.p.). On the issue of the the cult and intercession of saints in Calvin, see EIRE, *War against the Idols*, op. cit., pp. 195–233); Marie BARRAL BARON, "Érasme et Calvin au prisme du *Traité des reliques*", *Bulletin de la Société du Protestantisme Français*, 156.3 (2010), 349–71; Bruce GORDON, "Polity and Worship in the Swiss Reformed Churches", art. cit., pp. 510–19.

[21] See *Confessio Augustana*, xxi, in *Confessio Augustana. Das Augsburgische Bekenntnis* (1530), in *Bekenntnisschriften der evangelisch-lutherischen Kirche*, Göttingen: Vandenhoeck & Ruprecht, pp. 52–135. One can read a recapitulation of Reformation arguments against the cult of saints in Bullinger's first book, *De originis erroris libri duo* (1539), which emphasises "true" theocentrism against the Roman Church's multiplicity of divinities (Heinrich BULLINGER, *De origine erroris libri duo. In priori agitur de Dei veri iusta invocatione et cultu vero, de Deorum item falsorum religionibus et simulachrorum cultu erroneo. In posteriore disseritur de Institutione et vi sacrae Coenae domini, et de origine ac progressu Missae Papisticae, contra varias superstitiones pro religione vera antiqua et orthodoxa*, Tiguri: in officina Froschoviana, 1539). The topic of rejection of the saints made its presence known in all official documents of the Reformation, and in Protestant catechisms and confessions of faith. Besides its inclusion in the Augsburg Confession it had a place in the Calvinist Gallic Confession of 1559 and the *Confessio Belgica* of 1581 (PABEL, "Critique, Reform and Defence of Prayers to the Saints", art. cit., p. 94). The Anglican Church also rejected the cult of saints in 1563. Article XXII of the foundational *39 Articles* refers to the invocation of saints as "a fond thing vainly invented, and grounded upon no warranty of Scripture, but rather repugnant to the word of God" (in BARLETT, *Why Can the Dead do Such Great Things?*, op. cit., p. 91).

veneration and worship that a believer owed to God, and of devaluing the centrality of Christ, the *only mediator* between God and man.

Inter Sirtes: The Catholic Response

The first years of the Reformation saw an avalanche of Catholic controversial printed works on various polemical fronts. The question of indulgences, central to the first anti-Lutheran reaction, quickly became secondary in the face of the greater penetration of other topics of debate related to the sacraments, justification and works, free will, grace and papal authority.[22] Catholic response to the issue of the saints had been swift. *De veneratione sanctorum opusculum* by the Fleming Jodocus Clichtoveus was published at Paris in 1523; the author's intent was to demonstrate that the saints were worthy of receiving prayers and veneration, and that their ability to intercede was a belief with Scriptural support. A defence of mediation—with a synthesised exposition of Lutheran arguments—appeared in Johannes Eckius's *Enchiridion locorum communium adversus Lutheranos* (1525), which was regularly reprinted during the following years, as well as in Clichtoveus's own *Compendium veritatum ad fidem pertinentium contra erroneas Lutheranorum assertiones* (Paris, 1529).[23] In subsequent decades this dispute generated a continuous and ever-growing body of Catholic controversial texts, which constituted a cumulative body of arguments that became denser with each rewriting. The 1530s saw the publication of *De veneratione et invocatione sanctorum ac de honorandis eorum reliquiis brevis assertio*; some of its editions were published anonymously with a preface by Johannes Cochlaeus, and others appeared under the name

---

[22] Miriam U. CHRISMAN, "From polemic to propaganda: the development of mass persuasion in the late sixteenth century", *Archiv für Reformationsgeschichte*, 73 (1982), 175–95; Michael TAVUZZI, "Luther's Catholic Opponents", in *Martin Luther in Context*, Cambridge University Press, 2018, pp. 224–25. On Catholic controversialism, see the prosopography in Wilbrigis KLAIBER, *Katholische Kontroverstheologen und Reformer des 16. Jahrhunderts: Ein Werkverzeichnis*, Münster: Aschendorff, 1978; the panorama in Jay P. DOLAN, "The Catholic literary opponents of Luther and the Reformation", in *Reformation and Counter-Reformation, History of the Church*, vol. V, ed. by Erwin Iserloh, London: Burns & Oates, 1980, pp. 191–207; and the authors included in the general survey of Erwin ISERLOH, ed., *Katholische Theologen der Reformationszeit*, 5 vols, Münster: Aschendorff, 1984–1988. BAGCHI (*Luther's Earliest Opponents, op. cit.*, passim) paid special attention to German controversialism between 1518 and 1525, and Kai BREMEN (*Volkssprachliche Kontroversen zwischen altgläubigen und evangelischen Theologen im 16. Jahrhundert*, Tübingen: Niemayer, 2005) analyses controversialism in German. I know of no general survey of Catholic controversialism in Spain.

[23] I omit texts written in vernacular languages, given their scant distribution or impact outside Germany. On the confutation of Caspar Schatzgeger, Johannes Dietenberger and others, see BAGCHI, *Luther's Earliest Opponents, op. cit.*, pp. 155–59.

of Arnoldus Wesaliensis. Cochlaeus himself was the author of a certain *De sanctorum invocatione et intercessione deque imaginibus et reliquiis eorum pie riteque colendis, liber unus*, which I know exists in an edition of 1544.[24]

Outside Germany, Tommaso de Vio, Ambrogio Catarino, and Albert Pigghe also contributed to the topic, and works in defence of the cult of saints continued to be produced even after the close of the Council of Trent.[25] David Bagchi has pointed out that, because Lutheran criticism was reasonably moderate in comparison with other Reformers, the controversialists soon began to include in their confutations arguments that were not strictly his own.[26]

A common characteristic of the first Catholic controversialists was to weave together a pattern of Scriptural passages that could be used to respond to the argument *ex silentio Scripturae* and thus to establish the veneration of the saints upon the solid rock of Revelation. The Biblical foundation was crucial enough in this polemic that Clichtoveus, Eckius, Tommaso de Vio, and the rest made it their first and principal aim to create a mosaic of Scriptural passages. This method was also the most uncomfortable, one that revealed the contradictions and tensions in Catholic discourse. Thus, the controversy regarding saints largely resolved itself into two complementary strategies: establishing a body of passages and authoritative citations, and reinterpreting or "deactivating" the meaning of *mediator unus* in the Epistle to Timothy and in the passages that supported it in the Protestant body of argument. Regarding this common foundation, however, there are important shades of difference, which can be illustrated by the representative cases of Clichtoveus and Eckius.

---

[24] Arnoldus Wesaliensis, *De veneratione, invocatione et reliquiis sanctorum brevis assertio doctissimi quodam viri Arnoldi Vvesaliensis*, Moguntiae: excudebat Franciscus Behem, 1540, and Joannes Cochleus, *De sanctorum invocatione et intercessione deque imaginibus et reliquiis eorum pie riteque colendis, liber unus, Ioannis Cochlei Germani adversus Henricum Bullingerum Helvetium*, Ingolstadii: ex officina Typographica Alexandri Wucissenborn, 1544.

[25] Tommaso DE VIO (Cajetan), *De Sanctorum inuocatione Aduersus lutheranos iuxta scripturam Tractatus*, Parisiis: Regnault, 1531; Ambrogio CATARINO, *De certa gloria, invocatione ac veneratione sanctorum disputationes atque assertiones Catholicae adversus impios*, Lugduni: apud Mathiam Bonhomme, 1542. Albert PIGGHE, *Controversiarum praecipuarum in comitijs Ratisponensibus tractatarum, et quibus nunc potissimum exagitatur Christi fides et religio, diligens et luculenta explicatio*, Coloniae: ex officina Melchioris Novesiani, 1542. On the impact of the controversy in Italy, see Wietse DE BOER ("Trent, Saints and Images: A Prehistory", in *Trent and Beyond. The Council, other powers, other cultures*, ed. by Adriano Prosperi and M. Catto, Turnhout: Brepols, 2017, pp. 121–44), who surveys Italian conflicts and polemics, especially at the episcopal level, giving special attention to the reforming bishops like Pier Paolo Vergerio, Vittore Soranzo and Jacopo Nacchianti. De Boer highlights the importance of the Italian context, which acts as a complement to Hubert Jedin's perpective in underscoring the crucial role of the French delegation and of Charles de Guise in the conciliar decree.

[26] BAGCHI, *Luther's Earliest Opponents, op. cit.*, p. 154.

Clichtoveus's first purpose in *De veneratione Sanctorum* was to establish the legitimacy of the cult of saints on a foundation of revealed truth, the testimony of the Fathers and the magisterium of the Church, and lastly on weaker forms of authority and propriety (the moral order, for example).[27] Still, Clichtoveus is clearly uncomfortable with hagiographical literature—he describes it as a mix of *impietas*, *credulitas*, and *error*—and with the difficulty of managing the faith of simple folk or rightly moderating and directing the religious sensibilities of the ignorant. Thus, the *debita veneratio* required a delicate balance, and Clichtoveus's argumentation—as he himself affirms—followed a path *inter Sirtes*. In fact, the controversy about the saints frequently involved proposals from Catholic theologians for deep purification at the heart of the Church, and at times, suggestions for possible third ways (e.g., Clichtoveus, *De veneratione*, 18^r) or intermediary formulae like Albert Pigghe's slogan calling on the Church to *eradicate abuses and retain the truth* (*Controversia*, cciv).[28] Clichtoveus's most theologically important argument, which he develops in the first two chapters (*De veneratione*, 4^r–9^v), is his attempt to establish on Biblical grounds the saints' ability to intercede with God. This required in every case an analogical reading of Scripture or an abrupt transfer of meaning: it required him to postulate, for example, that the term *amici* or *amici Dei* could always be understood as referring to the

---

[27] Sam KENNERLEY ("Students of History, Masters of Tradition: Josse Clichtove, Noël Beda and the limits of historical criticism", *Renaissance Studies*, 52.1 (2019), p. 64) depicts Clichtoveus as the best-selling doctor of the Paris Faculty of Theology in the early sixteenth century. The issue of saints is important in his output. He wrote a life of St Louis, and in 1518 he participated in the debate about Mary Magdalene against Jacques Lefèvre d'Étaples. The prologue against *Lutheriana impietas* relates Luther's position to that of Wycliff, as arising from the same workshop. Baños indicates that Clichtoveus's *De veneratione* might have been written as a response to Lonicer's treatise, also from 1523, against the veneration of the saints (BAÑOS, "Lutero sobre la hagiografía", *art. cit.*, p. 13).

[28] This raises the question as to how far one can accept the arguments of the critiques against simple uses and customs. Some controversialists, like the Italian Sylvester Prierias, understood that critiques of *practices* in the cult of saints (e.g., pilgrimages) always had ecclesiological implications, to the extent that they undermined the authority of the Church that sanctioned them. All issues relating to uses and customs can be transformed into a problem of discipline or a question of ecclesiology, that is, as questioning the authority and capacity to regulate practice. Against this Italian controversialist posture, the thesis of Clichtoveus and Pigghe can be understood in fact as *third ways*. Pigghe conceded the existence of illegitimate forms of devotion, reproved pastoral negligence in cultic regulation, and concluded by inviting priests and bishops to correct abuses, errors, and superstition in order to promote a new (Catholic) form of veneration of the saints. On the third way of Diego Laínez and the Jesuit position with regard to the saints during the concluding years of the Council, see FABRE, "Une théorie en mouvement", *op. cit.*, pp. 14–15. See also Erika RUMMEL, "The Idea of Accommodation: From Humanism to Politics", in *The Confessionalization of Humanism in Reformation Germany*, Oxford University Press, 2000, pp. 121–49.

saints, or to interpret Old Testament passages in which certain persons transfer their favours to other persons as representative of the "transference" of saints' merits in intercession.

Clichtoveus produced a clearer synthesis a few years later in *Compendium veritatum ad fidem pertinentium contra Lutheranas assertiones* (1529). The modest number of Scriptural passages gathered in *De veneratione* had grown notably in the intervening years (114ᵛ-119ʳ),[29] as had the testimonies of the Fathers cited in favour of the saints. The section closes with a summary of Lutheran arguments and their authoritative sources, followed by a commentary on *mediator unus* (119ᵛ ss.). Here the exposition is constructed as opposing readings and Scriptural passages, like a diptych, in which the number (if not the clarity) of passages that support the saints contrasts favourably with those used by the Lutherans. Some of these (Deut. 6, 1 Kings 7, Isaiah 42) would in fact reappear in the *Censura Generalis*.

Johannes Eckius, the most pugnacious Catholic controversialist of the 1520s and 30s, took a different approach. His *Enchiridion... adversus lutheranos* of 1525, which brings together an overview of Lutheran doctrinal "disagreements," is remarkably updated and has a great capacity for synthesis. It is likely that the work remained a standard reference manual on Lutheranism even after the 1549 publication of Johannes Cochlaeus's copious commentaries, *De actis et scriptis Martini Lutheri*. In fact, between 1525 and 1575 there were at least 116 reprintings and translations of Eckius's *Enchiridion*. The work was organised as a series of controversies: each theme presented, in order, the Catholic arguments, the Lutheran arguments (under the heading *Obijciunt lutherani...*), and a point-by-point confutation.[30] Unlike Clich-

---

[29] Quite possibly from reading Eckius's *Enchiridion* (1525), which, as I will show below, offered a new collection of Biblical passages.

[30] Johannes ECKIUS, *Enchiridion locorum communium adversus Lutheranos*, Landshuti Baioariae, 1525. The first edition contained 28 topics of disagreement. In 1529, Eckius added one more. The order is important, because the first articles have to do with ecclesiology (the magisterium of the Church, the authority of councils and of the Pope) or they are about faith, salvation, and the sacraments (1–12). The rest of the articles (13–28) touch on Catholic practices: the first concern feast and fast days (xiv), the veneration of the saints (xv) and images of saints and the crucified Christ (xvi). On the arranging of the *Enchiridion*, see P. FRAENKEL, "Johann Eck und Sir Thomas More 1525–1526: Zugleich ein Beitrag zur Geschichte des *Enchiridion locorum communium* und der vortridentinischen Kontroverstheologie", in *Von Konstanz nach Trent*, ed. by R. Bäumer, Padeborn: Schöningh, 1972, pp. 481–92. There is a profile of Eckius as theologian and as the most fearsome controversialist in Erwin ISERLOH, *Johannes Eck (1486–1543): Scholastiker, Humanist, Kontroverstheologe*, Münster, Aschendorff, 1981, and in *Katholische Theologen der Reformationszeit*, vol. I, *op. cit.*, pp. 65–71. Eckius's participation in the Leipzig Disputation (1519) has been studied by Bagchi (*Luther's Earliest Opponents, op. cit.*, pp. 70–77).

toveus's confident approach, presenting a review of Biblical passages in support of the veneration of saints without reservations, Eckius recognised the difficulty of the task. In fact, he confirmed at the outset the absence of any unequivocal Scriptural teachings on the saints:

> Explicite non est praecepta sanctorum.

This was as much as to admit, partially or with reservations, the Lutheran idea of the silence of Scripture on the topic. It was at once a concession (as to what was explicit) and a non-concession (as to what was implicit) of the adversaries' positions (*Enchiridion*, 157). Thus, any search for Biblical passages to invalidate Protestant arguments was bound to be a reading between the lines and a discovery of truth that was only implicit, analogical, tralatitious, and never evident. Eckius employed a double argument to explain the absence of clear, explicit teachings: (1) there is no reference to the saints in the Old Testament because the Patriarchs were in limbo and the people of Israel already had a propensity for idolatry (so that it was necessary to remove occasions that might encourage it); (2) there are no references in the New Testament, lest the Gentiles should continue venerating mere humans (the *terrigenae*) as if they were gods. Moreover, it would have been impossible for the Apostles and Evangelists to teach the veneration of saints without falling into arrogance: they might seem to be requiring glory for themselves after their deaths if they encouraged such veneration. Therefore, in light of the "justified" lack of explicit teachings, Eckius could only pay attention to those that are implicit: in other words, his only recourse was to build a repository of passages that *indirectly*, or in a veiled manner, supported the intercession of the saints. A good example of this is his reading of Matthew 25:40 ("what you do to one of the least of my brethren, you do to me", "quandiu fecistis uni ex his fratribus meis minimis, mihi fecistis"), which in its original context awards eternal life to works of mercy that a person does for his fellows;[31] it allowed the *Enchiridion* (and later works) to *implicitly* support, by extrapolation, the idea that actions or merits have a kind of person-to-person power of transference. If the term *brethren* has not only its obvious meaning but also refers to good men, especially good men who have died, then what is offered to the *fratellus* would be offered to the saints and to God himself.

---

[31] The passage belongs to the "little Apocalypse" of Matthew, in which Christ addresses the saved so they might take possession of the Kingdom ("because I was hungry and you gave me to eat; I was thirsty and you gave me to drink…", etc.). The righteous ask Christ when these things occurred ("When did we see you hungry, and fed you?…"). Christ's reply closes the brief dialogue, "As many times as you did it to one of the least of these my brethren, you did it to me".

On the other hand, the six New Testament passages which, according to Eckius, supported Lutheran theses and called on Christians to pray directly to Christ or God himself are much clearer. The last of them is in fact the precept of *mediator unus* from the epistle to Timothy. It could be that, as happened with Clichtoveus's work, the sheer quantity of Biblical passages (allegedly) favouring the saints might compensate for the lack of textual clarity and power. In any case, the arguments of Clichtoveus and Eckius proceed along similar lines, though they are based on different perceptions of the possible readings supported by Scripture. They also differ regarding the ways to neutralise Protestant discourse's use of *mediator unus*. Clichtoveus proposes that Christ should be understood as the *one* mediator with regard to redemption, whereas, with regard to intercession, he would certainly be a mediator but not the only one (vid. II, xi, 72^r). Eckius, on the other hand, expands Christ's unique mediatorship to include the saints by virtue of the solidarity of the head and members of the Church; that is, he superimposes the Pauline passage with its metaphor of the (*one*) body in order to reduce multiplicity to unity. The Italian controversialists seem to favour Clichtoveus's approach of discoursing with an air of certainty, rather than Eckius's cautious recognition that, in the final analysis, *explicite non est praecepta sanctorum*.[32] At the same time, one does not always find that they manage to defuse *mediator unus*: the discomfort encountered by Catholic theologians trying to redirect the interpretation of this statement is clear even in the Tridentine decree *De veneratione*, which in fact includes it as an indirect statement summarising Reformed positions (Decr. 302).

Controversialism and Heresiology

What then was happening in Spain? How did its theologians view and express the *quaestio de sanctis*? W. Klaiber's classic bibliography of Catholic controversialism does not include Spanish authors despite the relevance of their theological schools, especially of Salamanca, and the significant participation of Spanish theologians in the Council of Trent. Perhaps the reason is that, except for a few works like that of Diego de Zúñiga, their polemical involvement did not take the form of concise, distinct treatises like

---

[32] Tommaso de Vio's *De invocatione Sanctorum* (in *De sacrificio Miss[a]e. De Communione. De Confessione. De Satisfactione. De Sanctorum inuocatione Aduersus lutheranos iuxta scripturam Tractatus*, Parisiis: Regnault, 1531) begins, for example, with the weight of the Lutheran affirmation ("Luterani invocationem Sanctorum aiunt ex Scriptura non haberi", III, G5) and continues by presenting two blocks of Biblical passages that would negate this: one dedicated to the invocation of the holy angels, and a second one dedicated to the invocation of holy human beings.

Clichtoveus's *De veneratione*, but were often included in major theological works or incorporated into commentaries on St Thomas's *Summa*. One need only recall that Melchor Cano's *De locis theologicis* (1563) closed with three exercises in controversy designed to be models of argumentation for theological professionals in the struggle against heresy, especially against the Reformers. It is unfortunate that no map has yet been created of the complex theological (as opposed to inquisitorial or political) reaction to Lutheranism in Spain, beyond generalities and commonplaces.[33] Here I shall restrict myself to designating a prime text, *Adversus omnes haereses* by the Franciscan Alfonso de Castro, which predates the censorial intervention of 1554 and illustrates the links between Catholic controversialism and the new heresiology of the School of Salamanca.

The *princeps* of the *Adversus omnes haereses* appeared in Paris in 1534. A few years later, in 1547, Castro published a no less extensive second treatise, titled *De iusta haereticorum punitione*. Beyond its discussion of the treatment of heretics, this work is often portrayed as a contribution to establishing the foundations of modern penal law. The *Adversus haereses* enjoyed an extraordinary circulation in Europe, thanks to its many editions and reprints that appeared in Paris, Lyon, Antwerp, and Venice, and subsequent translations into common languages in the eighteenth century. It differed from more recent catalogues of heretics, such as that of Bernard of Luxembourg, which followed the Augustinian model, being organised not by names of heresiarchs but by themes and concepts, creating the structural model for a new heresiology using historical, ecclesiological, and dogmatic elements. For example, Castro traced the history of heresies related to each concept (e.g., *Gratia* or *Eucharistia*), examined possible historical links, and included the conciliar pronouncements on each point of doctrine, with the result that the history of dissent could be viewed in parallel to the history of dogma.[34] Until Alfonso de Castro's death in 1560, his book was regularly updated in dialogue with contemporary events, either through incorporating new themes and

---

[33] For the Iberian world, we do not have any repertories like those of Louis Desgraves (*Répertoire des ouvrages de controverse entre catholiques et protestants en France (1598–1685)*, Geneva: Droz, 1984–1985) or Klaiber (*Katholische Kontroverstheologen*, op. cit.). On the other hand, we do have detailed studies of the reception and reading of Protestant texts, and of inquisitorial and pastoral (though not theological) answers to them.

[34] The ordering by topics and concepts had already been adopted by Eckius for his *Enchiridion*, but on a very small scale, to order and refute Lutheranism's polemical matters. In classical heresiology, this had been the structure (with variations) of the *Curatio Graecorum affectionum* of Theodoret of Cyrrhus and of St Epiphanius's *Panarion*. The models of Late Antiquity remain to be studied, as well as more modern ones, that could explain the composition of the vast thematic encyclopaedia that is the *Adversus haereses*.

entries or by expanding and modifying existing topics.[35] In the final edition published during Castro's lifetime (1556), there were at least 35 articles that described and confuted Lutheran positions. Thus, *Adversus omnes haereses* inserted the genre of controversy into the structure of heresiology, while at the same time tracing a kind of intellectual genealogy of dissident arguments. On the other hand, *De iusta punitione* was a juridical treatise that attempted to redefine how religious dissidence should be handled, and to influence imperial policy. The prologue was written shortly after Charles V's victory over the Schmalkaldic League at Mühlberg—at a moment, therefore, when it was possible from the standpoint of *Realpolitik* to see Protestantism as a religious movement in decline, whose influence in the collection of Habsburg territories had been partially deactivated by force of arms. In fact, in Castile at the midpoint of the century, there was a permeable border between heresy and sedition, possibly as a consequence of the Schmalkaldic War, and Charles V's correspondence reveals how far political disorder was associated with doctrinal dissent.

In the *Adversus haereses*, the entries about saints, images, and relics are partly an immediate echo of Catholic controversies of recent years.[36] The article titled *Sancti* in fact repeats the structure and strategy of the controversialists, whom Castro cites (giving special praise to Eckius and Cochlaeus). The text was updated and expanded in later editions, taking note of the works of Tommaso de Vio and Albert Pigghe, and of the failed Colloquy of Regensburg. Castro lists at the outset 25 authoritative Scriptural passages favouring the saints, although, unlike Eckius, he does not take notice of Lutheran arguments (as he did in the rest of the entries), nor does he take the trouble of reworking the meaning of *mediator unus* from the epistle to Timothy. Thus, the confutation simply omitted mentioning any Scriptural support for the opposition or tracing Protestant arguments beyond a general reference to the supposed uselessness of intercession. There are no substantial differences in argumentation or style between the controversialists and Castro; the latter only changed the framework or general structure that contained the discussion on the saints.

---

[35] Xavier Tubau has pointed out, for example, that the entry *Gratia* in the 1534 edition, slightly modified for the 1541 edition, was rewritten and expanded to include a *tertia haeresis* on this topic in 1556, referring to Luther. The length of the *Gratia* entry grows from one to 30 pages between 1534 and 1556. The text's growth parallels, in a way, the doctrinal development of Lutheranism, giving a response to it in each of the editions.

[36] Alfonso DE CASTRO, *Adversus omnes haereses libri XIV*, Parisiis: Iodocus Badius et Ioanni Roigni, 1534: see *Sancti*, 195ᵛ–197ʳ (in the 1556 edition, 156ᵛ–158ᵛ), *Reliquia sanctorum*, 201ʳ–203ʳ (explanded in 1556, 153ᵛ–138ʳ), *Imago* (138ʳ–139ᵛ).

Thus, at the beginning of the 1550s, the controversialists had established the battle lines of *theological* polemic about the saints almost exclusively on the field of Scripture, and had managed to define two paths of Bible reading: a Protestant one, organised around the sole mediation of Christ, and a Catholic one, whose quantity of texts underwent significant inflation between the 1520s and 1550s, perhaps using sheer numbers to compensate for a lack of clarity—a lack that Eckius recognised in his *Enchiridion*. The sets of passages that Eckius, Clichtoveus, and Castro collected are different, yet at least a dozen of the same Biblical references appear in all three. Their treatises show that early in the conflict there developed a fixed group of precise passages from Scripture for and against the cult of saints. One is therefore led to ask what impact and consequences this polemic had for the publishing and reading of Bibles. Do printed Bibles in fact manifest these reading itineraries in their summaries and indices? Are positions regarding the saints disseminated in marginal notes and metatexts? The *Censura Generalis*—like the indices of Louvain and some Parisian censures—provide an optimal instrument for analysing how the polemic regarding intercession made its way into Latin Bibles published after 1528.

From Louvain to Salamanca: Prohibited and Expurgated Bibles

The *Censura Generalis* or general censure of Bibles was printed at Valladolid in 1554. Until that moment, the 1551 Index of Prohibited Books had been the only one published in Spain. This was, barring a few additions, little more than a transcript of a 1550 catalogue of books prohibited or recommended by the Louvain Theological Faculty. The title of the Spanish edition reproduced Louvain's exactly: *Catalogi librorum reprobandorum et praelegendorum ex iudicio Academiae Lovaniensis.*[37] Louvain's indices had been published since 1546; they focused especially on university and school Latin books, and the method of control they proposed was aimed at the booksellers' market on

---

[37] Martínez de Bujanda reproduced the inquisitor Fernando de Valdés's letter from the end of 1550, which accompanied the Louvain Index that he sent to the Inquisition's districts for adoption as a catalogue of reference: "... y para que se guardase de tener y leer semejantes libros mandamos imprimir el dicho catálogo (de Lovaina) y al final del se pusiese el memorial de los libros que por el Santo Oficio estaban prohibidos en estos reinos" ("... and so that care should be taken not to possess or read such books, we order said catalogue (of Louvain) to be printed, and that it should include at the end a list of the books that were prohibited by the Holy Office in these kingdoms": in MARTÍNEZ DE BUJANDA, ILI, V, p. 59). We know of four editions of 1551: in Valladolid, Toledo, Seville, and Valencia, which have been partly described by Israel RÉVAH ("Un *Index* espagnol inconnu: celui édité par L'Inquisition de Séville en novembre 1551", *Studia Philologica, Homenaje ofrecido a Dámaso Alonso*, Madrid, 1963, vol. III, pp. 131–32) and exhaustively by their editor, MARTÍNEZ DE BUJANDA (ILI, V, pp. 66–69).

the geographical frontier of Protestantism. Bibles were a key part of all these indices: they came under the first catalogue heading and were the largest group of prohibited books. The reason given by the censors was that some of those in circulation were "corrupt" in their commentaries, while the editors of others referred openly to contemporary religious conflicts and took sides in doctrinal disputes or proposed a reading for a Biblical text that sanctioned a Protestant position. The concept of the "depravation" of Scripture was central to the discourse in the indices' preliminaries—perhaps the only place where the editors openly expounded their misgivings and purposes. The emperor Charles's very brief *Mandement* for the 1546 Louvain catalogue effectively assumed that "plusieurs imprimeurs ont corrompu les Bibles" and that they had changed "le texte et la lettre de la sainte escripture et y adioustant prefations, sommaires ou tables et annotacions mauvaises...".[38] The Faculty of Theology's epistle (1546) that served as a preface was even more radical: it condemned Bibles that "corrupted" the meaning of Sacred Scripture using additions, changes of placement, and biased omissions to the point where they became unrecognisable ("ita corruptus (sc. sensus) ut biblia vetera locis multis non agnoscas, tanta est diversitas", *Epistola*, 1546, Cc iii v). The later Louvain catalogues (1548, 1550, 1558) maintained and amplified the lists of Latin Bibles, which in any case formed their own distinct block.[39]

The first Spanish Index (1551), then, was not the work of the Holy Office. It did of course include a local section of Castilian books, but the main part was wholly imported from the imperial university most strongly implicated in regulating and managing heterodoxy and Lutheran books—many of which were published nearby in Flanders and Brabant.[40] The Holy Office's

---

[38] *Mandement*, in *Edictum Caesareae Maiestatis promulgatum anno salutis MDXLVI. Praeterea Catalogus et declaratio librorum reprobatorum a Facultate Sacrae Theologiae Lovaniensis Academiae Iussi et Ordinatione praenominatae*, Lovanii: Servatius a Sassen, 1546, Aav.

[39] The list of Bibles in the 1550 catalogue is, in the main, that of 1546, with the single addition of *Biblia sacra latina, juxta veterem et vulgatam edicionem...* (París, 1545) printed by Robert Estienne, which had been condemned by the Paris Faculty of Theology in 1549 (see Martínez de Bujanda, ILI, II, n° 233). For a chronological table of prohibited editions of the Bible and the New Testament in all the Louvain indices between 1546 and 1558, with their places and editors, see Martínez de Bujanda, ILI, II, pp. 65–67. In 1550, the Bibles were divided amongst Latin, Greek, German, and French (ILI, II, 440–41), and there is also a list of New Testament editions (ILI, II, 442). The editors of Latin Bibles that are prohibited come from only a few cities: in particular, Antwerp, Basel, Lyon, and Paris; secondarily, with just one Bible, Zurich.

[40] The four extant editions of the Spanish Index of 1551 are different from each other. The most complete is the Toledo edition (Martinez de Bujanda, ILI, V, p. 68), since it includes the Louvain paratexts and a section of prohibited books in *romance*. The 1550 Louvain Index also included a section of books recommended for teaching the various disciplines (Martínez de Bujanda, ILI, V, 65). Some editions retain, among the paratexts, the introductory letter

adoption in 1551 of the Louvain catalogue brought with it policies and reading practices that had been defined in the complex religious and publishing situation of the Low Countries, and that were part of the doctrinal and controversial tasks that the University of Louvain had assumed during the first decades of the sixteenth century. It also brought with it the fiery preliminary epistle of the Rector and may have contributed to encouraging misgivings in Spain about a *depravatio* of Latin Bibles (vernacular Scriptures having been prohibited as a whole) and about "good books" in which unacceptable theses had been inserted or intermingled. It is possible that importing the Louvain Index intensified in Spain a negative attitude toward Protestant editions of the Bible (before the appearance of heterodox groups in Valladolid and Seville) and those printed in Germany and France, and alerted censors to errors inserted in scholia, annotations, and summaries.

This section of Bibles proved to be of extraordinary importance. It not only affected the reading of the sacred text and its printed distribution in the Low Countries, but also decided the beginnings of the Spanish Crown's expurgatory policy, which was initially confined to this limited trial field.[41] The *Censura Generalis*, as the first experiment with structured expurgation, is linked to the reception of the Louvain catalogue, or, more precisely, with its newness as a censorial instrument, the vacillations of its use, and the protests raised by the first attempts at its implementation.[42]

Ignacio Tellechea and Jesús Martínez de Bujanda have argued that the 1554 *Censura generalis* was developed to resolve the many doubts arising from

---

from the rector of the University of Louvain, to which other local documents are added (for example, a letter-edict from the Toledo Inquisition, for the edition from that city). It should be pointed out that Bibles in the common language were entirely prohibited in the section of the Holy Office.

[41] See María José VEGA, "Buenas y malas biblias. La *Censura generalis* (1554) y los inicios de la política expurgatoria de la monarquía hispánica", in *Curiosidad y censura en la Edad Moderna*, ed. by Silvia-Alexandra Ștefan and Oana-Andreia Sambrian, Bucharest: University of Bucharest, 2020, pp. 14–52.

[42] In the months following the promulgation of the 1551 Index, letters from booksellers and questions sent to the Holy Office by bishops and inquisitors from local districts anticipated officious and alternative proposals for intervention in the presses, ones that would allow the keeping, reading, buying, and selling of Bibles and prohibited books as long as terms, passages, prologues, or proper names were selectively eliminated. The application of the 1551 Index must have been uneven (Ricardo GARCÍA CÁRCEL, *Herejía y sociedad en el siglo XVI. La inquisición en Valencia (1539–1609)*, Barcelona: Península, 1980, pp. 299–300; MARTÍNEZ DE BUJANDA, ILI, V, p. 70). Many of the consultations sent to the inquisitors are collected in AHN, *Inquisición*, lib. 574, with the register of letters from the Council to the tribunals of the secretariat of Castile between 1550 and 1555, and with the documentation relative to preparing the *Censura* of Bibles. Some of the most important documents have been extracted by MARTÍNEZ DE BUJANDA, ILI, V, 72–76.

enforcement of the Bible section of the Louvain catalogue, and to respond to the complaints of book-sellers, readers, monasteries, and universities, all of whom demanded that the Bibles on the list should be allowed to be used once they were corrected.[43] Surprisingly, the men in charge of enforcing the 1551 Index shared the perplexity felt by readers—a fact, incidentally, that is a significant clue to the weaknesses of the censorial system, which did not appear to function like efficient machinery, as is often believed, or that at least did not function that way at this moment or with regard to Latin Bibles. Instead, the inquisitors sent out consultations on practical and conceptual issues, politically restrained their own decrees, and responded to pressure groups, to organised guilds, and to particular interpretive communities. In fact, it was only with the help of the universities of Salamanca and Alcalá that they were able to fashion a reasoned response to the question of what to do with the Latin Bibles. Martínez de Bujanda suggests that the Council of the Inquisition may not have known all the editions included in the Louvain catalogue, or that, in some cases, it had not been concerned about them.[44] Perhaps the focus on prohibiting vernacular Bibles had led to a certain lack of attention to Latin Bibles; in any case, one cannot discount the possibility that the "malicious" Bibles that disturbed the Louvain theologians were not as high on the Spanish Inquisition's list of concerns.[45]

---

[43] See MARTÍNEZ DE BUJANDA, ILI, V, p. 77. In Fernando de Valdés's letter to the local inquisitors that accompanied the Louvain Index, they were urged to pay special attention to the Bibles: "y principalmente terneis attencion a que se recojan las biblias de las impresiones que van anotadas en dicho catálogo y el misal romano y diurnal que van añadidos al cabo" ("and you shall give principal attention to gather the Bibles from the printings that are noted in said catalogue, and the Roman Missal and Diurnal that are added at the end": in MARTÍNEZ DE BUJANDA, ILI, V, p. 60). The history and chronology of the consultations, which began with Domingo de Soto's in 1551, have been described by MARTÍNEZ DE BUJANDA (ILI, V 77–86), who includes and expands the conclusions from two previous writings by José Ignacio TELLECHEA IDÍGORAS ("La censura inquisitorial de Biblias de 1554", *Anthologica Annua*, 10 (1962), 89–142; "Biblias publicadas fuera de España secuestradas por la Inquisición de Sevilla en 1552", *Bulletin Hispanique*, 64 (1962), 236–47. The participation of the Salamanca Theological Faculty is particularly important to the process of correction and expurgation.

[44] Documentation examined by Vicente Beltrán de Heredia (1961) shows how frequently the Inquisition received requests for clarification regarding Bibles and, above all, the confusion regarding editions. It is possible that some of those listed in the Louvain Index had not even circulated in Spain. José Luis GONZÁLEZ NOVALÍN ("Inquisición y censura de Biblias en el Siglo de Oro. La Biblia de Vatablo y el proceso de fray Luis de León", in *Fray Luis de León. Humanismo y letras*, Salamanca: *Acta Salmanticensia*, Universidad de Salamanca, 1996, pp. 125–44) has shown, for example, that the Vatablo Bible circulated in Spain without any problem before the catalogue was published.

[45] The question of vernacular Bibles is outside the scope of this article. On the prohibition of Scriptural translations, which was not consistent across Europe, as well as on Bible censorship in Italy in the second half of the sixteenth century, see Gigliola FRAGNITO, *La Bibbia al rogo*.

The conclusions of the Salamanca and Alcalá theologians were finally published in 1554, under the title *Censura generalis contra errores, quibus recentes haeretici sacram scripturam asperserunt*. The *Censura* allowed the use of Latin Bibles published after 1528, so long as they were corrected within the span of sixty days. For this purpose, it contained a proposal for expurgating summaries, indices, scholia, and marginal notes. Since the Bible itself is a "flawless" text, the extensive preface to the *Censura* blamed Protestants for attempting to identify their own doctrines in the Scriptures using glosses and *tituli*, thus making the text say things that agreed with their impiety.[46] This is an old argument from the heresiology of Late Antiquity reworked by the Louvain censors (and, to a lesser extent, by the Paris doctors), that had been amplified with the invention of printing and Protestant publishing efforts. The work of review and examination encompassed 57 Bibles recently published by the presses of Lyon, Antwerp, Paris, Basel, Strasbourg, and Venice.[47]

La censura ecclesiastica e il volgarizzamenti della Scrittura (1471–1605), Bologna: Il Mulino, 1998. On the debate in Spain, see only Sergio FERNÁNDEZ LÓPEZ, *Lectura y prohibición de la Biblia en lengua vulgar. Defensores y detractores*, León: Universidad de León, 2003.

[46] *Censura generalis contra errores quibus recentes haeretici sacram scripturam asperserunt, edita a supremo senatu Inquisitionis adversus haereticam pravitatem et apostasiam in Hispania et aliis regnis et dominiis Caesarea Majestatis...*, Pinciae: ex officina Francisci Ferdinandi Cordubensis, 1554. The preface shows an understanding that the heretics' strategy was to sell their doctrine in prologues, commentaries, summaries, and indices of the Bible, as though it were the holy books' teaching: "sed nec vereantur nova nunc reperta techna usque adeo sacram Scripturam pravare tantamque illi vim inferre, ut iam ipsas sacras litteras loqui cogant quod illi volunt et quicquid impietatis commenti sunt [...] ut et sua falsa dogmata... dissemient et pro Sacra Scriptura venditent [...] Ita nunc adversus eruditiores graviorem pugnam meditentur, dum sua dogmata per annotationes, summaria et titulos sacro textui adscribentes, conantur ostendere aut eadem omnino esse cum divinis, ut manifeste ab ipsis eruta atque desumpta, utentes nimirum eorum fraude qui, cum clam venenum alucui praebere cupiunt" (*Censura generalis*, in TELLECHEA, "La censura inquisitorial de Biblias de 1554", *art. cit.*, p. 111). On the censure of summaries, indices, and marginal notes in the sixteenth century, see María José VEGA, "Obreros fraudulentos. La censura de sumarios, índices y géneros de la erudición en el siglo XVI", in *El arte de anotar. Artes excerpendi y géneros de la erudición en la primera edad moderna*, ed. by Iveta Nakládalová, Madrid-Frankfurt: Iberoamericana-Vervuert, 2020, pp. 185–212.

[47] The *Censura generalis* includes 55 Bibles, but there is a *peculiaris* censure added, specific to Robert Estienne's Paris Bible of 1545, whose New Testament is to be eliminated in its entirety, while *escasísimos errores* ("a very few errors") are to be expurgated from the Old Testament: this Bible is to be allowed for the utility of its scholia, *praesertim viris doctos, quibus plurimum prodesse possunt, sed ne rudes et illiterati decipiantur, pauca quaedam hic notare volumus, quae suspitionem aliquam haeresis praebere poterant*. This observation is interesting because it is one of the indication of the selective work of censorship according to the readership that would use it. As we shall see, this Bible had been already prohibited by the Faculty of Theology of the University of Paris. The end of the *Censura Generalis* includes in an appendix the prohibition of the Bible printed at Basel by Oporinus in March of 1554, translated by

Half the list came from the Louvain Index.[48] As for the rest, undoubtedly they must have been circulating in Spain at the beginning of the 1550s or, in a few cases, were suggested by the theologian-censors.

The Saints in the Censura Generalis

The *Censura generalis* listed 130 propositions that would need to be suppressed in the marginal notes, titles, summaries, glosses, commentaries, and indices of the Bibles submitted for inspection. The propositions referred in turn to an equal number of critical Scriptural passages where the metatexts could induce readings of the sacred text in support of Protestant theses. The majority concerned certain hot issues of anti-Lutheran polemic: essentially, justification by faith, free will, and—importantly though not primarily—the intercession of the saints. Paradoxically, the *Censura* in this way made public a divergent itinerary of Scriptural reading, in order from Genesis to the Pauline epistles. It also proposed a process of theological *notation* or *qualification*, since it identified and named the type of error into which each proposition fell, or (to put it another way) it graded its distance from a Catholic truth and the extent to which it contradicted that truth. Heresy—the most serious form of dissent—has a surprisingly minor place in the *Censura*. Only 15 of the 130 propositions receive the qualification of *haereticales*. Many more propositions were *suspectae* or *erroneae,* and the clear majority were denounced for ambiguity, equivocation, double meaning, or a biased and malicious interpretation of the sacred text. These, for example, are the *propositio vera sed detorta ab haereticis*, or the *propositio vera, sed in sensu haereticorum... erronea*; the *catholica, sed per eam male intellectum est...*; the *vera et catholica sed suspecta*, and the *impropria*, the ones that ought to be read cautiously (*caute legenda*), those which were true *sed cavenda haereticorum malitia*, or the one that must be expunged because it misinterpreted the text (*prava interpretatio*). This map of censures and notes shows that, from the Catholic viewpoint, (deliberate) ambiguity and new interpretive proposals were the key problem raised by a Protestant reading of the Bible. This fact implies a recognition, to some extent, of the fragility of the sources of doctrine. The repeated idea of *malitia*, of *prava interpretatio*, of meanings that are twisted or badly formulated, that are pulled in the direction of unexpected implications: all this places the issue of orthodoxy squarely within the field of hermeneutics. The continual use of adversative language

---

Sebastian Castellion; it may have come onto the market after the text of the *Censura generalis* had been completed.

[48] For a comparative table of Bibles that appear on the Louvain indices and the *Censura generalis*, see MARTÍNEZ DE BUJANDA, ILI, II, pp. 157–59.

(*vera sed... detorta, malitiosa, suspecta*, etc.) is a clear indication of the censors' discomfort in the face of the texts' support of both "true" and "wayward" theses. The qualifications also reveal that the censors' main objective was not heresy; rather, they seem interested in identifying a set of textual and writing practices. Along with condemning heresy, the preface of the *Censura* cites the primary objective of controlling interpretation and thereby controlling truth: *Censurae nostrae ratio ut non solum haeretica damnemus, sed admoneamus multa vere catholica trahi ab haereticis in pravum sensum* (Censura, B iiii). The difference between *damnatio* and *admonitio* implies a recognition of the hermeneutical difficulties confronting controversialists.

This is the context in which the 15 propositions, *calificaciones*, and critical passages on the saints given in the following table must be understood. Four of them concern images, while eleven—those that interest us here—have to do with the intercession of the saints:

No.	Text	Proposition	Theological note	Qualification
3	Deut 4	Dehortatio a quacumque similitudine adoranda. Et ibidem: imagines ne fiant quae adorentur, solicite rursum dehortatur	propositio erronea	Ex his scripturae locis et similibus deducere in lege nova non esse adorandas imagines ea adoratione qua Ecclesia Romana consuevit, ut haeretici deducunt, est error.
5	Deut 5	Solus Deus adorandus	propositio erronea	Haec propositio excludens adorationem sanctorum est erronea
6	Deut 6	Statuae subvertendae	propositio erronea	Haec propositio universaliter capta, non habetur in scriptura sacra, sed est error, tollens imaginem sanctorum.
13	Deut 13	Statuam seu imaginem prohibet	propositio erronea	Haec propositio docens esse tollendas imagines in nova lege, est erronea, praeterquam quod haeretici in contemptum imaginum eas appellant statuas.

No.	Text	Proposition	Theological note	Qualification
17	Iosuae 23	Hortatur populum ut soli Deo fidunt	propositio suspecta	Haec propositio est suspecta quae videatur negare invocationes et auxilia sanctorum.
18	I Reg 7	Corde soli Deo serviendum	propositio erronea	Haec propositio vera est, sed si per hoc vellint tollere interiorem venerationem sanctorum est error.
41	Ps. 80 (81)	Qui Deo credit, in nullo alio fidit	propositio erronea	Haec propositio cum aperte tollat invocationem et auxilium sanctorum est erronea.
45	Ps. 93 (92)	Solus Deus adiutor et salvator	propositio suspecta	Haec propositio quatenus dicit solum Deum adiutorem suspecta est, quod videatur tollere sanctorum et iustorum auxilia.
56	Es. 8	Fiducia in Deo, non in humano auxilio	propositio suspecta	Haec propositio suspecta est, quia videtur tollere invocationes et auxilia sanctorum.
59	Es. 30	A creaturis auxilium petentes, decipiuntur Similis est illa quae in aliis impressionibus in hoc loco habetur: Irascitur Deis si praeter ipsum humano consilio sive auxilio innitamur atque ideo eadem censura est plectenda	propositio erronea	Haec propositio in sensu haereticorum, scilicet quod non sint invocandi sancti erronea est.
61	Es. 43	Soli Deo fidendum	propositio suspecta	Haec propositio suspecta est quod videatur negare orando esse sanctos.

No.	Text	Proposition	Theological note	Qualification
62	Es. 45	Deus, cum sit creator omnium, ipse solus est invocandus	propositio erronea	Haec propositio est erronea, cum tollat invocatione sanctorum.
65	Es. 46	Execratur culturam imaginum insensibilium dominus	propositio erronea	Haec propositio, derivata a lege nova, est erronea, cum tollat venerationem imaginum.
120	Ad Heb. 12	Accedendum ad Christum qui solus est audiendus	propositio suspecta	Huius propositionis secunda pars suspecta est, cum videatur innuere nec audiendam ecclesiam, nec recipiendam doctrinam sanctorum.

In comparison to the polemic about sacraments, grace and justification, the issue of the saints occupied, theologically speaking, a secondary place—at least in the Spanish Inquisition's *Censura*—despite enjoying a primary place in the organisation of sacred time and space, in devotional practice, and in the ordering of the faithful's daily life. The saints, therefore, were secondary theologically but central culturally. The *Censura generalis* also offered a list of Biblical passages that were, as it were, magnetised by the Pauline idea of *unus Deus, unus mediator*, and that were reformulated using metatexts as an echo of that idea: *solus Deus, soli Deo fidunt, soli Deo serviendum, solus Deus, soli Deo fidendum*, etc. The summaries, marginal notes, and indices thus encouraged a familial sense (or rather, they *created* a familial sense through repetition of the formula *solus Deus*), establishing a tapestry of passages whose readings reinforced each other. The Pauline *Mediator Unus* is not included here because, obviously, it is not a metatext but part of the sacred text itself; nevertheless, it functioned as an invisible keystone for the interpretive edifice of expurgated metatexts, while remaining outside the structure.

Suspicion, Error, Heresy, and Blasphemy: How to Manage solus Deus

It is helpful to compare the qualifications in the *Censura Generalis* with the theological judgements of other authors and censorial colleges. In Alfonso de Castro's case, the mere presence of the entry *Sancti* in a book titled *Adversus haereses* raised (at least implicitly) the denial of saints' intercession to the level of heresy.⁴⁹ The *Censura Generalis* (1554), on the other hand, qualified it as *error fidei* or as the even more diffuse *propositio suspecta*, that simply recognises the (linguistic) ambiguity of the formulation *solus Deus*, which could imply a denial of veneration and devotion to the saints. Other Spanish theological treatises placed dissent regarding the mediation of the saints on an even lower level. One good example is Antonio de Córdoba's *Scholasticae Quaestiones* (1569), which lowers it to the category of *blasphemia*—very far, therefore, from heresy and well below errors of faith:

> Propositio blasphema est, quae convitium, aut vituperium iniuriam, vel irrisionem, aut derogationem, seu diminutionem honoris, vel excellentiae divinae vel alicuius ad Deum quoquo modo pertinentis infert, in se vel in modo dicendi. Qua re vituperia in Sanctos, in ecclesiam, in legem divinam, in sacramenta, in cultum divinum, et huiusmodi, quae ad Christum referuntur blasphema sunt.
>
> *Unde blasphemum est dicere, sanctos non esse colendos, nec orandos, nec posse iuvare devotos suos*, vel quod aeque fidendum est orationis cuiuslibet peccatoris viventis, sicut orationi cuiuslibet sancti aut etiam B. Virginis iam in celo regnantis, ut blasphemabat Lutherus. Item, quod religiones sunt laquei animarum, et quod sancti eas fundantes peccaverunt, ut blasphemabat Wicleff.⁵⁰

Propositio blasphema in the sixteenth century occupied the lowest place on the scale of dissent, below denial of minor certainties derived from custom and consent, and even below *offensio*, evil-sounding propositions, and *propositio seditiosa*. It was in fact on the borderline between minor forms of error, *injuria* to the sacred, and what were called sins of the tongue. Antonio de Córdoba's reflections, which appeared after the Council had ended, reasonably make one doubt the theological quality of the Tridentine declaration, which, upon close examination, does not contain the term *haeresis* with reference to those who disbelieve in intercession and the *debita veneratio*, but rather the less compromised and less defining term, *impietas*.

The Spanish Inquisition's *Censura Generalis* presents a contrast on this point with the Paris Faculty of Theology's pronouncement on Robert

---

[49] Denying intercession is in fact presented as *haeresis pestifera*, with the inclusion of some inherited references (such as an allusion to a certain Vigilantius who is known only from a mention by St Jerome, which was reproduced by Clichtoveus). His recent genealogy of heresy regarding the saints included the Waldensians, Wycliff, Huss, Luther, and Oecolampadius (Alfonso DE CASTRO, *Adversus omnes haereses*, 156ʳ).

[50] Antonio DE CÓRDOBA, *Quaestionarium Theologicum*, XVII, in *Opera Fr. Antonio Cordubensus, ordinis minorum regularis... Opera libris quinque digesta. I. Quaestionarium Theologicum. II. De ignorantia. III. De conscienctia; IV. Arma fidei et Ecclesiae sive de potestate Pape. V. De indulgentiis inscribitur*, Venetijs: ex officina Iordani Ziletti, 1569.

Estienne's editions of the Bible. The complex history of the Sorbonne doctors' corrections of Estienne's Bible has been recounted in detail by Elizabeth Amstrong and James K. Farge.[51] It is enough to recall here that the conclusion of the process was a list of *errores* to be printed with all the Bibles as a warning to readers, and later, a prohibition of the editions. The qualifications and censures of the Paris theologians were well known because Robert Estienne published in Geneva, in Latin and French, a lengthy confutation of each of the passages examined by the Faculty, the *Ad Censuras theologorum Parisiensium, quibus Biblia a Roberto Stephano typographo Regio excusa calumniose notarunt* (1552). The Paris case against Estienne is especially significant because the Spanish theologians also examined for the *Censura Generalis* his *Biblia sacra latina, juxta veterem et vulgatam edicionem* of 1545, which had been qualified and condemned in Paris in 1549 and prohibited in Louvain. It is useful to compare two examples from the *Censura Generalis* with the Sorbonne's qualifications and Estienne's refutations, because they show correlation on many points between the theologians of Paris, Louvain, and Salamanca on the subject of intercession. Here I will give the Biblical annotations first, the Paris censures second, and Estienne's confutations third, in italics:

> Annotatio: Deus timendus: et illi soli serviendum. Serviendum Deo soli. Deus solus adiutor et servator. In Bibliis 1528, 1532, 1534, 1540, 1545, 1546.
>
> Censura: Haec annotationes cum praeclusionis signo haereticae sunt, tollentes Sanctorum auxilium.
>
> [...] *Clara Scripturae verba sunt, Soli Deo servies, Deut. 6. c. 16. Matt. 4. b. 10. His censores dicunt everti auxilium Sanctorum, quod tamen ipsi pertinaciter tuentur. Soli Deo omnis honor et gloria, inquit Paulus. Cur pro Sanctorum cultu depugnant, quem a Spiritu Dei excludi fatentur? Porro haereticam vocare sententiam qua ex Lege et Evangelio transcripta est ad verbum, quam Deus scripsit suo digito, quam Christo ore suo protulit...*[52]

This censure concerns Deut. 6:13. It is worth noting that the formula *solus Deus adiutor et salvator* appears also in the *Censura Generalis*, which proposes its expurgation, not as *haeretica* but only as *propositio suspecta*. Estienne in his response is astonished that the Sorbonne would qualify as heretical an

---

[51] Elizabeth AMSTRONG, *Robert Estienne, Royal Printer: A Historical Study of the Elder Stephanus*, Cambridge University Press, 1954, pp. 170 ff. See also HIGMAN, *Censorship and the Sorbonne, op. cit.*, pp. 92–94, and James K. FARGE, *Orthodoxy and Reform in Early Reformation France. The Faculty of Theology of Paris, 1500–1543*, Leiden: Brill, 1985.
[52] Robert ESTIENNE, *Ad Censuras theologorum Parisiensium, quibus Biblia a Roberto Stephano typographo Regio excusa calumniose notarunt, eiusdem Roberti Stephani responsio*, Geneva: Robert Estienne, 1552, pp. 173–74.

annotation like *illi soli serviendum* which literally quotes the sacred text: in fact, *illi soli servies* appears, *ipsis verbis*, in the Gospel of Matthew. There are analogous cases in Psalm 44, Joshua 23:1, and 1 Chron. (1 Paralip.) 20:12; the censors reject these notes because Estienne "urges [the reader] to give worship only to God", as Luther had done, and this is a denial of the saints' patronage:

> Annotatio: Iosue dehortatur populum a commistione Gentium, ne alii adhareant et fidant *quam soli Deo*. Iosaphat propriae virtuti diffidens, *soli Deo fidit. In solo Deo sperandum*, qui solus salvat propter seipsum. In Bibliis 1532, 1534, 1540, 1546.
>
> Censura: Loci Scripturae quibus hae annotationes et similes adiacent, ut plurimum solum avocant et ab idolorum cultu et fiducia, *et populum ad unius Dei cultum invitant eadem*. In universum cum praeclusionis signo toties retito sic positae, *sunt falsae et conspirantes Lutheranis negantibus tam patrocinia Sanctorum quam merita operum*.[53]

The interest of these passages lies in the way they highlight how similar were the censorial actions of Paris, Salamanca, and Alcalá in identifying critical or dissident passages requiring expurgation; and at the same time, how they differed in the severity of qualification. The very same proposition could be *heretical* for the Sorbonne and *erroneous* or *suspect* for the Spanish Inquisition. One can thus identify a hard line regarding dogmatic qualification: that of Castro and the Paris theologians, for whom a denial of intercession was heresy. This means too that they implicitly raised the belief in intercession to the category of Catholic truth (*veritas Catholica*). This is in some way consistent with the strategy of Scriptural reading practiced by certain controversialists. There was also, then, a softer line: that of the *Censura Generalis* or of Antonio de Córdoba, in which the question of the saints remained outside the realm of heresy and Revelation. The censures of Paris and the Spanish Inquisition bear witness, in any case, to the impact of the *quaestio de sanctis* on Latin Bibles, and, at another level, to how censorial scrutiny was extended to paratexts and metatexts of Scripture. They also bear witness to the general spread of a strategy of vigilance that acquired distinct forms in each censorial jurisdiction while sharing objectives and procedures. The polemic surrounding intercession, which began with controversial writings in the 1520s, was transmitted to editions of the Bible only a few years later. Catholic reactions to Protestantism, therefore, should not be gauged only on the basis of theological writings, but also of censorial interventions and of Bible printing and reading.

---

[53] Robert ESTIENNE, *Ad Censuras, op. cit.*, p. 176.

Villegas' Deviation in the Compositional Criteria of his *Flos sanctorum*

Fernando Baños Vallejo
(Universitat d'Alacant, Spain)

One of the most successful literary genres ever printed were the compilations of lives of saints known in the Iberian Peninsula as *flos sanctorum*. Its origin lies in the *Legenda aurea* by Jacobus de Voragine, of which different vernacular translations were made early on, with the peculiarity that sometimes the translators omitted parts of the Latin text and added some local saints. The arrival of the printing press meant the continuation of this tradition until Alonso de Villegas established a turning point in the itinerary of the Spanish *flos sanctorum*, when he changed sources and adopted the Counter-Reformist models of Luigi Lippomano and Laurentius Surius, with the intention of obtaining recognition with a work that could be considered the "reformed *Flos sanctorum*". This is one of the landmarks in our goal of identifying the peculiarities of the Spanish post-Tridentine lives of saints. To this end, we thought we should first delve into the goals and procedures of this literature as the hagiographers themselves stated them in their prologues, before we analyze the content of their works. I have dealt with this topic in three previous articles.[1]

---

[1] This chapter is a continuation of my previous analysis of prologues of Spanish *flores sanctorum* from the sixteenth century, in which attention is paid to the hagiographers' statements within the context of the Protestant and Catholic Reformation and the controversy on saints. In Fernando Baños Vallejo, "Paratextos, ilustración y autoridad en los *flores sanctorum* castellanos del siglo XVI", *Versants. Revista suiza de literaturas románicas*, 65, 3, *fascículo español* (2018), 33–61, I analyzed the paratexts of Spanish lives of saints as an instrument of affirmation of authority. In Fernando Baños Vallejo, "Lutero sobre la hagiografía y los hagiógrafos sobre Lutero", *Studia Aurea*, 13 (2019), 7–40, I compared the prefaces

This time I will focus on Villegas, for he opened the way for the reform of the Spanish *flos sanctorum*. I will compare the prologues to his first and third parts paying attention to how coherent are the purposes he mentions in both books, and not only if they agree with each other, but also if both agree with the content of their respective books. We can perceive the distance between the strictness Villegas claims to have in the First Part of his *Flos sanctorum* (1578) and his laxity in the Third Part, eight years later (although it was published in 1588). However, we can affirm that this strictness was more a statement than a systematic implementation throughout the work. The conclusion will be that what from our contemporary perspective seems a clear contradiction, when analyzed within its context is not so, although there were excesses that even his contemporaries could see as such, since the author takes care to justify them, and there was even one particular narrative that was expurgated by the Inquisition.

Let us now examine his declaration of intent in the paratexts of the First Part:

Flos sanctorum. Primera parte (1578)

The title itself on the cover indicates that the book's content is in conformity with the reformed Roman Breviary:

> Flos sanctorum y historia general de la vida y hechos de Jesuchristo, Dios y Señor nuestro, y de todos los santos de que reza y haze fiesta la Iglesia Católica, conforme al Breviario Romano, reformado por decreto del Santo Concilio Tridentino.[2]

"According to the Roman Breviary" / Prevalence of a Cumulative Eagerness

In the dedication to King Philip II, Villegas points out conformity with the Roman Breviary as the main attribute of his work, and he wants it to be

---

of the main Spanish post-Tridentine hagiographers, Villegas and Pedro de Ribadeneira, with their European models and antagonists. In Fernando BAÑOS VALLEJO, "'Lanzarían grandes carcajadas': Lo apócrifo del *flos sanctorum* y la burla de los protestantes", *Rilce*, 36, 2 (2020), 428–52, utilizing the compilation of sources of the previous article, I delved into the concept of 'apocryphal' and its different categories in order to understand the rejection of apocryphal material by Catholic post-Tridentine hagiographers as the basis of a new critical hagiography that aimed at avoiding Protestant attacks and mockery.

[2] "Flos sanctorum and general history of the life and deeds of Jesus Christ, our God and Lord, and of all the saints to whom the Catholic Church prays and whose festivities it celebrates according to the Roman Breviary, reformed by decree of the Holy Council of Trent", Alonso de VILLEGAS, *Flos sanctorum*..., Primera parte, Madrid: Pedro Madrigal, 1588 (1ª ed. 1578).

considered the "reformed *Flos sanctorum*", by comparison with the reformed Roman Missal and Breviary produced as a result of the Council of Trent and issued by Pope Pius V for its establishment in the entire Catholic Church. If both were also adopted in Spain, despite the liturgical peculiarites of each diocese, says Villegas, it was thanks to Philip II, and thus the author beseeches the monarch to support also the dissemination of his reformed *Flos sanctorum*. The hagiographer claims to know that the king "ha desseado semejante libro, y que ha mandado a personas particulares le hiziessen",[3] and asks him, for he has spent many years working on this book on saints, to receive this work as the one that can bring to fruition the objective of reforming the book on saints who are mentioned in the Divine Office.

I believe that a current reader's most immediate interpretation of "conforme al Breviario Romano" ("according to the Roman Breviary") and the statements of the dedication would be to clearly understand that Villegas identifies his group of saints with those of the Roman Breviary. But he contradicts himself in the dedication when he announces that he will include Spanish saints and some extravagant saints, that is, who do not appear in the Roman Breviary. Indeed, if we assume that an association with the Roman Breviary means that any saint not included there would not be taken into consideration, Villegas is inconsistent, and his intention of having his book considered the reformed *Flos sanctorum*, the canonical reference, and complement to the saints' mentions in the Roman Breviary, is incongruous.[4] Nevertheless, careful analysis points to a less naive interpretation, if we consider that Pope Pius V himself, who issued the Roman Breviary in 1568 and abolished the particular breviaries of individual dioceses, monasteries and cloisters, nevertheless allowed that those that were older than 200 years and had been approved by the Holy See could still be in use. Thus, we can think that Villegas, using the flexibility shown by the Roman Church with some particular well-established breviaries, feels legitimized to indulge his eagerness for compilation and so to include both Spanish and some extravagant saints.

---

[3] "has long desired such a book and has even commanded some persons to write it". Greenwood erroneously understands that the king commanded Villegas himself to reform the *Flos sanctorum*. See Jonathan E. GREENWOOD, "Floral Arrangements: Compilations of Saints' Lives in Early Modern Europe", *Journal of Early Modern History*, 22, 3 (2018), 181–203, p. 194.
[4] "El libro dará mucho gusto a todos los que rezan el oficio divino, porque podrán qualquier día que rezaren de alguna festividad [...] venir a este libro y ver en él la letura y historia de aquella festividad o la vida de aquel santo cumplidamente" ("The book will give great pleasure to all those who pray the Divine Office, because they will be able to come to this book any day they pray for a festivity [...] and perfectly see in it the reading and history of that festivity or the life of that saint."). VILLEGAS, *Flos sanctorum*, Primera parte, *op. cit.*, p. 7 of the first prologue.

Thus seen, Villegas does not associate his *flos sanctorum* with the Roman Breviary to the exclusion of all other materials, but follows what we could call a cumulative criterion: first he wants to compile all the saints of the official Roman catalog, not only an arbitrary selection, but the whole of saints venerated in the Catholic world at large, which will constitute the nucleus of his book. Villegas affirms: "mi intento fue escribir de todas las solennidades y fiestas que celebra la Iglesia, conforme al Breviario reformado, hecho por orden del Concilio Tridentino".[5] However, this does not exclude the addition of more saints, national or extravagant. Regarding the "Spanish" saints (although it also includes Portuguese saints), when analyzing the specific prologue to this part, we notice that Villegas does not even feel the need to argue in favor of their inclusion: he assumes the interest and convenience of offering those narratives in a book addressed in principle to the faithful Spaniards. Conversely, we can perceive how Villegas justifies his acceptance of extravagant saints in the corresponding preface. He says that his desire is that his book may satisfy the most demanding readers ("whoever has this book desires or misses no other"), and it be greatly esteemed ("much to esteem and little to wish for") in two aspects related to Trent's regulation, at least substantially. The first is its exhaustive character, as we are seeing, that is, that the book contains all the saints in the Roman Breviary (those to whom "the whole universal Church prays"), which implies many more lives than those included in previous *flores sanctorum*, as well as (and this is not a response to Trent's injunctions) many lives of Spanish and some of extravagant saints.

Criterion of Authority. A Supposed Limit to the Cumulative Eagerness

The second virtue praised by Villegas imbued with a post-Tridentine spirit in his *flos sanctorum*, in the preface to extravagant saints, is the critical rigour in the selection of his matters and sources. He repeats what he had said in the previous paratexts: that the content of these lives is endowed with great "authority and truth". In sum: in the dedication to King Philip II there is a significant passage in which Villegas warns that apocryphal materials caused the foreigners' mockery, probably referring to Protestants:[6]

> en los libros deste nombre que ahora andan, se leen muchas cosas apócrifas, y agenas de toda verdad, léense también otras muchas tan faltas de la

---

[5] "My intention was to write about all the solemnities and festivities celebrated by the Church according to the reformed Breviary as ordered by the Council of Trent", VILLEGAS, *Flos sanctorum*, Primera parte, *op. cit.*, p. 6, prologue to the reader.

[6] See BAÑOS VALLEJO, "'Lanzarían grandes carcajadas', *art. cit.*

autoridad y gravedad que pide semejante letura, que antes provocan a irrisión que a devoción, las cuales dan bastante causa a gentes de otras naciones para que burlen de los españoles, porque en su lengua no tienen cosa grave y de autoridad, en materia de tanta importancia.[7]

The dedication also contains the assertion that his entire material, including his mentioned selection of extravagant saints, comes from serious and reputable authors ("autores graves y fidedignos"). Then in the first prologue, he affirms that his main sources, Lippomano and Surius, are also based on authors considered serious, very reliable and truthful ("graves, muy auténticos y verdaderos").[8] In the second prologue, he justifies the suppression of well-known passages in the lives of saints because he could not find them in any serious and reliable author ("autor grave y auténtico"). And he warns: "Yo solo pretendí escrevir lo que pude autorizar con autor o escritura auténtica y grave. Y lo mismo digo acerca de los milagros, que escreví los ciertos, y dexé los dudosos".[9] In the prologue to Spanish saints, where he also remarks on the quality of his sources, prestigious chroniclers among whom he highlights as his main model fray Ambrosio de Morales, he says:

> Y entienda el lector que si de algunos santos se dixere poco, que es porque no se sabe otra cosa cierta. Y escrivir lo que es dubdoso ya he dicho que en este libro no se permite, porque lleva por principal fundamento verdad y autoridad de lo que dize, para que el español le precie y el estrangero no le desprecie.[10]

Likewise, in the last exordium on extravagant saints, he defends the authority of these accounts, although somehow less than for the other saints. There is some contradiction here with his assertion on following rigorous criteria, for

---

[7] "In the books on this topic that are currently being sold, we can read many apocryphal and untrue facts, as well as other things so lacking in the authority and gravity required by such a topic that they rather incite laughter than devotion, and provide foreign people an occasion to mock Spaniards because they do not have in their language something serious and endowed with authority on such an important topic as this", VILLEGAS, *Flos sanctorum*, Primera parte, *op. cit.*, dedication.

[8] VILLEGAS, *Flos sanctorum*, Primera parte, *op. cit.*, p. 6 of the first prologue.

[9] "I only wanted to write what I could find in a reputable author or writing. And the same is true about miracles, for I included the undisputed ones and left out those considered dubious", VILLEGAS, *Flos sanctorum*, Primera parte, *op. cit.*, fol. 70^v of the second prologue.

[10] "The reader must understand that if do not say much about some saints, it is because we do not have reliable data about them. And writing what is dubious, I have said it is not permitted in this book, which is based on truth and authority so that the Spaniards may appreciate it and the foreigners not mock it", VILLEGAS, *Flos sanctorum*, Primera parte, *op. cit.*, fol. 1^v of the exordium to Spanish saints.

he is now accepting a reduction in authority, although later he claims that he has expurgated the most suspicious elements:

> Bien es verdad que los autores de algunas dellas son de menos autoridad que los alegados en las escripturas por el orden de los meses, cuyas fiestas celebra toda la Iglesia Cathólica, que esto fue parte para que no las celebrasse. Con todo esso tienen autoridad, y la que basta para que ánimos sin passión y malicia las reciban y estimen en mucho. Especialmente que yo hize en ellas lo que en las demás he hecho, aunque sean de autores gravíssimos, que es quitar algunas cosas impertinentes y aun sospechosas de que fueron puestas allí maliciosamente de gente que con ánimo doblado y dañado desseava desautorizar, assí a los que las escrivieron como a los de quien se escrivieron.[11]

At this point, we can perceive with clarity that Villegas gives preference to his eagerness for compilation over the credibility of his stories, and it happens that these two principles by their very nature tend to collide, and they create problems for many post-Trent hagiographers.[12] If Villegas is intent, as we have seen, on making his *flos sanctorum* superior to the previous ones in rigor, that is quality, maybe he does so by paying attention more to surpassing them in quantity: he includes all the saints of the Roman Breviary, that is, more than what other similar books included, with the addition of the Spanish and some extravagant saints (so that he cannot be accused of missing any). He had already announced these two qualities in his first prologue: the owner of his book will have narratives for all the festivities of the liturgical calendar and all the lives of saints compiled in previous *flores sanctorum* as well as many more added to them, with the advantage that everything is true, reliable, and authentic ("cierto, verdadero y auténtico").[13]

---

[11] "It is true that the authors of some of them have less authority than those used in the sections that follow the order of the months, whose festivities are celebrated by the entire Catholic Church, and this was precisely the reason why those were not celebrated. Even so, they have some authority, enough for people without passion and malice to accept them and esteem them much. Particularly because I did with them what I have done with the others, even those from very authoritative texts, namely I purged some impertinent and even suspicious things that were introduced into them by duplicitous and evil people who wished to discredit those who wrote them and those they wrote about", VILLEGAS, *Flos sanctorum*, Primera parte, *op. cit.*, fol. 62ʳ.

[12] See in this same book the chapter by Cristina SOBRAL; and BAÑOS VALLEJO, "Lutero sobre la hagiografía y los hagiógrafos sobre Lutero", *art. cit.*

[13] Villegas states that he includes all the saints of the Roman Breviary. According to Greenwood, these number 212. Ribadeneira will later surpass Villegas when he compiles in his 1610 edition 240 lives of saints, that is all the saints of the Roman Breviary at that time. Greenwood claims that before Villegas and Ribadeneira, Surius had organized his *De probatis sanctorum historiis* (1570) according to the Roman Breviary of 1568. However, I have not seen in Surius' exordium any reference to the Roman Breviary; GREENWOOD, "Floral

In this regard, there is in the First Part of Villegas's *Flos sanctorum* at least one problematic presence: a saint whose life was considered apocryphal from early on, for which reason he appears in Pius V's Breviary only with a prayer, without any biographical data. It is St George. In fact, the well-known and frequently quoted *Gelasian Decree*, so called because of its probably spurious attribution to Pope Gelasius I, although it dated back to the sixth century, includes a list of apocryphal texts and a list of acceptable texts, and although the acts of martyrs figure among the accepted ones, it excludes expressly from them the passion of St George and that other of St Cyricus and Julitta, because they were "composed by heretics". Hagiographers and learned clergymen usually knew that canon, which explains why Lippomano, Surius, Villegas and Pedro de Ribadeneira justify that their version or versions of St George's life are not the one that had been forbidden by the *Gelasian Decree*. Ribadeneira in particular, who had already mentioned Gelasius's censorship of hagiographies in his prologue, explains that if the Roman Breviary does not include specific readings for St George nor mentions his life and martyrdom, it is because of the decree's prohibition.[14] Ribadeneira doubts whether to include St George's life, but in the end he does so and eliminates the episode of his fight against the dragon, which does not appear in his sources. Villegas cannot resist including this episode, albeit briefly, despite the fact that his sources, shared with Ribadeneira, do not include it: "Ya avía dado muestra de ser hombre valeroso y de grande ánimo, en que passando por la ciudad de Berito, mató a un terrible dragón que hazía mucho daño en aquella tierra, ganando en este hecho inmortal fama".[15] He justifies this mention in a curious marginal note in which he recognizes that the mention

---

Arrangements", *art. cit.*, pp. 191–92, 194 and 197. Lorenzo SURIUS, *De probatis sanctorum historiis*, t. 1, Colonia: Gervinus Calenius and heirs of Quentelius, 1570.

[14] Villegas justifies this not in the account of St George's life itself but in his *exordium*: "Y assí, aunque allí se veda la vida de san Georje mártir, no es la que escrivió Simeón Metaphraste, que va en este libro, a la qual remito al letor, para que considere y eche de ver la autoridad y verdad que esta tiene; estando en esto, falta la que de ordinario deste santo se leía, dando cierto indicio de ser la que vedó el papa Gelasio" ("And so, although the life of St George the martyr is forbidden there, it is not the one that Symeon Metaphrastes wrote, which goes in this book, to which I refer the reader, so that he may consider and see the authority and truth that it has; in this way, the one ordinarily read about this saint is omitted, given a certain indication of being the one that Pope Gelasius forbade"). VILLEGAS, *Flos sanctorum*, Primera parte, *op. cit.*, pp. 5–6 of the first prologue. Pedro de RIBADENEIRA, *Flos sanctorum, o libro de las vidas de los santos. Primera parte*, Madrid: Luis Sánchez, 1616 (1ª ed. 1599), pp. 4 and 299.

[15] "He had already been shown to be valiant and brave when at the time he was passing through the city of Berito, he killed a terrifying dragon that caused great harm to that land, gaining immortal fame with this deed", VILLEGAS, *Flos sanctorum*, Primera parte, *op. cit.*, fol. 148ᵛ. "Berito" is Beirut.

of the dragon does not appear in his sources, but he is including it because of the authority of old paintings that represent him with the beast. Villegas is motivated by his desire to be thorough.

The other passion censored by the *Gelasian Decree*, that of St Cyricus and Julitta, is absent from the Roman Breviary, but is included in Villegas's compilation, although in the Third part of his *Flos sanctorum*, which is devoted to extravagant saints and persons illustrious for their virtue.

Flos sanctorum. Tercera parte (1588)

The complete title constitutes already a full justification:

> Flos sanctorum. Tercera parte. Historia general en que se escriven las vidas de sanctos extravagantes y de varones illustres en virtud, de los quales los unos por aver padecido martirio por Jesuchristo o aver vivido vida sanctíssima, los tiene ya la Iglesia Cathólica puestos en el catálogo de los sanctos; los otros que aún no están cannonizados, porque fueron sus obras de grande exemplo, piadosamente se cree que están gozando de Dios, en compañía de sus bienaventurados. De cuyos hechos assí de unos como de otros se puede sacar importante provecho para las almas de los fieles. Collegido todo de authores graves y fidedignos.[16]

Clear Prevalence of the Cumulative Eagerness

Published ten years after the First Part, the third one is the work examined here as proof of the process of relaxation of the initial orthodox criteria in the compilation of lives of saints. The very global conceptualization of the third volume does not follow the original idea of a reformed *Flos sanctorum* associated with the reformed Roman Breviary, for the lives it includes do not appear in the latter, and in numerous cases do not even belong to canonized saints; even more, some figures included in the compilation barely fulfill the attributes of sanctity. We will see later how Villegas justifies this work, but we can begin now by indicating that in the case of Cyricus' narrative, the three-year-old boy who behaves in the presence of the assassins of his mother Julitta

---

[16] "Flos sanctorum. General history in which are included the lives of extravagant saints and men illustrious in virtue, and because either they suffered martyrdom for Christ or they lived a saintly life, the Catholic Church has already included them in its catalogue of saints; the others, who are not canonized yet, we believe that they are already enjoying God piously in the company of the blessed because their deeds were exemplary. The deeds of both can be beneficial to the souls of the faithful. Everything has been compiled from serious and truthful authors", Alonso de VILLEGAS, *Flos sanctorum. Tercera parte...*, Toledo: Juan y Pedro Rodríguez hermanos, 1588.

with the integrity and maturity of an adult martyr, Villegas feels obliged to justify his inclusion, for he knows that this life is considered apocryphal by the *Gelasian Decree*. And he does so like Surius, his source, stating that the censored version is different than his.

We can see that Villegas does not constrain himself to the strict criteria of a critical revision of hagiography, perhaps best represented within Catholicism by Erasmus of Rotterdam and his approach in his life of St Jerome. This is already explicit in the title, for he does not call him saint but "distinguished doctor", and affirms that he writes his book using information from St Jerome's letters; and it is perceptible in the prologue, where he declares his compromise with truth and his rejection of the typical fictions of hagiography.[17] But let us go beyond Catholic reformers, given that Villegas and Ribadeneira see themselves as performing the same function as their models, Lippomano and Surius, that is, militants against Protestantism and its attacks and mockery of Catholic hagiography. If we go back to Villegas's dedication to the king, we can observe that his attempt to purge the apocryphal elements to prevent "other nations" from "mocking Spaniards", clearly points to Protestants' criticisms, as can be seen in Lippomano, who refers to the "heretics" who might laugh out loud ("lanzarían grandes carcajadas").[18] They may evoke attacks against the cult of the saints and hagiography like those coming from Luther, who, paradoxically, ended up promoting the publication of hagiographic compilations written with Protestant criteria. Luther, in his prologue to the *Vitae Patrum* written by Georg Major, one of his disciples whom he commanded to write this compilation, free of fantastic elements, highlights some extreme examples of fictitious hagiographies, "totally impudent", that cause the Church to be ridiculed, which as a result also happens in the end to the true miracles. He mentions explicitly the cases of Marinus, Euphrosyne and Simeon Stylites ("on the column") and says that there are many more cases similar to these.[19]

Given that post-Tridentine hagiography has a component of reaction to Protestant criticisms, it is interesting to see, for our purposes, if Villegas also included those biographies denounced as apocryphal by Luther in 1544. In

---

[17] Erasmus of ROTTERDAM, *Eximii Doctoris Hironymi Stridonensis vita, ex ipsius potissimum literis contexta*, Basilea: Johannes Frobenius, 1519.

[18] Luigi LIPPOMANO, *Sanctorum priscorum patrum vitae, numero centum sexagintatres, per gravissimos et probatissimos auctores conscriptae*, Venetia: Ad Signum Spei, 1551. See BAÑOS VALLEJO, "Lutero sobre la hagiografía y los hagiógrafos sobre Lutero", *art. cit.*, and BAÑOS VALLEJO, "Lanzarían grandes carcajadas", *art. cit.*

[19] Georg MAJOR, *Vitae Patrum, in usum ministrorum verbi, quoad eius fieri potuit repurgatae*, with a prologue by Martin Luther, Wittenberg: Peter Seitz, 1544.

my opinion, both could be expected, the Catholic hagiographer's avoidance to prevent Protestant critique, as Lippomano suggested, or the opposite, that is, that Catholic writers would reaffirm tradition, whenever it came from authoritative sources, as Surius does,[20] the author of the most canonical compilation of lives of saints in the Counter-Reformation, published with the support of Pius V himself. Villegas states that he is following Surius regarding two of the three lives stigmatized by Luther, that of Simeon Stylites (First Part, third section) and that of Marino or Marina (in the Third Part),[21] one of the women disguised as male friars, as well as Euphrosyne, also referred to by Luther.[22] On the life on Simeon Stylites,[23] Villegas recognizes at the beginning that he is not an example to imitate, but he includes it nonetheless because it is noteworthy. He is once again following a cumulative eagerness:

> También es verdad que cosas tales como aquí veremos que hizo, más son para maravillar que imitar, pues él pudo hazerlas con particular favor de Dios, y licencia para que las hiziesse, y otro haziéndolas podría ser causa de su muerte. Y esto no agrada a Dios, pues quiere que nos castiguemos, y no que nos matemos.[24]

Something similar happens in the introduction to the life of St Marina, about whom he warns us that, as it occurs with other lives of saints, there are aspects more to wonder about than to imitate ("más para admirar que para imitar"), as the fact that Eugenio takes his daughter María to a male cloister disguised as a male and that she remains there under this guise for a long time. He adds that this was done by a particular instinct of God, and otherwise would be badly done ("lo qual se hizo por particular instinto de Dios, que en otra manera era mal hecho"). We see that while Villegas gives up and includes cases that are more curious than exemplary, on the other hand he tries to compensate by adding didactic remarks to prevent the reader from deviating from the right doctrine.

---

[20] See BAÑOS VALLEJO, "Lutero sobre la hagiografía y los hagiógrafos sobre Lutero", *art. cit.*, pp. 28-29.
[21] In the entry entitled "San Eugenio monge y María su hija", Alonso de VILLEGAS, *Flos sanctorum. Tercera parte, op. cit.*, fol. 149ᵛ.
[22] The Euphrosyne referred to by Luther must be the transvestite from Alexandria by analogy with Marino or Marina and because of the legendary nature of the account. But the Euphrosyne included by Villegas in the extravagant section of the First Part is St Euphrosyne of Constantinople.
[23] His penitence on a column was parodied by Buñuel in *Simón del desierto* (1965).
[24] "It is also true that things such as those we will see he did are more for marvelling at than for imitating, for perhaps he did them with favour of God and license to do them, but another person could die doing them. And this does not please God, for He wants us to punish, not to kill, ourselves".

In addition to the lives mentioned above, denounced as apocryphal in the Catholic tradition or subject to Protestant criticism, and they are just a few examples, we can also pay attention more in particular to the most shocking section of those studied here: the addition of the Third Part devoted to men illustrious in virtue. In order to see the broadening of criteria used by Villegas, we will analyze the justification he offers in the prologue to the Third Part, on the one hand, and the figures who are most removed from the traditional models of sanctity based on martyrdom and religious life, on the other. We will pay attention to lives of lay people included by Villegas in his desire to create a mirror big enough but also closely related to them, in which the contemporary faithful could see themselves reflected.

As we have mentioned, it is necessary to examine in detail the prologue to the Third Part regarding the sources he mentions, an addition to those of the First Part, and the edifying purpose. Starting with the latter, Villegas defends the writing and publication of this Third Part using a biblical idea and quote: human life on earth is a struggle (Job 7. 1). There is no other way to achieve salvation than through struggling. Although Villegas does not mention here the Protestants, it is obvious that he is emphasizing the Catholic creed about the retribution of good works against Luther's five so-called "sola", and in particular the "sola fide" and "sola gratia" as means to salvation. Villegas goes on at length arguing that nobody is saved except through struggling, which is evident in the case of martyrs, both male ("some crucified, others beheaded; these are stoned, those flayed and the others burned") and female (who were also "guerreadas, combatidas y muertas": "battled, fought and killed"); but even those who live in the most absolute seclusion must fight against their weaknesses; and not even the Son and Mother of God were exempt from this struggle. Thus, the book he is presenting offers a compilation of particular examples of this idea: different types of struggle from the primitive Church to contemporary times, and several models that can fit all statuses and classes of persons. Let us underline the relevance Villegas gives in this book to variety and contemporaneity. The purpose, then, is the same he stated in the first prologue to the First Part: "Y porque a todos les quadra y es necessario el obrar bien para salvarse, a todos les quadra y conviene la historia de vidas de santos, porque todos hallarán en ella exemplos que imitar".[25] Villegas himself reminds us that he had already stated this idea in the First Part, although this

---

[25] "And because it is necessary for everybody and we all must act properly to attain salvation, the lives of saints are beneficial and necessary for everybody, because all can find in them models to follow", VILLEGAS, *Flos sanctorum*, Primera parte, *op. cit.*, p. 1 of the first prologue.

text of the exordium of the Third Part differs, logically, in his justification of these foreign stories ("historias peregrinas") as equally edifying:

> El importante provecho que resulta de la lección de vidas de sanctos ya en la primera parte lo signifiqué. Aora digo que si todos los libros en que se escriven vidas de sanctos son provechosos a las almas, este será provechosíssimo, lo uno porque de industria escogí vidas que dizen con todos estados y suertes de gentes, y lo otro porque son historias peregrinas, que a los muy leídos se les harán nuevas, juntamente con ser los hechos que se refieren en ellas, assí de tormentos y martirios que padecieron algunos mártires, tan extraordinarios, terribles y espantosos, como las asperezas y penitencias que sufrieron de su voluntad y gana sanctos confessores, hermitaños y solitarios; osadías y atrevimientos heroicos hechos por tiernas y delicadas donzellas; todo esto con atención considerado y ponderado por pechos christianos y devotos no es posible sino que harán en ellos effecto y provecho singularíssimo, dando desta suerte manjar y sustento a sus almas.[26]

Justifying these stories as edifying is problematic, as we will see, but it can be perceived in this very passage where it says that for them to be efficacious, they must be received by good Christians with praise and attention.

Regarding the choice of saints, his canon does not follow the Roman Breviary, as in the First Part, but the Roman Martyrology revised by cardinal Cesare Baronio and established for the entire Church by Pope Gregory XIII in 1584.[27] We can say that if Villegas wrote his First Part of the *Flos sanctorum* relying on the promulgation of the reformed Roman Breviary (1568), he now composes the Third Part based on the enactment of the reformed Roman Martyrology, offering a complement to the brief biographical references contained in it, which, according to Villegas, are read throughout Catholic

---

[26] "The paramount benefit from reading lives of saints I explained in the First Part. Now I add that if all books that contain lives of saints are beneficial for the soul, this one will be particularly beneficial, because of the care with which I chose lives that fit with all sorts and stations of people, and also because they are foreign stories, which will be new to those who have read already many, and also because the events described in them, torments and martyrdoms suffered by some of the martyrs, are so extraordinary, terrifying and atrocious as the harshness and penitence the confessors, hermits and anchorites underwent voluntarily; the boldness and courageousness of weak and young maidens; and if Christian and devout souls well consider and ponder on all of these things, these stories cannot but have a good effect and a most special benefit in them, thus offering sustenance and ambrosia to their souls".

[27] It is significant, as an example of how post-Tridentine hagiographers are interconnected, that Baronio used for his repertoire Villegas's First Part, which is proof that vernacular hagiography also influenced the hagiography written in Latin, something that was not frequent and is the opposite of our case here. See José ARAGÜÉS ALDAZ, "El santoral castellano en los siglos XVI y XVII. Un itinerario hagiográfico", *Analecta Bollandiana*, 118 (2000), 329–86, p. 367.

Christendom on the day dedicated to each saint and at the hour of Prime. But once again, we are dealing with Villegas' eagerness for compilation; he is not satisfied with an enlarged list of extravagant saints, but wants to add characters he calls "illustrious in virtue", because they are not included in the Roman Martyrology. His justification is that their biographies are also an example that heaven is attained with good works, with a life's struggle:

> el orden que tiene Dios puesto para communicar su cielo y admitir a él los mortales, que es por pelea y victoria, y que por este camino fueron los sanctos. Y para que más en particular se vea esto, servirá el presente libro, en cual se escriven vidas de sanctos y varones illustres en virtud, desde el tiempo de la primitiva Iglesia hasta el nuestro, y van de suerte que unos se alcanzan a otros, y, aunque por diversos medios, todos pretenden un fin, el cual alcançaron, que es ser bienaventurados. [...] Lo segundo hize esta mezcla porque ya que de presente no sean canonizados, possible es que andando el tiempo los canonizen, pues de ordinario passan muchos años para hazerse la canonización, junto con que no impide el no estar canonizados para lo que yo pretendo en este libro, que es provar que todos los buenos y que desean ir al cielo, le han de ganar por obras meritorias fundadas en gracia; y por exemplo de unos, otros los imiten y consigan el mismo fin.[28]

Villegas is right because some of the virtuous people he included were eventually canonized, although at a much later time, like Joan of Arc or Thomas More. But the truth is that comparing the criteria expounded in the prologues of the First and Third Parts, it is clear that Villegas has evolved to the point of contradicting himself: from utter rejection to dubious truth, for instance eliminating "dubious" miracles in the First Part, to including stories that present "some doubt" in the Third Part: "Bien es verdad que de unos por estar cannonizados, es el negocio certíssimo; y no estándolo otros, ay alguna dubda, mas consideradas bien sus obras maravillosas, sus victorias y triumphos, piadosamente puede creerse que están gozando de Dios".[29]

---

[28] "The order disposed by God to communicate his heavenly reward and admit mortals to it, through struggle and victory, was the road taken by saints. And so that this can be seen more clearly, I wrote this book, which contains lives of saints and men illustrious in virtue, from the time of the primitive Church to our times, in such fashion that they all rival each other and although they use different ways, they all had one goal, which they all achieved, which was being blessed. [...] Secondly, I chose these lives because although they have not been canonized yet, it is possible that they will be down the road, for it usually takes a long time; in addition, not being canonized does not hamper my intention in this book, which is that all good people and those who wish to go to heaven must attain this with meritorious works based on grace, so that their example may prompt others to imitate them and achieve that same end".

[29] "It is true that because some are canonized, the account is true; while the fact that others are not, offers us some doubts, although considering their wonderful works, victories and triumphs, we can believe piously that they are enjoying God".

Regarding sources, he is still relying on Lippomano and Surius to defend his choice of mixing canonized and non-canonized characters, for they had done it also, and to justify even writing a Third Part, for otherwise he would have left out in Spanish an important section of his Latin sources, selecting those lives most worthy of being known ("más dignas de ser sabidas") and more beneficial. He also indicates in the composition of this book he went beyond Lippomano and Surius, and has utilized other hagiographers like Juan Basilio Santoro (*Hagiografía y vidas de los santos del Nuevo Testamento*, 1585), as well as, and this is very significant because of his openness, chronicles of religious orders and even manuscript accounts.

Perhaps the clearest indication of this openness is the inclusion of lay "virtuous" people, since religious status represented the traditional model of sanctity (together with the older model of martyrdom). I suggest an analysis of eight cases, beginning with the humblest of them, lay ordinary females:[30]

In the first edition of the Third Part (1588) we were already told a miracle that proves Teresa López's sanctity, a woman married and born in Toledo. When lying in bed moribund, those present see some sort of Veronica with the face of Christ. Villegas highlights that this case is "confusión de los pérfidos hereges, que persiguen el sancto uso de las imágines, pues aquí se vee confirmado con milagro cómo el venerarlas es sanctíssimo, y que premia Dios a quien con devoción lo haze".[31] Villegas includes the notarized declarations of two priests who witnessed the miracle and summarizes information from four other witnesses, something that gives the impression of an official ecclesiastical process.

The other two lay women were added in the following year's edition.[32] The first is Bárbara de Santiago, married but a virgin. Although the account attributes to her virtuous good works like charitable alms or visiting the sick, as well as fasting and other strict acts, what is highlighted in her is her chastity, for she convinced her husband to preserve her virginity, despite sleeping in the same bed. At the end, we are told something she had in common with the Virgin Mary, for some texts had affirmed that the Virgin's beauty inspired

---

[30] See M. Mar CORTÉS TIMONER, "Censuras, silencios y magisterio femenino en la *Adición* a la Tercera parte del *Flos sanctorum* de Alonso de Villegas", *Specula*, 1 (2021), 183–210, pp. 188–89 and 195–98, in relation to the model of holiness represented by these three women, but also with regard to other women and specifically the "live saint" María de la Visitación, to which we will refer below.

[31] "To confound perfidious heretics, who even attack the use of images, for here we see confirmed with a miracle that venerating them is most holy and God rewards whomever does it devoutly".

[32] Alonso de VILLEGAS, *Flos sanctorum. Tercera parte...*, Toledo: Juan y Pedro Rodríguez hermanos, 1589.

chaste and not lewd desires.[33] That was also the case of Bárbara de Santiago's beauty: "y su lengua muy dulce, el aspecto de su persona causava juntamente amor y respeto, que ningún hombre que la mirara, por malo que fuera, se atrevía a dezirle palabra indecente".[34] Another element of sanctity offered by the book is that Francisco Escudero, the Jesuit confessor who wrote the life of this woman utilized as a source by Villegas, remembering her virtue after her death, he strongly felt the presence of her soul, communicating with him.

Ana de Cuéllar also preserved her virginity despite having been married for twenty-eight years. The most relevant episode is that thanks to her prayers to God and a procession she did entirely on her knees, her husband, who was agonizing unconscious, regained his senses to receive the sacraments and thus die in a state of grace. Villegas highlights Ana de Cuéllar's devotion and charity, for she cared until the end for an invalid woman who lay in bed and insulted her and treated her harshly; he also remarks on her sacrifices like the cilice, the scourge or using a stone for a pillow.

The other blessed lay people were already included in the first edition. I follow the order in which they appear in the book. While most of these accounts average three pages in length, that of Gonzalo Ruiz de Toledo, the protagonist of El Greco's painting known as "The Burial of the Lord of Orgaz", is five pages long. What makes him blessed is the miracle portrayed by the painter. After his death in 1323, his burial was attended by St Stephen and St Augustine, both of whom he had honored with the foundation of a monastery of the Order of St Augustine under the advocation of St Stephen. Don Gonzalo had been the tutor of Princess Beatriz, which gave his seignorial rank more relevance, and in addition to being rich but nonetheless virtuous, the merit that earned him celestial recognition was, according to Villegas, that "he had no sons, and spent his time and income in building temples, repairing some, and founding others".

The popular French maiden Joan of Arc was finally canonized in 1920, which justifies, although belatedly, Villegas's choice. Her most famous characteristic is her military leadership in the war against the British (Villegas calls her "warrior" in the rubric on her life) and her donning a male attire, which later would be used to accuse her. The attributes, though, of her sanctity, in addition to her virginal chastity, are God's call to lead the French troops and her death at the stake after being captured and falsely accused of witchcraft; she suffered an unjust execution with the strength and piety of

---

[33] Fernando Baños Vallejo, "Belleza y virtud en las vidas de María castellanas", *Medievalia*, 18, 2 (2015), 43–63, pp. 46 and 50–51.

[34] "And her speech was very sweet, and her beauty provoked at the same time love and respect, for no man who saw her, regardless of how bad he was, dared tell her anything indecent".

a martyr. Other attributes of sanctity mentioned by Villegas are her gift of divination, for she requests a singular sword that is being kept in a church that she had never seen before, and predicts the circumstances of her death.

The life of the famous Thomas More, presented in this book as a martyr of Henry VIII, is told in six pages that pay particular attention to his trial, with abundant use of dialogue and direct speech. Villegas is also validated with the subsequent canonization of Thomas More in 1933. He is characterized as an erudite student of Latin and Greek grammar, Philosophy, Law, Sacred Scriptures and author of works, among which *Utopia* is mentioned, a wise and ingenious speaker and an accomplished lawyer, which enabled him to be appointed chancellor to Henry VIII, and valiant enough to face death when he falls in disgrace after refusing to recognize the king as head of the English Church. His virtuous life full of vigils, fasting and prayer is also praised.

Juan de Dios, a fool, although canonized in 1690 (one new wise choice by Villegas), is the object of the longest of these accounts (11 pages long), one of God's fools studied by Aragüés.[35] As this scholar indicates, Lope de Vega included him some twenty years later in his sacred play *Juan de Dios y Antón Martín*. Villegas recounts his beginnings as a shepherd, his life as a soldier, his conversion after hearing a sermon in such radical fashion that he enters a state of holy folly, for he gets rid of the books and images he used to sell, runs throughout Granada almost naked and abases himself as much as he can as a form of mortification:

> Se entró en un lodaçal y se rebolcó en él, y puesta la boca en el cieno dava vozes confessándose por gravíssimo peccador. Salió de allí, y como estava corría por las calles principales de la ciudad dando saltos y haziendo muestras de loco y teniéndose por tal; los mochachos le davan grita, y tiravan tierra y lodo y otras inmundicias, y él con mucha paciencia y alegría lo suffría todo, pareciéndole gran dicha llegar al cumplimiento de sus desseos, que era padecer algo por el que tanto amava.[36]

He then was taken to an insane asylum for a few days, a place in which he decided to devote himself to serving the poor. Then there comes his phase, which

---

[35] José Aragüés Aldaz, "Locos y simples de Cristo en las letras de la Contrarreforma: vindicación de un tema hagiográfico", *Rilce*, 36, 2 (2020), 572–600. See also his chapter in this volume.

[36] "He entered a quagmire and rolled in the mud, and after licking it, he hollered aloud confessing that he was a sinner. He came out of there and ran through the main streets of the city, jumping and doing other deranged things and behaving like a fool; the children followed behind him yelling at him and throwing dirt and mud at him and other filth, and he suffered everything with much patience and happiness, for he thought it was good fortune to fulfill his wish, that is to suffer for Him Whom he loved so much".

occupies most of the chapter, as a founder of places to take care of the needy, from which activity a hospitaller order was created, approved by Pius V. Because of this last merit, and because he is a contemporary figure, Villegas justifies including him despite not having been canonized. His life is not lacking in prodigious events, such as surviving a devastating fire at the hospital after having rescued heroically the sick in his arms; or the fact that his corpse, not being embalmed, is well preserved after twenty years. "Quien se humilla será ensalzado" ("for whosoever abases himself shall be exalted") is the moral teaching of this story, summarized in Christ's dictum (Luke 14. 11) quoted by Villegas.

We will pay closer attention to the case of Baltasar Gérard, a murderer who is nonetheless, and to our surprise, presented as a martyr by Villegas.[37] He was a Catholic soldier from Burgundy, twenty-eight years of age, who killed the Prince of Orange, William the Silent in 1584. It is the first assassination of a head of state with a hand-gun, according to Lisa Jardine.[38] Villegas, obviously, does not give him the treatment of a saint, but includes him among the "men illustrious in virtue", although he makes clear several times that they are also "enjoying God", as he says in particular about Gérard. Coincidentally, six years later Villegas commits self-plagiarism and copies this entire account (except the introduction) in his Fifth Part.[39] Villegas mentions religious and political motivations, for he states, and repeats later when talking about Gérard's interrogation, that his decision to kill the Prince of Orange, although it cost him his own life (as it happened), was a consequence of his desire to serve God and his king and to benefit all Christians by beheading the Protestant rebellion. The truth is that in addition to these motivations, he also had an economic incentive because Philip II had put a price to the Prince's head, whom he considered not only the head of the Flanders rebels but also a traitor, for he had put his confidence in him when he appointed him Governor General of Holland, Zeeland and other territories. In addition, according to Jardine, although Gérard obviously could not claim the bounty, his family did. It was not the first attempt with a pistol on William's life, because in 1582 he had been seriously wounded by a Spaniard from Viscay called Jean Jauregay, maybe also motivated by money, although William

---

[37] The surprising presence of this murderer in Villegas's compilation was pinpointed without further analysis by GREENWOOD, "Floral Arrangements...", *art. cit.*, p. 195.

[38] Lisa JARDINE, *El atroz final del Príncipe Guillermo "El Taciturno". El primer asesinato de un jefe de estado a punta de pistola*, Madrid: Siglo XXI, 2008. It is a translation of *The Awful End of Prince William the Silent. The First Assassination of a Head of State with a Hand-Gun*, London: Harper Collins, 2005.

[39] Alonso de VILLEGAS, *Fructus sanctorum y quinta parte del Flos sanctorum*, Cuenca: Juan Masselín, 1594, fol. 179. The differences between the two versions are minimal: some changes of order and some abridged passages in *Fructus*.

survived in this occasion. These are facts provided by Jardine in his book, who also includes in the appendices the King's Edict and some Protestant accounts of the assassination of the Prince of Orange and the torture and execution of his killer.[40] In order to have an idea of how explicit Philip II's document is, we can just read the title:

> Proclama y edicto, a modo de proscripción, hechos por Su Majestad el Rey nuestro señor contra Guillermo de Nassau, Príncipe de Orange, como capitán en jefe y máximo perturbador de la Cristiandad, y especialmente de estos Países Bajos, y mediante los cuales todos quedan autorizados a herirle y a matarle, cual si fuere peste pública, con recompensa a aquel que lo hiciere y que asistiere o ayudare a ello.[41]

Villegas's account in the Third Part does not mention the economic incentive and characterizes the assassin with some resources he borrows from the hagiographic tradition. The first of these is the analogy between the killer's behavior and a biblical character, Eleazar, who decides to commit a suicidal action to defend his people: he goes under a war elephant to kill it and so is trampled by it (1 Maccabees 6. 43–46). Villegas compares this action to that of the "brave soldier" Gérard. He does not qualify him as a martyr unequivocally, but he is prudent saying that some do so while others reduce the category of his actions ("adelgazan el negocio") or just consider his behavior good and memorable. In any case, Villegas justifies including him among the virtuous men because of the incredible strength Gérard showed when facing horrible torture and death, with the added interest of being a contemporary story. The truth is that his account shows similarities with Christ's passion not only in the sequence of seizure, interrogation, torture, and cruel execution, but also in his composure, transcendent and hieratic attitude. The narrative also reminds us of many martyrs' passions through the use of the particular animal that accompanies the executioners, a male goat in this case, which is supposed to lick his wounds and to tear off pieces of his flesh ("pedazos de sus carnes"), but does not touch Gérard at all; and in particular through the suggested divine help to make him able to handle terrible tortures for days (whipping, hanging, burning, needles inside his nails and all types of vexations), "and it was a true sign that God preserved his life" ("y fue indicio cierto que Dios le conservava

---

[40] JARDINE, *El atroz final...*, *op. cit.*, pp. 30 and 32.
[41] "Proclamation and edict, in the manner of a proscription, made by His Majesty the King our Lord against William of Nassau, Prince of Orange, as the general captain and main disturber of Christendom, and particularly of the Low Countries, by which any person is authorized to wound and kill him, as a public scourge, offering a bounty to whomever does it, helps to do it or assist in doing it".

la vida"). He faced everything with serenity and calm ("serenidad y sosiego"), and his hieratic attitude in front of the governors reminds us of Christ's behavior in front of Pilate: "Lo que era de mi parte ya está hecho y acabado. Aora podéis vosotros, señores, hazer lo que os pareciere que es de vuestro oficio".[42] His executioners and enemies believe his composure is due to the devil's help, but he prays to God in the midst of his torments. In addition:

> Preguntávanle cómo no moría estando tan llagado, y respondía que los bienaventurados causavan su consuelo. Dezía otras palabras que eran ocasión a los mismos verdugos de derramar lágrimas y que se apiadassen dél. Afirmavan algunos de los presentes que era más que hombre. Otros le llamavan hechizero, y le preguntavan cuánto avía que encomendara su alma al demonio. Respondía con mucha paz y quietud que nunca él avía tenido trato o conversación con el demonio.[43]

His reaction to these insults was to be quiet and lower his eyes; he even thanked his judges for feeding him in jail and, like Christ did, prayed for them to God. He is also thankful for his sentence, just like St Cyprian of Carthague, bishop and martyr. He showed himself strong in the gallows:

> Lleváronle a executarla [la sentencia], y los pies quebrantados, los dedos casi sacados y todo él abrasado, llegó a la plaça y subió en un cadahalso, donde fue visto sus ojos claros, el color del rostro firme y constante, y mucho más su coraçón. Llegáronle a un palo o cruz, y no demudó el rostro, ni mostró señal de temor, teniendo presentes braseros de fuego y instrumentos de hierro espantosos.[44]

During the long and very cruel execution, he moves his lips in prayer and, although he is burned with red hot sheets and tongs, he does not become altered nor move, but continues praying and making the cross with his arms; and he continues with his prayers until they put him on a bench and cut him open in a cross shape, then they disemboweled him, ripped his heart apart

---

[42] "On my part, everything was finished and done. Now you can, my lords, you can do whatever is best fit to your profession".

[43] "They asked him how was it that he did not die after having received so many wounds and he responded that the saints gave him consolation. He said other things that caused the executioners themselves to cry and feel pity for him. Some witness affirmed that he was more than human. Others called him a sorcerer and wondered how long ago he had given his soul to the devil. He responded very calmly and peacefully that he had never talked to nor dealt with the devil".

[44] "They took him to the execution of the sentence and with broken feet, his fingers almost disjointed and burnt all over, he arrived to the square and went up the gallows, where they could see his clear eyes, the color of his face firm and constant, and much more his heart. He arrived in front of a pole or cross and he did not become altered nor showed any fear, even in the presence of fire and terrible iron instruments".

and threw it to his face, "y como si sólo tuviera boca y boz para lo que era virtud, no dio suspiro alguno, ni gimió, mas guardando siempre el color de su rostro grave y sereno, dio su alma al Señor".[45] This resilience is characterized as miraculous because it reminds us of the martyrs' strength, particularly in the context of a book of saints, and because there are many references to help received from heaven, even if Villegas does not explicitly speak of a miracle. It is also prodigious that Gérard's head, hanging on a pike on the walls of Delft, was more beautiful than the heads of many who are alive.

The last resource utilized by Villegas to characterize Gérard as a martyr is the analogy with St Proculus of Bologna, another soldier and true martyr executed in 519 according to the version compiled in Villegas's book, who, according to this author, did the same as the Burgundian soldier, that is, he killed an Arrian tyrant who persecuted Catholics. Thus Gérard's narrative, which began likening Gérard to the biblical character Eleazar, ends symmetrically making him an equal to St Proculus, and therefore Gérard is framed as a saint.[46] The miracle attributed to St Proculus is more marvelous and legendary than the execution of Gérard (which is also rather wonderful in itself), for St Proculus, as other cephalophore saints, stood up after being beheaded, took his head in his hands and entered the city in this manner. However, Villegas uses him as an argument from authority in favor of Gérard because his life is among those included by Surius and it appears in the Roman Martyrology. Because of this, Villegas also includes the specific life of St Proculus in the same Third Part, but in the section of extravagant saints. Going back to Gérard's passion, the hagiographer concludes, by analogy between both cases and because of the composure of the assassin when facing torment and death:

> Y así aviendo tenido el mismo intento Baltasar Guiarrars en matar al Príncipe de Oranje, y llevando los tormentos con que fue muerto con la paciencia que se ha dicho, piadosamente es de creer que está gozando de Dios, y así puede ir en este libro en el número de varones illustres.[47]

This is the end of the text devoted to this assassin, placing him among the virtuous men. The deviation from the initial criteria of the first production of his *Flos sanctorum*, published 8 years before the writing of this story, is

---

[45] "And as if his mouth and voice could be used only for something virtuous, he did not moan, but preserving the color of his face always grave and serene, he expired".

[46] In the *Fructus sanctorum y quinta parte del Flos sanctorum, op. cit.*, Villegas places St Proculus's example before Gérard's, precisely the opposite of what he does in the Third Part.

[47] "Thus, having Baltasar Guiarrars the same intention of killing the Prince of Orange, and suffering the torments that killed him with the patience we have described, one must believe that he is now enjoying God piously and therefore he can be included in this book among the virtuous men".

noteworthy, not only because of the category of the character involved, which is far removed from the consecrated models of sanctity, but also because of the different type of sources utilized. In the First Part the nucleus was composed of saints from the reformed Roman Breviary and the sources ought to be serious and reliable authors, as were his main models, the post-Tridentine hagiographers Lippomano and Surius. Conversely, in his Third Part, as I mentioned, Villegas used also references from the reformed Roman Martyrology and other hagiographical compilations, adding now chronicles of religious orders and even manuscript accounts. Thus, in the life of Gonzalo Ruiz de Toledo, he utilizes sources of this type (chronicles and reports), without mentioning the author, but at least identifiable because of where they are being held. However, the authority of the sources of Gérard's narrative represents the lowest category, because he does not identify them at all and only claims their truthfulness basing on, he says, they agree with other: "el caso como sucedió por relaciones diversas y que todas concuerdan en una cosa es desta manera".[48] Indeed, while this account can be more truthful than other lives of saints consecrated by the most renowned authors in the ecclesiastic tradition, nevertheless the lack of clarity about its sources makes us doubt that he is fulfilling his compromise regarding authority. This was a compromise that had been updated in the prologue to the Third Part in the following terms (referring to the added lives, marginal with respect to those taken from books of saints and canonical hagiographers): "a lo cual añadí otras historias de nuevo, sacadas de memoriales de mano, aunque de authores fidedignos".[49]

In view of the dubious hagiographic consideration of Gérard's life as "martyrdom", both because of its content and origin, we could wonder the specific motivations behind Villegas's incorporation of this story into his compilation. There could be reasons that coincide with those stated in the prologue to his Third Part: to offer an ample group of models that show many cases of how salvation can only be attained through good works and life struggle. As Villegas presents it, Gérard's case has the exemplarity of a "hero" who decides to die for his faith and his coreligionists. It also makes explicit the analogy with the biblical character Eleazar and with the martyr St Proculus. To this it could be added the exemplarity of patience and the serenity with which he suffers torment and his death sentence. The latter serves Villegas to show the proximity to St Cyprian martyr, and additionally all these characteristics

---

[48] "This case as it happened according to different accounts that agree with each other in the following manner".
[49] "To this I added other new lives, taken from manuscript reports, although the authors are trustworthy".

show the analogy with all other martyrs and with Christ himself. Within this context of elements that are typical of passions, we can also include the aspects that approach the events that take place in the story to the supernatural, to God's intervention, something that also justify the inclusion of this story.

In addition, we could consider other specific reasons not stated as such but equally evident. First, the enormous interest readers might have in a current and trending story (considering the religious, political, and military European context) that belongs to the conflict between the Catholic Spanish might and the Protestants. That contemporaneity makes the text close to what journalism is for us. Villegas places his story in time and space ("in the Flanders rebellions, at the same time this book was written"), but does not make explicit the interest I am referring to. Besides, this story serves Villegas to position himself in line with the Spanish Crown and the Papacy, something that can be made clearer with a contemporary event.[50]

In sum, the lay characters we have analyzed, and particularly the assassin, show that Villegas evolves towards a greater flexibility and even relaxes his criteria for including hagiographic material between the First and Third Parts. This can be explained because of the success of the first editions, which prompts him to increase the number of lives that go beyond his original design.[51] But also as a result of the evolution itself of hagiography after Trent and the canonical liturgical productions related the cult of saints, which show a move from restrictive criteria to recuperating certain cults. I am referring for instance to the fact that Surius claims to be less strict than his model, Lippomano;[52] or that some lives eliminated from the first reformed Roman Breviary are later incorporated again, and the fact that the Breviary will be overtaken as a reference for saints by the reformed Roman Martyrology. On the other hand, as we have just seen, there is a desire in Villegas to connect with contemporary times, as shown by Gérard's story as well as that of Juan de Dios, or the "santa viva" ("live saint"), the reason for the textual expurgation we will analyze now. These texts reflect the latest trends, and not only from a religious standpoint; they are live ideology. That is the only way we can explain the inclusion of a recent killer among the saints in the Third Part of the *Flos Sanctorum*.

---

[50] The best proof of Villegas's interest in Gérard's contemporary story is that in the volumes in which he talks about St Proculus and Baltasar Gérard, he devotes more space to the latter than to the former: in the Third Part, he devotes some 600 words to St Proculus while he uses 1,600 for Gérard's story; in the Fifth Part, he utilizes some 300 words for St Proculus and 1,100 for Gérard.

[51] See ARAGÜÉS ALDAZ, "El santoral castellano...", *art. cit.*, pp. 356–57.

[52] See BAÑOS VALLEJO, "Lutero sobre la hagiografía y los hagiógrafos sobre Lutero", *art. cit.*, pp. 25–30.

Let us finish with the expurgated text, not without indicating that Villegas already excused himself in advance in the prologue to the First Part as follows:

> Y si alguna cláusula o sentencia aquí se hallare, que por tener diversos sentidos, alguno dellos fuere erróneo, o sospechoso, digo que mi intento fue dezirlo a sentido católico, y no otro. Digo más: que assí en esto que aquí en este libro he escrito, como en todo lo demás que por escrito, o en público, o en otra cualquier manera he dicho, o dixere, he escrito, o escriviere, me sujeto a la corrección y censura de la santa madre Iglesia Romana, y de su cabeça, que es el Summo Pontífice, y de todos sus fieles ministros, y que estoy apercibido para me corregir siempre que me sea dicho, lo en que yo, como hombre, aya errado.[53]

Maybe these words are just a formula to show his discipline rather than a true expression of doubt or fear of making a mistake, but the truth is that one of his accounts was expurgated by the Inquisition, that devoted to a "live saint", María de la Visitación, a nun at the monastery of the Anunciada in Lisbon. It is part of the life of María de Ajofrín as one more testimony of Christ's stigmata on her body and as support of María de Ajofrín's stigmatas. Regarding the "live saint" María de la Anunciación (as Villegas calls her), he says that she has stigmata in her head, hands, feet and side: thirty-two holes in her head as if made by a crown of thorns; stigmata like roses, with a triangular perforation in the form of a nail in her hands and feet. Every Friday, five drops of blood flow from the stigmata on her side. Villegas must have been convinced of the truth of the story, for he states:[54]

> La [llaga] del costado vieron por orden del Summo Pontífice Gregorio décimo tercio algunas personas, y fueron officiales del Sancto Officio de la

---

[53] "And if a clause or sentence were to be found here that might have diverse interpretations and one of them would be wrong or suspicious, I state that my intention was to say it with a Catholic meaning, not otherwise. Item more: that in everything I have written in this book, as well as in everything I have ever written or said, or could write or say in the future, I subject myself to the censure of the Holy Mother Roman Church and its head, the Supreme Pontiff, and all its faithful ministers, and I am ready to accept any correction that they may indicate to me in everything I could have erred as human", VILLEGAS, *Flos sanctorum*, Primera parte, *op. cit.*, p. 8 of the first prologue.

[54] I use for the expurgated part Alonso de VILLEGAS, *Flos sanctorum. Tercera parte...*, Zaragoza: Pedro Puig and Juan Escarrilla, 1588, but with the addition of the men illustrious in virtue printed in Huesca: Juan Pérez de Valdivielso, 1588. The reason is that, curiously enough, the edition we have been using, quoted by ARAGÜÉS ("El santoral castellano...", *art. cit.*, pp. 356–57) as if it were the first, is already expurgated. Printing data of the first section are: Toledo, by Juan y Pedro Rodríguez hermanos, 1588, but the addition or second section indicates Toledo, Pedro Rodríguez (only) and two dates, 1587 at the beginning and 1588 at the end. Maybe both are false, for the expurgation was ordered in June of 1589.

> Inquisición, y el padre fray Luis de Granada y otros perlados de su orden, y sobre ello dio Breve el mismo Pontífice Gregorio, y yo le vi impresso y le leí.[55]

More than twenty years ago, Pierre Civil noted that this passage about the Portuguese nun had been expurgated (one page in total more or less). Mathilde Albisson has studied this topic recently[56] and states that the account was denounced to the Inquisition because it happened that the same year the Third Part was published, in 1588, the Portuguese Inquisition discovered that the nun's stigmata were false and she painted them with red ink. The censor who examined Villegas's text, Pedro López de Montoya, determined that the hagiographer had no malice whatsoever ("nengún género de malicia"), but nonetheless the Inquisition decreed the expurgation in June 1589, and it appears in the Index since Sandoval (1612).[57] Perhaps it was also a reason for censorship, as M. Mar Cortés Timoner suggests, the fiery defense that Villegas makes of the miraculous Christ's stigmata on women.[58]

In sum, when comparing the criteria Villegas used in his First and Third Parts, we see how far the author went: he began wanting to become the official Counter-Reformation Spanish hagiographer (and we must remember here that the first volume was dedicated to the Spanish monarch and the second to Cardinal Gaspar de Quiroga, General Inquisitor and Archbishop Primate of Toledo, that is the maximum Church authority in Spain), and, in opposition to this, he ended up being the author of a text expurgated by the Inquisition. He followed a path that can be explained by his change of criteria as a compiler, his becoming more relaxed, his cumulative eagerness, which in the end had more weight than a strict rigorous attitude when selecting hagiographic material. But Villegas was unstoppable, and this did not

---

[55] "Some persons saw her side stigmata under the command of Pope Gregory XIII, members of the Holy Office of the Inquisition and Father fray Luis de Granada and other prelates of his order, and the pontiff himself issued a Brief about this, and I saw it printed and read it".

[56] Pierre CIVIL, "Religiosité populaire et religiosité des élites à travers les *Flos Sanctorum* de la fin du XVIe siècle", in *Relations entre identités culturelles dans l'espace ibérique et ibéroaméricain*, ed. by Augustin Redondo, vol. 2, París: Presses de la Sorbonne Nouvelle, 1997, pp. 77–94 (pp. 88–89). Mathilde ALBISSON, "Una aproximación a la censura inquisitorial de la hagiografía en lengua vulgar del Índice de Valdés (1559) al Índice de Zapata (1632)", *Rilce*, 36, 2 (2020), 453–76. See also a new contribution by Javier BURGUILLO, "El éxito editorial del *Flos sanctorum* de Alonso de Villegas frente al control de la literatura hagiográfica después de Trento", in *Los agentes de la censura en la España de los siglos XVI y XVII*, ed. by Mathilde Albisson, Berlin: Peter Lang, 2022, pp. 303–40.

[57] Jesús MARTÍNEZ DE BUJANDA, *El Índice de libros prohibidos y expurgados de la Inquisición española (1551–1819)*, Madrid: Biblioteca de Autores Cristianos, 2016, p. 1096.

[58] CORTÉS TIMONER, "Censuras, silencios y magisterio femenino…", *art. cit.*, pp. 187 and 200–01.

prevent him from editing more volumes that he presented as additional parts of his *Flos sanctorum*; he will still write two more that include not lives of saints but sermons and exempla.

In any event, although Villegas went from rejecting "dubious" miracles to accepting stories that present "some doubt", and although we can perceive some contradictions even in his First Part, there is in all his volumes a coherent principle, that is his wanting to offer varied behavioral models for salvation through good works, as dictated by the Catholic creed and as opposed to Protestantism. To this end, he compiled models of the oldest and most consecrated saints in Church's veneration, as well as of the most recent ones, even with no accreditation, but who offer the attraction of connecting with the contemporaneity of Catholicism and the current Spanish interests.

Holy Folly and *Simplicitas* during the Counter-Reformation

A Context for Lope de Vega's *El rústico del cielo*

José Aragüés Aldaz
(Universidad de Zaragoza, Spain)

Holy Folly: Foundations

The Christian tradition of holy folly (or holy foolishness) includes a varied group of vital attitudes and theoretical reflections with more relevance in the Eastern than in the Western Church. The tradition varies depending on the mental condition of the protagonists (from intellectual limitation and extreme innocence to insanity), and whether this folly is real or feigned or has been attributed to them only by a hostile environment. In any of these cases, the holy fool gladly accepts to become the object of mockery and humiliation, and in return, his words and gestures can reveal a superior truth through paradox (and sometimes humor).

This tradition has an illustrious genealogy.[1] Without mentioning the indirect influence that some currents of thought such as cynicism had on it, its

---

[1] For a first approach, see Michel de Certeau, *La fábula mística (siglos XVI–XVII)*, Madrid: Siruela, 2006; John Saward, *Perfect Fools: Folly for Christ's Sake in Catholic and Orthodox Spirituality*, Oxford: Oxford University Press, 1980; Irina Goraïnoff, *Les fols en Christ dans la tradition orthodoxe*, Paris: Desclée de Brouwer, 1983; Sergey A. Ivanov, *Holy Fools in Byzantium and Beyond*, Oxford: Oxford University Press, 2008; and the articles by Donatien Mollat ("Folie de la croix I: Dans l'Écriture Sainte"), André Derville ("Folie de la croix II: Dans la tradition"), Thomas Špidlík ("Fous pour le Christ I: en Orient"), and François Vandenbroucke ("Fous pour le Christ II: en Occident"), in *Dictionnaire de spiritualité ascétique et mystique. Doctrine et histoire*, vol. 5, Paris: Beauchesne, 1964, pp. 636–44, 645–50, 752–61, 761–70. For Counter-Refomation Spanish literature, see José Aragüés Aldaz,

roots can be found in the Old Testament. There appears an essential motif for this tradition: the opposition between human knowledge, mere vanity in God's eyes, and divine knowledge, occasionally expressed through humble and paradoxical means.[2] In the Old Testament there developed one of its most influential models: the eccentric prophet, symbol of a divine call, perceived as a fool.[3] In sum, the Chosen One, according to Isaiah, had to be also someone "despised", obedient and silent in the face of humiliation, "brought as a lamb to the slaughter": someone, according to the book of Wisdom, subjected to mockery, whose life will be considered "madness" by those who are real "fools".[4] In fact, we do not lack accusations of madness of diabolic possession about Jesus himself. But it will be during his Passion when the announcement about the scorn for the Chosen one takes a clear form. In the Sanhedrin and in front of the high priests, Jesus receives the first mockeries and is slapped and spit on. In the praetorium, he is stripped of his clothes and dressed in a ridiculous attire worthy of a carnival king, and the soldiers bow to him in derision. Then, after obeying his Father, he suffers a humiliating death on a cross suitable for slaves, in addition to receiving again affronts by priests and soldiers. The devout contemplation and imitation of this humble and obedient Christ—disguised, taken as a madman or a charlatan—will be the two main pillars of the holy fool's tradition.[5]

There is no lack of other referents for this tradition in the New Testament. Among them, Jesus's entrance into Jerusalem riding an ass, which could give him the appearance of the king of fools of a carnivalesque procession, provided the traditional association of this animal (which is also present in the iconography of the Flight into Egypt of the holy family) with stupidity and comedy.[6] Other passages associate apparent ignorance with real knowledge of divine matters, asking men to return to a sort of "spiritual infancy": to a kid's ingenuity, to the innocence of Adam before he tried the fruit of

---

"Locos y simples de Cristo en las letras de la Contrarreforma: vindicación de un tema hagiográfico", *Rilce*, 36, 2 (2020), 572–600.

[2] See MOLLAT, "Folie de la Croix", *art. cit.*, pp. 636–38. And see Gen. 2. 17, 3. 1–17; Num. 22. 22–35; Job 5. 12–13; Ps. 94. 11; Prov. 9. 13–17; Isa. 5. 21, 19. 11–13, 29. 14; Jer. 9. 22–23; Dan. 1. 3–6, 2. 19–48; Bar. 3. 9–14.

[3] SAWARD, *Perfect Fools, op. cit.*, p. 1; Svitlana KOBETS, "The Paradigm of the Hebrew Prophet and the Russian Tradition of Iurodstvo", *Canadian Slavonic Papers*, 50 (2008), 17–32.

[4] Isa. 53. 3–7; Wis. 5. 3–5.

[5] Matt. 26. 67–68, 27. 27–31 and 33–34; Mark 14. 65, 15. 16–20 and 29–32; Luke 22. 63–65, 23. 11 and 35–37; John 18. 22, 19. 1–5. For the suffering on the Cross as an affront, see MOLLAT, "Folie de la Croix", *art. cit.*, p. 639. And see Mark 3. 21–22, 5. 40; John 7. 20, 8. 48.

[6] Conrad HYERS, *The Comic Vision and the Christian Faith. A Celebration of Life and Laughter*, New York: The Pilgrim Press, 1981, pp. 46–49. And see Matt. 2. 13–15, 21. 1–11; Mark 11. 1–11; Luke 19. 28–38; John 11. 12–14.

the tree of knowledge.⁷ This is a topic related to an eloquent image (the wise Child Jesus) and an idea that permeates the entire Gospels: the exaltation of humility and the condemnation of pride expressed in the Song of Mary ("He has put down the mighty from their thrones, And exalted the lowly") and in Jesus's words ("For whoever exalts himself will be humbled, and he who humbles himself will be exalted").⁸

The Holy Folly tradition found its final support in the first letter to Corinthians. There St Paul dealt again with the opposition between the "wisdom of this world", incapable of knowing God, and a "wisdom of God" who has chosen to save humanity through the "message of the cross" that they perceive as "foolishness" (μωρία). Using this opposition, St Paul articulates a paradoxical conviction: "The foolishness of God is wiser than men". Other important considerations derive from there. First, God's predilection for those less learned (which could sometimes see real stupidity as a sign of closeness to God). Secondly, the consequent need to "become a fool" in order to attain the real wisdom (a foundation for simulated madness or simplicity). Finally, the apostles' consciousness of having been turned, by God's will, into "a spectacle to the world", "fools for Christ's sake" (a model for accepting this claim with more complacency than resignation).

It is possible that in the epistle the concept of μωρία has a particularly restricted meaning that Welborn associates with the condition of a social type: the retarded or mentally challenged of low social class, object of public derision and a frequent character in theatrical mime (where as a "wise-madman" he can reveal uncomfortable truths). But the exegesis of St Paul's text opted for a more loose interpretation based on the semantic amplitude of the word μωρία in other contexts, which can refer to intellectual deficiency as well as insanity (μανία).⁹ And it is not important that the Vulgate chose a term with a restrictive meaning to translate this word ("stultitia" means "foolishness" or "silliness", not so much "insanity"): in the future, fools and madmen walked together the road of holy foolishness.

This road initially took them through deserts and villages in Syria and Egypt. There appeared the first fools (σαλοί), such as the nun of the

---

⁷ SAWARD, *Perfect Fools, op. cit.*, pp. 8–11; HYERS, *The Comic Vision, op. cit.*, pp. 78–79. See Matt. 11. 25, 18. 2–4; Luke 10. 21.
⁸ Luke 1. 46–55, 14. 11.
⁹ Laurence L. WELBORN, *Paul, the Fool of Christ: A Study of 1 Corinthians 1–4 in the Comic-philosophic Tradition*, London: T & T Clark, 2005. And see Frédéric LE GAL, "L'Évangile de la Folie Sainte", *Recherches de Science Religieuse*, 89 (2001), 419–42; Riemer ROUKEMA, "The Foolishness of the Message about the Cross (1 Cor: 18–25): Embarrassment and Consent", in *Studia Patristica*, 63 (2013), 55–68.

Tabennesiot monastery (later called Isidore) who feigned in the fourth century "madness and demonic possession", "cuffed and insulted and cursed and execrated" by the other nuns until her sanctity was discovered by a divine announcement. Or Mark of Alexandria in the sixth century (considered an idiot by everybody except Daniel, who thought of him as the only "man" worthy of this name in the entire city), and Simeon, "the Holy Fool", who left for the desert city of Emesa to mock and defy its inhabitants through his scandalous behavior (something imitated five centuries later by Andrew of Constantinople).[10] From there, the tradition would continue in Russian villages, through which the "holy fools" (юродивые) wander already from the fourteenth century and mostly in the sixteenth and seventeenth centuries: Procopius of Ustyug, Isidore of Rostov, Basil of Moscow, Nicholas of Pskov, among many others. All of them mortified their bodies, living alone as paupers, almost naked in winter, provoking with their eccentric behavior and the freedom of their words those around them—not without insults and blasphemies—who considered them prophets and revered them as saints after their death.[11]

As it was articulated in Byzantium and Russia, the figure of God's fool in these regions did not exist in the west. According to Kobets and Ivanov, the western God's fool is more moderate, given his relationship with his environment, more constructive and guided by a will to collaborate with the church and with a clear social responsibility. In the west, sacred folly is associated with humility and self-deprecation and usually it stems from repentance. There is then no place in it for the superposition of sanctity and sin that appears in the paradoxical behavior of the eastern saint (who in fact practices his asceticism in secret). In the orthodox church, foolishness is a condition that defines the sanctity of these individuals and thus creates an

---

[10] In addition to ŠPIDLÍK ("Fous pour le Christ", *art. cit.*) and DE CERTEAU (*La fábula mística, op. cit.*), see Sara MURRAY, *A Study of the Life of Andreas, the Fool for the Sake of Christ*, Borna-Leipzig: Noske, 1910; Vsevolod ROCHEAU, "Saint Symeon Salos, ermite palestinien et prototype des 'Fous-pour-le-Christ'", *Proche Orient Chretien*, 28 (1978), 209–19; Lennart Rydén, "The Holy Fool", in *The Byzantine Saint*, ed. by S. Hackel, London: Fellowship of St Alban and St Sergius, 1981, pp. 106–13; Kari VOGT, "La moniale folle du monastère des Tabennesiotes", *Symbolae Osloenses*, 62 (1987), 95–108; Derek KRUEGER *Simeon the Holy Fool: Leontios' Life and the Late Antique City*, Berkeley: University of California Press, 1996; Isabella Gagliardi, "I saloi, overo le 'forme paradigmatiche' della santa follia", *Rivista di Ascetica e Mistica*, 4 (1994), 361–411.

[11] See GORAÏNOFF (*Les fols en Christ, op. cit.*), IVANOV (*Holy Fools, op. cit.*) and ŠPIDLÍK ("Fous pour le Christ", *art. cit.*). We can also add, among others, Ewa M. THOMPSON, *Understanding Russia: The Holy Fool in Russian Culture*, Lanham (Maryland)-New York-London: University Press of America, 1987; and the articles in *Holy Foolishness in Russia: New Perspectives*, ed. by P. Hunt and S. Kobets, Bloomington: Slavica, 2011.

entire "hagiographic category". In the west, the traits of foolishness are just added to a sanctity derived from other qualities and shown, generally speaking, without ambiguity.[12]

All of this is mostly true. The adoption of holy folly in western saints is, in fact, lighter and more episodic. It even becomes occasionally a mere rhetorical device, always with the support of St Paul's words. In the west, it seems that speculation on holy folly is more frequent than its practice. But we should remember that in other cases irrational behavior defines categorically the relationship of the saint with his environment (particularly in the case of some of Christ's simpletons whose ingenuity has little to do with the intelligent "craziness" of eastern holy fools). We must insist on the fact that the tradition of holy folly is a special chapter in the history of western Christianity.

In the Middle Ages, signs of this tradition can be already perceived in the "savage men" ("gesta") of the sixth century in Ireland, or in St Romuald († 1025–1027), who elicited derision when proclaiming, as the Carthusians would do later, "the Gospel of good humor". Cistercians wanted to compare themselves with the child, the indigent and the idiot, accepting the invitation to become "God's jonglers" ("ioculatores Domini") that their founder, Bernard of Clairvaux († 1153) had offered all Christians having in mind Paul's letter. In St Francis's life there are accusations of foolishness and eccentric episodes related to his search for self-deprecation. His own thought seems to have been construed on some of the principles of the holy foolishness: appreciation for happiness and laughter, desire of extreme simplicity, brotherhood with marginalized people, identification with the derided Christ of the Passion. It is not strange that his followers called themselves "the world's fools" ("moriones mundi") and that many unlearned and simple people were counted among the first supporters: friar Gil and brother Felipe, Ruffino, John the Simpleton (who mimicked each of St Francis's gestures or postures, coughs or sighs) or friar Juniper, intent on cooking a meal that would last for 15 days for the whole convent by putting in the pot all sorts of unusual things (whole eggs, unplucked chickens) with the intention of having more time to pray. The Franciscan Jacopone da Todi († 1306) chose, instead, the road of feigned madness. An illustrious lawyer in his youth, he underwent a sudden conversion after the death of his wife, thus beginning a life full of eccentric episodes geared towards converting others: he put resin on and rolled in colored feathers to interrupt a wedding or appeared in the midst of the village festivities on four legs and laden with saddlebags. Giovanni Colombini

---

[12] Svitlana KOBETS, "Foolishness in Christ: East vs. West", *Canadian-American Slavic Studies*, 34 (2000), 337–63; IVANOV, *Holy Fools, op. cit.*, pp. 374–98.

(† 1367), founder of the Jesuates, made his followers go on piggy back insulting each other and made them carry him, tied up, hitting him and decrying his vile condition.[13] With gestures like these, the tradition of Christ's fools showed its connection to other manifestations of symbiosis of sacredness and foolishness, such as the *festum stultorum* celebrated under the Song of Mary, the *festum asinorum* in commemoration of the escape to Egypt and the *festum puerorum* in which a child was appointed bishop as a way to give childhood authority over the Church.[14]

Holly Folly: The New Times

The thirteenth–fifteenth centuries were the golden age of the tradition of holy folly in the west. This tradition will survive during the following two centuries overcoming obstacles and profiting on the other hand from some curious synergies. One of the obstacles was a growing social rejection of the phenomenon of madness which will relegate it beginning in the second half of the seventeenth century to spaces of exclusion and reclusion, according to Foucault's well-known explanation. Until that exclusion, however, madness lived a "long period of latency" in which it was related to "all the great Renaissance experiences".[15] The figure of the fool—with enormous satirical value—arose enormous curiosity in literature and in Renaissance and Baroque arts—this curiosity is the other side of the feeling of strangeness that provoked its final isolation. It is needless to list the works (before and after Shakespeare and Cervantes) that paid attention to the nuances of folly. But we insist that that same curiosity also spurred contemporary inquiry about Christian folly. It is not by chance that the most famous satire on human folly and stupidity—Erasmus of Rotterdam's *Encomiun moriae sive Sutltitiae Laus*—includes at the end an overview on sacred folly. In it, there are biblical reflections on the vanity of human knowledge, he quotes St Paul's texts on the folly of the Cross and there is a celebration of Christ's protection of

---

[13] VANDENBROUCKE, "Fous pour le Christ", *art. cit.*, pp. 763–64; SAWARD, *Perfect Fools*, *op. cit.* pp. 31–103; IVANOV, *Holy Fools, op. cit.*, pp. 374–98; Isabella GAGLIARDI, *Pazzi per Cristo: Santa follia e mistica della Croce in Italia centrale (secoli XIII–XIV)*, Siena: Protagon Editori Toscani, 1998; and Isabella GAGLIARDI, *Novellus pazzus. Storie di santi medievali tra il Mar Caspio e il Mar Mediterraneo (secc. IV–XIV)*, Firenze: Società Editrice Fiorentina, 2017.

[14] Harvey COX, *Las fiestas de locos*, Madrid: Taurus, 1983; HYERS, *The Comic Vision, op. cit.*, pp. 46–49; Max HARRIS, *Sacred Folly: A New History of the Feast of Fools*, Ithaca, NY: Cornell University Press, 2011.

[15] Michel FOUCAULT, *Historia de la locura en la época clásica. I*, México D. F.: FCE, 1976, pp. 13–74, especially p. 20.

children and the ignorant, as well as his predilection for the ass and the lamb: "Christ himself, in order to help human stupidity [...] became stupid himself ('stultum')", behaving "through the folly of the Cross ('per stultitiam crucis') and some idiotic and simpleton apostles ('idiotas ac pingues')", whom He encouraged to follow the example of children, lilies or small birds, "all of them simple and mindless things" ("rerum stupidarum ac sensu carentium"). Erasmus did not hesitate to mention insanity ("insania") in association with the fervor of prayer, which is very close to pathological craziness, or to remember "something similar to folly" ("quoddam dementiae simillimum") which the mystical person experiences in his loving rapture towards God and that is a prelude to the insanity of eternal life.[16]

Despite its interest, Erasmus's *The Praise of Folly* is probably not the most definite contribution to the tradition of the sacred folly from this period. More interesting is the content (and apparently ignored by scholars) of a work written a century later by the German Jesuit Mattäus Rader: *De simplici obedientia et contemptu sui*. The text was printed in Augsburg in 1610 as the author's second part of his *Viridarium Sanctorum* whose first part had been published in 1604.[17] In it, the reader could find numerous stories about simpletons and fools for Christ, having a complete overview of sacred stupidity in the West and Byzantium (the latter was well known by Rader). The interested reader could obtain this overview, in an incomplete form, from a group of other printed works scattered throughout. Among them we can mention John Climacus's *Scala Paradisi*, the *Vitae Patrum* attributed to Jerome or the more complete *Vitae Patrum* by Heribert Rosweyd (which added materials from Palladius's *Lausiaca* and Moschus's *Pratum Spirituale*), together with post-Tridentine lives of saints: the *Vitae Sanctorum* by Lippomano and Surius (1570–1575) and the *Flores Sanctorum* by Villegas (1578–1604) and Ribadeneira (1599–1601), translated into several European languages.[18]

The reader of these texts (in particular Rader's) would find in these works on sanctity and folly spiritual sustenance but also satisfaction of his curiosity. By 1600, those stories already had an old flavor. Yet they also were a sign

---

[16] ERASMO, *Elogio de la Insensatez*, LXIII–LXVIII, ed. by T. Fanego Pérez, Madrid: Akal, 2011, pp. 157–73.

[17] With the addition of one more Part, the *Viridarium Sanctorum Tripartitum* was printed in Munich in 1614 as part of the author's *Opuscula sacra*. In 1627, the *Viridarium* was printed by itself in Lyon. See Veronika LUKAS, "Rader, Matthaeus", in *Brill's New Pauly Supplements I I. Vol. 6: History of classical Scholarship. A Biographical Dictionary*, 2014, online; Alois SCHMID, "Pädagoge, Philologe, Historiograph: P. Mattäus Rader", in *Literaturgeschichte Münchens*, ed. by W. Fromm, M. Knedlik and M. Schellong, Regensburg: Verlag Friedrich Pustet, 2019, pp. 152–58.

[18] ARAGÜÉS ALDAZ, "Locos y simples de Cristo", *art. cit.*, pp. 581–86.

of tenacious heroism against the vulgarity of modern times: a way of opposing, from the point of view of Christian folly, the growing imposition of lay reason in European thought (an attitude somehow shared by the mystic, who adopts in his discourse the figures of "the fool, the child, and the ignorant").[19]

Obviously, they also had to overcome the suspicions that existed in the religious milieu towards the dangerous mixture of the comic and the burlesque. But the truth is that those caveats were stronger among Protestants, where Calvinists explicitly condemned the simulation of folly to feign sanctity.[20] Among Catholics, however, there was still space for an alliance among happiness, good humor and folly, from Erasmus's text (a real praise of happiness) to the lay version of this topic represented by the kind-hearted folly of a Christian knight: Don Quixote.[21]

Seen in this light, it is even possible that sacred folly acquired in the sixteenth and seventeenth centuries the character of a *sign* of the Catholic anchoring of this tradition. Despite its "eccentricity", the sacred fool has an *anima ecclesiastica*, as Saward claims, that practices total submission to the Church, as opposed to the heretics or the schismatics, who, lacking abnegation, prefer their personal opinions (the world's wisdom) to the truth revealed through the folly of the Cross.[22] That opposition to the proud wisdom of the heretics was even more significant in the case of God's simpletons, one of whose signs was the total submission to the conventual hierarchy. The unnegotiable affiliation of sacred folly and sacredness with obedience will have deep connotations during the Renaissance. So it also happened with another essential Baroque principle, the rhetoric of self-deprecation as it was understood in a treatise like Matthias Thanner's *Vera et profunda humilitas* (*True and Deep Humility*). The text offers a method to attain "self-hatred and self-deprecation", made explicit in the cover itself through the opposition between "wise stupidity" and "stupid wisdom", and illustrated with old and new examples from the tradition of the sacred folly, from Simeon of Emesa to the Tabennesiot nun, Jacopone da Todi and St Francis Xavier.[23]

---

[19] CERTEAU, *La fábula mística, op. cit.*, pp. 33–35. St John of the Cross explains the oblivion of the world during the mystic rapture using St Paul's opposition between God's and man's wisdom (*Cántico espiritual*, c. 26 (declaración), in *Obras Completas*, ed. by L. Ruano de la Iglesia, Madrid: BAC, 1991, p. 845).
[20] SAWARD, *Perfect Fools, op. cit.*, pp. 99–102.
[21] Hans Urs von BALTHASAR, "Locura y gloria", in *Gloria. Una estética religiosa*, vol. 5, Madrid: Encuentro, 1988, pp. 135–93.
[22] See Saward's French translation, *Dieu à la folie. Histoire des saints pour le Christ*, Paris: Seuil, 1983, p. 10.
[23] See VANDENBROUCKE, "Fous pour le Christ", *art. cit.*, p. 763, who mentions the treatise *De la sainte vertu d'abjection*, by Jean-Chrysostome DE SAINT-LÔ (1654).

This tradition had survived until the sixteenth century thanks to a handful of illustrious men: Thomas More († 1525), who kept his jovial spirit until he was executed, Felipe Neri († 1595), a paradigm of a desire for joviality and *festività*, or St Ignatius of Loyola († 1556), who imposed the idea of *imitatio* of a scorned Jesus in the Company of Jesus and the accompanying desire to "be considered as fools" ("ser tenidos y estimados por locos"), although "without giving occasion to it" ("sin dar ocasión para ello").[24] In the seventeenth century, the Jesuits assumed the message of their founder, although not always with the same conviction as Père Druzbicki, who defined the Company as a "company of stupid men and of those who profess stupidity". Druzbicki defended self-deprecation and self-abnegation, appealing to the rule of St Ignatius and the example of the apostles, as well as to that of Christ himself, who wanted "to be considered stupid", and of that famous nun from Tabennisi whose story was the colophon to his book.[25] With a similar approach, the idea of the Christian folly can be traced in the thought of Père Lallemant († 1635), and in all those influenced directly or indirectly by him. In it we find the disturbing figure of Père Jean Surin, deep in the hell of depression after an exorcism, who turned into a "fool for Christ" and was totally committed to God's will so that he could thus find a cure. There we also find the Jesuit missionaries in charge of the re-evangelization of Brittany (Le Nobletz, Maunoir) and all those mystics who were born out of that fervor: the noble woman Louise du Néant († 1694), imprisoned among the Salpêtrière's deranged, or the famous and almost illiterate Armelle Nicolas († 1671), considered a half-witted peasant, reduced every Holy Week to a stupefied state in order to achieve a sort of "spiritual death" every Holy Friday. In all of them we can find the firm will to share in Christ's shame, who made—as Père Guilloré states—a divine joke-king in the tragicomedy of his Passion.[26]

"Simplicitas"

Although they walk on the same road, the steps of the fool and the simpleton do not get mixed. The latter's steps are guided, in fact, by a virtue with a deep theological meaning: "simplicitas". Understood as an "absence of composition" and linked to perfection and unity, simplicity is, according to Thomas Aquinas, the first of God's attributes.[27] Projected onto man, this virtue is

---

[24] SAWARD, *Perfect Fools, op. cit.*, pp. 104–48.
[25] Gaspar DRUZBICKI, *De sublimitate perfectionis religiosae*, discourse XXIV, in *Opera omnia ascetica*, 2, Ingolstadt: De la Haye, 1732, pp. 535–38.
[26] SAWARD, *Perfect Fools, op. cit.*, pp. 149–84.
[27] There is a very large bibliography about this topic. See recent works on the topic by C. HUNEEUS ALLIENDE ("La simplicidad divina: fundamentos en la tradición ascética y mística", *Lumen Veritatis*, 10 (2018), 314–33), which includes some general overviews and

identified in the Bible with integrity and moral and religious purity referred to by the Hebrew terms "tam, tamim" ("perfect", but also "wholesome" and "intact"). This is the meaning reflected by the Greek term ἁπλός and the Latin words "simplex" and "simplicitas". It appears with this value in Psalms 15. 1–2 and is attributed to Job, "an upright and honest man", to Jacob and to David, who behaved with a pure heart ("tam"), that is "in simplicitate cordis". In the New Testament, the "healthy eye" ("simplex") is opposed in Christ's words, to the "evil eye".[28]

Identified with integrity, "simplicitas" is then opposed to the indecision of the "divided" or dubious soul and to the "duplicity" of a soul split in his attention to human affairs.[29] For Christians, simplicity is then the end of a road of ascesis and cleansing of corporal passions (and detachment from the occupations of false wisdom). With a similar meaning, the semantic field of simplicity floods the discourse on the mystic experience, understood as a process of purification or "simplification" of thoughts, a sort of emptying of the soul's images in the search to join the simple God.[30]

In a similar fashion, "simplicitas" is opposed from the beginning of Christian writings to the "duplicity" of the heart and tongue, to lying and hypocrisy, to feigning and malice. It will be opposed to affectation in language, in a scheme that originates with the praise of biblical "rusticitas" as Jerome does and it moves towards the occasional censure of rhetorical obscurity and dialectical sophistication.[31] Simplicity is thus identified with sincerity

---

specific works on Thomas Aquinas. See also Juan José HERRERA, *La simplicidad divina según santo Tomás de Aquino*, Tucumán: Universidad del Norte Santo Tomás de Aquino, 2011. And see *Summa theologica* 1ª, q. 3, a. 7. For the Counter-Reform period, see for instance Santiago ORREGO, "Simplicidad de Dios y pluralidad de atributos divinos según fray Luis de León", *Veritas*, 54 (2009), 90–111.

[28] Job 1. 1, 1. 8, 2. 3; Gn 25. 27; 1 Kings 9. 4; Mt. 6. 22–23. See Ysabel de ANDIA, "Simplicité, I: Écriture et Premiers Pères", in *Dictionnaire de spiritualité, op. cit.*, vol. 14, 1990, pp. 892–903, especially pp. 894–97.

[29] ANDIA, "Simplicité, I", *art. cit.*, pp. 898–900.

[30] C. HUNEEUS ALLIENDE, "La simplicidad divina", *art. cit.*; Michel DUPUY, "Simplicité, III: D'Eckhart à nos jours", in *Dictionnaire de spiritualité, op. cit.*, vol. 14, 1990, pp. 910–21. The idea of the imitation of Christ in the search for human simplicity appears in Rhenish-Flemish mysticism and in the influential *Perle évangélique* (sixteenth century). To a radical relinquishing of the soul as imitation of "God's holy simplicity", see the French spiritual writers of the seventeenth century (Benoît de Canfield, Simon de Bourg-en-Bresse, Jean de Saint-Samson). Francis de Sales advocates the simple "look" or "gaze" of God as a guide to our thoughts.

[31] Paul ANTIN, "*Simple* et *simplicité* chez Saint Jerôme", in *Recueil sur Saint Jerôme*, Bruxelles: Latomus, 1968, pp. 147–61. See also Vicente BOSCH, *El concepto cristiano de "simplicitas" en el pensamiento agustiniano*, Roma: Apollinare Studi, 2001; Vincent DESPREZ, "Simplicité, II: Monachisme ancien et médiéval", in *Dictionnaire de spiritualité, op. cit.*, vol. 14, 1990, pp. 903–10.

and purity, with plainness and humility, and it reaches its summum in some souls' ingenuity, like those of children. With the example of the evangelical appreciation of children, Christian literature invites us to recuperate the happy simplicity of children, likening it occasionally to Adam's innocence. The Shepherd of Hermas (second century), St Ambrose (fourth century), Philoxenus of Mabbug (sixth century), among others, insist on these associations that last until the sixteenth and seventeenth centuries, encouraged by the meditation on the sacred childhood of Christ and the devotion of the Child Jesus, in particular in some orders like the Franciscans and the Carmelites.[32] Even St John of the Cross understood that to become one with "God's wisdom" it was necessary to behave "like ignorant children".[33]

This praise of simplicity can be also embodied in men without formal preparation, the illiterate or the imbecile (ἰδιώτης), a condition the Sanhedrin appreciated in apostles Peter and John. Patristic and eastern monastic writers assumed God's predilection for the unlearned which continued in the following centuries. Of course, this praise of simplicity could be trivialized making one's own ignorance into a "captatio benevolentiae" in prefaces.[34] On the other extreme, several authors cautioned about a simplicity born exclusively out of one's intellectual lack. Unlike Greek and Hebrew, the Latin term "simplex"—and its vernacular derivates—also had a negative meaning from which Christian authors kept frequently away. Simplicity had its own rules. As the Gospels pointed out, the fight against evil required a combination of innocence with some sort of intelligence ("be as shrewd as snakes and as innocent as doves"). Simple-mindedness—St Vincent de Paul reminded us († 1660)—was not a virtue in itself, those priests who frequented "fools and jesters"—Jean de Saint-Samson said († 1636)—did not show "a reasonable and luminous simplicity", rather "a rash ignorance together with stupidity".[35]

Nevertheless, it is precisely this negative value of the term that allowed the perfect integration of "simplicitas" into the sacred tradition of stupidity. Within this tradition, the accusation of simplicity was received with as much appreciation as folly. In fact, simplicity can also be an attitude "feigned" by

---

[32] Sandra LA ROCCA, *L'Enfant Jésus. Histoire et anthropologie d'une dévotion dans l'Occident chrétien*, Toulouse: Presses Universitaries du Mirail, 2007; Michele DOLZ, *El Niño Jesús. Historia e imagen de la devoción del Niño Divino*, Jaén: Almuzara, 2010 (for Carmelite devotional readings, see pp. 123–39).
[33] ANDIA, "Simplicité", *art. cit.*, pp. 898–902; DUPUY, "Simplicité", *art. cit.*, pp. 915–16. And see JUAN DE LA CRUZ, *Subida del Monte Carmelo*, I, IV, 5, in *Obras completas, op. cit.*, p. 265.
[34] Guy OURY, "Idiota", in *Dictionnaire de spiritualité, op. cit.*, vol. 7, 1971, pp. 1242–1248. And see Acts 4. 13.
[35] *Oeuvres spirituelles et mystiques*, Rennes: Pierre Coupard, 1658, p. 739. And see Matt. 10. 16; VINCENT DE PAUL, *Entretien* 201 (quoted in DUPUY, "Simplicité", *art. cit.*, p. 915).

divine inspiration or perhaps the result of a real mental lack, conceived as a sacred stigma that gives a transcendent meaning to the words and acts of the chosen person. In this way, the simple saint is linked to the sacred fool, using as reference Paul's famous epistle, which, as we mentioned before, perhaps was alluding to the "stupidity" rather than the "folly" of preaching the Cross.

"Simplicitas" created its own literary tradition. One of its more important landmarks was John Climacus's *Scala Paradisi* († 649?), where there is a distinction between natural simplicity (that of Adam or of children) and simplicity as a result of obedience, represented by the likes of Simpleton Paul, a simple monk who behaved like an obedient ass (through an "animalization" of biblical origin which is frequent in monastic literature, taken to more extreme consequences by fools and simpletons in their discourses of self-humiliation).[36] Four centuries later, St Peter Damian († 1072) wrote his treatise *De sancta simplicitate scientiae inflanti anteponenda*. There we find the allegorical meaning of the ass jaw with which Samson defeated the Philistines (understood as a symbol of preaching of simple-minded and humble people), and a mention of the three children of the book of Daniel to whom Gog bestowed knowledge, and some cases of illiterate people who were converted to "the wise stupidity of Christ".[37] The *Epistola ad fratres de Monte-Dei* by Guillaume de Saint-Thierry († 1148) dates from a little later, which offers a canonical definition of "simplicitas" ("a will totally addressed to God that avoids to be enmeshed in this world's affairs"), based on the memory of God and preceded by St Paul's reflection on "God's folly, wiser than men".[38] This "holy simplicity" provided the title to St Francis's *Second Life* written by Thomas of Celano.[39] Caesarius of Heisterbach († 1240) devotes the sixth "distinction" of his *dialogus miraculorum* to "simplicitas". At the beginning of this book, there are biblical references to the dove and the "simple eye", the need to become "children" or the frequent comparisons to "God's jokesters". The chapter then advances *a contrario*, paying attention to the condemnation of lay and religious people dominated by malice. Among the examples provided, there are some of an extreme simplicity: canon Werboldo who could not count more than "if things were odd or even" (not knowing then about

---

[36] We use the anonymous Spanish translation *Escala Spiritual*, Lisbon: Ioannes Blavio, 1562, fols 140–42. For animalization, see VANDENBROUCKE, "Fous pour le Christ", art. cit., p. 761. And see Ps. 21. 7 and 72. 22.

[37] *Opusculum* XLV (*PL* 145, pp. 695–704).

[38] Monique SIMON, "Sancta simplicitas: la simplicité selon Guillaume de Saint-Thierry", *Collectanea Cisterciensia*, 41 (1979), 52–72.

[39] *Vida segunda*, CXLII–CXLVII, 189–95, in *San Francisco de Asís. Escritos. Biografías. Documentos de la época*, ed. by J. A. Guerra, Madrid: BAC, 1985, pp. 338–42.

the theft of two hams), a priest's concubine who jumped into an oven trying to find her salvation, for she believed a priest's command, or an old nun, "who was so infantile that she could not tell apart brutes and men".[40]

Despite their interest, the abovementioned texts can barely be considered a precedent for the key work on sacred simplicity: Mattäus Rader's *De simplici obedientia et contemptu sui*. This work, which includes materials from some of the previously mentioned works, is not only characterized by its length but because it purports to offer a complete itinerary, full of reflections, on this hagiographic topic. This integrating desire also sets it apart from later works, like the already-mentioned book by Carthusian monk Matthias Thanner, although the latter also borrowed materials from Rader.

Rader's work is a product of its time. Towards 1610 those old cases of simplicity and folly were considered interesting again, as we have mentioned. From its very title, Rader defines "simplicitas" as subordinated to two virtues that were essential in the Counter-Reformation discourse: self-deprecation and obedience. This subordination explains the division of the text into six chapters. Simplicity is dealt with in three chapters framed by the first two chapters on the benefits of obedience and a final one devoted, not by chance, to the example of simplicity offered by Christ's life. These high virtues offer a formal and conceptual frame to what is not just a journey through the curious and eccentric spaces of folly.

However, it is true that what has the most interest for the current (and also the contemporary) reader is precisely this journey. The third chapter has a revealing title ("saints who feigned simplicity and fatuity because of self-deprecation"), although it is very modest sounding considering all that is included in its more than one hundred pages. It also includes an opportune preface on the concept of "simplicitas", a quality God himself has, and which in human beings can be, according to John Climacus, either "innate" or "acquired", the latter giving occasion to the legitimation of a cautious "simulation of foolishness". Then Rader proposes a curious typology of "simple people" divided into six degrees: those, like children, who do not know how to lie nor simulate, those who achieve simplicity through obedience, those who like being ridiculed and wish to "be considered stupid", those who, rather than being an object of ridicule, laugh at people, those who are really "simple-witted", and finally those who are considered ignorant only because they follow Christ. It is only then that the reader finds a list of "simulated" fools and simpletons: beginning with the biblical reference David, who feigned folly to save his life, and the pagan examples of Solon, Brutus and Ulysses, or the

---

[40] *Diálogo de milagros*, trad. by Z. Prieto Hernández, Zamora: Monte Casino, 1998, pp. 467–525.

examples of Domna and Indes, martyrs of Nicomedia, or the nun Isidore, Mark of Alexandria, Simeon the Holy Fool, St Francis and his disciple friar Juniper, Jacopone da Todi and many more, old and contemporary.

In the fourth chapter Rader changes his discourse and pays attention to "those [...] considered simple, fools and crazy without any reason for it". This category includes the most relevant example, Christ himself, "considered, because of men's stupidity, as a fool, a deranged person, a charlatan [...] spat on, beaten, treated with affront and vexations just for fun". The fifth chapter offered an "appendix on the 'facta et dicta' of some simple-minded people", as promised in the title. It was conceived as many other contemporary collections of *exempla* although apparently geared towards the topic of folly: there we can read the story of Salaunus, a man so simple that he was only able to learn the first two words of the *Ave Maria*, or some images of Child Jesus fed by children, or about a simpleton who decided to be castrated for Christ. Mattäus Rader abandoned the topic of simplicity in the sixth chapter, devoted to the tacit model for all the pages of this book, Christ's humility, and accordingly he finished his book with a poem on the evangelical *dictum* so dear to the tradition of the divine folly: "he who humbles himself will be exalted".

Stages of Folly

It is not difficult to find in Lope de Vega's plays (1562–1635) some of the principles of the tradition we have analyzed in the preceding pages. Among them, the praise of humility, which is the main topic of *La humildad y la soberbia* or *La humildad ensalzada* (*Humility and Pride*, or *Humility exalted*). In it, this evangelical "dictum" is repeated as a *leitmotif*, as in other religious plays by Lope that include this same motto or the one that derives from the Song of Mary: "He has put down the mighty from their thrones, And exalted the lowly". One of these plays is about the life of St Juan de Dios (*Juan de Dios y Antón Martín*; c. 1511–1512). In it, the main protagonist undergoes a profound conversion that makes him confess his sins in public and throw himself in the mud. Considered deranged, he is taken to the Royal Hospital, where when asked about his condition ("Who are you?"), he responds with a laconic "a fool for Christ" (*loco de Cristo*).[41] The forcefulness of the answer (which does not appear as such in the source of the play) shows just by itself the knowledge Lope had of the tradition of Holy Folly. This was a tradition particularly dear

---

[41] Lope de VEGA, *Juan de Dios y Antón Martín*, ed. by G. Mazzochi, in *Comedias de Lope de Vega, Parte X*, vol. 3, Lérida: Milenio, 2010, pp. 1365–1508.

to him, beyond his predilection for feigned fools and simpletons as characters in many of his profane plays.[42]

Several echoes of this tradition can be seen in some of his hagiographic plays ("comedias de santos"). The one bearing the explicit title of *Los locos por el cielo* (*Fools for heaven*), written between 1598 and 1603, deals with the story of Domna and Indes, who feigned being crazy before their martyrdom.[43] The play on St Francis, *El serafín humano* (*The human seraph*; c. 1610–1612), abounds in references to folly. Of course, the saint's biographies included many of these references: the saint was treated as a fool by those around him, he threw himself in snow to quell his carnal desires about marriage and he asked friar Gil to humiliate him by putting his foot on his chest. Folly will reinforce its presence in the play thanks to the presence of an enigmatic character (introduced just as "a fool") who prophesizes the sanctity of Francis. In the play there is also the presence of sacred simplicity, represented by friar Juniper, whose "blessed simplicity" is opposed, according to Lope, to "false, astute, lying" human science. Friar Juniper plays a secondary role (that of "gracioso", an archetypical character in Spanish drama),[44] although he will be the main character of another play of disputed authorship that bears the crystal-clear title of *El truhán del cielo y loco santo* (*The rogue of heaven and holy fool*). We also do not know if Lope is the author of *El saber por no saber* (*Knowing for not knowing*) devoted to St Julián de Alcalá, also on the topic of holy simplicity. In any event, the topic also appears on other "comedias de santos" by Lope like the trilogy on St Isidore the Farmer, who is presented as "ignorant" and "foolish" ("necio") and whose "rustic simplicity" will defeat Envy in the end.[45] It also appears in a play from before 1607 devoted to the Franciscan St Benedict of Palermo, entitled *El santo negro Rosambuco* (*The black saint Rosambuco*). In it, the protagonist is a slave with barely any preparation, a "simple idiot, without any science", an example of obedience and

---

[42] Adrián J. SÁEZ, "Locos y bobos: dos máscaras fingidas en el teatro de Lope de Vega (con un excurso calderoniano)", *eHumanista*, 24 (2013), 271–92; José Enrique LÓPEZ MARTÍNEZ, "Locos y bobos fingidos: otra forma de representar (sin disfraz) en el teatro de Lope de Vega", *Atalanta: Revista de las Letras Barrocas*, 2 (2014), 53–95; Belén ATIENZA, *El loco en el espejo. Locura y melancolía en la España de Lope de Vega*, Amsterdam: Rodopi, 2009; Jonathan THACKER; "La autoridad de la figura del loco en las comedias de Lope de Vega", in *Autoridad y poder en el Siglo de Oro*, Madrid-Frankfurt: Iberoamericana-Vervuert, 2009, pp. 175–88.

[43] Lope de VEGA, *Los locos por el cielo*, ed. by E. Bassegoda, in *Comedias de Lope de Vega, Parte VIII*, vol. 1, Lérida: Milenio, 2009, pp. 305–427.

[44] Françoise CAZAL, "Un gracioso de comedia de santos: fray Junípero en *El serafín humano* de Lope de Vega", in *Pratiques hagiographiques dans l'Espagne du Moyen Âge et du Siècle d'Or*, Toulouse: Méridiennes, 2005, pp. 315–28.

[45] Lope de VEGA, *San Isidro, labrador de Madrid*, ed. by M. Morrás, in *Comedias de Lope de Vega, Parte VII*, vol. 3, Lérida: Milenio, 2008, pp. 1521–1658.

above all of self-deprecation. He calls himself "dumb" ("tonto") and "worm" and suffers patiently the constant insults of his antagonist, whom he asks to step on him and humiliate him, as St Francis did.[46]

Simple humility is also the topic of *San Diego de Alcalá* (1613), a comedy on the life of this Franciscan lay brother who began as a hermit showing his love for nature's creatures and ended up traveling as a missionary to the Canary Islands and later professing in the convent at Alcalá de Henares. There, miraculously he could understand Latin and respond to complex theological questions. Then Child Jesus taught him to read appearing on top of a breviary.[47] The play —in which the saint's illiteracy and religious fervor are opposed to the shrewdness and lukewarm faith of the "conversos"—[48] follows closely the biographies of St Diego, who had been canonized by Sixtus V in 1588, thus becoming the first saint canonized by the Church after the creation of the Sacred Congregation of Rites. His hagiographies alluded to his "simple" condition and described him as "ignorant and without formal preparation" ("ignorante y sin letras").[49] In this comedy, Lope exaggerated the simplicity of friar Diego to make it fit the model of the "simple for Christ", assigning to him some motifs and images that did not appear in his biography but came from a previous play entitled *El rústico del cielo* (*The heavenly rustic*). Indeed, the latter had explored the topic of sacred stupidity when dealing with the discalced Carmelite Francisco del Niño Jesús, a saint closer to the topic we are studying here.

A Perennial Childhood

El rústico del cielo was published in 1623 in the *Parte XVIII* of the *Comedias* by Lope, but must have been written only a few weeks after the protagonist's death on December 27, 1604.[50] In fact, perhaps it is the play that under the title *El hermano Francisco* (*Brother Francis*) was part of the repertoire of the theatrical company of Gaspar de Porres, in 1605, and was staged on July of that year in Ávila (and a year later in Salamanca). Lope knew personally Francisco

---

[46] Lope de VEGA, *El santo negro Rosambuco*, ed. by L. Giuliani, in *Comedias de Lope de Vega, Parte III*, Lérida: Milenio, 2002, pp. 397–501.
[47] Lope de VEGA, *San Diego de Alcalá*, ed. by T. E. Case, Kassel: Reichenberger, 1988.
[48] Joseph SILVERMAN, "Cultural Backgrounds of Spanish Imperialism as Presented in Lope de Vega's Play, San Diego de Alcalá", *Journal of San Diego History*, 24 (1978), pp. 7–23.
[49] The source of this play is probably not (despite scholars' assertions) the *Flos Sanctorum* by Pedro de RIBADENEIRA. It could be the *Tercera Parte de las Crónicas de la Orden de San Francisco* by MARCOS DE LISBOA (Salamanca: Alexandre de Cánova, 1570, fols 126ʳ–142ʳ) or a text close to it. But the simplicity of St Diego is something present on any biography from the period.
[50] Lope de VEGA, *El rústico del cielo*, ed. by J. Llamas, in *Comedias de Lope de Vega, Parte XVIII*, vol. 2, Madrid: Gredos, 2019, pp. 615–794.

del Niño Jesús, which could have inspired some of the play's details. The play reveals the knowledge of very precise information (as it would later appear in the biography written by friar José de Jesús María, published in 1624, or in the documentation regarding his beatification process), which suggests that Lope consulted some manuscript that included this detailed information.[51]

The figure of Francisco offered the right model for the construction of a play based on the motif of sacred stupidity. The documentation for his beatification insists on his "coarse condition and rustic wit" ("tosca índole e ingenio rústico") and on his "more infused than natural" prudence.[52] Friar José de Jesús María would highlight, in his prologue, the marvelous virtues of a person that was "so coarse and rustic in his nature, so unskilled, so uncapable". The first chapter of his biography refers to his parents' worries, for they considered him an "imbecile" ("tonto"), or to the shepherds' mockery, who saw him "as a simpleton" ("como un simple"). That "short wit" ("corto uso de razón") displayed in his childhood and adolescence is the surprising point of departure towards his sanctity as explored in the rest of the play, where his simplicity plays a smaller role.

Lope, considering how much he liked the motifs of sacred folly and simplicity, will highlight in the play his rusticity and identifies it with a sort of "spiritual infancy" full of happiness and opposed to the vanities of human knowledge, represented in the play by the behavior of the university students of Alcalá (endowed with an obscure character) and the malevolent astuteness of the characters named Pride and Devil. In *El rústico del cielo*, sacred stupidity becomes the character in the background that accompanies the rest of Francisco's virtues (mostly humility, charity, and obedience) and is exercised before and after his profession in the Carmelite Order. All of it closely follows a model of sanctity that Lope relates to its model, St Francis, in a play of identities suggested by their names.[53]

In the Dedication that prefaces the *Parte XVIII*, Lope reminds us that monarchs Felipe III and Margarita of Austria themselves had watched a performance of this comedy and he celebrates how much both appreciated Francisco and the "sacred simplicity with which he called them brother Felipe and

---

[51] LLAMAS, ed., Lope de Vega, *El rústico del cielo, op. cit.*, pp. 624–25. See José de JESÚS MARÍA, *Historia y virtudes del venerable hermano fray Francisco del Niño Jesús*, Uclés: Domingo de la Iglesia, 1624. Two short works had been published in 1605 and 1607 written by Rodrigo de Flores and Juan Sánchez de la Torre. See also *Tenor de los interrogatorios para la deposición y examen de testigos en la causa de beatificación*, n. d.
[52] *Tenor, op. cit.*, fols 1ᵛ and 4ʳ.
[53] For the relationship among "simplicitas", "Laetitia" and "hilaritas" in St Francis, see Jacques LE GOFF, *San Francisco de Asís*, Madrid: Akal, 2003, pp. 136–40.

sister Margarita". In this performance, there were also "many children from principal families" that entered the stage singing and receiving the bread that the actor playing the Blessed gave them, which was a "great proof of the sanctity of this heavenly rustic".

The language and the atmosphere of his sacred simplicity are pervasive throughout the play, in fact from its first verses. In an idyllic morning, two shepherds comment on Francisco's "simplicity", whom no teacher could teach the alphabet. Indeed, the protagonist appears on the stage asleep without being able to move or open his eyes. Once awoken, he confesses that he was dreaming that he flew towards heaven in what is the first foreshadowing of his future canonization in the play. In a forest, young Francisco asks for forgiveness from some "brother trees" that he is forced to fell (Diego de Alcalá also will ask forgiveness from the flowers he cuts for the altar in Lope's homonymous comedy),[54] and talks later with a gentleman who mentions the "strange" and "sincere" simplicity of he who is destined to be a saint according to the lines on his hand and his physiognomy. The funny comments by Francisco, however, are the preface to a tragic scene. Threatened with prison by a guard who persecuted some thieves, Francisco grabs a sling, like David, shoots a stone with it and kills the persecutor, without being completely conscious about his actions. This provokes his companions' insults ("brute"; "bestia") and those of his own father ("fool, ignorant, lost, [...] stupid"; "loco, ignorante, perdido, [...] necio"), who decides to send him to Alcalá to avoid punishment, despite Francisco's protestations to the contrary, because he does not think he is guilty ("imprison the stone, not me [...] For the stone hit him").[55]

The rural setting of the initial scenes contrasts with life in Alcalá and its university atmosphere, whose most sordid aspects Lope describes through a secondary plot that includes students and prostitutes in a picaresque atmosphere. On one of the streets, three students talk about the bad food at the inn and about the prostitutes they are after, using a jargon full of student vocabulary and double entendre. On stage, Francisco talks to God and praises the greatness of Creation. Feeling somehow ashamed for his audacity ("upon entering Alcalá, / I dare to study God"),[56] he will use in this same scene some of the *topoi* about sacred simplicity. For starters, he recognizes his ignorance which he declares with an eloquent image (perhaps first used by Lope in his poem *Isidro* and later repeated in other plays like *San Diego de Alcalá*, *San Isidro Labrador de Madrid* or *La niñez de San Isidro*): his inability to go

---

[54] Lope de VEGA, *San Diego de Alcalá*, *op. cit.*, vv. 297–320.
[55] Lope de VEGA, *El rústico del cielo*, *op. cit.*, vv. 411–13.
[56] Lope de VEGA, *El rústico del cielo*, *op. cit.*, vv. 622–23.

beyond the "christus del abecé", that is the cross on top of the "cartilla" ("notebook") used by children to learn to read.[57] That initial sign (that reminds us of the case of Salauno who could not memorize but the first two words of the *Ave Maria*) is a new foreshadowing of his canonization inasmuch as it implies his absolute "dedication" to the Cross, to God and therefore his rejection of anything related to human knowledge (represented by the letters he has not learned). In the next stanzas, Francisco evokes the shepherds' adoration to "the Lamb [...] meeker than any lamb", promising to have an everlasting devotion to the festivity of Christmas, something that remains firm throughout the play. After a new confession of his ignorance in theological matters, he offers himself to the service of God, "who is the highest learning". He does so with extreme humility ("do not despise my coarseness"), wanting to be a jester ("for the greatness of a lord / requires him to have a buffoon") or a "cat" and a "dog" in the service of the divine prince and the Catholic truth ("I will be / a dog that perhaps will bring you / game for you to eat. / I will be a cat for infidels / and with my rustic wit / I will hunt the mice / that are eating your papers"):

> Yo vengo a serviros pronto;
> no despreciéis mi rudeza;
> porque suele ser grandeza
> de un señor tener un tonto.
> Un perro y un gato cría
> un Príncipe; yo seré
> perro, que quizá os traeré
> caza que comáis un día.
> Gato seré de infieles
> con mis rústicas razones,
> y cazaré los ratones
> que roen vuestros papeles.[58]

At the end, he reminds us of his expulsion by his father, asking God to receive him as a "little orphan", thus reinforcing the almost childish condition that he exudes in the play. Next, Francisco runs into the priest and the sacristan

---

[57] José ARAGÜÉS ALDAZ, "El *christus* del abecé. El *Isidro* de Lope y el hallazgo de la simplicidad sagrada", in *Lope de Vega y la canonización de san Isidro*, Madrid-Frankfurt: Iberoamericana-Vervuert, 2022, pp. 175–243. See Miguel de CERVANTES, *Don Quijote de la Mancha*, II, 42 (ed. by F. Rico et al., Barcelona: Instituto Cervantes-Crítica, 1998, pp. 968–69) for a similar expression in Sancho Panza. Francisco de QUEVEDO will use this image to attack Góngora ("que aprendiste sin christus la cartilla") as part of his well-known satire about his lineage (*Poesía original completa*, ed. by J. M. Blecua, Barcelona, Planeta, 1990, 829, p. 1094).
[58] Lope de VEGA, *El rústico del cielo, op. cit.*, vv. 660–71.

of the church of St Justus and St Pastor (curiously the so-called "children saints"), who are immediately aware of the extreme ignorance of this "simpleton" and accept him as an altar boy. Lope introduces a new profane scene in order to demystify student life based on a comic inversion of the appearances of knowledge. In it, four students steal some pastries and begin to eat them, mocking the baker with a language full of syllogisms; nevertheless, he takes revenge pretending to have used donkey's meat to make the pastries, using a new "argument" ("all those who eat donkey's meat / become an ass"; "Todos los que comieren carne de asno / han de ser asnos") to celebrate his final victory: "Consider if there are more stupid and ignorant people than students".[59] In the meantime, the sexton of St Justus and St Pastor has confirmed Francisco's inability to help him with Mass or even his gluttony, shown in eating the sacred hosts, and fires him; then he tries to justify himself by appealing to God's generosity with the eucharist and thus making the sexton angry: "Brother, some of your things / are tiresome, / for sometimes you are learned / and sometimes you seem stupid" ("Hermano, cosas tenéis / que me tienen ya cansado, / que unas veces sois letrado / y otras tonto parecéis").[60] Francisco, abandoned, addresses God and then rebukes his own body ("you are an ass"; v. 824), and then he sits on the steps of the church (like Paul the Simpleton who spent night and day in front of St Anthony's hermitage), proclaiming there to have a childish condition that he shares with the two children saints to whom the temple is dedicated and with that Child Jesus who has become the teacher of the only thing he has been able to learn (the "christus" of the reading notebook):

> Señores niños, ¿por qué
> de su casa me han echado
> si otro niño me ha enseñado
> el cristus del abecé?
> [...]
> Niño Dios, Niño bendito,
> perdido diz que anduvistes,
> que por ganarme os perdistes,
> ¡ah, Señor niño, ah, chiquito!,
> mire qué perdido estoy
> en este suelo sentado,
> que aunque a edad de hombre he llegado,
> niño en la inocencia soy.[61]

---

[59] Lope de VEGA, *El rústico del cielo, op. cit.*, vv. 759–60 and 777–78.
[60] Lope de VEGA, *El rústico del cielo, op. cit.*, vv. 813–16.
[61] "My children lords, why have I been expelled from his house if other child has taught me the *christus* of my ABC's? [...] Baby God, Blessed Baby, they say you were lost, that you were

There Francisco hears a divine message: "Serve many / to please just One" ("Sirve a muchos / y agradarás a uno"). Following this advice, he wants to help in the hospital, and begs the priests for their mediation in the name of that "Blessed Child / who escaped to Egypt fearing Herod" (vv. 906–07), not without admitting once again his incompetence and comparing himself to a "tree" or to "marble" ("Para sentado nací. / No diferencio de un árbol [...] y en todo parezco mármol").[62] Being already a nurse at the Hospital de Altozana, the doctor will berate him as useless ("he does it all backwards"; "todo lo hace al revés"), which provokes an even more eloquent image expressed by the protagonist: a man created backwards. It is a carnivalesque image created with the double meaning of "corteza" ("surface", particularly of a tree, but also "rusticity", meaning "corto"):

> ¿Qué quiere?, naturaleza
> nos vistió de esta corteza
> [...]
> Los hombres vestidos son:
> unos por el haz están
> y otros del revés.
> Cuando deprisa se viste,
> ¿no se ha puesto por los pies
> alguna media al revés?
> [...]
> Pues así naturaleza,
> con prisa de algún disfraz,
> iba a vestirme del haz
> y vistiome esta corteza).[63]

In the final scene of the first Act, the friars of the convent reject the possibility of throwing him out, for he has increased the health of the sick and the alms by offering a great virtuous example.[64] The second Act confirms his model condition. At the beginning, students Jerónimo and Marcelo—a

---

lost in order to find me, alas Lord Child, alas Lord Child! Look how lost I am sitting on this floor, that although I have reached a mature age, I am a child in innocence" (Lope de VEGA, *El rústico del cielo, op. cit.*, vv. 837–40 and 861–68).

[62] Lope de VEGA, *El rústico del cielo, op. cit.*, vv. 900–04.

[63] "What do you want. Nature covered us with a bark [...] Men are dressed: some in the right manner, some backwards. If you get dressed quickly, haven't you put on your stocking upside down? [...] Likewise, nature, in a hurry to dress me, was about to do it rightly and did it backwards" (Lope de VEGA, *El rústico del cielo, op. cit.*, vv. 976–90).

[64] The episodes of the first act (the guardian's death, the service of St Justus and St Pastor, the divine announcement, the entrance into the Hospital de Antezana) appear in JESÚS MARÍA, *Historia, op. cit.*, I, 1–3, fols 1–15.

counterpoint to those unorderly students from the first scenes—talk about the virtues of Francisco, now appointed main nurse at the Hospital de Altozana, a real help for the poor, orphans and women in need, an example of humility, charity and prayer. A man who "writes and receives letters from the most important people in court, the most illustrious people in Spain"; vv. 1312–14), although it is still necessary to tie him to his ass when he rides it "to prevent him from falling down from it".

Francisco also declares in the second Act his "stupidity", feeling like an "ass", but he knows to thank God for having created him human, with the capability of speaking and an immortal soul, instead of having made him a "lizard or a porcupine [...] stone, tree, plant, herb or ivy", or "monkey or dog, cat, bear, cow, duck nor any other food" ("un lagarto o puercoespín / [...] piedra, / árbol, planta, hierba o hiedra / [...] / monte, mármol, fuente o prado / [...] / [...] no ser / mona ni perro, ni gato, / ni oso, ni vaca, ni pato / ni otra cosa de comer").[65] The happiness achieved helping others in the Hospital de Altozana is then associated with the recovery of his human dignity, to which his ability to read contributes, albeit "imperfectly" ("aunque mal").

But Francisco continues to be mostly a child. And that sacred and perennial childhood explains the name adopted after his religious profession (in a pure Carmelite tradition), as well as the permanent place that his devotion to the love of Child Jesus has in his biographies (before and after his profession), founded in the frequent invocation of his "sweet name" and in his spiritual conversion, plain and constant: "he talks to Him, deals with Him, gives everything for his Name, / and Francisco, in sum, is called / *of the Child Jesus*".[66] The student Jerome had summarized it at the beginning of the second Act when he remembered the protagonist's well-known devotion to the festivity of the Child Jesus—that is Christmas—something that makes him organize every year a splendid banquet for all the poor of the surroundings. The details of that meal are put in Jerome's mouth, something that is a celebration of the saint's custom of placing a figure of Child Jesus on top of the heaps of bread given to the poor. This pleasant image will reappear in a later scene (although not related to Christmas). In it, Francisco pretends to talk with an image of Child Jesus (endowing it with life, so to speak) and ask from it bread for

---

[65] Lope de VEGA, *El rústico del cielo, op. cit.*, vv. 1524–1537.
[66] "Con él habla, con él trata, todo lo da por su nombre, / y Francisco, en fin, se llama / del Niño Jesús" (Lope de VEGA, *El rústico del cielo, op. cit.*, vv. 1368–1379). For the love of Child Jesus, see *Tenor, op. cit*, fol. 2ʳ, and JESÚS MARÍA, *Historia, op. cit.*, II, 6, pp. 176–80, who refers also to the devotion of the "sweet name of Jesus". For the latter, see Valeriano SÁNCHEZ RAMOS, "El Dulce Nombre de Jesús: una devoción popular al Santo Nombre en los Ciclos de Navidad y Semana Santa", *Revista Vera Cruz*, 18 (2001), 5–12.

a needy pauper before singing with all those present. Lope is imitating (although turning it upside down) those delightful episodes of a Child Jesus fed by other "simple" children that were included in Rader's book.

Seen in this light, the piety of the saint acquires a deeper meaning in another episode—also inspired by real events—that has a child as a protagonist: that of a child conceived by a woman, Andrea, with her lover Montalvo—one of the baker's thieves—when her husband was absent, a child that she tells his husband is an orphan given her by Francisco. The deception has the complicity of the protagonist in a dialogue full of references to Child Jesus and whose goal is to protect the "simple" life of the innocent child, with a reference to Herod's persecution and the flight into Egypt.[67]

But the most celebrated sign of the spiritual infancy of Francisco is his devotion to Christmas and the banquet associated with it, whose preparations take up many scenes of the second Act.[68] There the protagonist goes to Madrid to beg alms from the king (the "older brother" for Francisco) and from "all the brother's people", conversing along his way there with the plants from the orchards ("brother radish", "sister eggplant", "brother parsley"), in a humorous version of the well-known Franciscan brotherhood with all beings, also documented in biographies about our Francisco.[69] Along his way, Francisco will naively purchase an ox, giving money in advance, with the condition that it will be delivered to him in Alcalá before the festivity, something that the owner—knowing that Francisco is "a good Christian and stupid" ("buen cristiano y bobo")– does not intend to do: "Was my ox a student for me to take him to Alcalá?" (vv. 1872–73). Once in Madrid, a duke's majordomo celebrates the "sacred simplicity" ("santa simplicidad") of someone esteemed by King Philip II himself. In the meantime, Francisco has returned to Alcalá with astounding rapidity, and finds there the ox he purchased the day before, which had escaped and arrived at the hospital, followed by his owner, who is not repentant. On Christmas Eve, which is approaching, the ox will be in the manger together with the mule, a role Francisco reserves for himself: "I am a mule, do not suffer, / the mule of Child Jesus, yes" ("mula soy, no tenga pena, / del niño Jesús sí"). After this "many children and youngsters"

---

[67] "Mi niño Jesús, mirad, / [...] / que anda Herodes tras un niño; / su simple vida guardad / [...] / mas llevarémosle a Egipto / con vuestro favor, mi Dios" (Lope de VEGA, *El rústico del cielo, op. cit.*, vv. 1454–1462).
[68] See *Tenor, op. cit.*, fol. 2ᵛ., and much closer to Lope, JESÚS MARÍA, *Historia, op. cit.*, I, 5–6, fols 16-23. For St Francis's preaching at Christmas, see CELANO, *Vida primera*, XXX, 84, and *Vida segunda*, CLI, 199, in *San Francisco de Asís, op. cit.*, pp. 185–93 and 344.
[69] *Tenor, op. cit.*, fol. 2ᵛ. For St Francis, see CELANO, *Vida primera*, XXI, 58–60, XXVIII-XXIX, 77–81, in *San Francisco de Asís, op. cit.*, pp. 177–78, 188–90.

surround him and he invites those "brother lambs" to sing some stanzas with a clear Counter-Reformist message: "What can I do to attain salvation? Believe and do good works" ("¿Qué haré para me salvar? / Creer y obrar"). Most certainly, this would give occasion for many children of notable families to come up to the stage, which Lope mentions in the dedication of the play. If that was the case, the dissolution of boundaries between spectator and spectacle, the festive atmosphere and the prominence of children would make the audience feel that this part was similar to the "obispillo" ("little bishop") festivity, a variant of the tradition of sacred stupidity to which the play belongs.

Lope dealt with Francisco's religious profession, as a lay brother of the Order of the Discalced Carmelites of the Blessed Virgin Mary at the beginning of the third and final act. This stands in contrast to the big role this period plays in the biographies of the saint. His profession happened when Francisco was more than fifty years old and after overcoming the reticence of Philip II himself and, according to the play, even the people from Alcalá, represented by some students who already know him as their "teacher", although Francisco keeps insisting on his rusticity and the need to tame his being a "coarse ass" with his religious profession. The action then moves to Valencia where the wedding between Philip III and Margarita of Austria has just taken place and where Francisco is living now with the intention of founding a house for repentant women.[70] Then the provincial of the Carmelites orders his transfer to Madrid, something that is miraculously delayed due to a storm, thus fulfilling Francisco's desire to remain three more days in Valencia. During his journey to Madrid, the "wise people" of Alcalá come out to welcome him, as we are informed by a conversation between Pride and the Devil, whom Francisco always calls—in the play and in reality according to his biographers—"the Mangy" ("el Tiñoso").[71] The last scenes present the latter's attempts to defeat the protagonist, to whom the heavens have revealed that he is to die on Christmas Eve, one more proof of his devotion, because "he dies when God is born", something the Devil considers "God's play" ("niñerías de Dios"). In the last scenes, Francisco lies unconscious during Christmas next to an image of "Pilgrim Child Jesus". Finally, after regaining consciousness, he gives bread to the poor, sings to the Virgin and Child Jesus and finally he gives his soul to God.[72]

The third Act thus offers a hasty summary of Francisco's last years. But it is also adorned with a precious passage that revolves around his love for Child

---

[70] For his religious profession and stay in Valencia, see JESÚS MARÍA, *Historia*, I, 9–26, fols 36–101.

[71] JESÚS MARÍA, *Historia*, I, 8, fols 27–35.

[72] For his transfer to Madrid (the moment of his relationship with Philip III and Margarita) and his last days, see JESÚS MARÍA, *Historia*, I, 28–38, fols 101–40.

Jesus. Francisco dialogues with his image, which reminds him of the shepherds that Child Jesus taught to read and likens them to the priests that affronted him during his Passion. Francisco consoles the image ("It seems that you are pouting! / No, no, no more of that, Child Jesus!" ("¡Parece que hacéis pucheros! / ¡No, no, Niño, no haya más!"), before once again likening childhood and Passion to the image of a crucified Christ that addresses his father with child's language ("taita", "papa").[73] Then the saint sings and dances in order to make Child Jesus laugh and finally he puts him down on a wooden cradle he has made himself and begins rocking him, although Francisco falls asleep first in an image that takes us back to the "topos" of the protagonist's sacred somnolence that appeared at the beginning of the play.[74]

The praise—implicit and explicit—of divine simplicity in these scenes and the resulting inversion of the appearance of wisdom take other forms in this third Act when the Devil appears on stage. Almost at the beginning of the act, Pride and the Devil dialogue about Francisco's winning humility, inspired by Child Jesus, "a tender child" ("niño tierno") who "displays his childish games" ("imprime sus niñerías"), and against which the "plenitude of science" of the fallen angel can do nothing. Then the Devil complains that a "Sanson" has arrived to Valencia, a "David turned into a feigned fool". Francisco then produces from inside his habit an image of Child Jesus "dressed as a pilgrim", offending a furious "Tiñoso": "with this the ignorant have more power / against me than the learned" ("con esto pueden los necios / contra mí más que los sabios"). Almost at the end of the play, the Devil recognizes his defeat by appealing to the essential principle of the tradition of the divine stupidity:

> Sabios del mundo, ¿qué hacéis?
> ¿qué imagináis? ¿qué buscáis?
> ¿en qué libros estudiáis,
> si esto en ignorantes veis?
> ¡Oh, gran Libro, Cristo, en quien
> tan alta ciencia se aprende,
> que algún sabio no la entiende,
> y un rudo la entiende bien![75]

---

[73] For the assimilation of childhood and Christ's Passion, see LLAMAS, ed., Lope de Vega, *El rústico del cielo, op. cit.*, p. 773. See also Lope de VEGA, *San Diego de Alcalá, op. cit.*, vv. 247–60, and *El Serafín Humano*, ed. by M. Menéndez Pelayo, *Obras de Lope de Vega*, X, Madrid, Atlas, 1965, p. 43.

[74] St John of the Cross also sang and danced holding a Child Jesus in his arms, according to Jerónimo de SAN JOSÉ, *Historia del venerable San Juan de la Cruz*, libro IV, cap. 11, ed. by J. V. Rodríguez, Valladolid: Junta de Castilla y León, 1993, pp. 452–54.

[75] "Wise men of the world, what do you do? What do you think? What are you looking for? Why do you study in books, when you can learn this from ignorant people? Oh you, great

It is this tradition that gives meaning to the play and all its scenes and links them to many plays written by Lope and other authors who came after him, like *El lego de Alcalá* (*The lay brother of Alcalá*), by Vélez de Guevara, also devoted to St Julián, or *El loco cuerdo, San Simeón, el santo loco* (*The sane fool, St Simeon, the holy fool*), by José de Valdivielso. The sole existence of these texts requires an overview analysis to shed a more definite light on their connection to the post-Tridentine hagiographic discourse. In any event, the memory of old and new examples of sacred stupidity played a relevant role in the Counter-Reformist advocacy of the virtues of obedience, abnegation and self-deprecation, and in the defense of the humble, the willing acceptance of the mysteries of faith, and the reaffirmation of Catholic anchoring in a tradition whose origins go back to the narrative of the Passion and St Paul's reflections on the "folly of the Cross".

Book, Jesus Christ, in whom can be studied such great science that a wiseman cannot understand it but an ignorant may know it well" (Lope de VEGA, *El rústico del cielo, op. cit.*, vv. 2830–37).

Hagiographical Theater and Counter-Reformation
Between Baroque Aesthetics and *Arte Nuevo*

Natalia Fernández Rodríguez
(Universidad de Sevilla, Spain)

Saints and the Comedia

The resolutions of the Council of Trent regarding the cult of saints and the devotional efficiency of religious images had a manifest influence on the emergence of hagiographic plays in the last quarter of the sixteenth century. Instead of the clear catechetical orientation of religious drama before, or rather as a complement to it, post-Trent plays assumed the role of living demonstrations or proofs of the Catholic *depositum fidei* questioned by Luther in three basic aspects: justification, eucharist and the cult of saints.[1] On December 3 and 4, 1563, the twenty-fifth and last session of the Council took place, which included the decree "De invocatione, veneratione, reliquiis sanctorum et sacris imaginibus" ("On the invocation, veneration, and relics, or saints, and other sacred images"). It was the final impulse to make the cult of the saints one of the flagships of Catholic doctrine against skeptical Protestantism. Among other things, it was an attempt to direct devotion *ad extra*

---

[1] Jesús Menéndez Peláez, "Teatro e Iglesia en el siglo XVI: de la reforma católica a la contrarreforma del Concilio de Trento", *Criticón*, 94–95 (2003), 49–67, p. 59. Although the dramatic genre *par excellence* dealing with eucharistic topics was the *auto sacramental*, comedies also contributed to its exaltation as a Catholic keystone.

Hispanic Hagiography in the Critical Context of the Reformation, ed. by Fernando Baños Vallejo, Hagiologia, 19 (Turnhout, 2022), pp. 101–126.
© BREPOLS PUBLISHERS   DOI 10.1484/M.HAG-EB.5.131992

(outward devotion) as a counterpoint to the interiority (inward devotion) defended in Reformist circles:

> And the bishops shall carefully teach this, that, by means of the histories of the mysteries of our Redemption, portrayed by paintings or other representations, the people is instructed, and confirmed in (the habit of) remembering, and continually revolving in mind the articles of faith; as also that great profit is derived from all sacred images, not only because the people are thereby admonished of the benefits and gifts bestowed upon them by Christ, but also because the miracles which God has performed by means of the saints, and their salutary examples, are set before the eyes of the faithful; that so they may give God thanks for those things; may order their own lives and manners in imitation of the saints; and may be excited to adore and love God, and to cultivate piety.[2]

The image, observed and perceptible, was the axis that drew the emotional gaze of the faithful and the demonstrative desire of Trent's theologians. The recognition of the exemplarity of the saint paralleled the image that represented him.[3] This valuing of the visual element together with a concept of the devotional experience as an act of collective participation and the need to re-create a Catholic pantheon that embodied the doctrinal principles derived from the Council, found a stark ally in the stage:

> The theological basis for the dramatic action is presented in two levels. First and foremost, the play is a biography of a saint or a major religious figure [...]. On a slightly more dogmatic but just as basic level, the *comedia de santos* presents the audience with a model of Christian moral and ethical behavior, as exemplified in the main character.[4]

Converted into a *dramatis persona*, the saint contributed to make that *los ojos de los fieles* (the faithful's eyes) focus on the foundations of the doctrinal Counter-Reformation building. But there was also something else.

The proliferation of saints in theater coincided with a progressive professionalization of the stage. Mercedes de los Reyes has already explained that the consolidation of *autos sacramentales* as the epitome of religious drama removed hagiographic topics from the Corpus Christi celebrations and placed

---

[2] James WATERWORTH, *The Council of Trent. The canons and decrees of the sacred and oecumenical Council of Trent*, London: Dolman, 1848, p. 235.

[3] It is a basis of the *translatio ad prototypum* (whoever venerates the image also venerates what the image represents) established by St Basil and developed by John Damascene. See José Luis GONZÁLEZ GARCÍA, *Imágenes sagradas y predicación visual en el Siglo de Oro*, Madrid: Akal, 2015, pp. 291–97.

[4] Donald C. BUCK, "Popular Theology, Miracles and Stagecraft in the *Comedia de Santo*: Cañizares' *A cual mejor, confesada y confesor*", *Dieciocho*, 5.1 (1982), 3–17, p. 6.

them in the profane commercial theater.⁵ Under the name of "comedia de santos" or "comedia hagiográfica" we include a heterogenous corpus of plays composed during a century and a half with different stage and dramatic conceptions. Their only point in common is the need to separate them from other genres of religious theater—in particular *autos sacramentales*—and, on the other hand, their display of a Tridentine vindication of the cult of saints from the dogmatic-demonstrative and devotional-affective point of view that characterized the Counter-Reformation spirit. Despite the numerous controversies caused by the most dramatic-theatrical elements of the genre and the bewilderment of the purists because these plays placed the saint within a clearly profane and not allegorical world, there were always voices that defended the genre not only because of the dramatic construction of the plays, the striking scenography and its success with the public but also because of how efficient they were to "mover afectos" ("move affections")–that is, the ultimate desire of the Tridentine program. "Cuántos me afirman que lloran más que en el más ardiente sermón!" ("How many people would let me know that they cried more than in the most ardent sermon!"),⁶ will exclaim Father Manuel Guerra y Ribera in 1682.

The impact of Counter-Reformation in the development of hagiographic theater is then a versatile phenomenon. First, it had to turn the exemplary embodiment of dogma represented by the saint into an incentive to devotion. Occasionally, though, this main goal was mixed with other forces not necessarily pious or at least not always favorable to cultivating devotion *a priori*, although they could end up *moving affections* in unexpected ways. In the next pages, we will delve into these questions using a representative corpus of Counter-Reformation hagiographic plays spanning roughly a century, from the beginnings of the *comedia de santos*, in the last quarter of the sixteenth century, to the end of the seventeenth century.

Taking as a point of departure the catalogue developed by Stefano Arata in 1996, scholars have insisted on the unquestionable value of the plays included in BNE Ms. 14767 to look at the reality of religious drama at the beginning of the post-Tridentine period.⁷ If we exclude the *autos* of the *Códice*

---

⁵ Mercedes DE LOS REYES PEÑA, "Constantes y cambios en la tradición hagiográfica: del *Códice de Autos Viejos* a las comedias de santos del siglo XVII", in Jean CANAVAGGIO (ed.), *La Comedia*, Madrid: Casa de Velázquez, 1995, 257–70.

⁶ Emilio COTARELO, *Bibliografía de las controversias sobre la licitud del teatro en España*, Granada: Archivum, 1997, p. 334b.

⁷ Particularly interesting is the work by Rosa DURÁ CELMA, *El teatro religioso en la colección del conde de Gondomar: el manuscrito 14767 de la BNE*, Doctoral Dissertation defended at the Universitat de València, 2016 (https://roderic.uv.es/handle/10550/51899). In addition to an exhaustive introductory study, it includes the edition of all the plays included in the Ms.

de Autos Viejos, the Ms. includes the extant hagiographic plays that are closest in time to the end of the Council of Trent. In general, it allows us to observe the confluence of different dramatic conceptualizations on their way to being consolidated into the *comedia* genre.[8] In order to value the concrete manifestation of the Counter-Reformation boost to the composition of plays on saints' lives in the Golden Age we use some of the plays included in this Ms. as an *a quo* date; more in particular, those devoted to saints whose theatrical trajectory includes at least two more versions during the seventeenth century—at the beginning and the end of the century—with the intention of illustrating the different stages in the development of the genre: *Comedia de la vida y muerte de San Jerónimo*, *Comedia de la vida y muerte de San Agustín*, and *Comedia de la vida y muerte y milagros de San Antonio de Padua*.[9] The saints involved—two from the fifth and one from the thirteenth century—are also symptomatic of the post-Tridentine desire to *reinterpret* the lives of older saints in order to make them into atemporal representatives of the Catholic truth. The other titles we have studied are the following: on St Jerome, *El cardenal de Belén* by Lope de Vega, and *El fénix de la escritura* by Francisco González de Bustos; on St Augustine, *El divino africano* by Lope and *El águila de la iglesia* by Francisco González de Bustos and Pedro Lanini Sagredo; and on St Anthony of Padua, *El divino portugués, San Antonio de Padua*, attributed to Juan Pérez de Montalbán, and *El divino portugués, San Antonio de Padua* by Antonio Fajardo y Acevedo.[10]

---

[8] Durá Celma, *El teatro religioso, op. cit.*, p. 10.

[9] The *Comedia de la vida y muerte de San Jerónimo* (fols 331r–346r) is composed of 2,057 verses. Durá Celma suggests that it was composed close to the time when the *comedia nueva* achieved success more than other plays in the collection (*El teatro religioso, op. cit.* p. 217); the *Comedia de la vida y muerte de San Agustín* (fols 262r–282r) is composed of 2,916 verses and José Aragüés Aldaz dates it between 1586 and 1597 (Lope de Vega, *El divino africano*, *Parte XVIII de Comedias de Lope de Vega, I*, coord. Antonio Sánchez Jiménez y Adrián J. Sáez, Madrid, Gredos, 2019, 377–741, p. 436). There are no data on its performances. Regarding the *Comedia de la vida y muerte y milagros de San Antonio de Padua* (fols 108r–122r), Durá Celma indicates that there is a reference to the performance of a play entitled *La vida y muerte de San Antonio de Padua* during the Corpus in Logroño in 1610 by the company of Inés de Lara that could be this one (*El teatro religioso, op. cit.* p. 342). In all cases we use BNE Ms. 14767.

[10] The autograph Ms. of *El cardenal de Belén* indicates that the play was written in 1610. At the end there appear several performance licenses dated between 1610 and 1614. It was first published in the *Parte Trezena* by Lope, 1620. We quote from Lope de Vega, "El cardenal de Belén", ed. by Natalia Fernández Rodríguez, in *Parte XIII de Comedias de Lope de Vega, I*, coord. Natalia Fernández Rodríguez, Madrid, Gredos, 2014, 845–1010. *El fénix de la escritura* is extant in a *suelta* from 1729, and it must have been written in the last quarter of the seventeenth century. We use the copy kept at the BNE T/14785/14. *El divino africano* was first published in the *Decimoctava de Lope*, 1623. Aragüés Aldaz points out that it must have been written c. 1608–1610 (*El divino, ed. cit.* p. 378). We quote from Aragüés

Regarding dramatic construction and compositional keys, a first approach to these pieces reveals the existence of two basic groups. In the first group, the saint's life is developed almost as in a *tableau vivant*, with a strong predominance of a 'demonstrative' intention and a paramount presence of dogmatic reflection with a preference to explicit affirmations rather than being integrated into the action. This adopts the form of direct accounts, debates among the characters or symbolic-allegorical scenes where the dogma is plastically represented. These pieces would seem to reformulate the directives of the "De invocatione" with a command that would read as "All the playwrights shall carefully teach this". In the second group, though, the interweaving of scenes and dramatic episodes brings together the different pious elements and the counter-reformist echo is then harmonically integrated into the play. It is the stage trajectory of the characters, that is the protagonists of an action, what sometimes exceeds by far the boundaries of hagiography and thus demonstrates *in fieri* the value of works for salvation. It is true that during the seventeenth century, the counter-reformist debate on justification joins forces with the topic of *De auxiliis divinae gratiae*, and in fact goes beyond Tridentine intentions by delving into the boundaries of human freedom from an speculative standpoint.[11] In general, the doctrine of justification, with the understandable modifications due to the theatrical nature of the plays, is integrated into the action as an existential example and moral encouragement: *propaganda fidei* rather than theological speculation, and above all dramatic vision. If in the previous case the stage worked in the service of the Counter-Reformation, now the Counter-Reformation is fused with a genre in which two complementary components come together in a

---

ALDAZ ed. (see previous footnote). *El águila de la iglesia*, written in collaboration by Francisco González de Bustos and Pedro Lanini Sagredo, was first published in the *Parte treinta y ocho de comedias nuevas, escogidas de los mejores ingenios de España*, Madrid, 1672. We use a copy kept in the BNE R/22691. *El divino portugués, San Antonio de Padua*, attributed to Pérez de Montalbán, must have been written between 1621–1623 (Juan Manuel ESCUDERO BAZTÁN, "Los entresijos dramáticos en las comedias hagiográficas de Pérez de Montalbán. El caso de *El divino portugués, San Antonio de Padua*", *Hipogrifo*, 3.2 (2015), pp. 135–47, p. 136). We use the copy kept at the BNE R/11269(12). The autograph Ms. of *El divino portugués, San Antonio de Padua*, by Antonio Fajardo y Acevedo, is kept at the BNE Ms. 14883. The date 1689 appears at the end of the text.

[11] Precisely the lack of determination of the Council on a fundamental theological problem such as the role of divine grace in human salvation spurred the so-called debate *De Auxiliis Divinae Gratiae*. Successive disputes arose in Valladolid in 1582 and came to an end, theoretically, in 1607 when Paul V imposed silence on this topic. This controversy went beyond the boundaries of the schools and continued during the entire century, and found in the stage an efficient method of dissemination, for undoubtedly the philosophical and moral interest of a reflection that is linked to the topic of human freedom had many dramatic possibilities.

more intense fashion: the consolidation of the *arte nuevo* and the impact of Baroque aesthetics.

The inflexion point did not take place in Lope's works, as we could have assumed taking into consideration that the date of both coincides with the establishment of the *comedia nueva*. There are significant differences between Lope's two plays and those from the end of the sixteenth century. They certainly exist. But if we must incorporate them into one of the two groups we mentioned above, both *El cardenal de Belén* and *El divino africano* are closer to the former.[12] In the play on St Anthony of Padua attributed to Pérez de Montalbán, written probably between 1621 and 1623, we can perceive some elements that will be fully developed only later with the dramatic solutions of the second half of the century. Despite belonging to its same generic type, the hagiographic comedy did not evolve at the same rhythm as the profane comedy did because the pulse of this hagiographic theater (as conceived in the years immediately after Trent) kept beating strongly even after the establishment of the all-powerful *arte nuevo*. Our goal here is to analyze how those different compositional options adopted by hagiographic plays in the sixteenth and seventeenth centuries define the dramatic and stage mechanisms with which the counter-reformist spirit manifested itself in all its dogmatic and devotional dimensions. After some preliminary notes on the updating strategies of the post-Tridentine attitude regarding the cult of saints, we will focus on the two mechanisms that contributed to shape from the stage the gaze of the faithful: the promotion of participatory devotion as a confluence of the revalorization of the image and theatricality; and the transformation of the *arte nuevo* and its being accommodated (from the stage also) to the demonstrative goals of the Counter-Reformation.

Conflict Updating and Catholic Militancy

Thomas J. Hefferman reminded us that the constant dialogue between two historical moments—that of the saint and that when his life is written—is at the base of the hagiographic narrative.[13] This was particularly intensified during the Counter-Reformation. The three pillars of the communicative dimension of the new hagiography—legitimizing militancy, dogmatic normalization, and state *dirigisme*—could be anchored, with minor restructurations, on the the lives of traditional saints. Thus, the frequently-mentioned

---

[12] ARAGÜÉS ALDAZ studies the many similarities between the manuscript play and Lope's comedy ("El divino", *ed. cit.*, p. 436).
[13] Thomas J. HEFFERNAN, *Sacred biography. Saints and their biographers in the Middle Ages*, New York: Oxford University Press, 1988, pp. 22–23.

renovation of the post-Tridentine books of saints did not consist only in the abundance of new contemporary saints as indicated by José Luis Sánchez Lora.[14] The old figures, even those from early Christian times, continued enjoying an unquestionable vitality during the Counter-Reformation because hagiographic writers recreated them and made them into living representatives of the paradigm of contemporary sanctity and true advocates of the Catholic cause. On one hand, they could reflect the doctrinal normalization defended since the Council; on the other, they could represent behavioral proposals. The "argument from tradition", understood as a strategy to connect past, present and future,[15] justified utilizing old lives and explained that, as modern saints do, old saints also came to fulfill a militant and demonstrative mission: "Se trata de demostrar que el Dios de los apóstoles y de los mártires es el mismo Dios que hoy otorga su respaldo a los católicos, de donde resulta ser esta la misma iglesia que aquella".[16] Even Alonso de Villegas himself, in the prologue to his *Flos Sanctorum*, legitimizes writing lives of saints with this same argument:

> Por lo qual nuestro providentissimo Dios, desde los principios de su Yglesia católica Christiana ha proveydo de personas que hiziessen en ella oficio de coronistas, poniendo en memoria y haziendo historias de los hechos heroycos y obras valerosas de santos martyres, a los quales de ordinario más que a los confessores en aquel tiempo hazia fiesta y celebrava sus muertes.[17]

From this perspective, the cult of saints itself—the third pillar of the Catholic *depositum fidei*—is rooted in old customs:

> Y aún tengo por cierto que las lecciones del Breuiario Romano, que contienen martyrios de santos, fueron tomadas de las mismas historias de los Notarios de Roma. Y fúndome en que el mismo san Dámaso dize que el Papa san Félix ordenó que las missas se celebrasen sobre las sepulturas de los mártires o en lugar donde hubiesse buena parte de sus reliquias. Lo qual

---

[14] José Luis SÁNCHEZ LORA, *Mujeres, conventos y formas de la religiosidad barroca*, Madrid: Fundación Universitaria Española, 1988, p. 378.
[15] Julio CARO BAROJA, *Las formas complejas de la vida religiosa (siglos XVI y XVII)*, Madrid: Sarpe, 1985, p. 100; SÁNCHEZ LORA, *Mujeres, op. cit.*, p. 378.
[16] "It is about demonstrating that the God of the apostles and martyrs is the same God that today gives support to Catholics and therefore this Church is the same as that one", SÁNCHEZ LORA, *Mujeres, op. cit.*, p. 379.
[17] "For this reason, our very provident God, from the beginnings of his Catholic Church, has provided us with people who have the role of chroniclers, keeping a memory and writing stories of the heroic deeds and valiant works of martyr saints, in whose honor back then there used to be festivities and they celebrated their deaths more than they did with confessors". Alonso DE VILLEGAS, *Flos sanctorum y historia general de la vida y hechos de Jesucristo*, Madrid: Pedro Madrigal, 1588, Prólogo al lector.

> fue como un principio o origen casi de canonizar a los santos, o a lo menos de honrarlos y celebrarles fiesta en la Yglesia Christiana.[18]

This sort of genealogical legitimation to the veneration of saints and their images is key in Villegas's book of saints. And there are numerous examples in which old spirituality and devotion are defined as direct antecedents of the new customs.

In that case, the simulacrum of direct experience[19] that is theater, converted the stage into a particularly efficient militant tool. On the stage, saints from other periods came to life and incorporated themselves into the time-space frame of the audience and clearly connected old and *current* religious conflicts. This updating power of the stage, supported by the present deixis, the use of verbal tenses and some other obvious strategies, made the *sectarian* enemies of the Church, the heretics or the gentiles project themselves onto the times of the conflicts between Catholics and Protestants. And this did not only happen in plays close in time to Trent. In *El águila de la Iglesia*, dated from the end of the seventeenth century, it is impossible to not understand St Augustine words as offering a clear Counter-Reformist meaning:

> Lo que Jerónimo y yo,
> amigo Alipio, decimos
> es lo mismo que la Iglesia
> siempre tiene y ha tenido.
> Lo que sigue la romana
> Iglesia es lo que seguimos.
> El pontífice es cabeza
> universal en quien Cristo
> puso el fundamento todo
> y los que no están unidos
> con él y sus tradiciones
> son, como sabes, podridos
> miembros, cuya corrupción
> es contagio del abismo.[20]

---

[18] "And I even consider to be true that the lessons of the Roman Breviary that contain martyrdoms of saints were taken from Roman contemporary witnesses themselves. I say so because St Damasus himself says that Pope St Felix ordered the celebration of Mass on the tombs of martyrs or wherever there were many of their relics. This was almost the beginning or origin of the canonization of saints, or at least of honoring them and celebrating their festivities in the Christian Church", *Flos sanctorum, op. cit.*, Prólogo al lector.

[19] Pavel CAMPEANU, "Un papel secundario: el espectador", in André HELBO (ed.), *Semiología de la representación. Teatro, televisión, cómic*, Barcelona: Gustavo Gili, 1978, 107–20, p. 115.

[20] "What Jerome and I, friend Alipius, say is the same as the Church has always defended and still defends. What the Roman Church follows, we also follow. The pontiff is the universal

The magisterium of St Augustine and St Jerome, directly or indirectly, was the support for the Church of Rome and the Papacy from the point of view of the argument from tradition: "es lo mismo que la Iglesia / siempre tiene y ha tenido" ("it is what Church / always defended and still does"). In addition, the explicit agreement of the two Church fathers is a Catholic tightening of ranks against a Lutheran Reformation that pitched one against the other.[21]

In any case, it is obvious that the most effective examples of this updating tendency are the explicit mentions to Luther and Lutherans in comedies whose action takes place centuries before they existed.[22] In our corpus, there are two clear examples separated by a period of thirty years: the anonymous comedy on St Augustine and the play on St Anthony attributed to Pérez de Montalbán. And it is not by chance that the characters who trigger the comparison belong to the popular tradition. In the anonymous comedy, it takes place in a scene in which two secondary figures, Mesero and Compadre (Innkeeper and Compadre), comment with fascination the recent baptism of St Augustine:

Compadre	¿Sabéis vos cómo seguía este hombre la herejía?
Mesero	¿Yo? ¡El diablo que lo sepa! ¿Quereisme tentar? ¿No hago harto en saber de un mesón?
Compadre	Pardiós que tenéis razón.
Mesero	Dios da a cada uno el pago que merece. No me meto en cuentos: yo soy cristiano, sea el que fuere luterano.[23]

---

head on whom Christ established the foundation of the Church and those who are not joined with him and his traditions are, as you know, rotten members whose corruption is a contagion from the abyss". González de Bustos and Lanini Sagredo, *El águila, op. cit.* fol. 38.

[21] Teófanes Egido, "Pablo y Lutero: antiguas y nuevas perspectivas", *Revista de Espiritualidad*, 67 (2008), 253–73, pp. 256–58.

[22] On the presence of Luther and Lutherans in the Spanish religious drama of the mid-sixteenth century, immediately before the first plays we have studied here, is interesting the study by Jimena Gamba Corradine, "Lutero en las *Cortes de la Muerte*: representar la herejía en el teatro español del siglo XVI", *Hipogrifo*, 5.2 (2017), pp. 381–402.

[23] "Compadre: Do you know how this man persecuted heresy? Innkeeper: Me? The Hell I know! Are you trying to tempt me? Haven't I learned enough knowing how to run an inn? Compadre: By God, you are right. Innkeeper: "God gives everyone what they deserve. Do not tell me stories: I am a Christian; let them be Lutherans is they so desire". *Comedia de la vida y muerte de San Agustín, op. cit.* fol. 270a.

In the other example, Fr. Domingo—one of the future martyrs of Marrakech—[24] is about to leave for Morocco to evangelize the gentiles and from his endearing condition as *gracioso*, he says:

> Herejes y luteranos,
> a veros parto contento.
> ¡Vive Dios y ha de vivir
> que os tengo de sacudir
> los palos de ciento en ciento![25]

Thus, using a conscious vulgar tone, Counter-Reformation militancy arrives on stage in order to connect directly with the sensibility of the audience and the intention of establishing a foundation on which to build the post-Tridentine *fábrica de santos* (factory of saints).[26]

Collective Devotion, "Theatricality" and the Baroque

Cécile Vincent-Cassy states that the protagonists of hagiographic comedies move in plays from the profane to the sacred until they become objects of cult.[27] The cult of saints, the third pillar of the Catholic *depositum fidei*, has an inescapable visual dimension linked to the venerations of images, to the extent that the compositional axis of the plays—and what unifies them despite their extreme variety—is showing a human being become venerable image. This journey from the profane to the sacred stated by Vincent-Cassy is the process by which a being as human as the audience itself raises above the quotidian to reach the realm of the supernatural. And above all, it served to justify the veneration of the image through a detailed explanation of why the saint was a saint.

That the technology used on the stage, something so criticized sometimes, had a demonstrative function was already explained by Elma Dassbach

---

[24] According to Villegas's version, friar Fernando, the future Anthony of Padua, was moved by the example of some Franciscan friars who were martyred in Morocco and whose bodies were transported to Coimbra, what made him profess as a Franciscan (VILLEGAS, *Flos sanctorum, op. cit.*, fol. 191ᵛ). Playwrights alter the chronology of this episode to accommodate it to their goals.

[25] "Heretics and Lutherans; I depart a happy man to see you. May God live long (and He will) that I will give you hundreds and hundreds of blows". PÉREZ DE MONTALBÁN, *El divino portugués, op. cit.*, p. 162.

[26] The term is used by Jean Claude SCHMITT, "La fábrica de santos", *Historia Social*, 5 (1989).

[27] Cécile VINCENT-CASSY, "La *Ninfa del Cielo* de Tirso de Molina ¿una comedia hagiográfica", en *El Siglo de Oro en escena: homenaje a Marc Vitse*, ed. by O. Gorsse & F. Serralta, 2006, 1091–1102, p. 1091.

years ago.[28] But the relevance of the visual elements in hagiographic comedies did not end with the stage props and attrezzo, even if they were integrated organically and efficiently into the demonstrative goal of the genre.[29] Severo Sarduy indicated that the Baroque work of art, literary or pictorial, is *inside out*, that is it shows its supporting frame, its underside—the painting on the way to becoming a painting, the book on the way to becoming a book.[30] We could say that hagiographic comedy shows the inner workings—man becoming image—and in this way it displays a Baroque visuality much before the desire for a total art took hold in the mid-seventeenth century. In addition, the immediate consequence of making visible the other side of things is the dissolution of boundaries between the observer and the observed, as Emilio Orozco indicated when defining 'theatricality'—the Baroque reason, according to Christine Buci-Glucksmann:

> Es repitamos una vez más la búsqueda de una expresión desbordante, de una emoción comunicativa; incorporar al espectador como ser vivo y real a una escena que se ofrece como tangible realidad con una plena intercomunicación espacial.[31]

From this to a participative and collective devotion as the strategy of unification as desired by Tridentine theologians there is only a short distance. The Baroque was not just the Counter-Reformation art, but undoubtedly some essential components of the Counter-Reformist spirit found their most immediate aesthetic channeling through the Baroque art.

It is true that in the most recent plays of our corpus we find some striking manifestations of that profuse staging that has been considered one of the elements that best characterize hagiographic plays. In *El águila de la iglesia*, to name a significant example, St Augustine's iconographic attributes are brought into the stage through a remarkable fly system at the end of the second act:

---

[28] Elma Dassbach, *La comedia hagiográfica del Siglo de Oro español. Lope de Vega, Tirso de Molina y Calderón de la Barca*, New York: Peter Lang, 1997, p. 85.
[29] Consequently, Esther Borrego defends that not all hagiographic comedies are characterized by a rich staging ("Espacios de santidad y puesta en escena: las primeras comedias hagiográficas de Lope (1594–1609)", *Tintas*, 5 (2015), 31–46, p. 32).
[30] Severo Sarduy, "Barroco", in *Obra completa II*, ed. by Gustavo Guerrero and Françoise Wahl, Madrid: Galaxia Gutenberg, 1999, p. 1239.
[31] "It is, let us say it once again, the search for an overflowing expression, a communicative emotion; the incorporation of the spectator as a living and real being into a scene that is offered as tangible reality with a full spatial intercommunication", Emilio Orozco Díaz, *El teatro y la teatralidad del Barroco*, Barcelona: Planeta, 1969, p. 146. On theatricality as the Baroque reason, see Christine Buci-Glucksmann, *Baroque Reason. The Aesthetics of Modernity*, Londres-Nueva Delhi: Sage, 1994.

Bajan tres ángeles de lo alto, uno con la iglesia, otro con una mitra y otro con el báculo.

Ángel	Agustino
	la majestad soberana
	de Dios, te entrega su Iglesia
	y obispo que seas manda
	de Hipona. Obediente admite
	aquestas insignias sacras.
Dale la iglesia	
Canta	Y sobre tus hombros
	de la Iglesia santa
	Atlante sustente
	el leve peso de la fe sagrada.
Dale la mitra	
Ángel 2	Ciña tu cabeza
	aquesta tïara
	con la cual corona
	sus príncipes la Iglesia soberana.
Dale el báculo	
Ángel 3	Deste pastoral
	báculo te encarga,
	con que regir puedas
	el imperio de ovejas tan cristianas.[32]

The scene is quite eloquent. In addition to the subtle mention of the legitimacy of the Catholic Church, the audience also observes how the saint's iconographic configuration derives from God's direct command. And they see it live on stage. Because beyond the apparatus of flying machines, the revelation on stage of the process of sanctity through a series of images is supported by an overwhelmed expression that appeals directly to the gaze of the audience. It is precisely in the 'theatricality' of devotion—of which the extreme staging is its final expression—where lies the emotional effectiveness of hagiographic

---

[32] "*Three angels come from above, one holding a church, another a miter and the third the staff.* Angel: Augustine, the Sovereign Majesty of God bestows the church on you and commands you to be bishop in Hippo. Be obedient and accept these sacred emblems. *He gives him the church.* Sing: And on the shoulders of the Holy Church may Atlas support the light weight of the sacred faith. Angel 2: May this tiara crown your head with which the Sovereign Church crowns its princes. *He gives him the staff.* Angel 3. Receive the care of this pastoral staff and may you rule with it the fold of such Christian sheep", GONZÁLEZ DE BUSTOS and LANINI SAGREDO, *El águila, op. cit.* p. 34.

comedies from their beginnings to the last examples of the late seventeenth century. It was about creating a content of admiration for the sacred image in which the saint himself took part and of which he became little by little an integral part until he turned into a venerable image.[33] Thus playwrights appealed to the audience's affects but also to their expectations and, above all, to their knowledge of iconographic traditions in order to make them participants in the action that was taking place in front of them. From a theatrical point of view, this could be achieved through sudden *apariencias*, an inheritance of the old medieval drama as Domingo Garcías Estelrich reminds us:

> Éstas podían situarse en cualquiera de los huecos del escenario y constituirse de diferentes maneras: un sencillo lienzo pintado, objetos colocados simbólicamente, figuras humanas inmóviles como estatuas y personajes que hablaban y salían del marco de la apariencia para incorporarse a la acción sobre el entarimado.[34]

The devotional contexts were usually framed visually either by showing a religious image—generally of Christ or the Virgin—or through the creation of *tableaux vivants* or pictorial spaces in which the saint was the protagonist or, in many occasions, by a combination of both.[35] Consequently, and again with the same updating purpose as the one seen above, this process of construction of a man-image activated the doctrinal principles and pedagogical purposes of the Counter-Reformation. The display, for instance, of a penitential aesthetics in both anonymous comedies on St Jerome and St Anthony of Padua, besides activating a myriad of (even conflictive sometimes) affective resources, refers to a clear position on the efficacy of satisfaction as developed in session 14 of the Council in November 1551:

> [...] even as no Catholic ever thought, by this kind of satisfactions on our parts, the efficacy of the merit and of the satisfaction of our Lord Jesus Christ is either obscured, or in any way lessened: which when the innovators seek to understand, they in such wise maintain a new life to be the best penance, as to Fake away the entire efficacy and use of satisfaction.[36]

---

[33] Durá Celma has noticed the tendency of hagiographic plays in the Ms. to include asides in which the saint appears on altars or tombs (*El teatro religioso, op. cit.*, p. 353).
[34] "These could be placed in any of the stage empty spaces and adopt different guises: a simple painting, objects symbolically placed, immobile human figures and characters that speak and come out of the *apariencia* and incorporate themselves into the action on stage", Domingo Garcías Estelrich, "La escenografía teatral en los inicios del siglo XIX", *BSAL*, 57 (2001), 211–20, p. 212.
[35] On pictorial spaces, see Natalia Fernández Rodríguez, "Imaginería sacra y espacios pictóricos en las comedias de santos de Lope de Vega", *eHumanista* 28 (2014), 628-42.
[36] Waterworth, *The Council of Trent, ed. cit.*, p. 103.

In the second act of *Vida y muerte de San Jerónimo*, an allegorical character Penitence bestows on the saint the penitential attributes—the cilice, the discipline, the skull and the crucifix—in a scene that resembles (without the use of stage machines) the one we just analyzed in *El águila de la Iglesia*:

Jerónimo	Pues el mundo en mí murió,
	vísteme, Señor, de ti,
	pues él murió, viva yo.
	Viva yo, mas yo ya no:
	vive Jesuchristo en mí.
Penitencia	Cíñete aquesta pretina
	de castidad y limpieza.
Dale el silicio	
	y con esta diciplina
	esa tu carne malina
	amansará su braveza.
Dale la diciplina	
[...]	
	Para que puedas tomar
	en cualquier cosa consejo
	y en ella siempre acertar
	acostúmbrate a mirar
	de contino en este espejo.
Dale la calavera	
	y en él verás claramente
	quién eres, quién has de ser [...][37]

Once again, the *in fieri* construction of a penitent St Jerome presents live to the audience a very fertile iconographic tradition, and at the same time it affirms the value of satisfaction as *imitatio Christi* in full agreement with the Tridentine decree.[38]

---

[37] "Jerome: Since the world has died in me, dress me, my Lord, with you; since He has died, may I live; may I live, but I am not I anymore, for Jesus Christ is living in me. Penitence: Put on this girdle of chastity and cleansing. *She gives him the cilice*. And with this discipline your evil flesh will tame its wildness. *She gives him the discipline*. In order to receive advice in everything and act always in the right way, you better become used to look constantly in this mirror (*She gives him the skull*) and you will see in it who are you and who you will become", *Vida y muerte de San Jerónimo, op. cit.* fol. 337ʳ.

[38] "Add to these things, that, whilst we thus, by making satisfaction, suffer for our sins, we are made conformable to Jesus Christ, who satisfied for our sins, from whom all our sufficiency is; having also thereby a most sure pledge, that if we suffer with him, we shall also be glorified with him", WATERWORTH, *The Council of Trent, ed. cit.* p. 103.

These scenes, half *tableau vivant*, and half theater, constitute some sort of augmented reality in which the supernatural is made visible in a space that is a continuation of that of the audience. "Turn your eyes on me", says Christ to St Augustine in the anonymous play before stimulating his imagination (and the audience's) with the memory of his crucifixion:

> Volved los ojos a mí
> y considerad quién soy,
> pues por vos como aquí estoy
> al pie de la cruz me vi.[39]

A few verses later, the scene represents a passage of the *Meditations* where the saint, already converted, integrates himself into an iconographic space or *tableau vivant*:[40]

> Toca la música y en el lugar que estará hecho para ello parece Agustino hincado de rodillas y a un lado un Cristo que le echa sangre del costado en los labios y al otro lado la madre de Dios que le echa del pecho leche.[41]

In the final apotheosis, he finally appears as a venerable image-body: "Toca la música y descubren a Agustino en un tabernáculo abrazado al pie de un Cristo y a la herejía echada a sus pies".[42] The movement that follows in an action that sometimes could seem sketchy, converges towards the integration of the saint into a devotional imagery reconstructed on the stage; a compositional key that appears again in both of Lope's plays, where the pictorial mediation of the final *apariencias* is perfectly explicit. Thus, in *El divino africano*:

> Descúbrase san Agustín vestido de obispo con su cayado, y la iglesia en la mano, como le pintan; la Herejía a los pies, con algunos libros.[43]

---

[39] "Turn your eyes on me and reflect on who I am, for I come to you looking the same as I did when I was at the cross", *Vida y muerte de San Agustín, op. cit.* fol. 269.
[40] Durá Celma calls *tableau vivant* the concrete example (*El teatro religioso, op. cit*, p. 353). The iconographic-pictorial projection of the episode is obvious and can be confirmed with some paintings from Van Dyck that will inspire Murillo's *San Agustín entre Cristo y la Virgen*, from 1664 (Museo del Prado) (https://www.museodelprado.es/coleccion/obra-de-arte/san-agustin-entre-cristo-y-la-virgen/ddc8d76d-4dc4-4164-b768-1ba7b3c4ee1b).
[41] "Music plays and in a place made for it Augustine appears on his knees and on one side a Christ, from whose side blood flows toward his [Augustine's] mouth, and on the other the Mother of God with milk issuing from her breast", *Vida y muerte de San Agustín, op. cit.* fol. 278ᵛ.
[42] "Music plays and Augustine appears in a tabernacle, embracing a Christ and Heresy laying at his foot", *Vida y muerte de San Agustín, op. cit.* fol. 282ʳ.
[43] "St Augustine appears dressed as a bishop with his staff and holding a church in his hands, as he is usually depicted; Heresy is at his feet, and there are some books", Vega, *El divino, op. cit.* v. 2948Acot. On the iconographic tradition about St Augustine and the concrete

And in *El cardenal de Belén*:

> Ángel   Roma venturosa, espera,
> que te le quiero mostrar,
> por que a retratalle aprendas
> y de esta suerte le pintes.
>
> San Jerónimo se descubra en unos peñascos, colgado el hábito y capelo de un árbol, con el canto en la mano, el pecho descubierto, el león a los pies y mirando a un Cristo.[44]

These are plays in which the dramatic development appears in retrospect as a dynamic gloss of the final image that brings together the iconographic tradition of both saints. And as the sermons devised in Trent,[45] they appeal to the audience's gaze and at the same time turn it into admiration. Also in the play on St Anthony of Padua attributed to Pérez de Montalbán, there appears at the end a pictorial space: "Al son de chirimías se descubre a un lado San Antonio con un niño Jesús en los brazos y al otro San Francisco con Cristo imprimiéndole las llagas".[46] But that is not all. Immediately afterwards, Friar Domingo comes out on the stage thanking Anthony's miraculous help and therefore hinting at his sanctity:

> ¡Qué gran maravilla!
> Admirado vengo.
> Cuando ya cansado
> mi brazo soberbio
> de matar contrarios
> contra el cielo opuestos
> cercado me vi
> de escuadrones fieros,
> dije: "Antonio santo,
> ayudadme", y luego
> pareció que airado
> me arrebató el viento

---

examples that have the same configuration of Lope's aside, see ARAGÜÉS ALDAZ, *El divino*, ed. cit., n. 676.

[44] "Angel: Fortunate Rome, hold on, for I want to show him to you so that you learn to represent him and paint him in that same fashion. St Jerome appears on top of some boulders, with his habit and galero hanging from a tree, holding a rock in his hand, a lion at his feet, and looking at a crucifix", VEGA, *El cardenal, op. cit.* vv. 2862–65.

[45] WATERWORTH, *The Council of Trent*, ed. cit., p. 235.

[46] "At the sound of the shawns, Saint Anthony appears at one side with Child Jesus in his arms and, at the other side, Saint Francis with Christ stamping the wounds on him", PÉREZ DE MONTALBÁN, *El divino portugués, op. cit.* fol. 174ᵛ.

> y en menos de un hora
> donde estoy me ha puesto.⁴⁷

The admiration for the saint integrated into the dramatic action itself, what we could call a meta-theatricalization of devotion, is what constitutes the final example of overflowing and converts into theater the Tridentine desire to make piety into an act of collective participation. In hagiographic plays, the episodes in which the characters *see* the saint are frequent, and thus they become witnesses of his sanctity and direct the audience's gaze towards what they themselves are *seeing*.

In the anonymous play on St Anthony of Padua and the one written by Fajardo y Acevedo, there is a miracle included in Ribadeneira's *Flos sanctorum*–but curiously not in Villegas's—that illustrates how some hagiographic plays also contribute (in their particular way) to the exaltation of Christ's real presence in the eucharist. According to Ribadeneira, following a dispute with Bovibillo, who "negaba la verdad del Santo Sacramento" ("negated the truth of the Holy Sacrament"), St Anthony took the consecrated host to a mule that belonged to the heretic and had not eaten in three days, and after hearing the saint's words the beast kneeled down "allí delante del Santísimo Sacramento" ("right there in front of the Holy Sacrament"). Then Ribadeneira comments:

> Con este tan evidente milagro quedaron todos los católicos consoladísimos y los herejes rabiosos y confusos, y su principal maestro, con quien había sido la disputa, ganado y convertido a la fe católica.⁴⁸

The probatory value of the miracle and its militant-updating projection are quite clear in the sense we mentioned above. And this will be preserved in the plays. But it is significant that, when bringing the episode to the stage, both playwrights decided to refer to it through the narration of a character and not make a scene with it. In the anonymous play, Friar Rugero asks another friar to tell him about the life and works of St Anthony for he is convinced that his "relación ha de ser cierta" ("account must be true") because this brother was a direct witness of the harshness of the saint's life.⁴⁹ The friar then tells him the miracle of the mule and the sacred host after putting it within the

---

⁴⁷ "What a great marvel! I come full of admiration. When I saw myself surrounded by fierce squadrons, after my strong arm was already tired of killing enemies who were opposed to heaven, I exclaimed: 'St Anthony, give me help'. Then it seemed that an irate wind snatched me away and took me to where I am now", Pérez de Montalbán, *El divino portugués, op. cit.* fol. 175ʳ.
⁴⁸ "With this conspicuous miracle, all Catholics remained consoled and the heretics rabid and confused, and their main teacher, with whom he had the dispute, became defeated and converted into the Catholic faith", Pedro de Ribadeneira, *Flos sanctorum o libro de las vidas de los santos*, 1761, p. 227.
⁴⁹ *Vida y muerte de San Antonio de Padua, op. cit.* fol. 115ʳ.

chronological context of the contemporary dogmatic debates, something that connects it directly to the Counter-Reformation:

> Aun no ha muchos años fue presente
> que con dañado pecho el sacramento
> de la Santa Quarestía no aprobaba
> a quien volver al tiempo pretendía.[50]

Up to this point there was nothing different than what was included in the *flos sanctorum*. Rugero's reaction is what makes a difference:

> Vamos, que ya del todo enciende
> un fuego espíritu[a]l que ya me abrasa
> y no he de dar paso hasta seguille
> imitándole en todo muy de veras.[51]

On the stage, the devotion itself is theatralized—or meta-theatralized to be more precise, as we indicated before—overflowing as a mirror toward the audience's world. What aspires to move the affections is not the bare narrative of the miracle, as in the *flos sanctorum*, nor its visual recreation as it so frequently happens in hagiographic plays, but the living demonstration of its exemplary efficacy. When in the very next scene St Anthony prays on his knees while Rugero watches him from a window, a true *mise en abyme* is being created in which the window opens a tunnel between the audience and the saint himself;[52] that visible transit, so to speak, between the quotidian and the transcendent implies the devoted adhesion to the venerated image. Not much before in the same comedy, St Anthony had climbed to a rock from which he preached some highway men amid a storm. The saint's intercession prevented the outlaws from getting wet and, impressed by the miracle, they reacted in a curious manner:

> No sea por ti movida
> más tu lengua, que aunque calle
> solo tu aspeto y tu talle
> reprehende nuestra vida.[53]

---

[50] "Not so many years ago, it was clear that the sacrament of the Holy Eucharist did not approve of whomever wanted to return to that time showing an evil heart", *Vida y muerte de San Antonio de Padua, op. cit.* fol. 115ʳ.

[51] "Let's go, for a spiritual fire is fully burning inside me and I will do nothing without following him and truly imitating him in everything", *Vida y muerte de San Antonio de Padua, op. cit.* fol. 115ʳ.

[52] On the metaphysical value of the visual representation of the window, see Víctor STOICHITA, *La invención del cuadro*, Madrid: Cátedra, 2011, p. 107.

[53] "Do not move your tongue anymore, for even if it is silent, your aspect and figure serve as a reprimand to our lifestyle", *Vida y muerte de San Antonio de Padua, op. cit.* fol. 113ᵛ.

The sinner prioritizes the saint's presence over his word, the efficacy of the image over the sermon, and affirms, in sum, the relevance of seeing and watching as an incentive towards repentance.[54]

Having a clear precedent in imaginative meditation, hagiographic comedy assumed the maxim *we can learn more with the eyes than with the mind*, included in a *Memorial* from 1598 addressed to Philip II.[55] And not only in terms of stage machines. Stage resources, whenever available, help achieve these goals with undoubted efficiency. But much before the sophistication of technical made them essential for the genre, playwrights found ways to capture and, particularly, guide the audience's gaze to wherever they desired; just like those figures typical of the Baroque period that show the spectator from within the painting itself the point towards which they should focus their eyes.[56]

The Transformation of the Arte Nuevo

One of the defining characteristics of the genre of hagiographic comedy from its beginning was the presence of profane elements that had nothing to do with the protagonist's biography. Love scenes and plots, comic vein, episodes of jealousy and honor ... were added to the pious lives and made the hagiographic genre into a true *sacro-profane mixture*. During the genre's long existence, even its harshest critics understood that the profane topics were a necessary element to keep the audience happy.[57] But this was not all. From the

---

[54] VILLEGAS stated the following about St Anthony of Padua, precisely with regard to the updating strategies we mentioned before: "Y públicamente muchos comovidos de los sermones que predicó en Padua una Quaresma se juntaron, y andaban por las calles diciplinándose. Y quedó de allí costumbre en aquella ciudad de hacerse estas diciplinas públicas en la Semana Santa. Y de allí lo tomaron en otras partes" (And many joined publicly, moved by the sermons which he preached in Padua during one Lent, and flagellated themselves in the streets. And from then on, the habit of self-inflicting these public disciplines in Easter pervaded in the town. And this same custom was taken in other places) (*Flos sanctorum, op. cit*, fol. 192ᵛ). The gloss insists on this: "El origen de las procesiones de diciplina en Semana Santa fueron los sermones de San Antonio" (The origin of discipline processions in Easter were Saint Anthony's sermons) (*Flos sanctorum, op. cit.*, fol. 192ᵛ). It was not about presenting old saints as the embodiment of some (and renewed) doctrinal principles, rather it was about referring to their influence to explain the genesis of some devotional practices particularly ridiculed by Protestantism.
[55] Javier APARICIO MAYDEU, *Calderón y la máquina barroca: escenografía, religión y cultura en El José de las mujeres*, Amsterdam: Rodopi, 1999, p. 60.
[56] On the semiotic effects of deictic figures and their relationship with directing the gaze, see Mieke BAL & Norman BRYSON, "Semiotics and Art History", *The Art Bulletin*, 73.2 (1991), 174–208, pp. 190–91.
[57] Already in 1613, Father Juan Ferrer, who was somewhat ambivalent about how much theater should be permitted, understood that some elements not necessarily edifying of this

very first hagiographic plays, the profane appears not only as a recreational element, but it has most of the time a clear probatory function following the dictates of Counter-Reformation principles. That happens, for instance, in the anonymous comedy on St Augustine when, almost at the very beginning, two suitors appear on the stage pursuing two ladies. From a structural standpoint, the scene marks a change location and places the action in front of the church where St Ambrose is preaching and where Monica tried to bring Augustine at the beginning of the play. But besides, the contrast between the two Christian and Manichean suitors, and their different attitudes in the face of temptation, are an almost didactic hint. None of them will be able to bring their initial desire to fruition, but while the heretic desists almost in a mechanical manner because his *sect* forbids him otherwise, the Christian acknowledges his mistake and repents, thus affirming the value of good works:

> Pues ¿cómo un bárbaro bruto
> sin Dios ni ley de razón
> guarda con tal devoción
> de su seta el estatuto
> y yo que sigo a mi Dios
> voy contra sus mandamientos
> con tan laçivos intentos?[58]

This didactic-demonstrative use of the profane is a remote seed that will end up flourishing as the true compositional key of the genre during the seventeenth century. From a structural and compositional point of view, we must point out that the plays of the first group underscore from the beginning the pious and supernatural meaning and only later profane scenes are introduced. In these comedies, the saint's world is described from the beginning, and the profane hints only appear occasionally in some scenes like the one we

---

hagiographic theater could be harmless and even beneficial: "Y aunque en ellas haya algunas veces dichos graciosos que entretengan y alegren el auditorio, sin haber en ellos cosa que pueda provocar a deshonestidad ni lascivia, no por eso estas gracias y donaires contradicen con el argumento de lo que se representa, pues en estas tales representaciones de edificación y recreación es justo que haya lo uno y lo otro, porque con lo uno se recree y divierta el ánimo cansado con las ocupaciones ordinarias; y con lo otro salga enseñado y edificado" (And despite they sometimes include joyful sentences that entertain and amuse the audience, they do not cause neither dishonesty nor lust, and they are not contradictory with the plot represented, for in such representations of instruction and entertainment, both aspects must appear, because one thing refreshes the mood, exhausted by daily occupations; and the other educates and instructs it) (COTARELO, *Bibliografía, op. cit.* p. 250b).

[58] "How is it possible that a brute Barbarian without any law nor reason nor God might keep the rules of his sect with such great devotion, while I, who follow my God, act against his commandments with such lascivious desires?", *Vida y muerte de San Agustín, op. cit.* fol. 266ʳ.

analyzed before. The plays from the second half of the seventeenth century, on the other hand, begin with the profane and then they capture the transcendental dimension and give it priority, either with ironic interventions or supernatural appearances or through a miracle's mediation. Consequently, the saint is part of a universe construed from the *arte nuevo* and because of this the basic components of the comedy are subjected to a process of transformation in order to adapt them to a new goal that was not reduced (it could not) to the entertainment dimension. It is then that the Counter-Reformation spirit seems to dissolve itself under the impulse of a dramatic poetry that, strictly speaking, could be used to express it even with more intensity.

As an immediate effect of the full integration of the protagonist into the universe created by the playwright, the typical *comedia nueva* characters moved around the supernatural coordinates of the saint, so that the transcendent dimension of their lives is made visible with more or less intensity. In the play attributed to Pérez de Montalbán, starting in the second act there develops a love plot between the suitor, Federico, and Rosamira, a married lady. When they come out on stage, they converse on human love under the guise of Petrarchan idealization although it only hides a mundane feeling. The sudden appearance of Friar Domingo urging them to go to St Anthony of Padua's sermon is rather eloquent:

> Sus palabras escuchad
> y tened dellas memoria
> si queréis gozar la gloria
> con Dios en su eternidad.
> No os arrepintáis después,
> pues que mi voz os replica.
> Venid, venid, que predica
> el divino portugués.[59]

Anthony preaches in the main square "porque en la iglesia / no hay gente que le oiga", ("because in the church there are no people to listen to him") and the pedagogical spirit of the Counter-Reformation lies in this active search of the faithful to whom transmit sacred teachings. Above all, the dramatic action in progress is where we find confirmation of the efficacy of preaching for the sinner's repentance, something which in essence implies an affirmation about the existence of free will. Anthony's sermon occupies the second act and part of the third, and from the beginning the sensationalist reflections

---

[59] "Hear out his words and keep them in your memory if you want to enjoy for eternity the glory with God. Do not regret it later, for my voice insists to you: Come, come, the Divine Portuguese is preaching", PÉREZ DE MONTALBÁN, *El divino portugués, op. cit.* fol. 166ᵛ.

on the incarnation of Christ and the *memento mori* make us foresee Rosamira's change of heart. The Devil expresses it in the following manner after he comes out dressed, as usual, as a "lover":

> A Rosamira enlazada
> entre mis lazos tenía,
> mas hoy la esperanza mía
> pienso que sale engañada.
> A oír de Antonio el sermón
> ha venido. Claro está
> que, oyéndole, dejará
> los lazos de mi prisión.[60]

That is exactly what happens, tacitly, when the lady dismisses Federico at the beginning of the third act. It is not a sensationalist conversion nor a literal *rasgarse las vestiduras* (tearing of clothes) as it happens with other repentances on stage. It is a simple scene of lover's scorn that could be very well part of a dagger and sword comedy. However, in a universe that lies between the quotidian and the supernatural and where the Devil himself acts as a scene director, Rosamira's words acquire a different meaning. The profane is turned upside down and ends up highlighting by itself the key elements of the Counter-Reformation spirit. We can see it with more clarity in Fajardo y Acevedo's play, also on St Anthony of Padua. The comedy begins in this case with a typical situation of the *arte nuevo*: Leonor, dishonored by Lope de Atayde, is in search of vengeance and her friend Violante, Fernando's sister, the future Anthony of Padua, recommends her to keep her travails in secret. But after another blunt rejection by Lope, in the second act, Leonor confirms her goal:

> Cielos, hombres, plantas, fieras,
> pues el honor he perdido,
> verá el mundo en mi venganza
> el más trágico prodigio.[61]

This framework, typical of the comedy genre, is put in the service of an exemplary goal to the point that Leonor, a genuine dramatic creation, will embody—always through a poetic filter—the Counter-Reformist doctrine of justification. Already in the first scenes, her reaction was ironic when

---

[60] "Rosamira and I were entwined in an embrace before, but today my hopes will be deceived. She has come to hear Anthony's sermon. It is obvious that after hearing him she will abandon the bonds of my prison", PÉREZ DE MONTALBÁN, *El divino portugués, op. cit.* fol. 167ʳ.
[61] "Heavens, men, plants, brutes, since I have lost my honor, the world will witness with my vengeance a most tragic prodigy", FAJARDO Y ACEVEDO, *El divino portugués, op. cit.* fol. 25ᵛ.

Violante and her father lamented Fernando's departure (he had gone to preach to Morocco):

> Parece que con su nombre
> el corazón se me alegra.
> Algún misterio escondido
> en este nombre se encierra.[62]

Leonor's strange feeling was nothing but divine grace's first call.[63] The active presence of the supernatural is immediately revealed when the Devil, Plutino, appears and confirms his true intentions:

> El padre de la mentira
> soy e intenta mi cautela
> perseguir esta familia
> por haber nacido della
> este Antonio, este enemigo
> cuya virtud me atormenta.[64]

Then, Baby Jesus alerts Anthony himself: "El común enemigo / a tu padre persigue: yo le amparo".[65] The honor plot devised at the beginning disappears when the true transcendent meaning of the conflict becomes clear. When Leonor reappears on stage after a two-year lapse, she is no longer a vengeful lady who wishes the death of the person that dishonored her, but a repentant sinner who appeals to God's grace and to the value of good works:

> Si el cielo tiene un buen día
> cuando sus pecados llora
> el alma que arrepentida
> el favor de Dios implora.
> ¿A qué aguardo?[66]

Anthony's mediation, in a scene that occupies one hundred verses, leads a contrite Leonor to God's forgiveness. Thus, an emblematic character of the

---

[62] "It seems that my heart rejoices with his name. There must be some hidden mystery in this name", FAJARDO Y ACEVEDO, *El divino portugués, op. cit.* fol. 12ᵛ.

[63] Leonor's characterization, with the relationship between free will and divine grace in the background, refers (even through a poetic filter) to the debates *De Auxiliis* mentioned above.

[64] "I am the father of falsehood and my pretended care really wants to persecute this family because Anthony was born in it, the enemy whose virtue torments me", FAJARDO Y ACEVEDO, *El divino portugués, op. cit.* fol. 13ʳ.

[65] "The common enemy your father persecutes: I protect him", FAJARDO Y ACEVEDO, *El divino portugués, op. cit.* fol. 15ʳ.

[66] "If it is a joyous day for Heavens whenever a repentant soul cries for her sins and implores God's favor, what am I waiting for", FAJARDO Y ACEVEDO, *El divino portugués, op. cit.* fol. 46ᵛ.

arte nuevo—the dishonored lady who wishes for revenge—is redefined as a virtuous example to confirm, as if she were character from a book of saints, the efficacy of repentance:

> Dedícate a Dios gozosa,
> que te quiere para esposa,
> pues dio en el blanco tu tiro.[67]

Examples like Leonor's are the ultimate manifestation of the meta-theatralized devotion that we mentioned before. It's the comedy's characters (not the hagiography's) who demonstrate the *depositum fidei* through a suggestive exercise of poetization of the dogma.

Before we conclude, we could comment on yet one more illustrative example from the plays devoted to St Augustine. It is not by chance that the bishop of Hippo had such fertile dramatic life after the Council of Trent. Juan Manuel Forte Monge reminds us that the saint became a Counter-Reformation *auctoritas* in the fight against heresy.[68] That is why in the anonymous comedy and in *El divino africano* there are encounters between the saint and Heresy and Truth. In both, Heresy actively intervenes to guide a blind Augustine towards hell, and Truth frees him by removing his blindfold and allowing him to *see the light*.[69] This identification of blindness and sin (which will have a long iconographic projection) is also at the base of Augustine's characterization in *El águila de la iglesia*. In this case, it is filtered through one of the defining characteristics of the plot in the universe of the *arte nuevo*: the love plot in which Augustine acts as the main protagonist. Confused by Porcia's rejection (which he attributes to her having another lover), he rebukes her with typical *comedia nueva* words, although their confrontation has a deeper meaning:

Agustín	¿Quién puede ser? Dime, ingrata.
Porcia	Cristo, que es Dios verdadero.
Agustín	Ya lo quisiera verdad, que este no puede dar celos.

---

[67] "Devote yourself to God with happiness, for He wants you to be his spouse; you hit the target in the middle", Fajardo y Acevedo, *El divino portugués, op. cit.* fol. 50ʳ.

[68] Juan Manuel Forte Monge, "San Agustín, vencedor de herejes en el siglo XVI español", *Criticón*, 118 (2013), pp. 71–80.

[69] There is an essential difference between both scenes. While in the anonymous comedy the scene has an intrinsic allegorical nature, in *El divino africano* it is framed within one of Mónica's inner visions. See Aragüés Aldaz (*El divino, op. cit.*, n. 1251). There we are referred to several passages in Augustine's *Confessions* where there is an explicit mention of the intellectual *blindness* of St Augustine when he was young.

Porcia	Mira si querré otro alguno cuando por este te dejo.
Agustín	Bueno, cuando está esperando por ti en el campo (resuelto) Plácido, en quien vengaré mi agravio.
Porcia	¿Qué escucho, cielos? ¿Qué agravio?
Agustín	El que me ocasionas.
Porcia	Espera.
Agustín	En vano es tu intento.
Porcia	Ciego estás.
Agustín	Eres ingrata.[70]

Through the polyvalent symbolism of blindness, human love becomes a consequence of heresy. Augustine does not understand first voices coming from heaven that try to prevent the duel from taking place:

Voz	Ciego vas, Agustino, mal verás tu bien con amor lascivo.
Agustín	¿No ver mi bien? ¿Es error que en Porcia sigo mi bien?[71]

Then a storm unravels and prevents the two contendants from seeing each other. Amid all this turmoil, a vision appears that will move Augustine towards his final conversion:

¿Qué ilusión? ¿Qué fantasía
mis sentidos enajena?
Que aquello mismo que ven
es lo mismo que los ciega.[72]

---

[70] "Augustine: Who could it be? Tell me, ungrateful. Porcia: Christ, who is the true God. Augustine: I wish it were, for I cannot be jealous of Him. Porcia: You can see if I love another one, when I am leaving you for this One. Augustine: Well, now that Plácido is fully resolved and is waiting for you in the field. In him I will execute the revenge of my dishonor. Porcia: What am I hearing? What dishonor? Augustine: The one I receive from you, Porcia: Wait! Augustine: It is in vain. Porcia: You are blind. Augustine: You are ungrateful", GONZÁLEZ DE BUSTOS and LANINI SAGREDO, *El águila, op. cit.* p. 9.

[71] "You are blind, Augustine, and you will not be able to see what's good for you if you have this lecherous love", GONZÁLEZ DE BUSTOS and LANINI SAGREDO, *El águila, op. cit.* p. 10.

[72] "Such a dream? Such a fantasy that perturbs my senses? For they are being blinded by the same thing they are seeing", GONZÁLEZ DE BUSTOS and LANINI SAGREDO, *El águila, op. cit.* p. 11.

St Augustine's blindness, utilized from the beginning as an expression of heresy, is seasoned in a late seventeenth-century play with some comic ingredients and in the end it converges with human love as the epitome of sin. Hagiographic comedy challenges to some extent the archetypical nature of the *arte nuevo* and subjects it to a metamorphosis that opened its doors to dogmatic demonstration and devoted adhesion, although from the other side.

During the long life of the genre, hagiographic comedy was indebted to the directives established at the Council of Trent regarding the cult of saints. It could not be otherwise. The desire for a unification in faith that moved the Counter-Reformation could be channeled naturally through the possibilities offered by theater. In this article, we have tried to analyze the compositional mechanisms that in a varied but constant manner made the genre of hagiographic comedy since its beginnings into an aesthetic mold for the dogmatic and devotional objectives of the Counter-Reformation.

Delendus est Lutherus

The Triumph of the Saints and the Virgin Mary over Heresy in New Spain's Imagery

Alicia MAYER

Universidad Nacional Autónoma de México (UNAM)

Instituto de Investigaciones Históricas

In his celebrated *Historia de la Provincia de la Compañía de Jesús de Nueva España* (1694), the Jesuit historian Francisco de Florencia described how in 1579 Mexico City received several holy remains of diverse saints that Pope Gregory XIII sent as a gift to the faithful in New Spain "para que se introdujese en los recién convertidos la adoración de los santos con el culto de sus preciosas reliquias".[1] To celebrate the occasion of Rome's donation, a remarkable ceremony was held in the capital city, organized by the Society of Jesus, that had just been established in the Viceroyalty in 1572. A play called *Tragedia del triunfo de los Santos* was performed during the festivities and, amid its characters, it featured Martin Luther, the German reformer, as the anti-hero that defies the godly protagonists. The major topic of the drama was "hacer un elocuente tributo a la Iglesia siempre triunfante de las fuerzas del

---

[1] "To introduce the worship towards the saints to the newly converted with the cult to their precious relics". All translations are mine unless otherwise attributed. Francisco de FLORENCIA, *Historia de la Provincia de la Compañía de Jesús de Nueva España*, book V, México: Academia Literaria, 1955 (2nd ed.), p. 333.

Hispanic Hagiography in the Critical Context of the Reformation, ed. by Fernando Baños Vallejo, Hagiologia, 19 (Turnhout, 2022), pp. 127–161.
© BREPOLS PUBLISHERS   DOI 10.1484/M.HAG-EB.5.131993

mal" and, according to a witness, the performance "conmovió a los espectadores hasta las lágrimas".[2]

Years later, in March 1599, Dionisio Ribera Flores, canon of Mexico City's Cathedral and officer of the Inquisition, described in his *Relación historiada de las Exequias funerales de la majestad del rey Phillipo II*, how the Spanish king's obsequies were held in the Capital. The author heralded the power of the deceased monarch († 1598) and exalted his pious demeanor and his commitment against heresy. In Ribera's composition, Luther was portrayed as the worst heresiarch that had ever existed and was defined by the author as an inebriate "swollen toad". In the prelate's viewpoint, the ex-Augustinian friar was not only an ugly and depraved figure, but also a mistaken wretch, the personification of the most malevolent force. As Ribera reported, Philip II's homage was witnessed "por mucho concurso de gente [y] pareció por la novedad del lugar y aparato, un espectáculo digno de ser visto de todo el universo".[3]

In this way, Luther was introduced to an audience who did not know who he was. Even though "Protestant Christianity was hardly a factor in Spanish America", according to William Taylor,[4] Spain's authorities had longstanding worries that heresy could reach the American dominions and contaminate the colonial atmosphere with wrong propositions. In 1561, Archbishop Alonso de Montúfar wrote to king Philip II that he could rest sound because "Bendicto Dios, Nuestro Señor, que en lo que toca a la pestilencia luterana esta tierra está buena, hasta agora muy poco se ha sentido en ella, y eso poco que ha habido, con el favor de Nuestro Señor luego se ha puesto remedio en atajallo".[5] To convert the indigenous population of the Mesoamerican world to Catholicism and to destroy paganism were the priorities of the evangelizers

---

[2] "To make a tribute to the always triumphant church against the forces of evil". The play "moved the audience to tears". José ROJAS GARCIDUEÑAS and José Juan ARROM eds, *Tres piezas teatrales del virreinato*, México: Universidad Nacional Autónoma de México-Instituto de Investigaciones Estéticas, 1974, p. 21.

[3] "Seen by a great number of people [and] because of the novelty of the place and the setup, it was a show worthy of being witnessed by the entire universe". Dionisio RIBERA FLORES, *Relación Historiada de las Exequias funerales de la majestad del rey Phillipo II*, México: Pedro Balli, 1600, p. 165; Alejandro CAÑEQUE, "Imaging the Spanish Empire: The Visual Construction of Imperial Authority in Habsburg New Spain", *Colonial Latinamerican Review*, 19, 1 (2010), 29–68. On funeral arches, see pp. 44–51.

[4] William TAYLOR, *Theatre of a Thousand Wonders. A History of Miraculous Images and Shrines in New Spain*, Cambridge: Cambridge University Press, 2016, p. 559.

[5] "Regarding the Lutheran pestilence, blessed be God our Lord, this land is good [because] until now a tiny amount of it has been felt in it and of that little, with our Lord's favor there has been a remedy to stop it". Pedro GRINGOIRE (pseudonym of Gustavo Báez Camargo), "Protestantes enjuiciados por la Inquisición", *Historia Mexicana*, XI, 2 (1961), 161–79, p. 161.

and ecclesiastic officials in the new dominions. Because of New Spain's situation, the fight against heresy would only be a secondary goal. Why, then, would Martin Luther, a stranger in time and circumstances to the colonial world, appear in such important anniversaries as the King's funeral ceremony and a stage performance in the very far confines of the Spanish Indies? Moreover, why was this figure profusely –and so negatively—used in imagery and discourse in the viceregal period?[6]

This essay responds to the invitation that professors Carme Arronis and Fernando Baños at the University of Alicante made me to take part in the research project "La hagiografía hispánica ante la Reforma protestante" that searched for a global vision of the transformation in Hispanic hagiography from the sixteenth century. It aims to find answers to central questions: Did early modern hagiography change in response to the critiques made by Protestantism? If so, did the shifts obey Catholic reformist impulses, to Protestant incitement, or did it happen in a combined, coincidental manner? For my contribution, I was asked to analyze the footmark of Luther and anti-Lutheranism in the Viceroyalty of Mexico from the sixteenth through the eighteenth centuries, bearing in mind these perspectives. Specialized in hagiography and literature, all members of the symposium have an advantage over me: I have been mainly concerned with comparative history and history of ideas, particularly religious thought, but given this opportunity to discuss topics from a multidisciplinary aspect, I was eager to explore new interpretations while analyzing certain themes that I had only analyzed in part before in my book *Lutero en el paraíso* (2008).[7]

The reaction against Luther can be seen in many spheres in New Spain's reality: the political, the literary, the historical, the theological and the artistic. Leaving behind this ample thematic repertoire, I found the guidelines of

---

[6] There is no agreed-upon definition of the concept of imagery. While debate exists regarding a precise meaning, for the methodological purposes of this essay I have followed the Oxford Language Dictionary's guidelines. According to them, imagery refers to the visual symbolisms, visual images collectively, or to descriptive or figurative language (Online: Oxfordlearnersdictionaries.com/us/). The stance adopted in this paper is suggested by Asunción Lavrín, that refers to "el conjunto de procesos mentales que nos lleva a una comprensión intelectual del mundo interno" ("the set of mental processes that lead to an intellectual understanding of the inner world"). Asunción LAVRÍN, "El más allá en el imaginario de la religión novohispana", in *Muerte y vida en el más allá. España y América s. XVI–XVIII*, ed. by Gisela von Wobeser and Enriqueta Vila, México: UNAM-Instituto de Investigaciones Históricas, 2009, pp. 181–202. Antonio Rubial and William B. Taylor are scholars who have also examined the symbolic structure of New Spanish reality and its imagery in their various works.

[7] Alicia MAYER, *Lutero en el paraíso. La Nueva España en el espejo del reformador alemán*, México: UNAM-Instituto de Investigaciones Históricas, Fondo de Cultura Económica, 2008.

this academic gathering an opportunity to face a different challenge. What I believe to be motivating is to add the hagiographic component to this equation. It allows us to rethink how the Counter-Reformist ideological messages and symbols operated in the visual composites and in the written discourses, particularly where Luther is confronted with the Catholic saints and the Virgin Mary. These representations built a spacious, fascinating imagery in the colonial period, where life and thought were determined by the antagonistic truth between right and wrong, evil and good, sin and redemption. With the goals set by the seminar's directors in mind, I would like to discover not if art responded defensively to Protestantism, which is an obvious assumption, but what religious and cultural codes were followed to create the artistic and the discursive productions in New Spain. From there multiple secondary queries emerge: Were symbols and forms introduced as a result of the attack against Luther and Protestantism? In the same light, were religious practices and customs re-signified by instigation of Luther's movement? Were there theoretical concepts displayed in the Viceroyalty during the Counter-Reformation? Were new devotions originated and fomented in Spanish dominions as a response to Protestantism? Did the presence of the German reformer encourage change in the way sacred images of saints were worshipped and represented? How did Luther relate to Marian devotion?

To answer many of these topics in-depth, we require a book-length study. Because here our space is limited, we will discuss these questions in the light of a central hypothesis, which is that New Spain responded, in an implicit or explicit way, to the postulates of the Protestant movement, but did so according to the official patterns, codes and precepts set by Spain's policies regarding the use of images, set forth since the second half of the fifteenth century, which were updated after the Council of Trent (1545–1563). My desire is to explain how this program was carried out, among other ways, by promoting new as well as long-established traditional approaches to hagiographic representation in painting (iconography) and the written discourse, mainly sermons (rhetoric), where several saints and the virgin Mary were strong emblems against heresy. Luther's figure was "used" to convey a powerful message to viewers and readers as the number one enemy of Catholicism. To understand this antagonism, the interpretation of the written word plays a most important role, as discursive strategies explain the pictorial examples we have selected here to be analyzed. Therefore, we consider them as relevant primary sources for the present research. I want to show if the production, uses, promotion and reception of art and discourse from Medieval and Renaissance representations changed or were re-shaped in New Spain because of the attack on Protestantism. In part, I follow the conclusions of the key study of Felipe Pereda for the Iberian Peninsula,[8] while the present research focuses particularly on the colonial context, where a flood of European religious imagery was reproduced and adapted as products with transatlantic connections. Hence, painting and written treaties are the two vectors that make up the axis of our method for this historical review. The convergence between image and discourse will allow us to have a key understanding of the relationship between Catholic imagery and the Anti-Protestant reply in Mexico's colonial productions.

The manner in which Catholic understanding expressed itself in visual depictions and oral and recorded manifestations in New Spain has been discussed by several scholars on both sides of the Atlantic, among them Jaime Cuadriello, Antonio Rubial, Ilona Katzew, William Taylor, Luisa Elena Alcalá, David Brading, Paula Mues Orts, Alfonso Rodríguez G. de Ceballos, Sergi Doménech, Iván Escamilla and others. These works are benchmarks that deepen our way of understanding religious thought and practice in Mexico. These studies have paid less attention to analyzing in particular Luther's presence on canvases and the use given to this character in art and rhetoric. Despite being almost outside the central topics in the visual illustrations in New Spain, Luther's appearance, or rather what he symbolizes, cannot be ignored. Based on the primary sources and the scholarly literature that have been reviewed, we will investigate whether Luther and his confession encouraged—even though unintentionally—a change in the way sacred images were worshipped and depicted, and likewise in the manner saints were revered. To prove if the German reformer inspired—once again, intentionally or not—original cultural and religious guidelines of artistic representation, we must go through materials and documents that have been previously studied, and analyze in more detail recent findings that provide new insights in order to further test the hypotheses.

In sum, this article studies if certain devotions and other procedures originated in or were strengthened by Lutheranism. Finally, I am also interested in elucidating how New Spain forged itself a cultural identity through the dialectics between good and evil, Christ and Satan, orthodoxy and heresy, and so on, something that ended up building, from the figure of Luther as a "different other", an anti-hero in the Hispanic American mind. There are multiple examples of Luther's presence in the imagery and discourse in New Spain. Without pretending to be exhaustive, I will analyze here a selection

---

[8] Felipe PEREDA, *Las imágenes de la discordia. Política y poética de la imagen sagrada en la España del Cuatrocientos*, Madrid: Marcial Pons, 2007.

among a varied catalogue, specifically those which might be the most paradigmatic examples of the opposition between Luther, the saints and the Virgin Mary.

Catholic Heroes and Confessional Foes in Baroque Imagery

I

In the examples provided in the lines above, those where Luther stands out as part of New Spain's imagery at the dawn of the sixteenth century, the ex-Augustinian friar's presence responds to a strategic rhetorical stratagem that had a political significance.[9] In Francisco de Florencia's narrative, the Jesuits meant to honor the saints whose relics were revered, and at the same time praise the Society of Jesus, the order founded by Ignatius of Loyola in 1534 to serve the Papacy and extend the Catholic faith throughout the world in an ambitious missionary enterprise. The dignity of these virtuous persons was contrasted with the lowliness of the German "heresiarch", represented as the great enemy of the true religion, who was thus vituperated. In the second instance, Dionisio Ribera Flores aimed to make the pious king Philip II, considered in his time as the staunch champion of orthodoxy, *Rex Inclitus Fidei Defensori*, the antagonist of Luther, held responsible for the schism within the Universal Church.

The events that were described took place shortly after the reformist resolutions of the Council of Trent were decreed for the Catholic world.[10] Through them, the Church began a profound institutional renovation that meant to reaffirm its sacramental system and spiritual practices, reform the Papacy and establish new religious orders. This organic process was carried out by diocesan synods and provincial councils. Although it is true that the movement was an all-comprehensive reform in the Catholic sphere, its anti-Protestant aspect makes it also be known as the "Counter-Reformation".[11]

The Spanish Crown and Church sparked a whole smear campaign against Luther from the same moment that the Papacy condemned him in 1520 and after Luther defied the Imperial authority by rebelling against

---

[9] Rhetoric is the art used as a technique to arrange and produce discourse. It was fundamentally utilized to teach, move and delight the senses. Jaime H. BORJA, *Los indios medievales de fray Pedro de Aguado. Construcción del idólatra y escritura de la historia en una crónica del siglo XVI*, Bogotá, Colombia: Centro Editorial Javeriano, 2002, pp. 50–54.

[10] *El Sacrosanto y Ecuménico Concilio de Trento*, ed. by Ignacio López de Ayala, Barcelona: Imprenta de Antonio Sierra, 1848.

[11] There is much debate about the use of this terminology. For the discussion, see MAYER, *Lutero en el paraíso, op. cit.*, pp. 29–52.

Emperor Charles V, head of the Holy Roman Empire and at the time also sovereign of Spain.[12] From then on, the monarch and his successors set out on an unshakeable path to defend Catholicism with all human and economic resources. In August 1521, the same year that Luther was declared an outcast after the Diet of Worms, the Spanish captain Hernán Cortés conquered the city of Mexico Tenochtitlan, the heart of the Mexican empire. The Iberian presence in Mesoamerica marked the outbreak of Catholic Christianity into the New World. Since then, "European ways and things were selectively transferred and adopted" into the Hispanic American context.[13]

As part of the kingdom of Spain, New Spain was involved in the Catholic reformation program, which not only addressed doctrinal, liturgical and dogmatic issues besides the disciplining and training of the clergy, but also expanded Catholicism with an earnest missionary zeal. The movement also aimed to avoid the effects of the Protestant rupture overseas. Following Trent's decree of March 1547, that sought "to dispel errors and extirpate heresies", the First Mexican Synod of 1555 alluded to "the militant quality of the American [Mexican] Church" and determined that this institution, which had been recently planted abroad, was the devil's enemy and thus was compelled to fight against him in the New World.[14] On one hand, this battle would be fought in opposition to idolatry and paganism, and on the other it was directed towards preventing the menace of Protestant "contagion" in the Transatlantic dominions. Religion would be considered the primary vehicle for integrating the many and diverse ethnic groups present in the new realms. Yet, unity of belief and orthodoxy were also central themes to Spain since the times when the realm was ruled by the Catholic Monarchs, Ferdinand and Isabella, and later under the "Universal Monarchy" of the first Habsburg sovereigns.[15] Philip II believed that if the Catholic faith was lost in Europe, all his now worldwide states would be soon vanished. For this reason,

---

[12] Mark EDWARDS, *Printing, Propaganda and Martin Luther*, Minneapolis, Minnesota: Fortress Press, 2004, pp. 150–57; Peter BURSCHEL, "Das Monster. Katholische Luther-Imagination im 16. Jahrhundert", in *Luther zwischen den Kulturen*, ed. by Peer Schmidt and Hans Medick, Gotingen: Verlag, Vandenhoeck und Ruprecht, 2004, pp. 33–48.

[13] TAYLOR, *Theatre, op. cit.*, pp. 35–36.

[14] *Los Concilios Provinciales en Nueva España. Reflexiones e influencias*, ed. by Pilar Martínez López-Cano and Francisco Javier Cervantes Bello, México: UNAM-Instituto de Investigaciones Históricas, and the Benemérita Universidad Autónoma de Puebla, 2005; Alicia MAYER, "Política contrarreformista e imagen antiluterana en Nueva España", *Hispania Sacra. Revista Española de Historia*, LXVIII, 137 (2016), 31–43.

[15] PEREDA, *Las imágenes de la discordia, op. cit.*; Juan A. ORTEGA Y MEDINA, *Reforma y Modernidad*, in *Obras de Juan A. Ortega y Medina*, ed. by María Cristina González Ortiz and Alicia Mayer, México: UNAM-Instituto de Investigaciones Históricas-Facultad de Estudios Superiores Acatlán, 2013, pp. 55–76.

he emphasized that the cause of religion was for him the most important concern.[16] Consequently, any incursion of "schismatic sects" would threaten the political security of the Kingdom, not only in Europe but also beyond the Atlantic. Philip's aim was, at the same time, to recover for Christianity the German territories that had embraced the Evangelical creed and, above all, to avoid the expansion of Protestantism in the American hemisphere.

While this was pursued by Spain, the Council of Trent anathematized Protestant precepts. As Fernando Rodríguez de la Flor states, the negative perception of Luther was construed in the mental universe of the Catholic "confessional absolutism" of the Counter-Reformation.[17] The German monk was made the arch-enemy of Catholicism and the antagonistic model *par excellence* of Catholic values: in this fashion he made his way in colonial imagery. This figure in particular—probably only paralleled by John Calvin (1509-1564)—stood out quite negatively in people's minds. In his theological disquisitions, Diego Valadés (1533-1590), an outstanding Franciscan missionary, referred to Luther as the *Archihereticus Maledictus in Germania*, while chronicler Francisco López de Gómara (*c.* 1512-1572) defined him as "un personaje vehemente, mentiroso, pleitista, calumniador, tramposo, rudo, bufón, bribón y borracho que no contaba con virtud alguna".[18] Historians in New Spain praised the first religious persons to come to this hemisphere. The need for inborn, pious examples explains the spread of local hagiographies, and some characters, like friar Martín de Valencia, revered leader of the "Apostolic Twelve" Franciscans, considered a hero of the first missionary endeavor, were opposed to Luther.

On the other hand, new religious orders were created in the Counter-Reformation era, whose founders and promoters were promptly raised to the altars. Ignatius of Loyola, Francis Xavier, prime architects of the Jesuit order, and Teresa of Ávila, foremother of the Discalced Carmelites, were canonized in 1622 and other prominent figures of the ecclesiastical elite followed. Post-Tridentine Catholic prototypical personalities and symbols were profusely represented as *exempla* for generations to come.

---

[16] Geoffrey PARKER, "David or Goliath? Phillip II and his world in the 1580s", in *Spain, Europe and the Atlantic World. Essays in honour of John Elliott*, ed. by Richard L. Kagan and Geoffrey Parker, Cambridge: Cambridge University Press, 1995, pp. 259–60.
[17] Fernando RODRÍGUEZ DE LA FLOR, *Barroco, Representación e ideología en el mundo hispánico*, Madrid: Cátedra, 2002, p. 170.
[18] "A liar, a quarrelsome slanderer, trickster, rude fool and drunk man that had no virtue". Francisco LÓPEZ DE GÓMARA, *Annals of the Emperor Charles V*, ed. by Roger B. Merriman, Oxford: The Clarendon Press, 1912, pp. 125–26; Diego VALADÉS, *Assertiones Catholicae contra praecipuos aliquot haereticorum errores*, 1591, Manuscript. Vatican Library, Branch Ottoboniensis, 582–2366.

Luther considered biblical saints as models or examples for Christians, *exempla fidei*,[19] but he defiled the cult given to their paintings by considering it a perverse practice that praised false legends and derived from idolatry.[20] As a result, in Catholic view, he was flagrantly in league with the devil. However, notwithstanding the initial rejection of the Roman Church to its critics, it was shaken by the reformers's accusations and became more cautious in the process of canonizing virtuous characters from the second half of the sixteenth century. Despite the recommendations, after Trent new saints came along, and were promoted by ecclesiastic officials, as epitomes of Christian virtues, especially those that represented the spirit of Catholic reform in the new era, in opposition to the "nefarious" Protestant censures. Trent clearly pointed out that the honour which was shown to them referred to the prototypes which those images represented and not to the material image itself. Devotional models would still be considered useful "not only for the catechetical instruction of the faithful but also as a stimulus for the emulation of their lives and virtues through the expression of strong emotionality".[21] Also, on the Mesoamerican world in early colonial times, as in the Iberian Peninsula, a clear support of ecclesiastic officials towards the devotion to the Virgin Mary gradually led to the widespread worship of the Mother of God in her many dedications, especially that of the Immaculate Conception, meaning that Mary, through God's grace, was conceived free from the stain of original

---

[19] Suzanne KIMMIG-VÖLKNER, "Luther, the Virgin Mary and the Saints. Catholic images as a Key to Understanding the Lutheran Concept of Salvation", in *Martin Luther and the Reformation. Essays*, ed. by Harald Meller, Colin B. Bailey, et al., Germany: Sandstein Verlag, 2016, pp. 261–69 (p. 267).

[20] Martín Lutero, *La cautividad babilónica de la Iglesia*, in *Obras de Martín Lutero*, ed. by Carlos Withaus, 5 vols, Buenos Aires: Paidós, 1967–1977, p. 229. For analyses of Luther's theology, see, among others Teofanes EGIDO (prologue), *Obras de Martín Lutero*, ed. by Teófanes Egido, Salamanca: Editorial Sígueme, 2001, pp. 38–53; José María GÓMEZ HERAS, *Teología protestante*, Madrid, Biblioteca de Autores Cristianos, 1972; Adolfo GONZÁLEZ MONTES "Líneas estructurales de la teología de Lutero", in *Lutero y Reforma*, ed. by José Belloch Zimmerman and Ángel Rodríguez, Cáceres: Universidad de Extremadura – Banco de Santander, 1985, pp. 41–54; August HASLER, *Luther in der katholischen Dogmatik*, München: Max Hueber Verlag, 1968; *Luthers Theologie*, ed. by Julius Köstlin, 2 vols, Darmstadt: Wissenschaftliche Buchgesellschaft, 1968; Alister MCGRATH, *The Intellectual Origins of the European Reformation*, Oxford: Blackwell, 2004 (2nd ed.), pp. 103–16; Fernando BAÑOS VALLEJO, "Lutero sobre la hagiografía y los hagiógrafos sobre Lutero", in *Studia Aurea*, 13 (2019), 7–40 (pp. 12–13).

[21] Alfonso RODRÍGUEZ G. DE CEBALLOS, "Image and Counter-Reformation in Spain and Spanish America", in *Sacred Spain. Art and Belief in the Spanish World*, ed. by Ronda Kasl, New Haven-London: Yale University Press, Indiannapolis Museum of Art, 2009, 15-36, (p. 30); Gesa E. THIESSEN, "Luther and the role of Images", in *Remembering the Reformation*, ed. by Declan Marmion, Salvador Ryan and Gesa E. Thiessen, Minneapolis: Fortress Press, 2017, p. 184. Project MUSE. muse.jhu.edu/book/49654.

sin. In Mexico, the Virgin, in its title of Our Lady of Guadalupe, became "the prominent symbol of Mexican identity, providential unity and collective pride".[22] Strikingly, Luther was made the main antagonist in the face of Catholic values exemplified by the saints and the Mother of God.

II

During his lifetime, and contrary to what many Catholic adversaries acknowledged, Martin Luther emphasised the didactic and evangelical role of images and their importance in spreading the biblical messages, but he criticized what he thought to be an abusive, irreverent and idolatrous cult of images in Christianity. According to Gesa E. Thiessen's latest study of 2017, the German reformer acknowledged their relevance in remembering the Trinity and the saints. In summary, as this author states, Lutherans continued to worship in pre-Reformation custom.[23] Even though Luther was not a vehement iconoclast, and advocated moderate changes in the use of images, the Council of Trent responded harshly against him. In response, as Alfonso Rodríguez G. de Ceballos has observed, Trent consolidated the new religious culture of the Counter-Reformation, which "had as a visible and palpable consequence the multiplication of all kinds of images, cult images as well as miraculous, didactic, devotional, and processional ones".[24] The Jesuits were by far the leaders of a new strategy of communicating Catholic values. Jonathan Brown describes them as the "watchdogs of orthodoxy".[25] Their religious organization formulated a whole iconographical program which derived in a very successful means of indoctrination.

In his classic work (1921), *Der Barock als Kunst der Gegenreformation*, the German-Swiss art historian Werner Weisbach—and also more than a few later historians—pointed out that, because it opposed many of the Protestant premises, the Baroque was *par excellence* the art of the Counter-Reformation.[26] In a similar perspective, Francisco de la Maza argued that, if it

---

[22] TAYLOR, *Theatre, op. cit.*, p. 173.
[23] THIESSEN, "Luther and the role of Images", *art. cit.*, p. 168.
[24] RODRÍGUEZ G. DE CEBALLOS, "Image and Counter-Reformation in Spain and Spanish America", *art. cit.*, p. 29. Trent left many open questions regarding the representation of images according to the new policies of the Church and, thus, had inherent limitations. Its decrees in the field of art still had significant gaps in goals and methods. Systematic work, through years, led to models and guidelines.
[25] Jonathan BROWN, *Images and Ideas in Seventeenth Century Spanish Painting*, Princeton, New Jersey: Princeton University Press, 1978, p. 64.
[26] Werner WEISBACH, *Der Barock als Kunst der Gegenreformation*, Berlin: Paul Cassirer, 1921.

were not for Luther, this transcendent movement would not have existed. He maintained, as Weisbach did, that one effect of this long-lasting artistic and cultural process was its defensive character.[27] The so-called Baroque period, in its pervasive, cultural dimension in Europe, which several scholars date between 1570–1620 to the end of the eighteenth century, was one of social and political unrest, tension, a clash of ideas and antagonistic views, but still of enormous creativity and rich in aesthetic novelties.[28] In New Spain, although the central decades of the seventeenth century were highly conflictive, with many critical tensions in the colonial order, the pressure failed to cause the pathetic state of permanent warfare that existed in Europe. The sixteenth and seventeenth centuries marked an intense social interchange in the Viceroyalty and the development of a creole (*criollo*) or American-born mentality. It manifested in manifold ways, being one of them a particular religious affection and imagery. As William Taylor puts it, Baroque Catholicism was an expression of faith, social values, political relationships and engagements with objects of devotion.[29] Anthony Pagden has emphasized that in the colonial era the crux of cultural identity was of religious character, and it was an element that helped to bind relationships between the various parts that composed the empire.[30] As in Europe, in New Spain the Catholic Church elites framed a whole contextual universe to the social imagery and forged a solid ideology. Nevertheless, while Catholic orthodoxy became an essential trait of New Spanish essence, there were also not few features that gave this world singularity. As Jonathan Brown has observed in his classic work, *Images and Ideas in Seventeenth-Century Spanish Painting*, the Spanish Catholic Church (and we shall add its plant overseas) was not a monolithic institution. Following Antonio Domínguez Ortiz, Brown acknowledged several important distinctions in the organization of the Church (monastic and/vs parochial clergy) which considerably enhance the fields of study.[31]

The religious orders, the secular clergy and, most of all, the Society of Jesus, appointed the theological, symbolical and dogmatical elements necessary for authors and painters to efficaciously communicate their principles. Art

---

[27] Francisco de la MAZA, *El pintor Cristóbal de Villalpando*, México: Instituto Nacional de Antropología e Historia, 1964, p. 21.
[28] For Baroque traits and characteristics, see TAYLOR, *Theatre, op. cit.*, pp. 5–6; RODRÍGUEZ DE LA FLOR, *Barroco, op. cit.*, p. 23; José A. MARAVALL, *La cultura del Barroco*, Barcelona: Ariel, 1975, p. 34.
[29] TAYLOR, *op. cit.*, p. 6.
[30] Anthony PAGDEN, "Heeding Heraclides: Empire and its Discontents, 1619–1812", in *Spain, Europe and the Atlantic World. Essays in Honour of John Elliott*, ed. by Richard L. Kagan and Geoffrey Parker, Cambridge: Cambridge University Press, 1995, pp. 316–33 (p. 323).
[31] BROWN, *Images and Ideas, op. cit.*, p. 16.

was placed in the service of dogma. The response to Protestantism originated new patterns of representation since Trent's twenty-fifth session conclusions (4 December, 1563),[32] and especially with the precise, clear and instructive rules dictated by accredited writers[33] who endorsed proper depiction and display of images, as well as through the provincial councils and diocesan synods. They provided concepts to create the guidelines for the correct representation of the contents according to orthodoxy.

Spain had experienced a long-term fight with heterodoxy, as Jonathan Brown and later Felipe Pereda have neatly explained. In the Hispanic world, at the end of the fifteenth century, social, psychological and religious mechanisms oriented the use of images and the character of written discourses. Pereda argues that conflicts with racial and religious minorities in the Iberian Peninsula that opposed to external signs of devotion, forced the church and state authorities to elaborate a policy of inculturation where images played a very important role, along with preaching, before the watchful gaze of the Inquisition.[34] At that time, the targets of religious enmity were Jews and Moors who were suspected of practicing their religions after professed conversion to Catholicism. During the next two centuries, the objective moved to heresy, personified by Martin Luther. The historical-ideological frame of reference explains "the changing expressions of representation".[35] In the face of Protestant iconoclasm in Europe, images of Christ, the saints, church authorities and the Virgin Mary would be again mobilized and with renewed vigor. One more time, heterodoxy would be a topic in a leading position, this time in Baroque culture. Anti-Protestant propaganda reached the New World in the second half of the sixteenth century, but it was in the next generation when the post-tridentine clergy's efficacious indoctrination may be fully seen, with

---

[32] The Tridentine doctrine on sacred images is summarized by Alfonso Rodríguez G. de Ceballos in the following fundamental points: 1. That images, thanks to their faithful representation of the truth, be instructive and promote virtue, 2. That they be neither apocryphal nor suspect and thus lead to heterodoxy, confusion, or superstition, 3. That they be neither indecent nor profane in either dress or ornamentation, there by inciting devotion (decorum). "Image and Counter-Reformation in Spain and Spanish America", *art. cit.*, p. 20.

[33] As Alfonso Rodríguez G. de Ceballos also demonstrates, after Trent, a flood of literature on the subject of sacred images, very learned treatises as those of Gabriel Paleotti (1582), Johannes Molanus (1617), Vicente Carducho (1633) and Francisco Pacheco (1649) among others defined fundamental points regarding their use and representation, in a clear, precise and instructive way in the eyes of the faithful. "Image and Counter-Reformation in Spain and Spanish America", *art. cit.*, pp. 19–21. Pacheco formulated a guide to orthodox iconography in his famous *El arte de la pintura* (1649).

[34] PEREDA, *Las imágenes de la discordia, op. cit.*, p. 28.

[35] BROWN, *Images and Ideas, op. cit.*, pp. 14–15 and 55; PEREDA, *Las imágenes de la discordia, op. cit.*, pp. 26–29.

its rich proliferation of images and messages transmitted on canvases and from the pulpits in churches and in written treaties. Doctrinal expression aided interpretation of the many symbols in the paintings. Art became an effective instrument of Catholic propaganda to promote model saints, according to the precepts imposed by the Holy See and the Jesuits, the architects of the new Tridentine spirituality, with their strong religious influence. In Luisa Elena Alcalá's study on the uses and functions of images, the author shows how the Jesuit's pragmatic teaching balanced usefulness and aesthetics.[36]

In pictorial and sculptural representations, the divine and saintly were usually depicted as opposed to Satan and his followers. Hence, Luther was considered the devil's principal henchman and thus, in this manner, he appears characterized in the works of art. Luther, as an historical character, was not the principal focus of individual attention in colonial iconography and discourse. There was no intention to have him portrayed in a true or realistic way. As said earlier, he was treated as a rhetorical resource. By being constantly repeated, this Manichaean treatment became an archetype. Heretics—and Jews and Moors before them—were transformed into metaphors that represented dissent. To represent heresy, artists used a variety of standards, but almost all the references to the dichotomy between good and evil are staged in the so-called *Triunfos de la Iglesia* (the Triumphs of the Church). These were standardized paintings whose models were present in Medieval times and were re-defined in the Early Modern period. They flooded Catholic Christendom and explain the new "global" patterns of consumption, as they could be found in Germany, Flanders, Spain, and Hispanic America.[37] The catalogue of images in Europe and America show that the rivalry between Catholicism and Protestantism was an international concern.

Triumphs were usually large paintings, a lavish display of dramatical Baroque scenery, characterized by its narrative and dynamic composition. This type of "programmatic painting" as Jonathan Brown defines it,[38] was usually placed in the altars or walls in cathedrals, in parish churches, in oratories and in monastic cloisters for devotional purposes, but sometimes in more

---

[36] Luisa Elena ALCALÁ, "Acomodación, control y esplendor de la imagen en las fundaciones jesuíticas", in *Barroco Andino. Memoria del primer encuentro internacional*, La Paz, Bolivia: Viceministerio de cultura y Unión Latina, 2003, pp. 259–66 (p. 263); for this topic, also Santiago SEBASTIÁN, *Contrarreforma y barroco*, Madrid: Alianza Editorial, 1989, p. 13; Beatriz MARISCAL, "El programa de representación simbólica de los jesuitas en Nueva España", in *La producción simbólica en la América colonial. Interrelación de la literatura y las artes*, ed. by José Pascual Buxó, México: UNAM, 2001, pp. 51–66.
[37] Robert SCRIBNER, *For the Sake of the Simple Folk. Popular Propaganda for the German Reformation*, Oxford: Clarendon Press, 1994, pp. 63–65 and 115.
[38] BROWN, *Images and Ideas, op. cit.*, p. 65.

visible sites inside lay confraternities, for the instruction of the ordinary public. They represent the fullness of the propagandist conception of the Counter-Reformation, in accordance to the enforcement of church teaching and dogma. In fact, through these compositions, both the Spanish monarchy and the Catholic Church promoted their political and religious program, part of which was based on the traditional fundamentals of the ancient papal institution: pilgrimages, veneration of saints and relics, the use of revered images and statuary, adoration to the Virgin Mary were reaffirmed as spiritually commendable practices.[39] They were characterized, among other things, by the overload of figures, profuse allegory and symbolism. These paintings were narratives that carried out an apology of the Catholic faith, the Sacred Scriptures, Apostolic traditions, ecclesiastic authorities, and a continual defense of the sacraments, especially the Eucharist, against Protestant criticism. Serial, repetitive representation increased the efficacy of the message. Still, their intricate meaning was only fully understood by a few, more literate viewers.

The theme of the Triumphs is based on the last of the three stages of the church's undertaking: the militant (against enemies on earth), the purgative (phase of tribulation) and the triumphant (*non plus ultra* or eternal glory). This venture meant the apotheosis of the ecclesiastical hierarchy, the glorification of the sacraments and fulfillment of the precepts of the "true religion", and also implied that Satan and his minions (the heretics, schismatics, Moors and Jews) would had previously been defeated. Trent's position can be already seen in the guidelines of the Second Mexican Synod of 1565, where it says that:

> Obligación tenemos todos los fieles cristianos a creer que hay dos iglesias, la una se llama Iglesia triunfante, y la otra, Iglesia militante, la una donde para siempre viven en perpetuo gozo, y contentamiento, gozando de la clara visión de Dios, los que en este mundo, con el favor divino, triunfarán del mundo y del Demonio y de la carne y viven, como dice Isaías, en la hermosura de la paz y amistad de Dios.[40]

---

[39] Víctor Mínguez, "Los reyes de las Américas. Presencia y propaganda de la monarquía hispánica en el Nuevo Mundo", in *Imagen del Rey, imagen de los reinos. Las ceremonias públicas en la España moderna (1500–1814)*, ed. by Agustín González Enciso and Jesús Usunáriz, Pamplona: Ediciones de la Universidad de Navarra, 1999, pp. 231–57; Trinidad de Antonio, "Coleccionismo, devoción y Contrarreforma", in *Felipe II un monarca y su época*, Madrid: Museo del Prado, 1998–1999, p. 146; Mario Praz, *Imágenes del barroco. Estudios de emblemática*, Madrid: Siruela, 1989.

[40] "All faithful Christians must believe that there are two churches, triumphant and militant, one formed by those who live in perpetual enjoyment and contentment, enjoying the clear vision of God, constituted by those who in this world, with God's help, will conquer the world, the Devil and the flesh and live, according to [the prophet] Isaiah, in the beauty, the

The theme of the Triumphs was not conceived on American soil; they were a product of transatlantic connections and exchanges. The iconography was inspired in Peter Paul Rubens's (1577–1640) monumental tapestries for the Discalced Convent in Madrid. In New Spain, the notable painter Baltasar de Echave Rioja, taking Rubens's theoretical model, established in his *Triunfo* for the sacristy of the Cathedral of Puebla the patterns that needed to be followed by later painters. It was Cristóbal de Villalpando (*c.* 1649–1714) who gave the theme a monumental and impressive treatment.[41] (Figures 1 and 2).

In this wide operating theater, symbolically, Luther and the other heresiarchs became a necessary element of the composition. Consequently, they were transformed into actors who, at the bottom of the scene, played the role of forever condemned sinners. Sometimes labeled with his own name, which appears in a perfectly legible way in these settings, Luther personified the conflicting role that the Catholic authorities wanted him to perform: he represented evil, error and ignorance. A merely aesthetic response was not only expected from the audience, the lesser noticeable features tested their ability to discover a whole moral message conveyed in the interstices of the canvases. Luther was a warning sign for spectators, aimed to negatively impress the viewers attention. Hence, the observers were exhorted to follow the true religion by recreating vivid mental images that involved all the senses, emotions and feelings of awe and anguish. In this Baroque scenario, the "play" repeated itself throughout every corner of Catholic Europe and Spanish America. I have found different representations of the Triumphs of the Church in New Spain with an explicit reference to the German reformer. Here, we will soon analyze some of these examples.

The Counter-Reformation had two especially far-reaching agents: The Society of Jesus, the active, militant face of the Catholic renewal movement, headed by Ignatius of Loyola, followed by the great missionary Francis Xavier and the nobleman Francis of Borja, and the mystical forehead of the Discalced Carmelites, Teresa of Ávila. Painters in New Spain were most often commissioned by their patrons to produce works based on the lives of these egregious characters, who were canonized in 1622, except for Borja, who became a saint in 1670. These holy figures provided a fresh significance to

---

peace and friendship of God". Prologue, in Elena GERLERO, "Sacristía", in *Catedral de México, patrimonio artístico y cultural*, México: Fomento Cultural Banamex-Sedue, 1986, p. 395.
[41] I thank my colleague Iván Escamilla González for bringing this information to my attention. For the influence of the Flemish painter in New Spain, see Edward J. SULLIVAN, "European Painting and the Art of the New World Colonies", in *Converging Cultures. Art and Identity in Spanish America*, ed. by Diana Fane, New York: The Brooklyn Museum, 1996, pp. 28–41.

Catholic visual representation from the second half of the sixteenth century. Frequently, their iconography, with the symbols that described their deeds and achievements in the faith, was mostly accompanied by an allusion to the triumph over heresy and, particularly, to a character bearing the name of Luther. We will start by analyzing the Loyola sequences.

Ignatius of Loyola: Quintessence of the Catholic Champion

In Saint Ignatius of Loyola's canonization bull (1622), the Jesuits were meant to excel on two battle fronts: in the crusade against idolatry (paganism) in the American hemisphere, and in the fight against the Protestant schism in Europe. The aforementioned document further stated that:

> En la época en que fueron descubiertos nuevos mundos y en el Viejo se levantó Lutero para combatir a la Iglesia Católica, tuvo Ignacio de Loyola la idea de fundar una Compañía que se había de dedicar preferentemente a la conversión de los paganos y al rescate de los herejes [...] por esta razón ha venido a aumentar la lista de los santos.[42]

In New Spain, Saint Ignatius was highly praised by ecclesiastical officials, chroniclers, and preachers. Even Archbishop and Viceroy Juan Palafox y Mendoza, later, a declared enemy of the Society of Jesus, in his *Tratados Doctrinales* (1646), complimented Loyola by claiming that "para confusión y ruina de los errores de Alemania, levantó Dios por el mismo tiempo en la Iglesia a San Ignacio, y con él su valiosa Compañía, que puede justamente llamarse Ejército de la Iglesia".[43]

With frameworks supplied by the Jesuits, painters constructed visual compositions to exalt Loyola, following their dictates, together with the canons formulated since the Third Mexican Provincial Council of 1585, which stipulated that "the people preserve the memory of the Saints and venerate them, ordering the conduct of their life and customs in imitation of them".[44]

---

[42] "In the epoch whereby new worlds were discovered and in [Europe] Luther stood to combat the Catholic Church, Ignatius of Loyola had the idea to establish a Company that would be dedicated preferably to the conversion of the Pagans and the rescue from heretics [...] for this reason he increased the list of the saints", *Bullarium Cocquelines*, in Leopold VON RANKE, *Historia de los Papas*, México: Fondo de Cultura Económica, 1943, p. 430. Moreover, Ranke carries out an interesting comparison between Luther and Loyola, pp. 90–92.

[43] "God raised Saint Ignatius in the Church to confuse and ruin the errors of Germany, and with him his valuable Company, that can fairly be named as an army of the Church", Juan de PALAFOX Y MENDOZA, *Tratados doctrinales*, in *Obras del Ilustrísimo, Excelentísimo y Venerable Siervo de Dios Don Juan de Palafox y Mendoza*, 14 vols, vol. IV, Madrid: Imprenta de Don Gabriel Ramírez, 1762, chapter XXVII.

[44] As quoted in RODRÍGUEZ G. DE CEBALLOS, "Image and Counter-Reformation in Spain and Spanish America", *art. cit.*, 27.

Loyola's physical traits and character were already delineated by his biographer, the Jesuit Pedro de Ribadeneira. Miguel Cabrera (*c.* 1720–1768), one of the most famous painters in colonial-era and a man closely linked with the Jesuit Order,[45] copied Saint Ignatius portrait and at the same time contested heresy in a mid-size canvas that depicts the saint holding the Society's regulations, standing over a hideous harridan, biting her fist, with a bared left breast and snakes covering the right breast. This repulsive Medusa-like monster was in Renaissance art the iconic representation of envy, a deadly sin, and heresy (Figure 3).[46]

The theme of Christ or the saints rising over heretics and their books in a triumphant attitude was frequent in painting and sculpture, either in Catholic or Protestant imagery. Cabrera's piece on Saint Ignatius departed from models and prescriptions that came from Catholic Europe and were reproduced in Spanish American dominions. Among others, two European statues that are almost identical to Cabrera's version of St Ignatius of Loyola stand out: one in the Papal Basilica of Saint Peter in the Vatican, and another in the Cathedral of Cuenca (Spain). Cabrera's work followed the prototype: through these two figures, the saint and the rapscallion, he meant to personify the dual aspects of good and evil. The traditional attributes were followed by the master painter, except for the portrayal of the old harpy under the saint's feet, which in the Mediterranean examples holds a book that bears the name of Luther. The Mexican painting represented the impious character in the same dramatic way, but without the formal recognition from the artist who avoided labeling the Saxon "heresiarch's" patronymic on not one, but three of his erratic treatises (Figures 4, 5 and 6). The impact of the canons from Spain and Rome is clear, but in New Spain Luther's presence was mitigated, and a paler version of the polemic character was brought forward. Even though New Spanish topics and practices to represent the saints and Luther followed the same patterns as seen in early modern Europe, the contexts of both environs differed substantially in a way that the confessional rivalry was not fought in the New World. That could well be the reason why Luther was treated in a milder tone in the Viceroyalty than in Spain. In the colonies, he was recorded less often—or at least more indirectly. Church authorities in Mexico might have discouraged the explicit references

---

[45] Luisa Elena ALCALÁ, "Miguel Cabrera y la congregación de la Purísima", *Anales del Instituto de Investigaciones Estéticas*, XXXIII, 99 (2011), 111–35 (pp. 115–17).

[46] See BROWN, *Images and Ideas, op. cit.*, p. 76. The allegorical source for "Heresia", in Cesare RIPA, *Iconología*, Venecia: Presso Cristoforo Tomasini, 1645, p. 255. For "Envy", Andrea ALCIATI, *Emblemata*, emblem 71. mun.ca/alciato/index.html. Book of Emblems. The Memorial Web Edition in Latin and English. Accessed November, 2020.

to Luther to keep the Reformer out of the public's knowledge, being fearful to set the viewer's imagination in a wrong direction. There was no reason to contaminate the audience's minds with dangerous and pernicious ideas and bring forward controversial issues. The Council of Trent's provisions warned that hazards against faith or references to heretical opinions be avoided, because of the harm that could cause in the minds of the common folk. Even though enemies of the faith were not (if at all) in sight in New Spain, image makers were circumspect about how they presented the figure of a heretic to avoid misconceptions. Explicit theological information might induce an adamant pseudo-philosopher, a mere curious individual or, worse, the Indian neophytes, the latter considered vulnerable and tender plants in the faith, to embrace a misunderstanding. In consequence, a pragmatic orientation was given to these religious works of art. The intention was to warn against evil, idolatry, heresy, and apostasy. Suffice it to say that Loyola struggled with the devil, no matter his guise.

Miguel Cabrera is also the author of an impressive oversized painting that the artist prepared for the Jesuit Church (later the Temple of the Oratorians of Saint Philip Neri) in the city of Guanajuato (Mexico) (Figure 7). It, again, represents the triumph of the Church with Saint Ignatius as the principal character. Loyola appears standing on a golden chariot, in a perpetual combat against Satan. He holds the reins of a majestic quadriga that is conducted by a group of Jesuits in formal and holy procession. Each element present in the composition reflects a standpoint and a dogmatic definition. Cabrera created a spatial dimension where the higher location meant heaven and the low terrain the place for the fallen. From above, the Virgin in her character of Immaculate Conception looks over the scene, while deep down lie the threatening, misguided men under diabolical direction. In this way, the church warns the faithful against wicked deception. Luther and the rest of the heretics are "punished" for disrespecting the Catholic dogmas. Personified alongside a character with long donkey ears, the Saxon reformer and his followers symbolize stubborn ignorance and sin. This time Cabrera tagged Luther's name beside the figure next to an open book, the compendium of his pernicious doctrinal errors (Figure 8).

Sor Juana Inés de la Cruz, the famous Baroque poetess of the late seventeenth century, had already portrayed the heretics as ignorant fools who, the more they studied, the less they knew. She expressed that their opinions generated distorted and misguided assertions:

> Hace daño el estudiar, porque es poner espada en manos del furioso; que siendo instrumento nobilísimo para la defensa, en sus manos es muerte suya

y de muchos. Tales fueron las Divinas Letras en poder del malvado Pelagio y del protervo Arrio, del malvado Lutero y de los demás heresiarcas.[47]

Cabrera recreated in painting the same idea that Sor Juana brought forward almost a century earlier, that the "scoundrels" easily infected others with their false arguments, and they were contemptible cheats who had confused and corrupted the Christian word. The painter's two works exemplify not only the triumph of the doctrinal authority of the Church, but also the infallibility of the true religion, represented by Ignatius, where the enemies of orthodox Christianity are forever destroyed, vanquished and neutralized by the Catholic *Machina*.

Saint Teresa and the Discalced Carmelites' Enemies

As we noted earlier, the mystic, contemplative order of the Discalced Carmelites, founded by Saint Teresa of Ávila or Teresa de Jesús was the other stalwart of Catholic reform. In his biography of Saint Teresa written in 1587, the Jesuit Francisco de Ribera exalted the nun's prodigious virtues, and his work was crucial for the processes of beatification (1614) and canonization (1622) of the celebrated religious woman. Hagiographies were Catholic propaganda that conveyed a myriad of messages, among which narrative frequently presented Luther as an antagonist. The reason behind this effect was to lead to resistance and rejection of Protestantism. Ribera informed the reader that Teresa was born the 28th of March, 1515, when Maximilian was Emperor of Germany, grandfather of emperor Charles V, two years before "the damned Luther rose against the Church, something very convenient to the Divine Providence, because he would get the nuns out of their confinement, whilst Saint [Teresa] would make them come from everywhere called to convent life and to be consecrated to God".[48]

Several times, in her writings, Teresa referred to Luther's apostasy. She stated that one of the principal causes why she was moved to reform the Carmelite order was because she wanted the convents to become fortresses to defend religion against heretics, for all the souls lost in Europe. She also proclaimed: "contra todos los luteranos me pondría yo sola a hacerles entender

---

[47] "That happened to the holy Knowledge in the power of Pelagius, the obstinate Arius, the vile Luther and other heresiarchs". Sor Juana Inés DE LA CRUZ, "Respuesta a Sor Filotea de la Cruz", in *Obras de Sor Juana Inés de la Cruz*, 4 vols, vol. 4, México: Fondo de Cultura Económica, 1994, p. 463.

[48] Francisco de RIBERA, *Vida de Santa Teresa de Jesús*, Barcelona: Gustavo Gili, editor, 1908, p. 94.

su yerro [...] siento mucho la perdición de tantas almas".[49] For these and other reasons, the Carmelite nun, religious reformer and Spanish mystic would be held by the Catholic Church the central figure of a spiritual and monastic renewal movement, a natural opponent to Luther, who defied the paradigm of cloistered life and, in the eyes of Catholics, committed the atrocity of marrying a nun (Katharina von Bora).

At the beginning of the seventeenth century, the Spanish Church and the Cortes of Castile were forceful advocates of adopting Teresa as patron saint of Spain. First in 1617 and later in 1626, this process was encouraged in view of the great devotion towards her in "all these kingdoms of Spain, and especially in those of the Crown of Castile, where the saint was born and died and her uncorrupted body rests". The reasons for the vigorous promotion, besides her obvious merits, rested in that "this realm is mindful of the favours Our Lord has done it in having placed in these kingdoms such a holy and marvellous woman who has so honoured this nation".[50] As in the Peninsula, the official support of this figure was reproduced in the realms overseas.

In the Church of the Santa Veracruz in Mexico City there is an anonymous composition from the eighteenth century that exalts the Carmelite order with a complex allegory and intricate symbolism (Figure 9).[51] Mount Carmel is placed in the central part of the painting which, according to Santiago Sebastián, signifies the cosmic stage and the tie between heaven and earth.[52] On top rests the altar that was erected by prophet Elijah with the steer he offered to Jehovah in solemn sacrifice. On the left stand the founders of the ancient Carmelite order. The composition show a multitude of characters that appear in the set: male and female saints, priests, popes and venerated *personae*. All endorse orthodoxy by wielding the sacred writings and the works of the authorities. Then, we move to the earthly level where relevant figures of the reformed Order are represented, as Saint Teresa and John of the Cross (canonized in 1726). The lower scene is of particular interest.

---

[49] "I would alone battle against all Lutherans to make them understand their mistake [because] I deeply regret the loss of so many souls". RIBERA, *Vida de Santa Teresa de Jesús, op. cit.*, p. 97.
[50] I. A. A. THOMPSON, "Castile Spain and the Monarchy: The political community from *patria natural* to *patria nacional*", in *Spain, Europe, op. cit.*, pp. 144–45.
[51] Marcela CORVERA POIRÉ and Bulmaro REYES studied an engraved print that came to New Spain in the seventeenth century and served as a model to the mentioned canvas. "Decor Carmeli o Decoro del Carmelo", in *De Ávila a las Indias. Teresa de Jesús en Nueva España*, ed. by Manuel Ramos and Mario Sarmiento, México: Centro de Estudios de Historia de México-Carso, 2016, pp. 117–26. My thanks to Mario Carlos Sarmiento Zúñiga for bringing this information to my attention.
[52] Santiago SEBASTIÁN, *Espacio y símbolo*, Córdoba: Universidad de Córdoba, 1977, p. 16.

From the highest tower of the fortress the Carmelite nuns throw arrows to heretics whose heads protrude from the waters of a small stream, all bearing their names: Luther (Figure 10), Wycliffe, Huss, Calvin, Julian the Apostate and Peter Waldo. We must remember that the characters are not approached analytically, but in a rhetorical way. They are all visual signs, not providing any historical or chronological importance. According to the canons of the Counter-Reformation, the work transmits information descriptively and had a didactic purpose. It carries a moral message; the goal was to make a dogmatic apologue of the true religion that fights against the spiritual enemies by presenting the Discalced Carmelites, led by Teresa de Jesús, as the great defenders of Catholicism, since Biblical times, but also it represents the superiority of the reformed Order over schismatic errors.

Overwhelming Triumphs: The Chariot and the Vessel

The *Triumph of the Church* that Nicolás Rodríguez Juárez (1667–1734) made in 1695 for the Templo del Carmen in Celaya (Mexico) (Figure 11), based on contents of his brilliant predecessor Cristobal de Villalpando's stunning *Triunfo* for the sacristy of Mexico City Cathedral, is a powerful visual aid to devotion that was meant to cause enchantment. Overcrowded, with dramatic lighting, monumental dimensions, and profuse decoration, it is an authentic example of the Baroque expression of doctrinal and dogmatic instruction and orthodox guidance. The work exalts the sacred symbols—being the Eucharist the dominant element—represented through the custody and the communion wafer, the reminders of Christ's sacrifice[53] and the leading figures of the Christian religion. Commonly, the painters paid homage to the sacramental elements that were attacked by Protestants and the outstanding contestant authors of heterodoxy. Here, the disposition of the scenes is relevant. On the front plane of the picture, the Church is depicted as a woman with rich ornaments, while Saint Peter represents the Papacy. A group of angels support the pontifical tiara and the keys to heaven, giving the utmost importance to the Vicar of Christ's authority and power. Both preside on a throne over a saintly procession towards the arch of glory guarded by the members of the Carmelite order, in which Saint Teresa, Saint John of the Cross, Saint Elijah and others stand out. Many of them carry crosses. Carmelite saints receive the squad of popes and cardinals who defended Marian dogmas (principally, the composition is a promotion of the Immaculate Conception). Cherubs

---

[53] Lamberto FONT, *La Eucaristía. El tema eucarístico en el arte de España*, Barcelona: Seix Barral, 1952, pp. xliii–xliv.

bear a fountain and a mirror, attributes of the Virgin, and symbols of purity and justice.

As that of Rubens', Echave Rioja's and Villalpando's, Rodriguez Juárez's composition is placed on hierarchic levels. The upper setting alludes to the celestial realm, where the Holy Trinity presides. At the bottom of the painting, heretics, again, with their names labeled beside them, are crushed under the spins of the Roman Church's triumphant carriage. It is here that we find Luther, followed by Calvin, Beza and other leading figures of the Protestant Reformation, but also ancient apostates as Pelagius and Arius, who are defeated, and their repulsive works destroyed under the wheels of the golden vehicle (Figure 12). The characters represented the palpable presence of evil in the world, vices: hatred, discord, fury, blindness, ignorance, paganism and, of course, heresy.[54] The viewer might very well ignore the doctrinal arguments of the schismatic movements, but could witness that they were foes of a malignant kind. They stood as examples to drive people away from sin and to dissuade them from following the false religion of the enemies of the Church.

Another interesting version of the Triumphs in colonial art in Mexico is an anonymous painting of the eighteenth century that uses the traditional depiction of the victorious church as a ship (also found in Protestant propaganda of the time, against Catholics) (Figure 13).[55] The viewer's attention is directed to the large central scene where Saint Peter, who holds the helm of the vessel, successfully leads its destiny towards a safe port, while the wind spreads the sail with the label *Ecclesia Triumphans*. In the bow, raising his blazing sword, stands the Archangel Michael, who guides the ark to victory, with the founders of the leading religious orders, the Apostles and a plethora of other holy personages: saints, church authorities and the doctors of the Church, all described with their names. The ship storms through dangerous waters while the four evangelists witness the scene. Christ and the Virgin Mary guide the vessel of truth, and the dove of the Holy Spirit enlightens and shows the path. Below the main ship float two small boats, the *Navis haereticorum* and the *Navis scismaticorum*, guided by demons, dodging arrows, and fleeing from the ship of

---

[54] *Cristóbal de Villalpando. Catálogo razonado*, ed. by Juana Gutiérrez Haces, Pedro Ángeles, et al., México: Fomento Cultural Banamex-Conaculta, Instituto de Investigaciones Estéticas, 1997; José Julio GARCÍA ARRANZ, "Visiones y representaciones del mal en el imaginario emblemático hispano", in *Imagen y cultura. La interpretación de las imágenes como historia cultural*, ed. by Rafael García Mahíques and Vicente F. Zuriaga, Valencia: Universitat Internacional de Gandia, Universitat de València, Generalitat Valenciana, 2008, p. 747.

[55] Thanks to Museo Nacional del Virreinato in Tepotzotlan, Mexico, for granting permission to use this image. For the analyses of the painting, *Pintura novohispana. Museo Nacional del Virreinato. Tepotzotlán*, vol. II, México: Museo Nacional del Virreinato-Instituto Nacional de Antropología e Historia, pp. 188–89.

orthodoxy. Still more damned and swimming desperately are five characters that are signalled with their names to have them fully and unmistakably identified: Luther, in a muslim costume (Figure 14)[56] together with Beza, Calvin, Sabellius, and Arius, fighting to stay afloat in the raging sea, while the Church/ship victoriously leaves them drowning behind. While commenting on the allegory of Saint Peter's vessel, the preacher Ignacio Valderas noted that it made its way far from the storm and did not keel over "because of the winds of heresy".[57]

This painting is a good example of how art was reshaped after the sixteenth century Catholic Reform. The victorious vessel was a symbol since Medieval times, an emblem of the Church Triumphant taken from Saint Ambrose, meant to describe the persecutors which the militant church of Jesus Christ was subjected to in its dangerous voyage to the celestial Jerusalem. The parable became very popular in New Spain and was frequently exploited by many authors during the colonial era. Archbishop Palafox commented on it in his *Excelencias de San Pedro*.[58] Its topic was also amply used by preachers to praise the Virgin, the angels, the mediators and to extol the true religion over the subversions by Satan. A published sermon of 1670 reinforced its practicality when the author suggested that:

> Felizmente la nave de la Iglesia militante [viaja] al puerto y tranquilidad de la Triumphante, sin descaminarla en tanta confusión de olas, ni en la caliginosa noche de la fe en el estado de viadora ni perder de vista el rumbo, o norte fiel, que le enseñó la carta de marear de su confesión [...] tan recto lleva el camino esta nave llenando sus velas el viento favorable del Santísimo Sacramento y piloteándola Pedro con el timón de la fe [...] que entre escollos y errores y bajíos de tribulaciones al paso que parece que va más combatida y atónita navega más próspera.[59]

---

[56] Werner Thomas stated that, initially, Luther was associated with Judaism and the followers of Muhammad. Werner THOMAS, *La represión del protestantismo en España, 1517–1648*, Lovaina: Leuven University Press, 2001, p. 100. On Spain's conceptualization of its enemies, also Lauren BECK, *Transforming the Enemy in Spanish Culture*, Amherst, New York: Cambria Press, 2013.
[57] Ignacio VALDERAS COLMENERO, *Sermón de Nuestra Señora de Guadalupe*, México: Imprenta Nueva de la Biblioteca Mexicana, 1758, p. 45.
[58] PALAFOX Y MENDOZA, *Excelencias de San Pedro*, in *Obras, op. cit.*, vol. II, pp. 75 and 142.
[59] "Happily, the vessel of the militant Church travels to the port and tranquility of the Triumphant, without being mislead in so much confusion made by the waves, nor in the caliginous night of the faith, in the condition of traveler, without losing sight of the course, faithful north, shown by the sea chart of its confession [...] the ship carries it so straight-forward, the favorable wind of the most sacred Sacrament spreads its sails while Peter pilots it with the helm of faith [...] which between pitfalls and errors and shoals of tribulations seems to go more combative and stunned but more prosperously sails". Felipe GALINDO, *Oración Evangélica del gran príncipe de los apóstoles San Pedro*, México: Juan Ruyz, 1670, p. 6.

Themes like this one, taken from the Sacred Scriptures and History, were used to plan visual representations,[60] but also, after the sixteenth century schism, more characters and messages were introduced—mainly contemporary saints and new confessional enemies. As for the small figure that represents Luther, appearing with his name, but dressed as a Muslim, this shows the rhetorical use of the character, being equated with all dissident sects, as a stereotype of heterodoxy, confusion and doctrinal error.

Old Saints in New Frames: Two Medieval Saints against Luther

In a written sermon of 1781, Miguel Tadeo de Guevara emphasized that the Catholic Church had "sacred Doctors who with their pens assaulted the monsters that came out to combat against her".[61] This explains the subject of the monochrome religious plate of 1767, *Divus Thomas doctor Angelicus* by José de Nava (there is likewise a colored-version on canvas) in the city of Puebla (Figure 15). Also meant for didactic purposes, in this visual doctrinal defense the engraver paid tribute to Saint Thomas Aquinas (1225–1274), the Italian Dominican philosopher in the tradition of Scholasticism and Doctor of the Church, who was in several points disproved by Luther, together with Aristotle, in his *Heidelberg Thesis* (1518).[62] Trent granted a privileged situation to Thomism, the medieval philosophical school that is one of the most transcendent foundations of dogmatic teaching of the Church. In the image, Saint Thomas appears seated in a chariot and, while he receives the Holy Spirit's inspiration, he carries the Blessed Sacrament, the living body of Christ, as a symbol of truth. There are medieval depictions of the triumph of Thomas Aquinas, like that of Lipo Memmi (1323), where the Saint stands above a dejected Moor. Others include a fallen Jew among the condemned, as was customary in Medieval Europe. After the sixteenth century German Reformation, Luther was chosen to join the group of the ancient heterodox enemies. In Nava's print he is there represented, or, shall we say, only the

---

[60] Santiago SEBASTIÁN, *Emblemática e historia del arte*, Madrid: Ediciones Cátedra, 1995, p. 83.
[61] Miguel Tadeo de GUEVARA, *Visita sin despedida que hizo María Santísima de Guadalupe al Reyno para la estabilidad y firmeza de la iglesia americana*, México: Imprenta Nueva Madrileña de Don Felipe de Zúñiga Ontiveros, 1781, p. xvi.
[62] In 1520, Luther fully rejected Saint Thomas' explanation of Eucharistic transubstantiation, which stated that the mutation of the substance displaces that of the bread and wine into the body and blood of Christ, leaving only its accidents (species). T. Aquinas in IV Sentence 11, 11, quoted by PEREDA, *Las imágenes de la discordia*, op. cit., Pos 4539, Kindle Book. As for Luther, bread and wine does not change, but are maintained, but the sacred form is Divinity itself (consubstantiation). See Martin LUTHER, *On the Babylonian Captivity of the Church*. wordpress.com/2013/05pdf. Accessed October, 2020.

reformer's head, as he is shown decapitated (Freud would say castrated)[63] and "vomiting" his errors.

The Catholic world felt that Luther stood against Scholastic theology, when he wrote the *Disputatio contra scholasticam theologiam* (1517),[64] the work where he exposed that the Thomistic concepts should not be articles of faith. He also stated that a true reform was impossible if Canonical law and Scholastic theology and philosophy were not uprooted once and for all. Luther's arguments were viewed by the Dominican order and thus by the whole Catholic Church as an uproarious challenge to the Saint's *Summa Theologica*, considered the quintessence and summit of Christian doctrine.[65]

Saint Thomas showed the leadership of the Catholic Church as also the holy character that appears in another painting, this one from the cloister of the convent of Calpulalpan (Mexico) that shows Saint Nicholas of Bari (270–343), the early Christian bishop of Myra (Asia minor), standing on top of a book in which back is written the name of Luther (Figure 16). This legendary gift-bearing person, miracle worker and protector of children and sailors, who lived in the time of the Roman Empire, was apparently a whipper of ancient heretics too, like Arius, whom it is believed he slapped in the face for his attack on Trinitarianism.[66] Both works show how Baroque art used medieval figures as *exempla*, only placed in a different context, being nonetheless a successful display of anti-Lutheran propaganda.

The Mexican Virgin against the Leviathan

Circa 1775, the distinguished theological scholar, Patricio Fernández de Uribe denounced:

> Entre los innumerables errores que como otros tantos mortales venenos confeccionó Lutero para corromper o inficionar a los pueblos, no fueron los

---

[63] Sigmund Freud's title is *Das Medusenhaupt*, 1940.
[64] *Martin Luthers Werke. Kritische Gesamtausgabe*, 59 vols, vol. I, Weimar: Hermann Böhlau, 1883 and subsequently, pp. 221–28; Ricardo GARCÍA VILLOSLADA, *Martín Lutero*, vol. II, Madrid: Biblioteca de Autores Cristianos, 1976, pp. 235–36.
[65] On the subject, see Martín Lutero, *La cautividad babilónica de la Iglesia, op. cit.*, p. 186. Denis JANZ, *Luther on Thomas Aquinas. The Angelic Doctor in the Thought of the Reformer*, Stuttgart: Franz Steiner Verlag, 1989. EGIDO, *Obras de Martín Lutero, op. cit.*, p. 53. Heiko OBERMAN, "Via Antiqua and Via Moderna: Late medieval prolegomena to early reformation thought", *Journal of the History of Ideas*, 48, 1 (1987), 23–40 (pp. 26–28).
[66] Jean BLACKER, Glyn S. BURGESS, and Amy V. OGDEN, Wace (Introduction and Notes), *The Hagiographical Works: The Conception Nostre Dame and the Lives of St Margaret and St Nicholas*, Leiden: Brill, 2013; https://www.britannica.com/biography/Saint-Nicholas. Accessed on October, 2020.

> menos perniciosos los que vomitó contra el culto y adoración que la Iglesia y los fieles todos tributan a las imágenes de los Santos y especialmente de la Madre de Dios.[67]

So far, we have focused on the saints that the Catholic Church promoted as symbols to stand against Protestantism. Now, I will explain some strategic purposes to attack heresy where the figure of the Virgin Mary played a definitive role. After the German schism of the sixteenth century, the devotion to Mary was enhanced by the Tridentine church, when Protestant criticisms were directed to Catholics for the way they worshipped the Virgin.[68] Luther differed from other more radical Protestant interpreters on the perception of Mary; he defined her as a remarkable human being, an example of faith, love and fear of God, a model of virtue, modesty and obedience, who had humbly received grace from the Almighty. He referred to the Virgin as "the sweet and most blessed Mother of God", and above all, she honored her divine motherhood: *Ego nihil sum quam fabrica, in qua Deus operatur.*[69] What he opposed was devotion given to her as if she were the Divinity and, for the faithful, to plead for her help and invoke her aid and intercession. For the ex-Augustinian friar, reverence should be given only to God, and Mary should not be an object of cult. The proper homage was not to adore her as an icon, which would be a form of idolatry, much less with external forms of piety. Many Protestant leaders also questioned the attribute of the Virgin as Immaculate Conception, the belief that the Mother of God had perpetually been kept from original sin.[70]

The Counter-Reformation reacted to Protestant interpretations and stressed Mary's role as intercessor, co-redeemer, and mediator. Marian fervor was already a benchmark of Hispanic spirituality in Medieval Spain, and paragon of the Catholic Church. After all, her image in the monastery of Guadalupe in Extremadura became one of the foremost centers of Christianity in Castile in the fifteenth century, and images of Christ's mother

---

[67] "Amidst the innumerable errors invented by Luther, together with other mortal venoms to corrupt and infect the nations, not least among them were those which he vomited against the cult and worship, which the Church and the faith render to images of the saints and especially to the Mother of God". This sermon was not published until the nineteenth century. J. Patricio FERNÁNDEZ DE URIBE, *Sermones*, 3 vols, vol. II, Madrid: Editado por Ibarra, 1821, p. 55.

[68] PEREDA, *Las imágenes de la discordia*, op. cit., p. 20. For the Lutheran view of Mary, see KIMMIG-VÖLKNER, "Luther, the Virgin Mary and the Saints", art. cit., p. 261.

[69] *Martin Luthers Werke*, op. cit., vol. 7, p. 573. Also see *Das Magnificat verdeutschet und ausgelegt* (1521), in EGIDO, *Obras de Martín Lutero*, op. cit., p. 192.

[70] Suzanne STRATTON, *La Inmaculada Concepción en el arte español*, Madrid: Fundación Universitaria Española, 1989.

flooded the Peninsula in paintings and engravings, especially directed to convince religious dissidents. After Trent, again, its support responded to clear political goals; this time it was outlined as the prominent symbol of Spain Triumphant of the Austrian Habsburg dynasty over its confessional enemies. Late-Medieval practices were replicated in the New World context. The image of the *Tota pulchra* came to New Spain with the missionaries.[71] The Third Mexican Synod (1585), following the historic precedents of Spain's Marian adherence as well as the ideological post-Tridentine patterns of representation, determined that "especial devoción sea dada a la gloriosísima Virgen como a universal abogada y Señora nuestra",[72] for which it was mandatory to augment and bring forward its cult in all the cathedrals and churches of the Archbishopric and Province of New Spain. Mary's promotion was done through various channels: art (painting and sculpture), written treaties, and oral, persuasive preaching in the church pulpits. In sum, a text-supported iconography widely circulated in the Americas. According to William Taylor, nearly a thousand sermons were published in the seventeenth and eighteenth centuries and many of them focused on Marian themes,[73] particularly in the advocacy of the Immaculate Conception. The oral and, especially, the printed exhortations, at large rhetorically effective, played a crucial role to convey messages that helped to enrich Marian "theology of image".[74]

Another popular representation of Mary in Europe since Medieval times was that of the Woman of the Apocalypse. Conforming to tradition, a celestial lady appeared to Saint John the Evangelist on the Isle of Patmos (Greece) bearing a complete message of redemption. In iconography, the woman appears descending on Earth, standing on a crescent moon, dressed in a talar blue robe with star embroidery, her hands together in prayer, crowned, and surrounded by sun rays. She is also presented with wings, as an eagle, beating and smashing the head of the infernal dragon, according to Saint John the Evangelist's Book of Revelation, meaning that her pureness triumphs over evil.[75] The vision of Mary as *Mulier amicta sole* is frequent in Medieval

---

[71] Sergi DOMÉNECH, "La recepción de la tradición hispánica de la Inmaculada Concepción en Nueva España: El tipo iconográfico de la *Tota pulchra*", in *Espacio, tiempo y forma. Revista de la Facultad de Geografía e Historia*, 3, Serie VII Historia del Arte (2015), 275–309.
[72] "Special devotion be given to the most glorious Virgin as universal advocate and as Our Lady". Mss. Bancroft Library, Berkley, M–M 266, título 18.
[73] TAYLOR, *Theatre, op. cit.*, p. 17.
[74] PEREDA, *Las imágenes de la discordia, op. cit.*, p. 29.
[75] Francisco de FLORENCIA, *Estrella del Norte de México. Historia de la milagrosa imagen de María Santísima de Guadalupe* (1688), Guadalajara, México: Don Agustín de la Rosa, editor, Imprenta de Juan Cabrera, 1895, p. 130.

exegesis as an emblem of the Church triumphant,[76] and her image and symbol continued during the Baroque period. At the beginning of the seventeenth century, a Mexican preacher had maintained that the Virgin Mary "adorned and beautified the militant Church represented by the moon beneath her feet and the light behind her back".[77]

In Mexico, an icon that embraces both attributes, that of the Immaculate Conception and the one of the Woman of the Apocalypse, is Our Lady of Guadalupe of Tepeyac (Figure 17)[78] or Guadalupe-Tonantzin, in allusion to her pre-Hispanic equivalent, the mother earth and the deity of fertility. All the metaphorical aspects of the archetypal figure are there present, except for the light brown color of her face, which underlines her racial status (*La Virgen morena*). This devotional image was made, together with her counterpart, the Virgin of Remedios, a symbol of the spiritual and political conquest of Mesoamerica. As stated by William Taylor, Guadalupe was the most widely recognized and revered image in Mexico City during the colonial era, and still is one of the most (if not *the* most) relevant symbols of Mexican spirituality. Her shrine is an attractive sanctuary since those days, with an important flow of fervent pilgrims. Taylor adds that Guadalupe, as a whole, "sanctified both an American identity and the authority of the colonial system, affirmed the unity of that society and carried a message".[79] Devotion towards this icon was promoted with verve by the ecclesiastical hierarchy throughout the viceregal period and became an endearing part of creole mentality and, eventually, of the entire population of New Spain.

The myth of Guadalupe is an American-born essential founding tradition. Her attractive demeanor does not totally rest in the painting itself, but in the powerful narrative of her supernatural legend. Describing it very briefly, the narrative stated that, in December 1531, the Virgin appeared several times to an Indian named Juan Diego shortly after the Conquest of Mexico. He was on his way to receive catechism and passed through the hill of Tepeyac, in the northern part of Mexico City. She asked the man to collect flowers in the field, usually scarce at that time of the year. He was able to gather many beautiful, radiant roses and took them to the Archbishop

---

[76] Sergi DOMÉNECH, "Iconografía de la mujer del apocalipsis como imagen de la Iglesia", in *Imagen y Cultura, op. cit.*, vol. I, pp. 578–79.

[77] Alonso del CASTILLO, *Sermón predicado en el convento de Santo Domingo [...] en la salutación angelina del Ave María*, México: Bernardo Calderón, 1636, p. 13.

[78] Elisa VARGASLUGO, "Iconología guadalupana", in *Imágenes guadalupanas 4 siglos*, México: Centro Cultural Arte Contemporáneo, 1987, p. 59 and subsequent; STRATTON, *op. cit.*, pp. 46–47; Luis MONREAL Y TEJADA, *Iconografía del cristianismo*, Barcelona: El Acantilado, 2000, pp. 166–72.

[79] TAYLOR, *Theatre, op. cit.*, p. 293.

Juan de Zumárraga, as the holy lady directed. When Juan Diego unfolded his cloak in the prelate's presence, the picture of the Virgin became miraculously printed on the humble cloth. Zumárraga conformed with the Lady's wishes and placed her portrait in a shrine.

The Sacred Original is an example of a very successful type or model of devotional imagery. The cult's development has been widely documented by several contemporary scholars, many of whom are often concerned in analyzing it from a socio-historic, an iconographic or historiographic approach. To the best of my knowledge, fewer have investigated in depth the *Guadalupana* symbols as instruments to attack or confront Protestantism. Elsewhere I have described the intrinsic relationship between the Virgin of Guadalupe as a portent against heresy, in its polisemic visual and discursive aspects.[80] This notion had already been suggested by Marina Warner, when she analyzed how the Virgin was a legitimizing identity against religious dissidents,[81] and by Mexican historian Edmundo O'Gorman who in 1986 suggested that Our Lady of Guadalupe of Tepeyac was "the most conspicuous offspring of the Counter-Reformation in New Spain".[82] More recent studies have tested O'Gorman's once convincing argument. In iconography and devotional aspects, the figure of Mary battling against the serpent or dragon was fostered in Europe long before Trent, as can be seen in Dürer's woodcuts and, in general, the Mother of God was praised by Spain's Catholic kings and ecclesiastical authorities in the Peninsula, which, according to Alfonso Rodríguez G. de Ceballos had a close relationship with how the devotion to the Virgin Mary, and particularly to *Guadalupanismo*, was expressed in Mexico. Undoubtedly, the image of Guadalupe in New Spain meant to attract the Indian neophytes to the Christian faith, following the endeavors of the secular clergy, but it also worked out as a charismatic stronghold of truth for the population, to prevent them from falling into heterodox assumptions.

In the written sermons that refer to Mary in New Spain, Luther and Calvin are frequently mentioned, especially in the works that apply to Guadalupe. The American-born Spaniards or *criollos* set forward the belief that

---

[80] Alicia MAYER, *Flor de Primavera Mexicana. La Virgen de Guadalupe en los sermones novohispanos*, México-Alcalá de Henares: UNAM-Instituto de Investigaciones Históricas-Universidad de Alcalá de Henares, 2010; MAYER, *Lutero en el Paraíso*, *op. cit.*, chapter VIII.
[81] Marina WARNER, *Tú sola entre las mujeres. El mito y el culto de la virgen María*, Madrid: Taurus, 1991, p. 384.
[82] Edmundo O'GORMAN, *Destierro de sombras. Luz en el origen de la imagen y culto de Nuestra Señora de Gudalupe del Tepeyac*, México: Universidad Nacional Autónoma de México, 1986.

the Virgin appeared in Mexico to protect its inhabitants and preserve the *patria* (the Fatherland) from idolatry, heretic contamination, and Europe's current ills. The circumstance that she preferred this site to make her prodigious revelation to a modest Indian, recently converted to the Catholic faith, a neophyte who was thus integrated to Spanish colonial society, bears a powerful message as an indubitable sign of God's election of New Spain. In 1693, Juan Millán de Poblete, dean of the Metropolitan cathedral, as well as other preachers, claimed that Spain and its colonies were "free from the tares of heresy" thanks to Mary's protection, who acted as a "machine against Lucifer".[83] Her apparition and shelter made New Spain, in creole's perspective, a unique heavenly kingdom, a world far away from the confessional troubles in Europe. This notion of paradise was an essential part of colonial religious culture.[84]

The link between Guadalupe and heresy is not explicit in the works of art. To study this peculiarity, the historian must review the primary sources looking for details or clues that are rarely patent in the paintings. Certain colonial treaties emphasize the full meaning behind the images and reveal a wider foreground in their narrative. Among art historians, Jaime Cuadriello has showed that the sacred icon of Guadalupe is a true hieroglyph that offers several possible interpretations and helps us to decipher the meta-discourse embedded in the image-text relationship.[85] Many of these insights were given by colonial writers themselves. In 1748, Alonso Moreno, dean of the Cathedral in Mexico City noted that Luther was contemporary to the Virgin of Guadalupe's apparition (1531) and to the founding of the Society of Jesus (1534), a fact that, according to him, was a milestone for the Church's militant crusade to counteract the advance of heresy: "Mary came to Mexico to dissipate the thick darkness of gentilism and avoid the heresies of Luther, Calvin and their henchmen".[86] A word was also set forward announcing that Mary of Guadalupe had the faculty to "scare the bloody wolves, beasts and serpents which are

---

[83] Juan MILLÁN DE POBLETE, *Patrocinio de María Santísima*, México: Viuda de Bernardo Calderón, 1693, pp. 4–7; Luis de CARTAGENA, *Sermón que el obispo de Cartagena predicó [...]*, Sevilla: Herederos de Tomás de Haro, 1708, pp. 11–12.

[84] Antonio RUBIAL, *El paraíso de los elegidos. Una lectura de la historia cultural de Nueva España* (1521–1804), México: Fondo de Cultura Económica-Universidad Nacional Autónoma de México, 2010; Alicia MAYER, *Lutero en el paraíso, op. cit.*, pp. 311–86.

[85] Jaime CUADRIELLO, "Los jeroglíficos de la Nueva España", in *Juegos de Ingenio y agudeza. La pintura emblemática de la Nueva España*, ed. by José Pascual Buxó, México: Museo Nacional de Arte, Consejo Nacional para la Cultura y las Artes, 1994, pp. 84–109; Jaime CUADRIELLO, *Maravilla Americana. Variantes de la iconografía guadalupana. Siglos XVII–XIX*, México: Patronato Cultural de Occidente, 1989, p. 71.

[86] "Parecer" de Alonso Moreno. In Antonio de PAREDES, S. J., *Authentica del Patronato*, 1748, n/e and n/p.

enemies of justice and divine law", keeping Spain's colonies free, in peace and security.[87] José Patricio Fernández de Uribe later described that "at the same time that Luther in Europe sought to eradicate the cult of images and to suppress the power of Mary, God granted America an image of this Holy Virgin miraculously painted as an effective means to establish the true religion".[88] In 1777 bishop Francisco de Lorenzana y Butrón, a prominent church leader, added that "when in Europe the evil Luther, Calvin, Bucer, and other vomits from hell separated from the bosom of the church many provinces, Our Lady [of Guadalupe] doubled these here in land and inhabitants".[89] The victory of right over wrong, good over evil, light over darkness, and orthodoxy over heresy was explained through the struggle between the Virgin of Tepeyac and Luther. The authors contrasted these morally antagonistic characters using a profuse content of metaphors. Repeatedly, the preachers in New Spain pleaded her favor to, "throughout her miraculous image, ensure the defense of all the Kingdom against her opponents, the Lutherans".[90] This could surprise for the eighteenth century, but, again, Luther was used for a rhetorical purpose, to represent all confessional foes, past and present. The "Lutherans" then generally represented the Protestant enemies of Spain during the War of the Spanish Succession (1702–1713), the armies from Holland and Britain in the War of the Austrian Succession (1740–1748) and the Seven Years War (1756–1763). Our Lady of Guadalupe was considered in colonial times as a warrior-protectress, especially after 1737 when it was believed she had a merciful intercession to dispel a deadly epidemic, shortly before she was proclaimed patroness of Mexico.[91]

In a myriad of sermons, the Virgin is presented victorious over a serpent or a seven-headed dragon (a version of the mythological Hydra). In 1712, Juan Castorena y Ursúa, theologian and canon of the cathedral of Mexico City, as several other ecclesiastic authorities of the period, equated the

---

[87] Manuel ARGÜELLO, *Acción de Gracias a la soberana Reina del Cielo María santísima de Guadalupe [...]*, México: Imprenta de la Viuda de Miguel de Ribera, 1711, p. 12.
[88] FERNÁNDEZ DE URIBE, *Sermones, op. cit.*, p. 56.
[89] Francisco Antonio LORENZANA, *Oración a Nuestra Señora de Guadalupe*, México: Joseph Antonio de Hogal, 1770, p. xix.
[90] José ARLEGUI, *Sagrado Paladión del americano orbe: Sermón [...] a María Santísima de Guadalupe*, México: Imprenta de la Viuda de Joseph Bernardo de Hogal, 1743, p. 8.
[91] According to David Brading, this also coincide with the period of maximum apogee of the Mexican Church (1730–1747). David BRADING, "Tridentine Catholicism and Enlightened Despotism in Bourbon Mexico", *Journal of Latin American Studies*, 15 (1983), 1–22 (p. 2). Also, David BRADING, "La devoción católica y la heterodoxia en el México borbónico", in *Manifestaciones religiosas en el mundo colonial americano*, ed. by Clara García and Manuel Ramos, México: INAH-CONDUMEX-UIA, 1997, p. 49.

infernal monster with heresy.[92] In the original portrait of Guadalupe (the Sacred Original), the deadly serpent is absent. Instead, the Virgin stands on top of a crescent moon supported by the Archangel Michael. As stated by some preachers of that time, this showed that the Lady of Tepeyac had already triumphed over evil. Bishop Lorenzana y Butrón stoutly declared that the beast at the Virgin's feet was missing in the miraculous image because she previously had destroyed the heresies symbolized in the hellish animal.[93]

Apocalyptic iconography had significantly extended in Europe during the Renaissance, both in Catholic and Protestant environments, long before the cult to the Virgin of Tepeyac initiated in New Spain. German painter Albrecht Dürer's (1471–1528) versions of the prophecy of Saint John the Evangelist stand out in his magnificent fourteen woodcut prints (1498). Remarkably, the imagery of Dürer is suggested in New Spain well into the end of the colonial period. The symbolic treatment that the artist gave in one of his works to the eagle-woman that defeats the seven-headed Hydra, meant as a representation of chaos and wrong in the Old Testament, is the model that the Mexican painter Gregorio José de Lara followed in the eighteenth century to create the "Visión de San Juan en Patmos Tenochtitlán" for the Dominican temple of San Juan Coixtlahuaca (Oaxaca). Here, the Virgin of Guadalupe as *mulier amicta sole*, is represented with wings, facing a sort of inoffensive or naïve Leviathan (Figures 18 and 19). The abundant symbolism present in the Vision of the Apocalypse provided such a rich source of themes for art and discourse that many figural subjects could be added. This explains why Luther was equated with the dragon destroyed by the woman dressed by the sun of the prophecies, or with the Hydra, the mythological poly-cephalous creature whose poisonous breath killed all living creatures. According to legend, the Hydra had seven or nine heads and, when they were cut off, a new one sprouted in its place, making it immortal. Johannes Cochlaeus (1479–1552), Catholic author and Luther's ideological debater, made the most famous allusion to Luther as the seven-headed Hydra (1529), symbol of evil and the devil, that turned into a very used rhetoric model.[94] Later, the renowned Jesuit philosopher Fran-

---

[92] Juan CASTORENA Y URSÚA, *Parabién de las letras a las armas. Oración gratulatoria, panegírica [...] que predicó*, México: Juan Joseph Guillena, 1712, pp. 10–14.
[93] LORENZANA, *Oración a Nuestra Señora de Guadalupe, op. cit.*, p. xix.
[94] Leif GRANE, "The image of Myth and Reality", in *Seven-Headed Luther. Essays in Commemoration of a Quincentenary 1483–1983*, ed. by Peter Newman Brooks, Oxford: Clarendon Press, 1983, p. 232; BURSCHEL, "Das Monster. Katholische Luther-Imagination", *art. cit.*, p. 41.

cisco Suárez (1548–1617) stated that there were in his time so many heretic sects that "they can hardly be counted, and there are as numerous heads as opinions".[95] Some authors in colonial New Spain, like Juan de Palafox y Mendoza, shared these impressions and replicated this theme.[96] Also Patricio Fernández de Uribe recalled that "Luther and Calvin, as seven-headed Hydras, go on aborting and prodigiously reproducing monstrous heresiarchs".[97] A whole message is conveyed in an anonymous eighteenth century painting that depicts the Archangel Michael, the seven-headed dragon and the Virgin of Guadalupe (Figure 20) that echoes Francisco Pacheco's famous treatise *Arte de la Pintura* (1649), were a clear description of all these symbols are exposed, as follows:

> La más célebre pintura de San Miguel es cuando se pinta peleando con el demonio; y cuando venció este dragón, y lo derribó del Cielo, *y a todos los que lo siguieron*. Este es el príncipe que peleó antiguamente contra el rey de Persia en defensa del pueblo de Dios y ahora es el defensor de la Iglesia.[98]

Naturally, there were different levels of understanding of the various symbolisms that the Church wanted to transmit, depending on how a person approached the multiple concepts. Biblical exegesis, theological expositions, dogmatic arguments, and narratives were not for the common folk, but for the literate. The learned were the audience that could read and reflect on what had been written by the most erudite. But, ultimately, the Church's purpose was to reach most people, and to have an overwhelming impact with a massive message. What was relevant in all the examples here analyzed was to make the people understand that Protestantism was a menace that had multiple evil effects on someone who embraced this doctrine, leading to rejection towards its premises. These materials show how effective rhetoric was because it paved the way for a more clear comprehension of the entire notion the church officials wanted to convey. In other words, images and printed sermons were interconnected and, together, they formed a successful display of anti-Lutheran and anti-Protestant propaganda.

---

[95] Francisco SUÁREZ, *Defensa de la fe*, vol. IV, Madrid: Instituto de Estudios Políticos, 1971, p. 621.
[96] PALAFOX, *Obras, op. cit.* vol. II, book I, p. 373.
[97] FERNÁNDEZ DE URIBE, *Sermones, op. cit.*, vol. III, p. 191.
[98] "The most famous painting of Saint Michael is when he is pictured fighting against the devil; and when he defeated this dragon; and threw him out of Heaven, *and all those that followed*. This is the prince that formerly fought against the king of Persia in defense of God's people and now is the protector of the Church". The underlined part is mine. Francisco PACHECO, *El arte de la pintura. Su antigüedad y grandezas*, Sevilla: por Simon Faxardo, impresor, 1649, pp. 550-51.

Conclusions

Five hundred years ago, Martin Luther changed the path of medieval Christianity at the same time that the American world beyond the Atlantic appeared in the European consciousness. In this essay, I have explained the apparently incomprehensible and yet sustained presence of Luther in colonial painting and discourse during the viceregal period in New Spain, especially in those topics that referred to particular saints and the Virgin Mary. The figure of the Saxon reformer was rhetorically used by the Mexican ecclesiastic officials as a symbol of evil, error and misguidedness. The seemingly devilish-like nature of the German ex-Augustinian friar became a stereotype, in opposition to the Catholic holy characters, paragons of goodness and virtue. We can affirm that Luther determined the self-consciously identification of the creoles with anti-Protestant, Christian values represented by the Catholic champions.

Luther appeared in the imagery of the colonial world as a result of the cultural confrontation between Catholicism and Protestantism, where the Mexican church used the Reformer as an antagonistic character to defend orthodoxy. His presence undoubtedly served a strategic purpose. Through visual and discursive strategies, the Church and the State imposed the ideological messages of the Catholic Reformation that were so imperative to convey. In a highly efficient way, the post-Tridentine Church set forward old and new notions and programs that circulated in the Iberian Peninsula since medieval times. Traditional iconography was reinterpreted to fit the new times and ideology. Ultimately, Trent tried to introduce its own principles with specific codes of action and communication, together with acts of legislation, cultural cohesion, and religious uniformity. For some time, the institution specified concepts and defined practices, topics, rites and beliefs. It put emphasis on the practice of the sacraments (especially the Eucharist), in the worship given to Mary, in the veneration of saints and images, in the power of indulgences, the value of relics and processions, the role of the Church as intermediary and in collective religiosity. It attacked heterodoxy and anathematized "heretical" propositions. These "codes" were massively communicated throughout different strategies and contributed efficaciously to indoctrination.

Specific questions were set forward in the introduction of this essay. One of them refers to how hagiographic representation in viceregal art changed because of the Reformation. The first conclusion is that, for the particular paintings we have analyzed, the so-called Triumphs of the Church, the saints and the Virgin Mary, their aesthetic framework and methods have all Mediterranean precedents. The various interpretive strategies used Medieval European canons, copied its official religious models, employed terms coined in the Old World before the Reformation and did not include indigenous components and stylistic categories specific of the Mesoamerican life. The Council of Trent restored or reframed old patterns within the context of the sixteenth-century Catholic reform. The difference from previous uses and customs in the Iberian Peninsula rest on the fact that the new saints of the Counter-Reformation were promoted and, as for the antagonistic characters, conventional iconographic models such as Jews and Muslims were substituted or joined by the new enemies of the faith, the Protestant reformers. Nevertheless, hagiography in the early modern era did not primarily respond to Protestant criticism, though that was a secondary effected. In this sense, Luther, considered as the spokesperson of Protestantism, leader of all schismatics, was introduced in post-Tridentine depiction of saints, just as previously Moors and Jews have been used in artistic representation in Spain at the end of the fifteenth century. After Trent, the exemplary persons elevated to the altars were turned into attractive motives, according to the new circumstances, whereas Luther and the reformers that followed him were introduced as symbols of evil. More than Martin Luther, it was the religious and political movement created after him what propelled new cultural prototypes in Europe and was transplanted to the Spanish Indies with colonization. In this view, post-Tridentine concepts did not alter the route of artistic representation as it was expressed before the Baroque period, but they provided new elements of representation based on the new saints of the Counter-Reformation and on the Protestant dissidents.

The way Luther was perceived in colonial times had long-term consequences for Latin American identity. His absence from American geography did not prevent him from becoming a figure firmly engraved in the consciousness of the New Spanish population. The whole concept of "otherness" (the heterogeneous) can be seen throughout what Luther represents in viceregal imagery, as a non-identifying trait of New Spain. Despite how unusual it may seem and the geographical distance and strangeness of the German world for Hispanic America, there was a forceful response to Luther and his movement in the colonial realm. As the paradigm of evil, the German reformer permeated into the psyche of the population and came to be embedded in the religious and political culture of these remote regions of the Spanish Empire. All this happened through the work of image makers, theologians, ecclesiastic authorities, poets, writers, historians and magistrates who fought against Luther with the pen, the preaching, and the paintbrush.

Acknowledgements: I want to thank Iván Escamilla González for his insightful comments on the topics of this essay.

THE TRIUMPH OF THE SAINTS AND THE VIRGIN MARY

Fig. 1: Peter Paul Rubens, *The Triumph of the Church* (Museo del Prado, Madrid, Spain [ca. 1625])

Fig. 2: Cristóbal de Villalpando, *The Triumph of Religion* (Sacristy, Metropolitan Cathedral, Mexico City [1686])

Fig. 3: Miguel Cabrera, *Saint Ignatius of Loyola*
(Museo Nacional de Arte, Mexico City [ca. 1750-1760])

Fig. 4: Camillo and Giuseppe Rusconi, *Saint Ignatius of Loyola* (Basilica of Saint Peter, Vatican City [1733])

Fig. 5: Manuel Álvarez de la Peña, *Saint Ignatius of Loyola*
(Cathedral Church, Cuenca, Spain [ca. 1755])
(Photo Alicia Mayer)

Fig. 6: Manuel Álvarez de la Peña, *Saint Ignatius of Loyola* (detail)
(Cathedral Church, Cuenca, Spain [ca. 1755])
(Photo Alicia Mayer)

Fig. 7: Miguel Cabrera, *The Triumph of the Church*
(Church of Saint Felipe Neri, Guanajuato, Mexico [eighteenth century])

Fig. 8: Miguel Cabrera, *The Triumph of the Church* (detail)
(Church of Saint Felipe Neri, Guanajuato, Mexico [eighteenth century])
(Photo Julio César León Morales)

Fig. 9: Anonymous, *Allegory of the Carmelite Order*
(Church of the Santa Veracruz, Mexico City [ca. 1692])
(Photo Alicia Mayer, best image available)

Fig. 10: Anonymous, *Decor Carmeli* (print, detail)
(Museo del Carmen, Mexico City [seventeenth century])
(Photo Courtesy of the Instituto Nacional de Antropología e Historia)

THE TRIUMPH OF THE SAINTS AND THE VIRGIN MARY

Fig. 11: Nicolás Rodríguez Juárez, *The Church Triumphant* (Carmelite Convent in Celaya, Mexico [1695])

Fig. 12: Nicolás Rodríguez Juárez, *The Church Triumphant* (detail) (Carmelite Convent in Celaya, Mexico [1695])

Fig. 13: Anonymous, *Triumph of the Church* (or *of the Faith*) (Museo Nacional del Virreinato, Mexico [eighteenth century])

Fig. 14: Anonymous, *Triumph of the Church* (or *of the Faith*) (detail) (Museo Nacional del Virreinato, Mexico [eighteenth century])

Fig. 15: Joseph Nava, *Divus [Saint] Thomas Doctor Angelicus* (engraving) (Puebla, Mexico [eighteenth century])

THE TRIUMPH OF THE SAINTS AND THE VIRGIN MARY

Fig. 16: Anonymous, Saint Nicholas of Bari
(Convent of Calpulalpan, Tlaxcala, Mexico [eighteenth century])

Fig. 17: The Virgin of Guadalupe, The Sacred Original
(Basilica of Guadalupe, Mexico City [sixteenth century])

THE TRIUMPH OF THE SAINTS AND THE VIRGIN MARY

Fig. 18: Albrecht Dürer, The Woman of the Apocalypse (prophecy of Saint John the Evangelist) (woodcut/print [ca. 1498])

Fig. 19: Gregorio José de Lara, *Vision of Saint John the Evangelist in Patmos-Tenochtitlan*
(Coixtlahuaca, Oaxaca, Mexico [eighteenth century])

Fig. 20: Anonymous, Saint Michael holding the banner of Santa María de Guadalupe
(Museum of the Basilica of Guadalupe, Mexico City [eighteenth century])

The Evolution of the Figure of St Michael the Archangel

From Medieval *Flos sanctorum* to New Spain's Hagiography (*c.* 1480–1692)

Marcos CORTÉS GUADARRAMA
(Universidad Veracruzana, Mexico)

The figure of St Michael the Archangel appeared from very early on in New Spain. In fact, Motolinía tells us that in view of the desolation caused in the territory by the ten plagues immediately after the conquest had been accomplished,[1] the first twelve Franciscan friars who arrived in 1525 adopted St Michael the Archangel as their captain and chieftain, and to both him and Gabriel they sang a Mass every Monday. This tradition later continued until the very moment when the *Historia de los indios de la Nueva España* was being written between 1536 and 1541.[2]

However, if we want to understand this act by the Franciscan friars and therefore the establishment and evolution of the figure of St Michael the Archangel in New Spain, we must go back in time. This article covers a timespan from the end of the fifteenth century to the end of the seventeenth century. Its goal is to review the transformation in the Archangel's characterization in the written culture from the Spanish late Middle Ages to New Spain's Baroque. In

---

[1] His words are influenced by a millenarism construed with the discourse of apocalyptic literature, in particular the book of Daniel and St John's Revelation. Antonio RUBIAL GARCÍA, *La hermana pobreza. El franciscanismo: de la Edad Media a la evangelización novohispana*, México: Universidad Nacional Autónoma de México, 1996, p. 127.

[2] Fray T. de BENAVENTE "MOTOLINÍA", *Historia de los indios de la Nueva España*, ed. by Mercedes Serna and Bernat Castany, Madrid: Real Academia Española, 2014, p. 25.

essence, this characterization was born out of a medieval view that considered him the victorious leader *par excellence* of the cosmic conflagration between good and evil, until he was re-construed, after the major schism of the Christian church that took place in the sixteenth century, as an institutionalized celestial being with great influence and power who advocates for Catholics.[3]

In order to meet our goal, we will analyze the following materials. On one hand, among the Iberian Peninsula works that reflect on the incorporation of the Archangel within the readings of the Christian liturgical calendar, we will analyze two *Flores sanctorum* (*c.* 1480 and 1580) as examples of collective hagiography based in the medieval source *par excellence* for these type of texts, the *Legenda aurea* by Jacobus de Voragine; and two entirely-reformed *Flores sanctorum* based on post-Tridentine sources written by Alonso de Villegas (1578) and the Jesuit Pedro de Ribadeniera (1599). On the other hand, among the works written and/or published in New Spain, I will use, as an example of a chronicle of the evangelization written by a friar using different textual materials, Jerómino de Mendieta's *Historia eclesiástica indiana* (1525–1604); a text written by a friar in one of the pre-Columbian languages, the *Diálogo de doctrina christiana* by Friar Maturino Gilberti (1559); a text written by schooled indigenous people, the *Codex mexicanus* (*c.* 1590); a Counter-Reformist work focused on the figure of St Michael the Archangel, *De la devoción y patrocinio de San Miguel, príncipe de los ángeles, antiguo tutelar de los godos y protector de España*, by Nieremberg (Madrid, 1643, although we will use a copy printed in Mexico that same year by the widow of the printer Bernardo Calderón); the *Vida de la Venerable madre Isabel de la Encarnación* (1675) by the Licenciado Pedro Salmerón, an example of a hagiography from New Spain; and finally the *Narración de la maravillosa aparición que hizo el arcángel san Miguel a Diego Lázaro de San Francisco, indio feligrés del pueblo de S. Bernardo de la jurisdición*[sic] *de Santa María Nativitas*,[4] by the American-born Jesuit Francisco de Florencia, who was inspired by Nieremberg's work.

Although the range of texts we are studying is rather large, this is the only way we can understand the dimensions of a tradition about the Archangel and its evolution for different purposes and readers on both sides of the Atlantic. Even so, it is clear that there are many more texts that deal with the figure of St Michael and our intention is not to include them all in our

---

[3] "Abogado de las Repúblicas de la tierra" (Advocate of the world's republics), was called by Juan Eusebio NIEREMBERG in *De la devoción y patrocinio de San Miguel, príncipe de los ángeles, antiguo tutelar de los godos y protector de España*, México: Viuda de Bernardo de Calderón, *c.* 1643, p. 9.

[4] Francisco de FLORENCIA, *Narración de la maravillosa aparición que hizo el arcángel san Miguel a Diego Lázaro de San Francisco*, Sevilla: Thomás López de Haro, 1692.

study.[5] However, by covering some two hundred years we want to encourage reflection and further analysis of the other texts that we cannot include here. Finally, we hope to increase the bibliography devoted to this important Christian figure, who has a large presence in New Spain's art and architecture, about whom there exist several books devoted to cathedrals and paintings but not so many devoted to the analysis of the evolution of religious textual materials in the pre- and post-Tridentine Hispanic world.

St Michael the Archangel: A Medieval Apocalyptic Characterization

In the *Flos sanctorum con sus ethimologías* (c. 1480) it is said that St Michael the Archangel is present in some doctrinal readings and in the lives of some saints compiled throughout the Christian liturgical calendar: in the festivity of the "Resurrection of the Lord";[6] in the festivity of "How the Cross was found";[7] St Christine;[8] and the Assumption of Mary.[9] In addition, some miracles take place in his churches[10] and in natural spaces consecrated to him, mainly mountains.[11] Generally speaking, he is characterized in all these festivities as a messenger who can announce and execute God's commands, and bring to his presence men's souls, including the Virgin Mary herself. He can also bring with him those martyrs whom God considers deserving of this merit.

This repertoire based on the *Legenda aurea* helped shape his literary figure within the pre-Tridentine hagiographic discourse and therefore within the late medieval Christian cosmovision: a festivity at the end of September (29 September) whose protagonist stands out because of his leadership over other archangels (Gabriel, Raphael and Uriel) thanks to his fight and victory against a dragon.[12] Clearly, this event is a representation of the symbolic struggle against good and evil (Lucifer and the Antichrist[13]). Undoubtedly, this endowed him, more than his miracles—which join together the two

---

[5] These are mainly other versions compiled in the *Flores sanctorum* printed from 1497 to 1578.
[6] *Flos sanctorum con sus ethimologías. Lo maravilloso hagiográfico*, ed. by Marcos Cortés Guadarrama, Xalapa: Universidad Veracruzana, 2018, p. 306.
[7] *Flos sanctorum con sus ethimologías*, op. cit., p. 362.
[8] *Flos sanctorum con sus ethimologías*, op. cit., p. 432.
[9] *Flos sanctorum con sus ethimologías*, op. cit., p. 499.
[10] *Flos sanctorum con sus ethimologías*, op. cit., pp. 341–42.
[11] FLORENCIA, op. cit., p. 64, devotes chapter XVI to the question of why St Michael the Archangel appears in high places, mainly mountains.
[12] A conceptualization that derives from the Biblical apocalyptic discourse: Ap 12. 7–9.
[13] "Según dice el profeta Daniel: 'Se levantará en el tiempo del Anticristo, lidiará por los escogidos de Dios y los defenderá'", *Flos sanctorum con sus ethimologías*, op. cit., p. 595.

natural spaces consecrated to him, mount Gargano in Italy and mount Saint-Michel in France—with a unique quality above all the other saints of the Christian liturgical calendar, making him into a divine power that stands second only to the interceding power of the Virgin Mary herself.

In addition, and in parallel to this, this medieval narrative includes a paramount element that although is not an article of faith, constitutes a universally accepted opinion within Christian angelology. The idea of an individual guardian angel for each soul is a topic that has interested great theologians like St Jerome,[14] and also a topic analyzed in one of the most important books on angelology in the medieval Hispanic world from the late fourteenth century: the *Libre dels àngels* by Francesc Eiximenis.[15] This aspect of Christian angelology, also present in the *Flos sanctorum con sus ethimologías*,[16] will be inherited by the first apparitions of angels in the constitution of the Indian Church. Approximately in 1596, Jerónimo de Mendieta began writing his *Historia eclesiástica indiana*, construed with pre-existing textual materials. There is a section entitled "De los prodigios y pronósticos que los indios tuvieron antes de la venida de los españoles, acerca de ella" that includes a curious anecdote about an angel that came to offer peace to one of the Indians captured by the Aztecs and who were to be sacrificed:

> Uno de los primeros evangelizadores de esta nueva Iglesia dejó escripto en un su libro, que cuando ya los españoles venían por la mar para entrar en esta Nueva España, entre otros indios que tenían para sacrificar en la ciudad de México en el barrio llamado Tlatelulco, estaba un indio el cual debía ser hombre simple y que vivía en la ley de la naturaleza sin ofensa de nadie (porque de éstos hubo y hay entre ellos algunos que no saben sino prejuicio): este indio, sabiendo que lo habían de sacrificar presto, llamaba en su corazón a Dios, y vino a él un mensajero del cielo, que los indios llamaron ave del cielo porque traía alas y diadema, y después que han visto cómo pintamos los ángeles, dicen que era de aquella manera. Este ángel dijo a aquel indio: "Ten esfuerzo y confianza, no temas, que Dios del cielo habrá de ti misericordia; y di a estos que ahora sacrifican y derraman sangre, que presto cesará el sacrificar y el de derramar sangre humana, y que ya vienen los que han de mandar enseñoreándose en esta tierra". Este indio dijo esas cosas a los indios de Tlatelulco, y las notaron. Y este indio fue sacrificado adonde ahora está la horca en el Tlatelulco, y murió llamando a Dios.[17]

---

[14] *Comentario a Mateo*, XIX, lib. II.
[15] Francesc EIXIMENIS, *Libro de los ángeles*, Burgos: Fadrique de Basilea, 1490 (1392 in Catalan), fol. CXIXr.
[16] *Flos sanctorum con sus ethimologías, op. cit.*, p. 599.
[17] "One of the first evangelizers of this new church wrote in his book that when the Spaniards were sailing towards New Spain, among other Indians that were kept to be sacrificed in the

Influenced by the discourse of other literary religious genres, such as the miracle narratives of hagiography, Mendieta's words are a prefiguration of the idea of a guardian angel for the individual protection of souls, even for indigenous people on the verge of converting to Christianity even if they still do not know it. That is, what is being narrated is the creation of the idea of a guardian angel for an Indian who, although pagan, deserves a visit suitable to a virtuous Christian. In addition, the episode offers the interpretation of the western Christian cosmology as it was supposedly received by the first schooled Indians, who at first saw birds in the sky but, after having contact with the first images of angels, ended up accepting that they were in fact the incorporeal Christian beings. This set the frame that would shape the narratives about St Michael the Archangel in New Spain during the seventeenth century: his apparitions to virtuous Indians were endowed with a childhood innocence. In Mendieta's passage, the angels are also intermediaries between God and humankind. The first Franciscan preachers were intent on disseminating and establishing these qualities and their meaning. As an example, we can mention the work of a French Franciscan, Friar Maturino Gilberti.[18]

Certainly, the first preachers' intention of highlighting the relevance of angels, and in particular that of St Michael the Archangel, can be read in the *Diálogo de doctrina christiana* (1559) by Gilberti.[19] At the end of this book—which created problems for his author on account of some dangerous opinions that apparently could be interpreted as seemingly Lutheran—[20]we

---

Tlatelulco neighborhood in Mexico City, there was an Indian who must have been rather simple and who lived following nature's law without offending anybody (there were and still are some of them who only know how to cause damage). A messenger from heaven came to him, called *heaven's bird* because he had wings and a crown, and after they learned how we depict angels they claim he was one of them. The angel told the Indian: "Be hopeful, do not have fear, for the God in the heavens will take pity on you; and tell those who now sacrifice and spill blood, that this sacrificing and blood-spilling will soon come to an end, and that those who come to be lords after taking possession of this land are on their way here". The Indian communicated these things to the Indians of Tlatelulco and they took note of them. And he was sacrificed where now stand the Tlatelulco gallows, and he died invoking God", Jerónimo de MENDIETA, *Historia eclesiástica indiana*, intro. by Antonio Rubial García, México: Consejo Nacional para la Cultura y las Artes, 2002, p. 313.

[18] He was seventy-three years old in 1559 and claimed to have learned seven indigenous languages and have a specialization in Tarascan.

[19] Maturino GILBERTI, *Diálogo de doctrina christiana en lengua de Michoacán*, México: Juan Pablos, 1559. This book bothered the bishop of Michoacán, Vasco de Quiroga, and was persecuted by the Inquisition in a legal process that lasted seventeen years (from 1559 to 1576). The documents about the case can be read in Francisco FERNÁNDEZ DEL CASTILLO, *Libros y libreros en el siglo XVI*, México: Fondo de Cultura Económica, 2017 (1ª ed. 1914), pp. 1–37.

[20] In question was whether in this text (written in an indigenous language) he said that no images whatsoever should be worshipped, even a Crucifix or an image of the Virgin Mary, given that the Crucifix, the Virgin Mary and the saints serve to remember God's greatness.

can find examples of two "gloriosos santos" ("illustrious saints"), St Eustache and St Alexius; then, a reference to "Del glorioso príncipe san Miguel y de su excelencia y oficios" ("the illustrious prince St Michael and his excellence and actions");[21] as a colophon to the voluminous book, the author writes about "El ministerio de los ángeles" ("the angels' ministry").[22] The choice of saints and the celestial authority selected by the author are clearly related to his French origin, for it is well known that these three saints enjoyed a significant cult in medieval France.

His version of the life of St Michael Archangel (written in Purepecha or Tarascan) and included in a typical humanist genre, the dialogue, includes one of the first engravings depicting the Archangel and printed in New Spain (see Figure 1). The source of Friar Gilberti's text is the same we find in the Spanish translations of the *Flos sanctorum* based on Voragine's text. In concrete, it seems close to the family of printings identified as Compilation A or *Gran Flos sanctorum*, which later included reworked materials printed between 1516 and 1580 in a collection known as *Flos sanctorum renacentista*.[23] In the encounter and dialogue between a young disciple (*hurenguareri*) and a great master (*hurendahperi*) who is traveling on a road, some of the qualities of angels are defined in a metaphorical sense with the intention of explaining the truths of the Christian doctrine.[24]

In *Diálogo de doctrina christiana* we are offered a characterization of St Michael Archangel that derives from medieval sources and conceptualizations, in which hierarchy and authority played an obsessive role on the narrative construction.[25] As proof of this, we can mention the fact that in Friar Maturino's book there is a subchapter devoted to St Michael entitled:

See FERNÁNDEZ DEL CASTILLO, *Libros y libreros, op. cit.*, p. 21. The Inquisition arrived in Mexico in 1571, with the same intention as it had in Europe: defending the Catholic religion and culture from any suspicion of heresy. William Taylor calls the sixteenth century the 'Protestant period' of this institution in New Spain, intent on protecting Christian beliefs. Mayer indicates that in the seventeenth century fear of Protestantism receded as an ideology capable of infecting New Spain, but not the suspicions about the Crypto-Jews. See Alicia MAYER, *Lutero en el Paraíso: La Nueva España en el espejo del reformador alemán*, México: Fondo de Cultura Económica, 2012, p. 145.

[21] GILBERTI, *Diálogo de doctrina christiana, op. cit.*, fols 308ᵛ–314ᵛ.
[22] GILBERTI, *Diálogo de doctrina christiana, op. cit.*, fols 314ᵛ–317ᵛ.
[23] José ARAGÜÉS ALDAZ, "Los *Flores sanctorum* medievales y renacentistas: brevísimo panorama crítico», in *Literatura medieval y renacentista: líneas y pautas*, ed. by Natalia Fernández Rodríguez and María Fernández Ferreiro, Salamanca: La Semyr, 2012, pp. 349–61.
[24] See Franco MENDOZA, "Maturino Gilberti traductor: *Diálogo de doctrina christiana en la lengua de Mechuacan*", Doctoral Diss. Defended in 2008, and directed by Miguel León-Portilla.
[25] Jacques LE GOFF, "El hombre medieval", in *El hombre medieval*, ed. by Jacques Le Goff, Madrid: Alianza, 1990, p. 37.

"Del primer officio de sant Miguel que fue echar a Lucifer y a los suyos del cielo empíreo" ("On St Michael's first job which was expelling Lucifer and his cohort from heaven").[26] This information, in view of the linguistic difficulties of those who engaged in the so-called spiritual conquest of Mexico, must have been highlighted by each preacher or reader.

This apocalyptic hierarchy lies also at the base of the last book on saints that derived from Voragine's text, the *Flos sanctorum renacentista* by Pedro de la Vega,[27] published in 1580.[28] The hierarchy is alluded to directly in this rubric: "Comiença la historia de los aparecimientos del glorioso arcángel sant Miguel y de la disposición y orden de las hierarquías de los ángeles" ("Here begins the story of the apparitions of the illustrious Archangel St Michael and the arrangement and order of the hierarchies of angels"). In addition, there is an episode of paramount relevance for the understanding of the literature about St Michael the Archangel that developed in New Spain in the seventeenth century:

> E la tercera vez apareció el arcángel sant Miguel en Roma, en tiempo de sant Gregorio papa, porque como sant Gregorio estableciesse las Ledanías mayores, que son del día de sant Marcos por una grant pestilencia que andava en Roma, que era llamada inguinaria, y rogasse devotamente al señor por la salud del pueblo, apareció el ángel de Dios sobre un castillo que era llamado entonces "El castillo de Adriano", y alimpió un cuchillo que tenía ensangrentado, y metiolo en su vayna. E viendo esto el bienaventurado S. Gregorio, entendió que el Señor Avía oydo la oración del pueblo y suya, y edificó en aquel castillo una iglesia a honrra de los ángeles: y es llamado aquel castillo hasta el día de hoy: el castillo de sant Miguel. Este aparecimiento es celebrado a ocho días de mayo con el aparecimiento que fue hecho en el monte Gargano.[29]

---

[26] GILBERTI, *Diálogo de doctrina christiana*, op. cit., fol. 309ʳ.

[27] He is intent on correcting and prolonging as well as finally establishing under his name an editorial tradition that lasted seven decades and during which only minor corrections were added to a book of saints that date from 1516. See José ARAGÜÉS ALDAZ, "Para el estudio del *Flos sanctorum renacentista* (I). La conformación de un género", in *La hagiografía entre historia y literatura en la España de la Edad Media y el Siglo de Oro*, ed. by M. Vitse, Madrid-Frankfurt: Iberoamericana-Vervuert, p. 121.

[28] Pedro de la VEGA, *Flos sanctorum. La vida de nuestro Señor Jesu Christo, de su Santísima Madre y de otros santos según el orden de sus fiestas*, Sevilla: Fernando Díaz, 1580.

[29] "And the third time St Michael Archangel appeared in Rome was at the time of St Gregory Pope, because as St Gregory had established the Greater Litanies, which take place on St Mark's day because of some plague that existed in Rome called inguinal and he prayed devoutly for the people's health, God's angel appeared on top of a castle which was called then Adrian's Castle and cleaned a bloody knife and put it in the scabbard. And when blessed St Gregory saw this, he understood that the Lord had heard people's prayer and built in that castle a church dedicated to the angels. And that castle has been called St Michael's Castle

Although this appears in Voragine's (the apparition happened on 8 May), our first text analyzed here, the *Flos sanctorum con sus ethimologías*, does not include the exact date. Perhaps the Spanish medieval cosmology did not need such reminders, but towards the end of the sixteenth century the celebration of the festivity was well established. And this is important to understand how years later the apparition of the archangel was institutionalized each 8 May, as we will see.

In addition, Pedro de la Vega's work circulated in New Spain.[30] On page CCXIXr there is one of the most spectacular engravings of St Michael the Archangel (Figure 2) included in a book of saints.[31] In it, we can perceive all the elements that constitute the textual category of *mirabilia* in a narrative of the saint's life that insists on his fight against the devils, his contact with the Christians' souls and his power as army's commander in favor of those who are removed from sin. Looking at the iconographic and iconological aspects of this engraving, we can deduce that there was a saturation of *mirabilia* aspects that by the second half of the sixteenth century caught the attention of the Inquisition, who started discrediting some versions of saints' lives in the *Flores sanctorum* because of their lack of historic truth.[32] Proof of this is the fact that the first *Flos sanctorum* printed in 1556 or 1558 in Zaragoza was included in the *Index librorum prohibitorum*.[33] This censure happened several times in New Spain during the sixteenth century. For instance, in 1561 there was a process against "Antón, sacristán" ("Antón, sexton") for the theft of some forbidden books that had been requisitioned and were being kept in the

---

to this day. This apparition is celebrated on May 8, together with the apparition on Mount Gargano", Vega, *Flos sanctorum, op. cit.*, fol. CCXXr.

[30] There is a copy at the Biblioteca Nacional de México, the oldest book of saints preserved there. There is an older one in the Palafoxiana, printed in Seville by Juan Gutiérrez in 1568.

[31] The same engraving had been used a few pages before (LXIIv) to illustrate the narrative of the history of the festivity of St Gabriel in March. Of course, this was a mistake, for the elements of this engraving correspond to the life of St Michael. We also know that printers, to save money, recycled engravings and used them in several sections of a same book, or even as part of different literary genres.

[32] Mathilde Albisson, "Una aproximación a la censura inquisitorial de la hagiografía en lengua vulgar: del índice de Valdés (1559) al índice de Zapata (1632)", *Rilce*, 36.2 (2020), 453–76.

[33] With all certainty the year was 1556; this was because in the first edition of the *Index* it was written "1558", while the mistake was corrected in the second edition. Thus, the date of "1556" remained. In Quiroga's *Index* of 1583, there also appears "1556", one more reason why perhaps this is the correct date. See Carme Arronis Llopis, "El Tractado de la vida de Christo: sobre prohibiciones 'hagiográficas' del índice de Fernando de Valdés (1559)", *Hispania Sacra*, LXXI, 144 (2019), 481–82. This theory is right because in 1586 the Holy Inquisition of the New Spain declared forbidden in the "Villa de Valladolid" the "*Flos santorum* zaragozano, impreso en el año de 1556". See Fernández del Castillo, *Libros y libreros, op. cit.*, p. 325.

church of Zacatecas, perhaps among them a copy of the 1556 *Flos sanctorum*. The sexton defended himself in the following manner:

> Preguntando, cuántos libros fueron los que este confesante tomó de las dichas petacas, y para qué efecto los tomó e cuántos dispuso de ellos.

> Dixo: que no tomó más de uno e que no lo tomó para leerlo sino porque tenía muchos santos[34] y para verlos, e que antes que este confesante tomase el dicho libro, vió que Hierónimo, hermano de este confesante, y Martín, indios, tomaron de las dichas petacas seis libros.[35]

This passage shows that owning books does not imply reading them but enjoying them as objects, particularly when they include images, as those we identify with the story of St Michael the Archangel. However, in this case it is clear that there is an intention to avoid any suspicion implied by reading a forbidden book. The sexton accuses two Indians of being responsible for the theft and describes himself as innocent because he asked them for the books back and inquired the reason for their behavior. What is interesting is that the Indians did not want the books to read them, but to look at the images:

> Dixo: que al tiempo que este confesante dio los dichos libros a los dichos trompeteros, les dixo, que para qué lo llevaban, que se los volviese, pues sabía que eran prohibidos, y ellos le respondieron que no los querían para leer sino para verlos, y aunque este confesante se los pidió muchas veces, nunca los quisieron volver.[36]

Regarding ownership of *Flores sanctorum* by indigenous *caciques* in the sixteenth century, I have worked on the topic in another article.[37] Apparently,

---

[34] Because in Spanish the term "santo" can mean a "printed image" or "an image in a printed publication" (*DRAE*), maybe this is not a reference to saint's images strictly speaking.
[35] "To the question how many books he took from the chests and for what purpose and how many he used, he responded: That he only took one, and not to read it but because it had many images and wanted to see them, and that before he took the said book he saw that Jerome, his brother, and Martin, both Indians, took also six books from these chests", FERNÁNDEZ DEL CASTILLO, *Libros y libreros, op. cit.*, p. 40.
[36] "He said: at the time the accused gave the books to the trumpeters, he inquired the reason why they were taking them and asked them to return the books, for he knew they were forbidden, and they responded that they did not want to read them but to look at the pictures, and although the accused asked them for the books back many times, they never wanted to return them", FERNÁNDEZ DEL CASTILLO, *Libros y libreros, op. cit.*, p. 41.
[37] Marcos CORTÉS GUADARRAMA, "Un *Flos sanctorum* y un *Contemptus mundi* entre los bienes de un indígena de la Nueva España a finales del siglo XVI: una aproximación a la hagiografía hispánica ante la Reforma protestante", in *Patrimonio textual y humanidades digitales IV. El Renacimiento literario en el mundo hispánico: de la poesía popular a los nuevos géneros del humanismo*, ed. by Javier Burguillo and Aarón Rueda Benito, Salamanca: SEMYR & IEMYR, 2021, pp. 87–105.

laying blame on the indigenous population was a resource frequently utilized by Spaniards to avoid punishment.[38] In addition, in 1586 the Inquisition of New Spain was uncomfortable with the old printed editions of this work,[39] what makes sense if we remember that eight years before Villegas's modified *Flos sanctorum* was already in circulation, a book of saints whose poetics can be explained because of its intention to adhere to the tenets of the Council of Trent (1545–1563) and its connection to the more modern sources written by Luigi Lippomano and Laurentius Surius, thus eliminating the archaic features related to Voragine—and therefore all suspicion that could justify its prohibition. This in what regard intentions, for I have studied how Villegas does not depart from the *mirabilia* that he says to reject, at least not in a book that was utilized to teach about devils.[40]

From this moment on, narratives about St Michael the Archangel will have very different characteristics than those belonging to the Hispanic late medieval tradition. It is crucial for Villegas to not begin with a description of the metaphysical aspects we commented in other testimonies before—even the engraving that illuminates his narrative is more austere in comparison to that in Pedro de la Vega's *Flos sanctorum* (see Figure 3). On the contrary, his account begins with the well-known biblical story of Saul, king of Israel, and the affront he received from the giant Goliath; and how the meek shepherd David was the only one that came to the announcement that promised great rewards to whomever was victorious.[41] Then Villegas explains his parable:

> Dibuxo maravilloso es éste, de la batalla que hubo en el cielo entre los Ángeles, de que siempre que se haze dellos fiesta, es bien se haga memoria, y por ser una hazaña famosa que hizieron, y en que los buenos se señalaron.[42]

The battle between a giant and a humble shepherd—seen respectively as Lucifer and St Michael by the modern hagiographer—is the symbolic account

---

[38] We can attest this in other cases compiled by FERNÁNDEZ DEL CASTILLO, *Libros y libreros, op. cit*. It is important to recall that the Inquisition of New Spain did not have jurisdiction over the indigenous. What is particularly interesting here, based on the inquisitorial proceedings, is the social interaction between humans with diverse ethnic background.
[39] FERNÁNDEZ DEL CASTILLO, *Libros y libreros, op. cit.*, p. 333.
[40] Marcos CORTÉS GUADARRAMA, "Un caso de interés para la demonología originado en la hagiografía: san Germán y su evolución por los *Flores sanctorum* pretridentinos y postridentinos", *Hispania Sacra*, LXXIII, 148 (2021), 351–59.
[41] Alonso de VILLEGAS, *Flos sanctorum y Historia general de la Vida y Hechos de Iesu Christo*. Toledo: por la viuda de Juan Rodríguez, 1591 (1ª ed. 1578), fols 330ᵛ–331ʳ.
[42] "This is a great depiction of the battle that took place in heaven among the angels, because of which we always celebrate their festivity, and it is good to remember it because they accomplished a great deed in which the good stood out", VILLEGAS, *Flos sanctorum, op. cit.*, fol. 331ʳ.

of the struggle against the enemies of the Catholic church. This parable is offered from the point of view of the reform that took place in one of the literary genres more popular at the time and its consequences will be seen in New Spain. In addition, within the Indian church, it was adapted to the realities and demands of one of the territories farthest away from the Spanish crown, with an indigenous faithful population seen from very early on as breastfed children[43] and endowed with a growing consciousness of *criollismo* that will constitute their own identity, construed through a series of advocations and local miracles. Its ultimate goal is to declare that New Spain deserves all the virtues of a New Jerusalem;[44] a territory of Catholic victory that deserves sanctity or an even better place than Europe, corrupted by Lutherans embodied in a figure that represents evil itself: Luther.[45] This would become the canonical discourse—among other texts that narrated the lives of venerable New Spain inhabitants who were considered saints by many American individuals—thanks to the figure of St Michael the Archangel narrated from the postulates of the Jesuit Company, whose members were responsible, among other things, for defending the Catholic church, as we will see.

St Michael the Archangel: A Counter-Reformist Characterization in New Spain

We have mentioned that the postulates of the Jesuit Company[46] were crucial for the consolidation of the statutes of the Council of Trent.[47] This mission was not only accomplished in Europe, but also in the American viceroyalties since the Company arrived in Peru in 1568 and then in New Spain in 1572. Thus, since the end of the sixteenth century, the Jesuits of the first American generation, like Joseph de Acosta (1540–1600), were intent on creating a theology for the Indian church. Their mission in the Perú viceroyalty was fundamental for this purpose and as a result we have the *De procuranda indorum salute* (1588). In this work, Acosta affirms—twice—that the preachers intent on going to America should not have the slightest doubt about the catechism

---

[43] "Con la leche de la fe en los labios" (with the milk of faith on their lips), MOTOLINÍA, *Historia de los indios, op. cit.*, p. 181.
[44] The archangel was considered an angelic patron of Israel, while Samael was its enemy. See Antonio RUBIAL GARCÍA, "Invención de prodigios. La literatura hierofánica", *Historias. Revista de la dirección de estudios históricos del INAH*, 69, (2008), 121-32.
[45] MAYER, *Lutero en el Paraíso, op. cit.*, p. 15.
[46] They can be read in St Ignatius's *Ejercicios espirituales*.
[47] Pilar GONZALBO AIZPURU, *La educación popular de los jesuitas*, México: Universidad Iberoamericana, 1989, pp. 11–24.

(as it had been established in Trent) and the Protestant calumnies regarding the sacraments, against whom they should stand firm:

> Quien desempeña el oficio de cura de los indios tiene bien claro en el catecismo del Concilio de Trento lo que hay que saber: primero sepa exponer, de acuerdo con la capacidad de los oyentes, las verdades del credo y principales misterios de fe; después los mandamientos de Dios, cómo se cumplen y quebrantan, y lo que pertenece a la comprensión y práctica de los sacramentos [...] No desconocemos las numerosas y graves definiciones dadas por la Iglesia misma en materia de sacramentos en el magno y ecuménico Concilio Tridentino contra las insolentes calumnias de los innovadores.[48]

In this second phase of evangelization,[49] Acosta demanded that all preachers going to America focus on three aspects to transmit God's mysteries: will, faith and conversion.[50] Of course, this preoccupation was not exclusive to the Jesuits, for they were also transmitted in different levels by the other religious orders that arrived to New Spain in the sixteenth century, as can be seen in the case of the Franciscan Maturino Gilberti; and also in the part of the *Codex mexicanus* (c. 1590) devoted to the saints of the Catholic church, there appears one of the first representations of St Michael the Archangel sketched on amate paper by a schooled Indian (Figure 4). However, as I have demonstrated in the case of a work by the Italian Jesuit Ludovico Bertonio,[51] it was members of the Jesuit Company who took the lead in their systematic interest in creating and disseminating ascetic, theological and scientific works in Spanish America and even in other continents[52] with the intention of benefiting pedagogy and an interest in teaching that had no precedents. In this sense, they will utilize with rhetorical and narrative talent the figure of St Michael the Archangel following Acosta's three concepts since the end of the sixteenth century (will, faith, and conversion).

---

[48] "Whoever is a priest among Indians has included in the Trent catechism all that must be known: first, the exposition, according to the audience's capability, of the truths of the Creed and the main mysteries of the faith; then God's commandments, how to follow them or break them, and what pertains to the understanding and practice of the sacraments... We do not ignore the grave and numerous definitions given by the Church regarding the sacraments in the great and ecumenical Council of Trent against the insolent calumnies of the innovators", Joseph de ACOSTA, *De procuranda indorum salute*, Madrid: Consejo Superior de Investigaciones Científicas, 1984, pp. 209, 357.

[49] The first was done by soldiers themselves and not by evangelizers. Acosta laments these abuses. ACOSTA, *De procuranda indorum, op. cit.*, p. 359.

[50] ACOSTA, *De procuranda indorum, op. cit.*, p. 363.

[51] Marcos CORTÉS GUADARRAMA, "Una *Vida de Christo* en aimara (1612) a partir del *Flos sanctorum reformado* de Alonso de Villegas", *Rilce*, 36.2 (2020), 527–47.

[52] Jonathan E. GREENWOOD, "Readable Flowers: Global Circulation and Translation of Collected Saints' Lives". *Journal of Global History*, 13 (2018), 22–45.

An example of this, regarding the topic of conversion, is the Christianization of the festivity of Tezcatlipoca, who, in the pre-Columbian cosmology, reminded St Michael's cosmic mission because of the unavoidable presence of the devil defeated at the feet of the winner and because he shared with him popular veneration.[53] In fact, Acosta writes in his *Historia natural y moral de las Indias* (1590) that the celebration of this important deity in the Mexica pantheon took place in May, "que es el tiempo en que aquella tierra hay más necesidad de agua. Se comenzaba su celebración a nueve de mayo, y se acababa a diez y nueve" ("at the time when there is more need of water in that land. It began on 9 May and ended on the 19th").[54] Curiously, following the impetus of the cult of the Archangel Michael's apparition proposed by the Jesuit Juan Eusebio Nieremberg in his work, there is a coincidence between the eve of the festivity of Tezcatlipoca and the apparition of St Michael the Archangel (May 8), whose main miracle in New Spain is related to the miraculous apparition of water. But let move slowly with our proof.

In 1599, Jesuit Pedro de Ribadeneira's *Flos sanctorum* was printed, where there was also "La fiesta de la Dedicación de San Miguel arcángel". Leaving aside a narrative tone influenced by Renaissance humanism—which is so characteristic of Villegas's prose—[55]the Jesuit is much more frugal in his beginning. For him, it is important to highlight right from the very first lines the two aspects involved in the celebration of the archangel: one on September 29, a celebration of one of the church's patron saint and defender;[56] the other one on May 8, because he appeared on top of mount Gargano to be honored by Christians. Later Ribadeneira's text engages in a long theoretical question on the nature and category of angels and why they must be honored, thus being very different from the literary penchant that characterizes the other Counter-Reformist *Flos sanctorum*, Villegas's. Even so, there is a passage that will help us understand that angelology, and in particular why the legend of St Michel the Archangel became richer and by then, in

---

[53] Gonzalbo Aizpuru, *La educación popular, op. cit.*, p. 99. Tezcatlipoca (the term means 'a smoking mirror'), like St Michael the Archangel, is one of the protagonists in a cosmic struggle, in this case against Quetzalcóatl. See Miguel León-Portilla, *La filosofía náhuatl estudiada en sus fuentes*, México: Universidad Nacional Autónoma de México, 1966, p. 125.
[54] Joseph de Acosta, *Historia natural y moral de las Indias*, ed. by Edmundo O'Gorman, México: Fondo de Cultura Económica, 1962, p. 272.
[55] Villegas quotes the Zeuxis myth in order to justify his poetic construction in his third part of the *Flos sanctorum* (1587). See Cortés Guadarrama, "Un caso de interés para la demonología", *art. cit.*, in press b.
[56] Pedro de Ribadeneira, *Flos sanctorum, o libro de las vidas de los santos*. Primera parte, Madrid: Luis Sánchez, 1616 (1ª ed. 1599), p. 665.

Ribadeneira's work, it had become a narrative topic endowed with great malleability in comparison to its medieval versions:

> Por esto en las divinas letras [los ángeles] se llaman soldados de Dios, exército del Señor, Príncipes de las Provincias, Presidentes de los pueblos, guardas y maestros de los hombres [...] Llámanse luz, por su gran claridad y sutileza, llámanse fuego y carbones encendidos: porque son ardientísimos y abrasados en el amor. Llámanse estrella de la mañana, porque así como las estrellas corporales hermosean el cielo visible e así ellos más excelentemente adornan el supremo e intelectual cielo. Llámanse trono de Dios, porque en ellos reposa, y tiene su asiento. Llámanse piedras preciosas y encendidas, porque encienden con sus oraciones, amonestaciones, y consejos, nuestras almas, para que apetezcan y busquen las cosas santas y preciosas del cielo, y menosprecien las de la tierra. Llámanse Sol, porque alumbran el mundo; columnas del cielo, porque le sustentan; carros de Dios, ciudadanos de paraíso: y finalmente amigos e hijos del mismo Dios. Por todos estos títulos debemos nosotros invocar a todos los santos Ángeles, alabarlos, e imitarlos, y con más especial devoción al Capitán de todos ellos, y Príncipe de la Yglesia, san Miguel.[57]

This list of adjectives written by Ribadeneira in the first edition of his *Flos sanctorum*[58] is an open field for the imagination of other Jesuit hagiographers devoted to what was the main literary topic of their times. Although we know that Nieremberg will revise and continue Ribadenaira's mission, as an author he will insist not so much in the reform of a text born in the Middle Ages like the *Flos sanctorum*, but in the creation of other works more attuned to the times such as the *Vidas ejemplares y venerables memorias de algunos claros varones de la Compañía de Jesús* (1643–1647) (where he includes a life of Ribadeneira himself), and a book about the figure of St Michael the Archangel: *De la devoción y patrocinio de San Miguel, príncipe de los ángeles, antiguo tutelar de los godos y protector de España*.

---

[57] "Because of this (the angels) are called soldiers of Christ in the Bible, the Lord's army, Princes of the Provinces, People's Presidents, Guardians and teachers of humankind... They are called light because of their brightness and levity, they are called fire and burning coal because they are most ardent and burning in love. They are called morning star because just like corporeal stars make the visible sky beautiful, likewise they adorn the supreme and intellectual heavens in a most excellent manner. They are called God's throne because he rests in them and takes seat on them. They are called precious and ardent stones because they light up with their prayers and warnings and advice our souls so that they may desire and search for the holy and precious things of heaven and scorn those of this world. They are called sun because they enlighten the entire world. Heaven's columns because they support it; God's chariot, citizens of paradise, and finally friends and children of God himself. With all these names we must call all the holy angels, praise them and imitate them, and more devoutly their captain and prince of the Church, St Michael", RIBADENEIRA, *Flos sanctorum, op. cit.*, p. 670.

[58] Dedicated to the Queen of Spain, Margarita of Habsburg.

The book's intentions are explained in the paratexts that accompany it. It is a project that Nieremberg himself engaged in for the benefit of the kingdoms of Spain. The main idea is based in the enormous benefit other republics faithful to the archangel have enjoyed and the author asks us to remember what he has done for Spain: in 589, thanks to a 3-day fast, King "Recaredo", his court and 62 bishops gathered in Toledo and were "antecedentes a la Aparición de S. Miguel, que cae a ocho de Mayo, en el cual se convirtió del Arrianismo a la Fe verdadera. Del qual ayuno resultó la perpetuidad de constancia de la Fe Católica de España".[59] Nieremberg recommended this to his contemporary Spanish priests interested in the common good, remembering that St Michael the Archangel himself ordered a third of the angels (part of his army) to fight against the Muslims on Santiago's side in the legendary battle of Clavijo, thus securing a victory for the Spanish Christian. The Jesuit regretted that at present this celestial authority was somewhat forgotten, to whom Spain owed so much. He even recommends in the same year his book was printed (Madrid, 1643): "hazer en su honra una Procesión, o alguna otra demostración, y assentar para adelante mayor recurso y estimación de su Patronazgo".[60] It is clear that just like the archangel helped Spain against the Arabs,

> así también ahora que no tenemos peligro de moros, sino de heregias, Dios que nos quiere defender dellas a dispuesto que acudamos al medio por donde antiguamente nos defendió de las mismas, que fue su gran Privado san Miguel, Patrón de los Católicos.[61]

Nieremberg's intentions were perfectly reinforced by a royal rule desire to accept the institutionalizing of the apparition of St Michael the Archangel to take place every May 8 in every place of the kingdom and for all subjects. The first to receive such command would be the "arzobispos, obispos y prelados" ("archbishops, bishops, and prelates"). The ceremony and official character recommended for this event would be consecrated with a: "Procesión general a la iglesia que huviere de su devoción, y si no a la más principal, y que se ayune su víspera" ("general procession to the church under his patronage or the main church, having fasted on the eve").[62]

---

[59] NIEREMBERG, *De la devoción y patrocinio de San Miguel, op. cit.*, fol. XVr.
[60] NIEREMBERG, *De la devoción y patrocinio de San Miguel, op. cit.*, fol. XVII.
[61] "Likewise, now that we are not under the Muslim danger, but the danger of heresies, God, who wants to defend us from them, has determined that we must use the means he used to defend us before, that is the help of his great confidant St Michael, patron saint of Catholics". NIEREMBERG, *De la devoción y patrocinio de San Miguel, op. cit.*, fol. XVIII.
[62] NIEREMBERG, *De la devoción y patrocinio de San Miguel, op. cit.*, fols XIX–XX.

The royal rule took place when Juan de Palafox y Mendoza was the viceroy and archbishop of New Spain (1600–1659), a personality that, as we can surmise because of the administrative positions he occupied, was fundamental for the history of New Spain as shown in his decisions. Towards 1643, when Nieremberg's book was published, Palafox y Mendoza was devoted to the institutionalization of the apparition in 1631 of the archangel in Tlaxcala. In fact, Jesuit Francisco de Florencia states that since the year 1632 the sanctuary of San Miguel del Milagro was credited for this apparition, after having being examined three times about this matter.[63] However, only in 1643 "el ilustrísimo don Juan de Palafox y Mendoza" issued a decree to find the truth with the intention of promoting the cult and devotion to the "holy archangel".[64] The cult adopted an institutional dimension never seen before, so much so that the *criollo* Jesuit author thinks pertinent to include a copy of the archbishop's decree inside the pages of his book.

In the context of a Counter-Reformist and political strategy that re-utilized the archangel as the victorious champion of the Catholic church, we have already mention that the printing business of the window of Bernardo de Calderón in the City of Mexico[65] published a version of Nieremberg's book. Item more, considering that it had been printed in Madrid during the 10 years for which Nieremberg had been granted a privilege, we can consider Paula de Benavide's edition as an illegal edition.[66] If we use the arguments I have developed in these pages, it is clear that the widow of Bernardo de Calderón experienced a financial gain from a book that was easily sold, for its content offered depth and historical support to a legendary and marvelous narrative about an apparition occurred in 1631 in Tlaxcala.

The legendary elements of this apparition were construed with the main *topoi* and motifs of the hagiographic literature of New Spain. Particularly with those narrative elements present in the apparitions of the most important virgins of New Spain: the Virgen de los Remedios and the Virgen de Guadalupe. Similarly to what happens with the legends of these virgins, St Michael the Archangel also appeared to a virtuous and innocent Indian, on 8 May, with the addition of an element that was necessary for the time of

---

[63] FLORENCIA, *Narración de la maravillosa aparición, op. cit.*, p. 82.
[64] FLORENCIA, *Narración de la maravillosa aparición, op. cit.*, pp. 83–84.
[65] Arturo VILLASANA BALTASAR and Guadalupe RODRÍGUEZ DOMÍNGUEZ, "Un subterfugio editorial mexicano del siglo XVII: la edición contraecha de la viuda de Bernardo de Calderón", *Biblographica*, 2: 2 (2019), 70–96.
[66] If that was the case, it would be a problem that pertained more to the civil authorities than to the Inquisition, which was worried about persecuting heretical ideas rather than the problems derived from bad editorial practices. VILLASANA BALTASAR, "Un subterfugio editorial mexicano", *art. cit.*, p. 92.

drought in which the apparition took place: the miraculous finding of water that had the power to cure different diseases.[67]

Although the miraculous apparition of water was intrinsic to some lives of saints, including the most fantastic ones,[68] in the institutionalization of this festivity with its marvelous water, every 8 May, there is a coincidence with and substitution of the festivity of Tezcatlipoca at a time of drought, which took place, as Acosta reported some 150 years before, from 9 May through 19. With this the viceroyalty of New Spain attained a double purpose: on one hand, making official the festivity of the apparition of the archangel, as requested by Nieremberg, and with it his clear intention of defending Catholicism; secondly, it had a local interest, eliminating idolatry once and for all through the celebration of a powerful advocation on the eve of day devoted to the also powerful pre-Columbian god Tezcatlipoca, a cult that probably still existed at this time of the year, which also happened to be the most important time in the high Mexican plateau because of the drought.[69] In addition, 34 km away (some eight hours by foot) from San Miguel del Milagro (Tlaxcala) there lay the old sacred city of Tianguismanalco (Puebla), where Tezcatlipoca was venerated.[70]

The official character of Palafox's and Mendoza's intentions had an influence in other hagiographers interested in giving impetus to the canonization of other venerable people from New Spain who were perceived locally as saints. This impetus ended up in failure each time, as has been already studied.[71] That was the case of the hagiographer Pedro Salmerón, who wrote the *Vida de la venerable madre Isabel de la Encarnación* (1675). It is a hagiography under the guise of a biography with the typical elements of the genre and a Baroque aesthetic character.[72] Almost at the end of the narrative on the Carmelite nun,[73] the hagiographer digresses in a chapter to inform the reader

---

[67] FLORENCIA, *Narración de la maravillosa aparición, op. cit.*, p. 83.
[68] Marcos CORTÉS GUADARRAMA, "Fuera del canon de la Legenda aurea: la vida de san Antolín en los *Flores sanctorum* castellano medievales", *Archivum*, 66 (2016), 7–44.
[69] We shouldn't forget that in 1629, a date close to that of the archangel's first apparition, the *Tratado de las supersticiones y costumbres gentílicas que oy viven entre los indios naturales desta Nueva España*, by fray Hernando Ruiz de Alarcón, was published, a compilation of some spiritual practices impossible to eliminate even from the schooled Indians.
[70] Richard NEBEL, *Santa María Tonantzin Virgen de Guadalupe. Continuidad y transformación religiosa en México*, México: Fondo de Cultura Económica, 2002, pp. 89–90.
[71] Antonio RUBIAL GARCÍA, *La santidad controvertida. Hagiografía y conciencia criolla alrededor de los venerables no canonizados de Nueva España*, México: Fondo de Cultura Económica, 2001.
[72] RUBIAL GARCÍA, *La santidad controvertida, op. cit.*, pp. 38–65.
[73] She engaged in great fights against the devil and suffered a terrible illness that provoked her horrible pain until her death.

about the most efficacious remedies she used to heal her horrible pains and the terrific visions and evil fits that tormented her: water and dirt from the place where the glorious archangel St Michael appeared four leagues outside of Puebla de los Ángeles, the native town of the nun.

Pedro Salmerón compares Mother Isabel de la Encarnación with other Catholic saints[74] and gives her a halo of sanctity by comparing a moment of her life with the archangel's. The audacious passage derives from the fact that, according to Francisco de Florencia, Salmerón himself had written in 1645 a brief text about the archangel's apparition in Tlaxcala.[75] Thus, chapter XII of the third part of the hagiography is the account of a legend encouraged since the 1530s: an adolescent Indian, virtuous and exemplary, Diego de san Francisco, who had been taught Catholicism since he was young by his parents, receives the miraculous apparition of the archangel "y le dixo, que en la parte que ahora está la fuente, cabasse, y descubriría el agua de ella, que lo dixesse a los vecinos, porque avía de ser muy saludable, para sus necessidades" ("who told him to dig where now the fountain is, and he would find water, and told him to inform his neighbors about it, for it was very healthy, so that they could use it for whatever they needed").[76] The account continues and the devils of medieval hagiography are substituted (as expected in the Counter-Reformation) by those of illness.[77] The *mirabilia* elements appear as we could expect: we are told that the water was endless despite not having a natural source.[78] The account ends saying that the miracles performed by this miraculous water "que era menester un libro entero para escribirlos, sanado muchos enfermos, coxos, tullidos, ciegos" ("would need an entire book to describe them, for they cured many sick, lame, cripple and blind"). This invitation was accepted seventeen years later by the Jesuit Francisco de Florencia (1620–1695). In fact, his *Narración de la maravillosa aparición que hizo el arcángel san Miguel a Diego Lázaro de San Francisco, indio feligrés del pueblo de S. Bernardo de la jurisdición*[sic] *de Santa María Nativitas* will be one of the most original works written in the Spanish world at the end of the seventeenth century, devoted to St Michael the Archangel as an advocate of Catholicism for the Spanish Crown.

---

[74] Among them St Teresa de Jesús and St John of the Cross. On the other hand, he also compares her to fray Luis de Granada and even Job, to the point of calling her a Second Job. See Pedro SALMERÓN, *Vida de la madre Isabel de la Encarnación, carmelita descalza, natural de la Ciudad de los Ángeles*, México: Francisco Rodríguez Lupercio, 1675, p. 17ᵛ.
[75] FLORENCIA, *Narración de la maravillosa aparición, op. cit.*, pp. 2, 7–8.
[76] SALMERÓN, *Vida de la madre Isabel, op. cit.*, fol. 96ᵛ.
[77] CORTÉS GUADARRAMA, "Un caso de interés para la demonología", *art. cit.*, en prensa b.
[78] SALMERÓN, *Vida de la madre Isabel, op. cit.*, fol. 97ᵛ.

At the beginning of this book there is an engraving of the archangel dressed as a defending soldier—keeping the devil at bay with a lance at his feet (Figure 5)—inspired in an engraving by Hieronymus Wierix, from 1619, entitled *Quis sicut Deus?* (Who like God?) (Figure 6). We must not forget this, for it has already been studied how since the end of the sixteenth century there were images in circulation inspired in a different iconographic tradition of the archangel that began with the engraving from 1584 by Wierix (Figure 7) based on a design (*c.* 1580) by Martin de Vos, where an angel points to heaven with his right hand and the left one holds a palm leaf. This image would be widely disseminated in the Spanish world, with Mexican examples in the paintings of St Michael in the cathedrals of Cuautitlán and Oaxaca, dating from the end of the sixteenth century and the first decades of the seventeenth.[79]

With this work, the *criollo* Jesuit Francisco de Florencia disseminated throughout Europe, from the printing press of Thomás López de Haro in Seville (1692), the marvelous apparition of the archangel in Tlaxcala, New Spain. His narrative is based on the solid literary tradition we have reviewed that undoubtedly included the archangel among the most important members of the celestial court and therefore a great sign of distinction for the land (in this case the writers') that deserved such a spiritual wonder.

After a Baroque-looking dedication,[80] there begins the new addition by Florencia, who did not forget to praise and thank the achievements of Nieremberg's work, who in 1643 wrote before him with the intention of consecrating the archangel as one of the "Principales ministros celestiales" ("main celestial ministers").[81] In addition, he offers the relevant philological data that Nieremberg himself, in the second edition of his work, included the account that Florencia is about to recount with some additional details.[82] However, despite this indebtedness, in the work of the New Spanish Jesuit we do

---

[79] See César Esponda de la Campa and Orlando Hernández-Ying, "El Arcángel San Miguel de Martín de Vos como fuente visual en la pintura de los reinos de la monarquía hispana", *Atrio*, 20 (2014), 8–23; Mario Ávila Vivar, "La iconografía de san Miguel en las series angélicas", *Laboratorio de arte*, 28 (2016), 243–58.
[80] The work is dedicated to Manuel Fernández de Santa Cruz, bishop of Puebla de los Ángeles the year the text was published. The *criollo* Jesuit develops a complete metaphor between the bishop's last name and the instrument with which the archangel defeated the devil: the "Santa Cruz" (Holy Cross), making use of a large and erudite knowledge of references from the utilization of the Holy Cross in the coat of arms of the city of Marseille (together with three fleur-de-lis) to Nieremberg's account in his continuation of Ribadeneira's *Flos sanctorum*: the life of St Procopius, to whom St Michael appeared on a Cross, according to Surius's, "para significar quánta concussación tenía san Miguel y la Santa Cruz para hazer el bien a los hombres". See Florencia, *Narración de la maravillosa aparición, op. cit.*, p. IIIr.
[81] Florencia, *Narración de la maravillosa aparición, op. cit.*, p. 1.
[82] Florencia, *Narración de la maravillosa aparición, op. cit.*, p. 2.

not find the resentment towards Protestants and other heretics with which Nieremberg had began his work. Florencia's book focuses exclusively in extolling the apparition of the archangel in Tlaxcala, New Spain, and the miraculous water of this sanctuary. He also insists in the use of Counter-Reformist sources with which the books of saints were modernized. Thus, the name of the German Laurentius Surius—on whom both Villegas and Ribadeneira based their works and whose book has already been studied within the context of the European controversy on hagiography and the Reformation—[83]is constantly mentioned in support of the *criollo* Jesuit's discourse. From this point of view, it is possible to say that Florencia's work is the result of the splendor of Catholicism that Nieremberg had aspired to forty-nine years before by placing all the kingdoms of Spain under the advocacy of the archangel. Indeed, the triumph of Catholicism is so absolute that Florencia does not even bother to insist on it. On the contrary, his discourse is devoted to the validation and praise of the presence of New Spain—through the archangel's manifestation—in a world order in which America had been subordinate to Europe.

Final Considerations

Using the textual sources we have analyzed, there was an evident transformation in the hagiographic literature that narrated the apparition of St Michael the Archangel. After the Reformation, there was the most radical transformation of this celestial figure in favor of his institutional and irrevocable use in benefit of Catholicism. His advocacy is seen as a prefiguration, according to Nieremberg, of Catholicism's absolute triumph in all the lands of the Spanish Crown. This fact can be observed in certain significant acts on the part of some American subjects at the time of Michael's apparition (a date that, as we have studied, was established—with the support of a previous textual tradition—by Nieremberg's work in 1643). Thus in 1684, Carlos de Sigüenza y Góngora stated that every 8 May, during the festivity of St Michael the Archangel, the Licenciado Santiago de Zuri-Calday, the owner and oldest chaplain of the Convento Real de Jesús María, and chamber secretary to the most illustrious and excellent D. fray Payo Enríquez de Ribera, archbishop of Mexico and viceroy of New Spain, liberally bestowed a dowry of 600 pesos upon two noble orphaned girls.[84]

---

[83] Fernando BAÑOS VALLEJO, "Lutero sobre la hagiografía y los hagiógrafos sobre Lutero", *Studia Aurea*, 13 (2019), 7–40.
[84] Carlos SIGÜENZA Y GÓNGORA, *Paraíso Occidental*, ed. by Margarita Peña, México: Consejo Nacional para la Cultura y las Artes, 2003, pp. 90–92.

By this time, the fear of Protestants is more a literary memory for a few erudite than a real and feared enemy in flesh and blood. In 1684, Sigüenza y Góngora himself said, when talking about the year Marina de la Cruz was born and about her good principles (founding nun and donor for the future generations of the Convento Real de Jesús María in Mexico City):

> [1536] Célebre en las historias de los tiempos, así porque en él le fue cortada la cabeza a la impía Ana Bolena, mujer de Enrique VIII, rey de Inglaterra, habiéndola antes convencido de incestuosa con su propio hermano, como también porque en él comenzó Calvino a enseñar a los de Ginebra su falsa secta y se concordaron las dos mortalísimas pestes del universo Bucero y Martín Lutero, presidiendo éste a un conciliábulo de 300 ministros en Wittemberga.[85]

The fear of Protestants had turned into a literary idea more and more deprived of real significance, as we can see in the last quote. Catholicism had won in the Spanish world and it should not surprise us that in Francisco de Florencia's work there is very little of Nieremberg's animadversion against the heretics; on the other hand, what we find is an exhortation to offer the apparition of St Michael the Archangel in Tlaxcala as an event that, being so providential, gave great prominence to New Spain within the global order.

However, and paradoxically, the orthodox New Spanish devotion to St Michael will become blurred after eighteenth-century secularism. Indeed, after the multiplication of images, churches, advocations, miracles, and large numbers of devoted faithful in New Spain, the IV Mexican Provincial Council of 1771 will rule about the inappropriateness of the Archangel's images.[86] This provision will not eradicate the cult of St Michael in Tlaxcala, still alive today.[87] In sum, the analysis of the evolution of the figure of St Michael the Archangel through a variety of hagiographic sources (pre- and post-Tridentine sources from Spain and New Spain) from the end of the fifteenth to the end of the seventeenth century has allowed us to interpret a component of Mexican culture that, to some degree, is still extant in the twenty-first century.

---

[85] "[1536] It was famous in contemporary histories because the impious Anne Boleyn, Henry VIII's wife, king of England, was beheaded after having convicted her for incest with her own brother, and also because Calvin began teaching in Geneva his false sect and there took place the two most lethal plagues of all, Bucero and Martin Luther, the latter presiding over a secret meeting of 300 priests in Wittenberg", SIGÜENZA Y GÓNGORA, *Paraíso Occidental, op. cit.*, p. 122.

[86] GONZALBO AIZPURU, *La educación popular, op. cit.*, p. 99.

[87] Eduardo MERLO JUÁREZ and José Antonio QUINTANA FERNÁNDEZ, *Quién como Dios, san Miguel del Milagro*, Puebla: Universidad Popular Autónoma del Estado de Puebla, 2009.

Appendix

Figure 1: "St Michael the Archangel", fol. 308ᵛ. Engraving from the *Diálogo de doctrina christiana en lengua de Michoacán*, printed by Juan Pablos, México, 1559

Figure 2: "St Michael the Archangel", fol. CCXIXr. Engraving from the *Flos sanctorum* printed by Fernando Díaz, Seville, 1580

Figure 3: "St Michael the Archangel", fol. 331ʳ. Engraving from the *Flos sanctorum* by Alonso de Villegas, printed by the widow of Juan Rodríguez, Toledo, 1591

Figure 4: "St Michael the Archangel", *Codex mexicanus* (*c.* 1590), Bibliothèque Nationale de France (detail)

Figure 5: "St Michael the Archangel". Engraving from the *Narración de la maravillosa aparición que hizo el arcángel san Miguel a Diego Lázaro de San Francisco*, by Francisco de Florencia, printed by Thomás López de Haro, Seville, 1692

Figure 6: "St Michael the Archangel". Engraving by Hieronymus Wierix, 1619

Figure 7: "St Michael the Archangel". Engraving by Hieronymus Wierix, 1584, based on a sketch by Martin de Vos

Catalan Lives of Saints after Trent (1575–1602)

Carme ARRONIS LLOPIS
(Universitat d'Alacant, Spain)

It is well known that one of the doctrinal consequences derived from the Council of Trent was the revision of hagiographic material in response to the Protestant controversy on the cult of saints. However, regarding certain contexts there are still few studies that analyze this production looking at specific changes on the narratives, or the compilers' intention when composing new hagiographic collections, which they frequently stated in their paratexts. It is certainly a work that still needs to be done for texts written in Catalan context, an area where otherwise there are studies that analyze the new production as a result of local devotion, a sort of *patriotic hagiography*, whose main intention was to highlight the sacred peculiarity of the territory as an essential part of its idiosyncrasy.[1] Nevertheless, here we will study the first Catalan compilations after the Council of Trent and will pay particular attention to the efforts made by the authors to accommodate the material to the new criteria. Thus we will be able to see how the post-Tridentine Catalan hagiographic production is in tune with other European Catholic initiatives, frequently characterized by their anti-Protestantism.

---

[1] See Pep VALSALOBRE, "Elements per a una Catalunya sacra: sobre alguns aspectes de l'hagiografia de l'edat moderna catalana" in *Vides medievals de sants: difusió, tradició i llegenda*, ed. by Marinela Garcia & M. Àngels Llorca, Alacant: IIFV, 2012, 99–122, and Xavier TORRES, "La ciutat dels sants: Barcelona i la historiografia de la Contrareforma", *Barcelona: quaderns d'història*, 20 (2014), 77–104.

Hispanic Hagiography in the Critical Context of the Reformation, ed. by Fernando Baños Vallejo, Hagiologia, 19 (Turnhout, 2022), pp. 189–214.
© BREPOLS PUBLISHERS   DOI 10.1484/M.HAG-EB.5.131995

A Medieval Book of Saints in a Post-Tridentine Period: The Flos sanctorum *from 1575*

In 1575, the printer Jaume Cendrat obtained a license, signed by Philip II's lieutenant Hernando de Toledo, to print exclusively and for a period of ten years a work known as *Flos sanctorum* (entitled *Flor del sants* in this edition), the vernacular version of the medieval *Legenda Aurea* by Jacobus de Voragine. This edition, printed in collaboration with Cendrat and Eulàlia Montpezada (widow of the printer Pere de Montpezat), was the last edition of the medieval book of saints that appeared in Catalan in the press after a long tradition that had started in the incunabula period.[2] It had been not published for 25 years, since the printer Pere de Montpezat, between 1548–1549, had made the previous edition (today lost). The context of these two editions, in what pertains to the concept of the cult of and devotion to saints, was considerably different.[3]

The 1575 edition was published after the end of the Council of Trent, in one of whose last sessions, number 25th, which took place on 3 and 4 December, 1563, on "the invocation, veneration, and relics of saints, and on sacred images", the devotion to saints in the Catholic Church had been reaffirmed. The value of saints as mediators to obtain divine grace was thus highlighted, insisting, though, that only God was in charge of granting it; it was also underlined the exemplary value of saints' lives and the benefit received from the cult of their relics and images, which served to reinforce the faith of their devotees. The tradition of venerating saints was then ratified, a fervor that was now vindicated as a differential fact of the Catholic spirit with regard to the Protestant *heresy*. In addition to reinforcing the dogmatic and doctrinal aspects in view of the contemporary controversies, the task of undertaking reformed practical changes regarding their devotion took now concrete form.

During the Council sessions, there were discussions on the quality of the devout texts, in particular regarding apocryphal and not well-proven content

---

[2] There are two incunabula editions in Catalan (one of 1494 and the other *c.* 1490–1494), as well as 5 from the first half of the sixteenth century (1514, 1519, 1524, 1547 and 1548–1549). See Carme ARRONIS LLOPIS, "La tradició editorial del *Flos sanctorum* català en el Cinccents", *Magníficat. Cultura i literatura medievals*, 8 (2021), 229–302.

[3] There are no extant copies of this edition printed in Barcelona by Pere de Montpezat, and we only have news about it from old descriptions by bibliophiles; however, their information allows us to guess that there was a connection between the 1548–1549 and the 1575 editions. It is not at all surprising, for the widow of Montpezat—who continued with the business after the death of her husband—participated in the 1575 edition made in collaboration with Jaume Cendrat. But because we ignore the details of this lost edition, we cannot determine which structural changes (order of chapters, suppressions, etc.) appear exclusively in the 1575 edition. (ARRONIS, "La tradició editorial del *Flos sanctorum*...", *art. cit.* pp. 261–62).

in hagiographic texts. This had been denounced by many Catholic reformist theologians since the beginning of the century, but undoubtedly it was the Lutherans' mockery of the quality of hagiographic books what spurred Catholics to undergo their revision.[4] The context of this discussions is key to understanding the main lines of action of Catholic hagiographers in the second half of the sixteenth century throughout Catholic Europe. This can be seen in the publication of the reformed book of saints by Luigi Lippomano, bishop of Verona (1551-1560).[5] This publication embodied the Tridentine spirit: it had a controversial nature that lay behind the goal of recuperating the authenticity of the hagiographic texts by eliminating everything considered *apocryphal*, that is, written by unknown or dubious authors, and it was made explicit in the prologue the need to exclusively use old and renowned sources (the more the better), that is illustrious authors respected by all, even by the heretics, so that the latter could not laugh at them.[6]

In the Council of Trent, the liturgical and paraliturgical texts were not revised, but several directives were issued on how to do it, and the Vatican See was charged with reforming the *Roman Breviary* (1568) and the *Roman Missal* (1570), in order to make the Catholic rites uniform, suppress some practices considered heterodoxical and revise the texts that referred to the saints they included. Other complementary works were also printed soon, such as Usuard's *Martyrology* revised by Johannes Molanus (1568), the "official" *Roman Martyrology* by Cesare Baronio (1584) or the publication of the complete text of the *De probatis sanctorum historiis* by the German Carthusian monk Laurentius Surius (1570-1575), a real keystone of the reformed post-Tridentine hagiography.

Since Trent, also, there was a call to pastoral responsibility, in particular regarding bishops and archbishops, to watch over the correct teaching of the faithful in each diocese and the application of the Council's directives. The Tridentine decrees were issued in Catalonia at the Provincial Council of Tarragona of 1564-1565, which was convened by archbishop Ferran de Loaces; in the diocese of Barcelona, bishop Guillem Caçador convened the Synod of

---

[4] On this topic, see Fernando BAÑOS VALLEJO, "Lutero sobre la hagiografía y los hagiógrafos sobre Lutero", *Studia Aurea*, 13 (2019), 7-40, and Fernando BAÑOS VALLEJO, "'Lanzarían grandes carcajadas': Lo apócrifo del *flos sanctorum* y la burla de los protestantes", *Rilce: Revista de Filología Hispánica*, 36.2 (2020), 428-52.
[5] *Sanctorum priscorum patrum vitae, numero centum sexagintatres, per gravissimos et probatissimos auctores conscriptae*, 8 vols, 1551-1560. See Sofia BOESCH-GAJANO, "La raccolta di vite di santi di Luigi Lippomano: storia, struttura, finalità di una costruzione hagiogràfica", in *Raccolte di vite di santi dal XIII al XVIII secolo. Messaggi, strutture, fruizioni*, ed. by Sofia Boesch-Gajano, Fasano di Brindisi: Schena, 1990, 110-30.
[6] BAÑOS VALLEJO, "Lanzarían grandes carcajadas...", *art. cit.*, p. 442.

Barcelona on April 6, 1566, after which it was ordered to deans and rectors of parishes to post announcements on the church doors informing the faithful of the issuing of the Tridentine decrees. A few years later, in 1573, the new archbishop of Tarragona, Gaspar Cervantes—who had attended the Council in person—ordered the publication of the *Instruccions y advertiments molt útils y necessaris per a les persones eclesiàstiques y principalment per als qui tenen cura de ànimes*, with the intention of disseminating the Tridentine spirit among the priests (the second edition of this work was printed precisely by Jaume Cendrat and Eulàlia de Montpezat also in 1575). The application of the decrees began taking place in later provincial councils (1577–1578 and 1584), under the responsibility of each diocese's bishop. Since this moment, and until the first decades of the next century, synods were celebrated in each diocese periodically, and in some cases annually (as in Barcelona between 1570–1575),[7] although the enactment of reforms was not always immediate.[8]

In this climate of exaltation of Catholic identity signs and the application of the decrees of Trent, printers Cendrat and Montpezada, no doubt, saw an opportunity to bring to the market a new edition of the text published 25 years before, precisely motivated by the value age and tradition had given that volume. In fact, in the license, it is highlighted that it was an old work that had been translated into Catalan a long time ago.[9] Indeed, the 1575 edition inherited all the editorial tradition that existed, including the consolidation of some tendencies such as increasing the content of the original Voragine's book with new chapters. This had become a characteristic tendency of the textual transmission of the *Legenda Aurea* in the Romance languages. Also in the case of Catalan, and since the incunabula period, each new edition had incorporated novelties as a marketing device, usually the addition of

---

[7] José Luis Betrán, "Entre el orden y el desorden: el clero diocesano barcelonés de la contrarreforma (1564–1700)", *Studia Historica. Historia Moderna*, 40, 1 (2018), 185–232, pp. 196–97.

[8] There were, for instance, many difficulties when adopting the new canonical Missal, for in the Missal of the Diocese of Barcelona dated from the end of the fifteenth century there were many masses considered heterodoxical like that offered to St Sigismund in favor of the sick with fever. It seems that the old rites had not entirely disappeared by the beginning of the seventeenth century: in 1596, bishop Dimes Lloris still demanded the removal of the old Missals and that Mass not be officiated with them (M. Socorro Paradas Pena, "El obispo de Barcelona en el tránsito del siglo XV al XVI: Pere Garcia (1490–1505)", *Pedralbes: Revista d'història moderna*, 13/2 (1993), 123–32, p. 128); in the Diocese of Barcelona, later bishops insisted in the adoption of the Roman Missal during the first half of the seventeenth century (Martí Gelabertó Vilagran, *La palabra del predicador. Contrarreforma y superstición en Cataluña (siglos XVII–XVIII)*, Doctoral Diss., Universitat Autònoma de Barcelona, Departament d'Història Moderna i Contemporània, 2003, p. 308).

[9] Arxiu de la Corona d'Aragó (ACA), Cancilleria: Reg. núm. 4702, fol. 267r.

some chapters of interest for contemporary readers: mostly lives of regional saints, lives that enjoyed a deep-rooted devotion, lives of founders of religious orders, etc. Consequently, the 1575 edition offers Voragine's nucleus of lives with many modifications: 25 original chapters have been suppressed and more than 40 have been added (five of which in this edition).[10]

However, we cannot consider the 1575 edition as just one more of the various published in the first half of the century, because this one has some characteristics that single it out among the Catalan *Flores sanctorum*. It seems that the editors, conscious about the particular doctrinal context of the edition, wanted a renowned copy editor from the city to take care of the edition. This was Pere Coll, doctor in Sacred Theology and prior of the Dominican convent of Santa Caterina de Barcelona, another fact highlighted in the license. Nevertheless, this is far from a *reformed* book of saints, because it is still a reedition of the medieval text with some sixteenth-century additions of different types. However, detailed analysis allows us to confirm that there have been several interventions in the text due to the main post-Tridentine directives regarding hagiographic revisions, and a certain effort has been paid to adapt the text to the new criteria of authority and authenticity demanded by the Church, which makes us consider this edition as a *transitional* book of saints.[11]

We can identify at least three ways of intervention on the text which show a will to revise and accommodate hagiographic material: the addition of a prologue that has a clear post-Tridentine sensibility; a revision of the text paying attention to apocryphal passages; and an improvement of the doctrinal character of some episodes with the inclusion of authoritative voices or biblical verses.

---

[10] The edition of 1575 added the lives of St Ivo, St Basil, St Francis of Paola, St Odile and a chapter devoted to the death of 10,000 martyr knights. These chapters must be added to those already added in previous sixteenth-century editions, most of them involving Catalan saints (such as St Matrona, St Severus, St Maginus, etc.), or deep-rooted devotions in the Principality or, particularly, in Barcelona, like saints Justus and Pastor, St Elmo (patron saint of sailors), St Bertrand, St Honoratus, St Sigismund, etc. (See ARRONIS, "La tradició editorial del *Flos sanctorum*...", *art. cit.* p. 267).

[11] In a post-Tridentine Portuguese context, there is also a revision of the medieval books of saints. The archbishop of Braga, the Dominican Bartolomeu dos Mártires, who had attended the Council and had contributed to the approval of the decrees on the veneration of images of saints, put the also Dominican Diogo do Rosário in charge of doing this revision. Thus he published the *Historia das vidas e feitos heroicos e obras insignes dos sanctos: cum muitos sermões & praticas spirituaes, que servem a muitas festes do anno* (Braga, 1567), which enjoyed a true success (1577, 1590, 1622, 1647, 1681), and which, as in the Catalan case, also included a little Portuguese compilation that narrated the lives of martyrs from the first times of Christianity through contemporary saints like Queen Isabel of Portugal. (On this book of saints see Cristina SOBRAL, "Um legendário à saída de Trento (Frei Diogo do Rosário, 1567)", *Studia Aurea*, 11 (2017), 253-72 and SOBRAL's chapter in this book.)

For the first time in the Catalan tradition of *Flores sanctorum*, the edition is prefaced by a brief prologue—whose authorship is not clearly stated—that justifies the benefit derived from reading lives of saints. This declaration of intentions clearly agrees with the goal of validating the cult of saints, and also can be seen as a consequence of the controversy on *sola fide*, for it insists quite frequently on the need to do good works. The prologue includes some *topoi* on the benefit of reading saints' lives that appear in other prologues of the Hispanic tradition, but what makes this preface unique are details such as referring to the authority of masters to reinforce some arguments (Thomas Aquinas, Escotus, Bonaventure, etc.), or legitimizing this publication by indicating that it is a command of the Church to organize compilations such as this one so that the faithful can find in them exemplary models, in a clear reference to the Tridentine decrees.

In addition, towards the end of the prologue it is explicitly stated that the text has been revised: purged of "superfluous" elements and reinforced with other "necessary" additions. Although this statement might seem one more *topos*, present also in other previous editions, this time we can confirm that it has been revised in depth to introduce some *improvements* from a contemporary perspective.

Thus, one of the interventions is paying attention, as we mentioned before, to apocryphal passages. The revision does not seem exhaustive nor systematic, and in each case a different solution has been found. In general, the editor is respectful with the text of the Catalan *flos sanctorum*, but he has revised it comparing it to a good Latin edition, what allows him in some cases to recuperate references that appeared in Voragine's text on the apocryphal nature of some passages and which had been eliminated in the previous vernacular versions: "E llig-se en una història dels grecs *apòcrifa* que l'àngel li donà del fust en què pecà Adam [...]".[12]

In other cases, however, the entire passage considered apocryphal has been eliminated, such as the episodes of the midwives who helped the Mother of God in the chapter on Christ's nativity, an anecdote that came from the *Gospel of James* and was considered apocryphal since the late Middle Ages, although need to expunge it was not clearly stated until 1614, the year of the publication of the appendix to the 1612 *Index* by Inquisitor Bernardo de Sandoval.[13] Nonetheless, in this 1575 revision the text was already eliminated,

---

[12] "In an *apocryphal* Greek story we read that the angel gave him some of the tree with which Adam sinned". Excerpt from the chapter entitled "Del trobament de la creu" (fols LXXII^v–LXXIII^v), fol. LXXII^v.

[13] See Bernardo de SANDOVAL Y ROJAS, *Appendix prima ad Indicem librorum prohibitorum expurgatorum*, Madrid: Luis Sánchez, p. 865.

although with little stylistic care, for the suppression was not accompanied by a revision of the text and there is an abrupt anacoluthon. With better or worse skill, it is clear that there was caution to avoid material of dubious provenance or not documented by *serious* authors or endowed with proven authenticity, which was one of the main efforts of the editor.

On the other hand, a close reading of this compilation, comparing it with previous editions, allows us to confirm that, despite the fidelity of the text compared to that of previous editions, some sections have been rewritten or augmented. That is the case of chapters with passages where a doctrinal point needed to be clarified, and the exposition of concepts has been made lighter, the syntax has been simplified and authoritative authors have been used to reinforce the doctrinal points. The chapter on the Purification of the Mother of God, for instance, is one of those modified completely to facilitate its reading, and also throughout the chapter its doctrinal content has been reinforced: using masters that interpreted some of the narrated episodes; including the Biblical verses on the episode that offer a particular reading of the evangelical facts; and even indicating the exact source of Biblical verses that were already in the text.[14]

This brief analysis, then, makes clear that the content of this *Flos sanctorum* published after Trent does not ignore the directives there approved regarding the adaptation of this material to the new Catholic needs. Its editor, the Dominican Pere Coll, was conscious of the dangers involved in the re-edition of a medieval text: he had to eliminate passages from dubious origin, use *auctoritates* to strengthen some doctrinal points and accommodate the structure and style whenever necessary; and even if he tried to assume these goals, it seems he did not do it consistently nor systematically. His intervention on the texts is moderate and some times the modifications have been introduced coarsely and without a coherent narrative solution. Despite these changes, the bulk of the book is essentially the fourteenth-century medieval work including the elements that gave occasion to its discredit like unproven etymologies, scarce indication of sources, little historical rigour, lives that only consist of miracles (that is material for admiration and not edification), etc.

The 1575 edition, thus, reflects the last efforts of local editors and theologians to keep as valid a calendar of saints of medieval origin at the new spiritual and theological crossroads of the last third of the sixteenth century, although its modifications were not enough to accommodate a medieval text

---

[14] In fols xxxxiv^r–xxxxv^r of the 1575 edition there is an example of additons of this type compared to previous editions of the text.

to the new critical standards expected from hagiography in that new post-Tridentine period. In fact, there was no later edition despite the fact that the license Jaume Cendrat attained allowed him to publish this book of saints in exclusivity for ten years.[15] We will not see another Catalan edition in the early modern period. Three years later, the reformed *Flos sanctorum* by the Toledo priest Alonso de Villegas was published (1578), soon followed by 4 more volumes (published between 1583 and 1594); as well as the *Flos sanctorum* by Jesuit Pedro de Ribadeneira (vol. 1 in 1599, vol. 2 in 1604), both following the model of Lippomano-Surius, an improvement over the medieval compilations that also took into consideration the new theological premises and methodological hagiographic criteria accepted by Catholic Europe. These two Spanish books of saints were very successful throughout the Peninsula as well as in other regions, for they were translated into other European languages. In a Catalan milieu, they satisfied the desires of a reading public that in some circles was already bilingual and could read Spanish without much difficulty. It is relevant that Jaume Cendrat himself printed several volumes of Villegas's Spanish *Flos sanctorum* in Barcelona: the third volume in 1588 (devoted to extravagant saints and virtuous men), and the fourth in 1590 (this one includes sermons for the different festivities of the liturgical cycle).[16]

In the Catalan context, there was no general compilation written in Catalan equivalent to these, which does not mean that there were not similar initiatives geared towards a revision of hagiographic material. However, these efforts focused on regional hagiography. As examples of this we can mention the *Vides de sants de Catalunya* by the Jesuit Pere Gil (*c.* 1600), and the *Historia general de los santos y varones ilustres en santidad del Principado de Cataluña*, by the Dominican Antoni Vicenç Domènec (printed in Barcelona in 1602 and in Girona in 1630). Indeed, the few decades that separate the latter from the Catalan *Flos sanctorum* and the first compilations of local saints are enough to offer us a very different spiritual context.

At the end of the sixteenth century, the progressive introduction of the Tridentine spirit in the dioceses is a fact which took the form of punctual reforms particular to each place. From the point of view of hagiographic revisions, the model of the *reformed books of saints* had become established and the new compilations were being disseminated throughout. They are the model, although do not include all the existing devotions. What remained to

---

[15] ACA, *Cancilleria*: Reg. núm. 4702, fol. 267ᵛ.
[16] In order to fully grasp the great reception of Villegas's work, in less than 15 years between 1586 and 1600 and only in Barcelona, there were twenty editions of its different volumes, many times printed by the main printers in the city such as Cendrat, or Damià Bagès, Francesc Trinxer, Hubert Gotard, Jeroni Genovés, etc.

be done was enlarging these compilations, revising what the first reformed books of saints have still not accomplished, which was also conceived, as we will see, as a way to putting a stop to the Protestant heresy.

The "Reformed" Compilations of Local Saints

It should not come as a surprise the desire of Catalan hagiographers to examine and disseminate accounts of their local saints and of those that, while they were not Catalan, had a deep-rooted devotion in the region. Indeed, the interest for local hagiography was not new nor exclusive; in the Catalan context, we have been able to identify it with the development of the printed *flos sanctorum*, for each edition increased the number of chapters devoted to local devotions, a tendency that also existed throughout Catholic Europe in the fifteenth century, and received a new boost after Trent. It was a milestone when in 1573 Johannes Molanus made explicit the need for each region to take care of their "suae nationis Sanctos",[17] as he did with his *Indiculus Sanctorum Belgii*, an addition to Usuard's Martyrology that he completed in 1568. Molanus paid particular attention to local saints whose relics were still preserved, probably trying to legitimize their authenticity and vindicate their cult as patron saints of several communities. Indeed, most dioceses engaged in similar initiatives to revise their *own* hagiographic material and disseminate it. The image we obtain from all these efforts is that of a deeply Catholic Europe and the testimony of faith offered by the first martyrs adopted a new meaning in the context of the wars of religion.

On many occasions, the bishops themselves promoted actions geared towards a revision of the authenticity of the local relics and the investigation of the known facts about the lives of the local saints, which were alive and present for the faithful as an exceptional heritage. The chrorographic work *Descripción de las excelencias de la muy insigne ciudad de Barcelona*, by Dionís Jeroni Jorba, printed in 1585, is a proof of this.[18] Among the long list of treasures and particularities of the city, he highlights the care taken to preserve the relics and venerate the festivities devoted to local saints, among whom he mentions St Severus, St Vitalis, St Pacian, St Olegarius, St Eulalia and St Matrona,

---

[17] Johannes MOLANUS, "Epistola dedicatoria", *Indiculus Sanctorum Belgii*, Louvain, 1573, fol. 3ᵛ.
[18] This was not the last time, for the historic-patriotic sermon by the doctor in Theology Onofre Manescal pronounced in 1597 at the Barcelona See and published some years later is another clear proof (see Onofre MANESCAL, *Sermó vulgarment anomenat del sereníssim senyor don Jaume segon*, Barcelona: Sebastià de Cormellas, 1602). In it, he devotes a long section to remembering Catalan local devotions of "indígenas y naturals" saints (fols 72ʳ–72ᵛ), as well as those of "de altres nacions" and whose relics are kept in Catalonia (fols 72ᵛ–74ʳ).

"patron saints of the city".[19] Jorba also highlighted his devotion for bishop Joan Dimes Lloris, in whom he emphasized his erudition and other virtues such as his confessional eagerness and special care with which he honored local devotions (pp. 6ᵛ–7ʳ). Indeed, this bishop promoted some initiatives to encourage the cult of saints from Barcelona such as the canonization of Olegarius and Raymond of Penyafort or the study of the authenticity of the relics of local saints. In this last task, he had the help of the Jesuit college and in particular of the Jesuit Pere Gil, who in fact was put in charge by bishop Dimes Lloris of verifying the authenticity of the relics of St Pacian, rejected as false,[20] and of recuperating and encouraging the cult of saints from Barcelona.[21]

The Jesuit Order from the very beginning contributed to the task of revising hagiographic texts taking it as one more aspect of its ideological struggle against Protestants.[22] In fact, Laurentius Surius himself had the collaboration of the Jesuits from Cologne to increase the hagiographic material available and wanted his compilation to be more inclusive than restrictive chronologically and geographically.[23] Many of the first compilations of local saints in Europe were the work of Jesuits. Thus, in Portugal, Jesuit Álvaro Lobo wrote the *Martirológio dos Santos de Portugal e festes geraes do Reyno: recolhido dalguns autores e informações por alguns Padres da Companhia de Jesu* (Coimbra, 1591), which was presented as some type of complement to the *Roman Martyrology* and followed the example of Molanus, who was explicitly quoted in the Prologue (fol. 3ʳ). Also the Sardian Jesuit Giovanni Arca wrote a compilation of local saints entitled *De sanctis Sardiniae* and composed of three parts, two of which were devoted to Sardinian martyrs and the third to confessors (Cagliari, 1598); a little later, the Irish Jesuit Henry

---

[19] Dionís Jeroni JORBA, *Descripción de las excelencias de la muy insigne ciudad de Barcelona*, Barcelona: Hubert Gotard, 1585, fol. 7ʳ. In the second edition (Barcelona: Hubert Gotard, 1589), which included some changes and additions, to the list of patron saints of the city are added St Sebastian and St Roch (fol. 13ʳ). Although they are not Catalan, their devotion was very well established in the region because they were considered protectors against the plague; precisely in 1589, there was a great plague which can explain that their popularity was even greater at the time.

[20] See Àngel FÀBREGA GRAU, "El P. Pedro Gil SJ († 1622) y su colección de vidas de santos", *Analecta Sacra Tarraconensia*, XXXI (1958), 5–25, p. 6.

[21] José Luis BETRÁN, "Culto y devoción en la Cataluña barroca", *Jerónimo Zurita*, 85 (2010), 95–132, p. 100.

[22] It is not by chance that the Bolandist Society and his *magnum opus Acta sanctorum* will be done within the Company.

[23] Serena SPANO MARTINELLI, "Cultura umanistica, polemica antiprotestante, erudizione sacra nel "*De probatis Sanctorum historiis*" di Lorenzo Surio", in *Raccolte di vite di santi dal XIII al XVIII secolo. Messaggi, strutture, fruizioni*, ed. by Sofia Boesch-Gajano, Fasano di Brindisi: Schena, 1990, 131–41, p. 140.

Fitzsimon wrote his *Catalogus Præcipuorum Sanctorum Hiberniæ*, (Rome, 1611). The compilation known as *Vides de sants de Catalunya* (*c.* 1600) by Pere Gil is one more eloquent testimony of this.

The Hagiographic Notes by Jesuit Pere Gil

Pere Gil (1551–1622) was a reputed and erudite theologian and historian, an important figure in the Company of Jesus and in general in contemporary Barcelona.[24] He is the author of several works, some of them of an edifying nature, devised as individual exercises for lay people.[25] His main work, though, was his *Història cathalana*, apparently unfinished and kept in manuscript form. It was composed of several volumes: the first was devoted to the *Història natural* (geography) of the land; the second to the *Història moral* (devoted to the historical facts of its inhabitants); the third, which has not been preserved, was devoted to the *Història eclesiàstica* and a fourth was devoted to the *Vides dels sants de Catalunya* and other territories and of which we only have some notes.[26] It seems that Pere Gil applied—at least at the beginning— the Jesuit model based on a historical division in three parts to describe the particularities of a territory, as other members of the Jesuit Company had done,[27] and followed the same theological and epistemological foundations

---

[24] He was the director of the College of Betlem in Barcelona (1594–1597; 1603–1607 and 1616–1619) and the College of Palma de Mallorca (1611–1615); Provincial of Aragon (1619–1622); a highly reputed theologian who acted as representative *ad litem* in the canonization processes of St Ignatius at Barcelona, Manresa and Montserrat (1595 and 1606) and in the beatification of St Francis of Borja (1611). In addition, he was the right hand of several bishops, particularly Joan Dimes Lloris; he was the confessor of viceroys and other important local personalities; he counseled several institutions of the Principality; and was a member of the Inquisition. See a brief biography in Rodolfo GALDEANO CARRETERO, "Historiografia catalana i model jesuític: la *Història moral de Cathalunya* by Jesuit Pere Gil (1550–1622)", *Recerques*, 70 (2015), 35–60, pp. 44–45.

[25] For instance an *ars moriendi*, *Modo de ajudar a ben morir, als qui per malaltia, ò per justícia moren* (Barcelona, 1605, Joan Amelló); or a translation of the *Imitatio Christi* (Barcelona, 1621, Sebastià Mathevat), a key work of the reformed spirituality and crucial for the development of St Ignatius's sensibility.

[26] See the edition of the first volume in Josep IGLÉSIES, *Pere Gil, S. J., (1551–1622) i la seva Geografia de Catalunya, seguit de la transcripció del Libre primer de la Història Cathalana, en la qual se tracta de historia o descripció natural, ço es de cosas naturals de Cathaluña*, Barcelona: Quaderns de Geografia, 2002 (reed. 1949); and the second volume in Rodolfo GALDEANO CARRETERO (ed.), *Pere Gil i Estalella, Història moral de Cathalunya: Llibre segon de la Història cathalana*, Barcelona: Institut d'Estudis Catalans, 2017. In this work, Galdeano (p. lxxiv), using internal references from the other two parts, partially reconstructs the contents of the Ecclesiastical History.

[27] Among the precedents we can mention the *Historia natural y moral de las Indias* by José de Acosta (Seville, 1590, with a reedition in Barcelona the following year and the authorization of Gil himself), or the *Naturalis et moralis historia del regno Sardiniae* by Giovanni Arca

which made explicit the success and triumph of Catholicism throughout history and served as an implicit answer to the Protestant advance.[28]

The hagiographic notes we have preserved are composed of some 70 folios attached to the first volume devoted to the Geography of Catalonia.[29] They begin with an introductory chapter that includes his methodological principles, utilized by him and that must be utilized in general, when writing lives of saints; then he offers a list of these lives classified in three sections: lives of Catalan saints (fols 16^r–39^r), which includes twenty from different Catalan dioceses, particularly Barcelona; virtuous Catalan characters, not canonized (fols 40^r–46^v), which includes nine chapters; and a final section, numbered differently, that includes more than one hundred martyrs from all over the Iberian Peninsula (fols 1^r–25^v).[30] The narratives have different length and some of them are unfinished[31] or have only the chapter rubric.

We have no certainty about how the preserved lives of saints would have been integrated into the volumes. Judging by some references in the first volume, perhaps the section devoted to the "Vidas dels sants de Cathalunya que foren naturals o visqueren o moriren en ella, o las relíquias principals dels quals se troban en Cathalunya, extensament referidas",[32] would have been part of the third volume devoted to the ecclesiastical history of the land; on

---

(written between 1598 and 1604, which remained unpublished). While this historiographic model is used mostly for descriptions of the New World, Jesuits from different provinces proposed similar projects for their territories. (GALDEANO, "Historiografia catalana i model jesuític", *art. cit.* pp. 46, 50).

[28] Other Jesuits wrote works with a similar intention but a more universal approach, like Giovanni Botero—already as an ex-Jesuit—*Le relazioni universali* (published in several volumes at the end of the sixteenth century), later translated into Spanish by the Dominican Jaume Rebollosa, and printed in Barcelona (1603, 1610, etc.). Curiously, Botero began with a description of the Iberian Peninsula and the Principality of Catalonia, a land at the border of the heretic territory of Huguenot France (BETRÁN, "Culto y devoción en la Cataluña barroca", *art. cit.*, p. 97).

[29] Pere GIL, *Vides dels sants de Catalunya*, Biblioteca Pública Episcopal de Barcelona, MS 235. See a codicological description in FÀBREGA GRAU "El P. Pedro Gil", *art. cit.*, that includes a transcription of chapter 2 and the list of lives of saints contained therein.

[30] In a marginal note, it says that, before the section devoted to Spanish saints, there must be included another chapter also within a Spanish context: "Falta aquí c. 4, Dels primers bisbes que los apòstols sant Pere i sant Pau enviaren a Espanya, com està en lo lib. 3 de la Història Ecclesiàstica" ("Ch. 4 is missing to be devoted to the first bishops that apostles St Peter and St Paul sent to Spain, which is part of book 3 of the Ecclesiastial History") (GIL, *Vides dels sants de Catalunya, op. cit.*, "Sants d'Espanya", fol. 1^r). In fact in the manusucript the two previous folios are blank.

[31] Occasionaly he indicates in the margin that research must be done to find information, or some author must be consulted.

[32] "Lives of saints from Catalonia who were born or lived or died there or whose main relics are kept there", GIL, *Vides dels sants de Catalunya, op. cit.*, fol. 13^r.

the other hand, in the second volume, he also alludes to the existence of a fourth volume devoted exclusively to lives of saints.[33] Everything points to the fact that Pere Gil modified his original plan as he gathered more material and perhaps he considered these lives as sufficient to put them all together in a semi-independent volume: a fourth volume devoted to the Hispanic context in which Catalan martyrs had a relevant place. While it went beyond the thematic coherence of a Catalan hagiographic project by including Spanish saints in the third section,[34] the result would help the book's pastoral mission which was to be achieved with information and narratives on lives of saints revised critically that would withstand the discredit given to this topic by Protestants.

Gil's hagiographic compilation follows completely Trent's directives on this matter. Before the saints' lives, he mentions the spiritual benefits that come from reading them, and makes explicit the critical rigour used in the accounts. Because the beginning is missing, we ignore the content of the prologue and the benefits described in the first chapter,[35] but in any event its existence allows us to consider that the work follows the Catholic dogma regarding the debate on the cult of saints vs. the Protestant *solus Christus* and *sola fide*. In chapter 2, devoted to "Dels modos ab los quals se poden y deuen saber y escriurer las vidas dels sants ab certitut moral que tinga auctoritat",[36] Gil makes clear that the criteria he has used to legitimize his stories and avoid the inclusion of apocryphal contents are those also followed on other parts of Catholic Europe, and when he justifies the revision of these accounts he makes clear that refuting Protestants is one of the main motivations behind

---

[33] GALDEANO, *"Història moral de Cathalunya", op. cit.* pp. lxxii–lxxiii.

[34] Also at the end of volume II, devoted to the History of Catalonia, he includes some chapters that address other peninsular kingdoms (Asturias, León, Castile, Galicia, Navarra, Portugal...) (see GALDEANO, *"Història moral de Cathalunya", op. cit.* p. cii.), that is, he goes beyond the Catalan regional borders. It seems that his *modus operandi* is more inclusive than restrictive. The fact that this material has a different pagination can be seen as suggesting a different formal division for his material. Other books of saints also had different page numbers for each section, as is the case in Villegas's or in Domènec's.

[35] At the beginning of the second section he says: "En lo prescedent quadern, que és lo primer, se escriu lo pròlech y lo primer capítol: De las utilitats que resultan de legir las vidas dels sants (fol. 13^r); i també per donar pas al capítol segon: Declaradas en lo precedent capítol algunas de las moltas utilitats que resultan de la contínua y devota lliçó de las vidas dels sants [...]" (in the previous section, which is the first, there is a prologue and a first chapter: On the utility derived from reading lives of saints (fol. 13^r); and it also introduces the second chapter: The previous chapter referred some of the many benefits derived from the continuous and devote reading of lives of saints) (GIL, *Vides dels sants de Catalunya, op. cit.*, fol. 13^r).

[36] "The manners in which we can and must know and write the lives of saints with an authoritative moral certainty", GIL, *Vides dels sants de Catalunya, op. cit.*, fol. 13^r.

his work, because it is presence of apocryphal elements what had motivated their scorn about lives of saints:

> en lo present segon capítol tractem dels modos que en Roma, Itàlia, França, España y altres províncias de la cristiandat se tingueren y observaren per a dar auctoritat a las cosas que de las vidas y martyris y morts gloriosas y miracles dels sants havian en los setgles venidors de restar en memòria dels cristians; [...] los historiadors que en històrias dels sants, per affesió o pietat indiscreta, escriuen las cosas duptosas per certas, y fingen o atribueyxen miracles a alguns sants ab pochs fonaments y poca certitut dels miracles, cometen gran peccat y gran sacrilegi, y fan més dany a la Iglésia santa del que·s pensan, per donar occasió als heretges de burlar-se de las històrias dels sants quant troban en ellas las cosas incertas o no verdaderes; com sabem per relació verdadera que alguns malvats heretges de Alemanya, Inglaterra y altres parts han fet libres y escrit contra las vidas compostas per alguns catòlichs de alguns sants, en los quals trobavan cosas falsas o apòcrifas o incertas o duptosas [...][37]

He also reminds us that bishops have the pastoral responsibility to watch over the revision of each diocese's hagiography to preserve this tradition from the mockery and slander of heretics.[38]

This desire to avoid scorn and slander is an argument we find explicitly indicated in the prologues of the main Catholic books of saints, such as the prefaces to Lippomano's and Surius' works, or in Villegas',[39] what bespeaks of the combative character of the first post-Tridentine books of saints, which, in the case of Gil, also coincides with his own convictions, for he had expressed a desire to engage actively in the ideological struggle to answer the Protestants' postulates.[40]

The methodological criteria he proposes to revise the lives of saints are in full agreement with those of other previous and contemporary

---

[37] "In the current second chapter we will study how Rome, Italy, France, Spain and other Christian provinces acted with regard to giving authority to how the things pertaining to the lives, martyrdoms, glorious deaths and miracles of saints would be kept in the memory of Christians in the centuries to come; ... historians who (because of partisanship or indiscreet piety) consider dubious things as true in the lives of saints, and who fake and attribute miracles to saints with little foundation and little certitude about their miracles, they commit a great sin and sacrilege and harm the church more than they think, for they give heretics occasion to mock lives of saints when they find in them uncertain or false things, as we know from some books that some evil heretics from Germany, England and elsewhere have written against the lives of saints composed by some Catholics where they found false or apocryphal or uncertain or dubious things", GIL, *Vides dels sants de Catalunya, op. cit.*, fol. 13^r.
[38] GIL, *Vides dels sants de Catalunya, op. cit.*, fols 13^r–13^v.
[39] See these statements in BAÑOS, "Lanzarían grandes carcajadas", *art. cit.* pp. 442, 445, 447.
[40] Gil, in 1582, had communicated to the provincial of his order his desire to go to Germany or France to fight the heresy (GALDEANO, "Historiografia catalana i model jesuític", *art. cit.* p. 43).

Counter-Reformation hagiographers, and can be seen in some of the arguments he poses to justify the need for rigour and authority, for we can read them *mutatis mutandi* in the prologues to other books of saints, such as allusions to the *Gelasian Decree* and to Pope Clement's recommendations, which we can find in the prologues written by Villegas and Ribadeneira. Gil, in order to expurgate these lives of apocryphal elements and endow them with authority and historical accuracy, enumerates seven principles on which every hagiographic text must be based: on the accounts of martyrs' lives written by the notaries of the primitive church; on the processes to determine the martyrdom; on the writings of the doctors of the Church; on the breviaries, missals and offices of churches; on the old martyrologies and books of saints that have great reputation; on the ecclesiastical tradition; and on the papal bulls of canonization and their respective processes.[41]

What separates Gil's exposition from the statements of other vernacular books of saints is its comprehensiveness and systematicity in the exposition of these arguments; perhaps we could wander whether they respond to a didactic purpose, for despite representing conventional erudition, they want to be also intelligible.[42] In addition, he offers some argument we do not find in other books of saints in his sixth criterion, "the conformity of the Churches in the lives of the saints", regarding the value of some devotions even if they are not supported by any *serious* or renowned author. Gil states that if they are deeply-rooted beliefs which have been accepted for a long time by local Churches, its validity can be legitimized; an argument which is crucial to approve some devotions of local saints, consecrated places related to them or some relics.

That is precisely the criterion applied, for instance, to validate the existence of some devotions, such as those associated to the relics of the so-called "holy corpse" of "the child of the monastery of Cluny of Sant Pere de Casserres" (Vic);[43] regarding this story, he states that he has not found any written testimony and he only has the oral account of the local inhabitants.[44]

---

[41] We can read an exposition of the criteria in FÀBREGA GRAU, "El P. Pedro Gil", *art. cit.* pp. 12–14.
[42] We can remember that Gil was Master of Theology in the Jesuit College for 20 years, and director on several occasions of the College at Betlem.
[43] In 1573, this monastery was joined to the College at Betlem in Barcelona as a source of revenue for its keeping. It is not strange that Gil, as director, would be interested in legitimizing the relics venerated there.
[44] "He-la oÿda de personas vellas naturals de aquella terra de Osona, <o que habitavan> cerca del monestir, las quals la referian per tradició y memòria de altras personas" ("I have heard it from old inhabitants of Osona, or those who lived next to the monastery, and who had heard it as memory and tradition from other people") (GIL, *Sants de Catalunya, op. cit.*, fol. 44^v).

However, beyond concrete details, he thinks it must be true that something miraculous happened to the child and it was related to the foundation of the monastery, which is the reason that his relics had been preserved there.

In general, though, he wants to offer legitimacy to the hagiographies he has compiled regarding the information found in the main sources, which he quotes carefully. Among his sources, we can mention traditional martyrologies and references to semi-contemporary historians like the Hieronymite Ambrosio de Morales. Consequently, some *new* narratives only add precisions on some anecdotes or make clear some information about the saints' biographies (place of birth, date of birth, etc.); others, though, differ greatly from previous versions.[45] Undoubtedly one of Gil's main characteristics is that he is not just a compiler but on many occasions, particularly in the first two sections devoted to Catalan devotions, he has compared different testimonies for each case. First, he usually offers a summary of all the information found in the renowned sources; but if there are discrepancies among them, he usually takes the side of the most truthful or best founded. In other cases, when the information is confusing or unknown, he offers his own opinion based on the different hagiographic information he has found:

> Destos y altres testimonis de historiadors se trau certament que estos sinc sants moriren en España [...], però no señalan ni declaran la província de España en la qual patiren martyri, ni lo any en lo qual moriren. Yo he feta alguna diligència acerca de assò, y considerades algunes circumstàncies (salvo sempre millor parer), me he persuadit que patiren martyri en Cataluña, y si bé no·m determine particularment en la vila o ciutat, però crec y tinc per a mi que patiren en Clobliure, o Rosas, o Empúrias o Gerona, o un lloc per allí cerca de aquestos. Per lo qual me mouen les següents rahons [...][46]

After each life, he usually offers some information on the saint's relics, or devotions related to his cult, and he also adds some facts relevant for encouraging that cult. For instance, after talking about the life and relics of St Maginus

---

[45] It could be easily proven with the story about St Severus, already included in the 1524 edition of the *Flos sanctorum*; in it there are anecdotes about the lives of bishops Severus of Barcelona and Severus of Ravenna, while in Gil's narrative the live of the Catalan bishop has been purged of extraneous episodes. See the study of this case in Carme Arronis Llopis, "Sever de Barcelona en la primera hagiografia reformada", *Specula. Revista de humanidades y espiritualidad* 1 (2021), 153–82.

[46] "It can be deduced from these and other testimonies of historians that these five saints died in Spain... although it is not mentioned in which region they suffered martyrdom not the year in which they died. I have strived to find information and considering some circumstances I am persuaded to think that they were killed in Catalonia, and while I am not certain about the place, I believe it was either Cotlliure or Roses or Empúries or Girona or any other place near these. And the reasons are...", Gil, *Sants de Catalunya, op. cit.*, fol. 26ᵛ.

of Tarragona, as well as the spring related to his martyrdom, he adds the following to contribute to his devotion among the faithful of Barcelona:

> En Barcelona y ha un monestir de monjas nomenat dels Àngels, en lo qual y ha una capella y altar de sant Magí, y las monjas del dit monestir acostuman entre any o casi tot lo any, tenir aygua guardada <de la font> de sant Magí per als malalts.[47]

Particularly interesting is the chapter devoted to Sant Pacià and the unfruitful search for his relics in which he participated at the request of bishop Lloris, what allows him to offer his first-hand testimony of why they were considered spurious: "Digué lo senyor bisbe a mi, Pere Gil, que yo·ls tragués [els óssos]. Fou posada una taula ab una tovalla de altar, y yo·ls traguí tots ab mes proprias mans sens deyxar res en dita cayxa".[48]

In some cases, the chapters are unfinished and we only have the chapter title that offers information about their content. Particularly incomplete is the second section devoted to "hòmens il·lustres de Cathalunya en sanctedat de vida y glòria de miracles, los <quals> no són sants canonizats per la Iglésia, ni escrits en los martyrologis, però són tinguts y reverenciats com a sants en molts llochs de Cathalunya".[49] It is composed by only nine narratives, and four of them only include the title with a blank space to be filled in later. Regarding the other five, three of them are written in Latin (according to Gil they were taken from Franciscan Francisco Gonzaga's chronicle), and only two are original and written in Catalan (they are devoted to Olegarius, bishop of Barcelona, and to the child's relics in the monastery of Sant Pere de Casserres de Vic). We should not be surprised by a section devoted to the will of legitimizing devotions that while not having been recognized yet, they have moved people's piety or have served as an example. Also Villegas' third volume includes an addition with lives of "men illustrious in virtue".[50] Once again, there is an agreement between Gil's doctrinal interests and those of

---

[47] "In Barcelona there is a monastery of nuns called Dels Àngels in which there is a chapel and altar of sant Magí, and during the year or almost all the year these nuns keep there some water of sant Magí's spring to cure the sick", GIL, *Sants de Catalunya, op. cit.*, fol. 17ᵛ.

[48] "The bishop ordered me, Pere Gil, to bring the bones. A table was covered with an altar mantel, and I put them all by my own hand, without leaving nothing in the box", GIL, *Sants de Catalunya, op. cit.*, fol. 30ᵛ.

[49] "Catalans illustrious for their sanctity of life and glorious miracles who have not been canonized nor included in martyrologies but are considered as saints and revered in many places in Catalonia", GIL, *Vides dels sants de Catalunya, op. cit.*, fol. 40ʳ.

[50] Alonso de VILLEGAS, *Flos Sanctorum: Tercera parte y Historia general en que se escriven las vidas de sanctos extravagantes y de varones illustres en virtud*, Toledo: Juan and Pedro Rodríguez, 1588, "Addición a la tercera parte del Flos sanctorum: en que se ponen vidas de varones illustres los quales, aunque no estan canonizados, mas piadosamente se cree dellos que gozan

other contemporary authors like Villegas and Ribadeneira, for all of them are inclined to include diverse materials in order to enlarge their compilations with the intention of legitimizing the numerous pious devotions that existed everywhere.

Pere Gil, then, while paying particular attention to Catalan saints, and especially to those of the diocese of Barcelona and its devotions, was not restricted geographically but included information about other peninsular martyrs, making clear on many occasions the inaccurate details about them transmitted by other historians. For him it was about revising the hagiographic material and offering both religious and lay people narratives that were updated and revised according to the best authors, and he did not hesitate to add a section of foreign saints ("from other provinces of Spain"), because his interest about local saints in the first two sections of the book was not exclusive. In his hagiographic work there are two tendencies at once: on one hand, a will to legitimize, revise and disseminate the cult of local saints understood as the exceptional heritage of the sacred history of the land and a demonstration of its Catholic roots; on the other, the need to pay attention to the emergency of the Catholic task to revise and compile lives of saints, regardless of their origin. Both tendencies contribute to the extolling of the Catholic cause by improving the narratives' quality and adding more instances to the list, what contributed indirectly to counteracting the expansion of the *heresy*.

The Catalan Book of Saints of the Dominican Antoni Vicenç Domènec

While the Jesuits had a relevant role in revising hagiographic material after Trent, they were not the only religious order to do so.[51] Others, like the Orders of Preachers, which had been in charge traditionally of compiling hagiographic narratives and accounts of the illustrious men of the order that were considered exemplary, continued with this task, putting now a special emphasis on the application of criteria of authority and historical reliability that the topic required.[52] In Spain, a clear example was the *Historia ecclesiástica, y flores de santos de España*, by Basque Dominican Juan de Marieta (Cuenca:

---

de Dios, por aver sido sus vidas famosas en virtudes, según lo coligió de auctores graves, y fidedignos el maestro Alonso de Villegas", Barcelona: Jerònim Genovés i Jaume Cendrat, 1588.
[51] See different examples in Sofia BOESCH-GAJANO & Raimondo MICHETTI, *Europa Sacra. Raccolte agiografiche e identità politiche in Europa fra Medioevo ed Età Moderna*, Roma: Carocchi, 2002.
[52] In SOBRAL's chapter in this same volume, we are reminded of the pastoral work developed by the Preachers Order through hagiographic compilations since the thirteenth century.

1594),[53] which enjoyed an important editorial success and had a prologue written by Villegas himself. Marieta contributed to this task by paying exclusive attention to the Spanish context. Even more restricted geographically was the Dominican Antoni Vicenç Domènec, who paid only attention to the devotions of the Catalan Principality: *Historia general de los santos y varones ilustres en santidad del Principado de Cataluña*, published in Barcelona in 1602 and reprinted in Girona in 1630.[54]

It is interesting to mention that he was born at Girona and became a Dominican priest at the convent of Santa Caterina de Barcelona in 1580, the same convent where Pere Coll had been director a few years before, the copy-editor of the 1575 *Flos sanctorum*. Perhaps we can assume in him a formation that paid attention to revising hagiographical material, the need to gather materials to legitimizing devotions and a desire to rescue them from what he considers "so unfair oblivion". The first news we have about his life come curiously from the chapter added to the beginning of the second edition of his book of saints and which is in itself a sort of hagiography of the author.[55] Domènec, according to this, was a model of virtue and, among other graces, it was attributed to him (while he was still alive) a miraculous power to cure the sick. In fact, when he died in 1607, his fame of sanctity was such that his burial was delayed three days because of the number of devotees who came to kiss and farewell the friar.[56] However, in the narrative there are only brief mentions to his work as compiler and what is highlighted it is his effort to gather the information.

Domènec's work aimed at being a comprehensive compilation of Catalan saints' lives from the first martyrdoms to almost contemporary virtuous men. His work is divided into two books, a first (fols 1^r–124^r) organized according to the festivities of the calendar,[57] devoted to canonized saints; and a second (fols 1^r–97^r) devoted to illustrious men in sanctity who had not been

---

[53] Juan de MARIETA, *Historia eclesiastica y flores de santos de España: en la que se trata de todos los santos mártires que ha avido en ella desde los tiempos de los apóstoles hasta aora y de los santos confesores, pontífices y no pontífices del mismo tiempo*, Cuenca: Juan de Masselin, 1594.

[54] Antoni Vicenç DOMÈNEC, *Historia general de los santos y varones ilustres en santidad del Principado de Cataluña*, Barcelona: Gabriel Graells i Giraldo Dòtil, 1602.

[55] "Vida y costumbres del venerable padre fray Antonio Vicente Domènec, de la sagrada religión de Predicadores", en Antoni Vicenç DOMÈNEC, *Historia general de los santos y varones ilustres en santidad del Principado de Cataluña*, Girona: Gaspar Garrich, 1630, no p. As we are told, the information comes from the "procés autèntic" (an authentic process) kept at the ecclesiastical court in Girona [p. 1].

[56] Fèlix TORRES AMAT also includes these data, *Memorias para ayudar a formar un diccionario critico de los escritores catalanes y dar alguna idea de la antigua y moderna literatura de Cataluña*, Barcelona: Imprenta de J. Verdaguer, 1836, p. 214.

[57] At the beginning of the work, however, there is a table of the lives included in the compilation listed by dioceses, what allows us to see the total number for each of them.

canonized,[58] which includes more than 40 lives organized according to monastic orders or by dioceses (in the case of bishops). In the work of Pere Gil (and Villegas), there was a similar section—although very brief and without any type of organizing principle—and in fact almost all the instances selected by the Catalan Jesuit are also part of Domènec's work,[59] what proves that these devotions were deeply rooted and shows identical interest in legitimizing these virtuous models that the faithful perceived as closer to them.[60]

Domènec's intention is rather clear: to unequivocally indicate the large number of saints with whom God blessed the land, which, according to him, made it special, although not well known to others. In fact, this is the reason he provides for having written the work in Spanish: to give it a greater dissemination beyond the borders of the Principality, although he claimed to write it in a Spanish that could be understood by the natives.[61]

Despite the linguistic change, Domènec's work is full of patriotism, as it happened with the historiographic discourse pronounced by Onofre Manescal in the cathedral of Barcelona in 1597,[62] and that was also printed, like Domènec's work, en 1602.[63] Both authors vindicate the need to make known the Catalan sacred heritage, which they considered little known and recognized. Some scholars, like Valsalobre or Torres,[64] have seen in Domènec's book of saints a response to Juan de Marieta, considering the little attention paid by the Basque author to Catalan devotions.[65] The Catalan Dominican does not make explicit if his work responds to anything, either to Marieta's work—he never refers to it—or to other Spanish books of saints, despite the fact that the seven years he claims to have devoted to his work are precisely the time elapsed after the printing of the Basque's *Historia*. However, it seems that his vindication is general and that with his effort he wanted to contribute

---

[58] DOMÈNEC, *Historia general de los santos, op. cit.*, "Prólogo al lector".
[59] Exceptions to this are the narrative on the relics of the "infant" of the monastery of St Pere de Casserres in Vic (fols 44ʳ-44ᵛ), who was related to the Jesuit College in Barcelona, and that of the Beatus from Organyà of the Convent of the Avellanes of Lleida, of which we only have the rubric title (fol. 46ʳ).
[60] On the devotion for these exemplary models of virtue, who were closer to the readers, see Fernando BAÑOS in this book.
[61] DOMÈNEC, *Historia general de los santos, op. cit.*, "Prólogo al lector".
[62] VALSALOBRE, "Elements per a una Catalunya sacra", *art. cit.*, p. 112.
[63] See note 18.
[64] VALSALOBRE, "Elements per a una Catalunya sacra", *art. cit.*, p. 112, and TORRES, "La ciutat dels sants", *art. cit.*, pp. 80-81.
[65] Marieta includes slightly more than a dozen devotions, which he considered the main ones: Pacian, Severus, Cucuphas, Matrona and Eulalia of Barcelona; Fructuosus and Thecla of Tarragona; Felix and Narcissus of Girona; Ot, Ermengol, and Justus of Urgell, Anastasius of Lleida, etc.

to the common Catholic cause. In fact, when in his prologue he describes the different types of lives of saints included in his work, he says that occasionally he has not included some because they are already included in the *flos sanctorum*, which seems to refer to Villegas's work,[66] and only includes new data about them. That is, he wants to complete already-existing information.[67]

On the other hand, it has not been mentioned that Domènec, like Gil and their previous models, explains his book as part of the need to combat and refute the heretics, and these are in fact the arguments with which he begins his prologue to the reader when justifying the need for his work:

> Quien cosiderare el bárbaro furor con que los hereges de nuestros tiempos se han atrevido a las reliquias de los gloriosos santos en la mísera Alemaña, infelice Inglaterra, y nuestra vezina Francia, no necessitará de que le acumule largas razones en este prólogo para declarar los motivos que pudo tener un español y religioso de la orden de Santo Domingo para dar defendidas del injusto olvido las santas memorias de los que, viviendo y muertos, tanto illustran su patria. Que, amigo lector, viendo a Dios perseguido y blasfemado en sus santos, ¿quién, después de dirretido en lágrimas de sentimiento, revestido de fortaleza del cielo, no se bolverá un fiero león de mança paloma por estarle al lado y en tan importante ocasión defenderle?[68]

In addition, he also reminds us of the benefits of reading lives of saints and the need for their intercession, thus implicitly refuting the Protestants' arguments. He also includes other reasons utilized by Catholic theologians, such as appealing to biblical authority, particularly referring to the biblical verses they saw as proof of the saints' intercession in the debate against the Protestants.[69] That is, Domènec's work, like Gil's, has a latent combative spirit that characterizes the first generation of hagiographers.

---

[66] He explicitly refers to the *Flos sanctorum* several times, so that the reader can find there complementary information.

[67] In Domènec's "hagiography", it is highlighted that his devotion for saints was such that he would have liked to complete his field work with a trip to the Principality of Catalonia to find information about hermitages and devotional houses, and he would have liked to do something similar in France and Italy ("Vida y costumbres del venerable", *op. cit.*, [p. 3]).

[68] "Whoever considers the deranged fury with which heretics have nowadays attacked the relics of glorious saints in miserable Germany and unhappy England and our neighbor France, does not need long explanations in my prologue about the motivations of a Spaniard and member of the Order of St Domingo to defend from unjust oblivion the holy memory of those who dead and alive illuminate their land. For, my reader friend, after seing God persecuted and blasphemed in the person of his saints, who won't turn—melting with painful tears and endowed with strength from heaven—from meek dove into a lion so that he could be by His side and defend Him in such important occasion", DOMÈNEC, *Historia general de los santos, op. cit.*, "Prólogo al lector".

[69] On this controversy, see the chapter by María José VEGA in this book.

Like Pere Gil, Domènec also revised and completed previous materials and those from recognized sources with those from his own research. But Domènec wants a comprehensiveness that we do not see in the Jesuit, something that took him to travel through Catalonia several times during seven years to explore archives in all the dioceses:[70]

> por enterarme de la verdad [...], porque no se me passase cosa por alto, inquiriendo escripturas antigas de mano por los archivos de las yglésias, monasterios, ciudades, villas y lugares; autos de dotaciones de monasterios, de catedrales, episcopologios deste Principado; y muy particulares escripturas antigas del Archivo Real de Barcelona; de todo lo qual he sacado gran parte de mi *Historia*, sin fiarme sino de solo lo que desta suerte he visto por mis ojos, allende de algunas particulares vidas que he sacado de autores graves, como Laurencio Surio, San Antonino de Florencia, San Gregorio Turonense, Vincencio Valvacense, César Baronio, Lipomano y otros muchos.[71]

His field research explains that we find in the book many local and conventual lives with little or scarce information about them. Domènec is cautious about them and regrets the little diligence shown by *old authors* when keeping memory of them. For instance, regarding St Nazarius, whose relics were kept at the Monastery of Sant Miquel de Cuixà, he says that we do not know much about him, not even his Order, because of the negligence of old authors;[72] or about St Calamanda Virgin, from Calaf, about whom nothing is clear: "De dónde fue natural santa Calamanda, ni qué martyrio padeció, no lo he podido averiguar, por lo qual no puedo dexar de añadir un toque a las quexas del antigo descuido, tantas vezes repetidas en esta *Historia*".[73] His compilation is thus a very personal work, interspersed frequently with comments about the material he has gathered.

Regarding lives from recognized authorities, he mentions his sources at the beginning. Comparing with other contemporary hagiographers, we could remark on his use of medieval Dominican authors such as Anthony of

---

[70] This effort is highlighted in the books's authorization by his superior, Gaspar de Vió, prior of the convent of Santa Caterina, as a guarantee of the authenticity of the informations therein contained.

[71] "To know the truth...because I did not want to have anything amiss, I searched through old manuscripts in churches, monasteries, cities, villages, and lists of bishops of this Principality, and specially through the old writings of the Royal Archive of Barcelona, only trusting in what I saw myself, besides some lives I took from renowned authors such as Laurentius Surius, St Anthony of Florence, St Gregory of Tours, Vincentius Valvasensis, Cesare Baronio, Lipomanus and many others", DOMÈNEC, *Historia general de los santos, op. cit.*, "Prólogo al lector".

[72] DOMÈNEC, *Historia general de los santos, op. cit.*, "Libro primero", fol. 2ᵛ.

[73] "Where was St Calamanda born I was not able to find out, and therefore I have to complain about the old negligence, so many times mentioned in this History", DOMÈNEC, *Historia general de los santos, op. cit.*, "Libro primero", fol. 12ʳ.

Florence or Vincent of Beauvais; and there are also frequent mentions to the *flos sanctorum* by Petrus de Natalibus (very discredited in the seventeenth century by the Bollandists for his scarce hagiographic value). Consequently, it frequently happens that he reproduces verbatim the narratives from medieval sources, although with the care to always indicate them. For instance, that is the case of his acount of Maginus of Tarragona (fols 78ᵛ–80ʳ). He begins the episode mentioning his sources, which in this case are St Jerome, Cesare Baronio, the Roman Martyrology and the 1575 Catalan *Flos sanctorum*, as well as a booklet with his life printed in Barcelona in 1595 with license, and a book of "authentic" miracles kept at the St Maginus' sanctuary. Nevertheless, the resulting narrative is the same as what is included in the 1575 text (and which had already been included in the 1547 edition), translated *ad pedem litterae*. That is, there are no substantial changes in content, although the discursive strategies used in the story offer an impression of legitimacy that makes it different from previous compilations.

Although he does not explicitly mention the criteria used by devout tradition to legitimize devotions—as Pere Gil does—he does so when confirming local venerations about which there is no written testimony. That is the case, for instance, about the cult in the Vic region of St Sigismund, son of the king of Burgundy, about whom he says:

> La venida de san Sigismundo a España no la escriven San Gregorio Turonense, ni san Antonino, ni otros historiadores franceses o de otras naciones. Pero tampoco no lo niegan, y assí no ay que dudar de una tradición tan grande como tenemos desto.[74]

Even more, he refers some devotions about the Burgundian saint, as the one that considered him a protector against fever, and in order to legitimize it he has no doubt to offer as evidence his own personal experience:[75]

> dize Zacharías, abreviador de Surio, que los que tienen calenturas, si hazen dezir una missa a honra deste santo, luego son curados. Esto (a lo que se cree), se ha de entender en el lugar de su sepultura y no siempre, sino ordinariamente y casi siempre. [...] Haze grande fiesta en este día [...] en su

---

[74] "The arrival of St Sigismund to Spain does not appear in St Gregory of Tours, St Anthony or other French authors or from other countries. But they do not deny it either, therefore we should not doubt about the great tradition we have about it", DOMÈNEC, *Historia general de los santos, op. cit.*, "Libro primero", fol. 38ʳ.

[75] However, the reform of the Missal of 1570 had eliminated some heterodoxical practises related to masses offered to saints, as those celebrated in the diocese of Barcelona to St Sigismund for the cure of fever (see GELABERTÓ VILAGRAN, *La palabra del predicador, op. cit.*, pp. 306, 308). Also in the life of Domènec, included in the second edition of the book of saints, he reflects about this episode ("Vida y costumbres del venerable", *op. cit.*, [p. 1]).

yglesia de Villadrau, en el obispado de Vique, donde (como tenemos dicho) hizo vida heremítica. En esta capilla de Villadrau a hecho el santo muchos milagros, pero por negligència grande de los padres antigos ay poca memoria dellos. Acuerdome aver oydo de mi madre que, siendo yo pequeño estava quebrado, y ella me encomendó a este bienaventurado rey haziendo cierto voto, y que presto quedé libre de aquella enfermedad, de tal suerte que por la misericòrdia de Dios nunca la he tenido después.[76]

Another particularity of Domènec's compilation is the blurry boundaries he established between hagiography and local history, something that is not just peculiar about his work.[77] Thus, he includes in the first book two chapters devoted to the conquest of Girona by Charlemagne, a story which, we are told, was included in the sermons preached in the See of Girona the second Sunday of Lent.[78] Domènec uses this occasion to provide proofs of the participation of the emperor in the conquest, doubted by some historians who, according to the Dominican, were wrong.[79] He also devotes a chapter to the life of the "most devoted" Charlemagne, "great servant of God", canonized by Antipope Paschal III in the twelfth century and worshipped as such in many German regions.[80] For Domènec, the sanctity of the emperor is a proven fact and he offers several arguments accordingly.[81] Perhaps his insistence in establishing links between the Catalan counts and the French dynasty was due to an attempt to endow Catalan history with an aura of sanctity. Towards the end of the second book, he also devotes a chapter to the "His Serene Highness and devoted Prince" Ramon Berenguer IV,[82] about whom he laments

---

[76] "Zachary, abridger of Surius, says that those suffering from fever, if they request a mass to be said for this saint, are immediately cured. This is believed to happen at the place where he is buried, and not always, but almost...There is a great festivity on his day...at the church of Viladrau, in the bishopric of Vic, where (as we have said) he lived as a hermit. In this chapel, he has performed many miracles, but the great negligence of the old fathers did not keep a memory of them. I remember having heard my mother that I was sick as a child, and she commended me to this saintly king making a promise to him and I immediately got well, so that I have not suffered this dissease ever since", DOMÈNEC, *Historia general de los santos, op. cit.*, "Libro primero", fol. 40r.

[77] We have seen the reverse example in other historical works such as Jorba's or Manescal's, that we have mentioned before, which include the sacred history of the territory as an inherent part of history. And it is very evident that the difference between the two was rather blurry at the time (Simon DITCHFIELD, "Historia Sacra between Local and Universal Church", in *Europa Sacra. Raccolte agiografiche e identità politiche in Europa fra Medioevo ed Età Moderna*, ed. by Sofia Boesch-Gajano & Raimondo Michetti, Roma: Carocchi, 2002, 405–09).

[78] DOMÈNEC, *Historia general de los santos, op. cit.*, "Libro primero", fols 21r–24r.

[79] DOMÈNEC, *Historia general de los santos, op. cit.*, "Libro primero", fol. 21v.

[80] DOMÈNEC, *Historia general de los santos, op. cit.*, "Libro primero", fols 8v–11r.

[81] DOMÈNEC, *Historia general de los santos, op. cit.*, "Libro primero", fols 10v–11r.

[82] DOMÈNEC, *Historia general de los santos, op. cit.*, "Libro segundo", fols 89v–93v.

that there has been no process to canonize him on account of the miracles attributed to him, although "han sido tan descuydados los escriptores antigos en escrivirlos, que quieren que sus maravillas las entendamos el día del juyzio, y no agora".[83]

Domènec's work, for all these reasons, happens to be a very interesting compilation. On one hand, he wants to apply the critical method required of all hagiographic material, that he mainly understands as finding proofs in recognized sources; but sometimes, these sources have authority for him only because they are old—very old manuscripts, as he says sometimes.[84] On the other hand, his main objective is to gather all the information he has amassed, putting it in writing before it is lost forever, and this in practice means that much of that information is incomplete or confusing. His real goal is not to disqualify and exclude but to preserve and keep any news regarding the existing devotions of the Principality.

Tentative Conclusion

Even though in the post-Tridentine Catalan context there was no general reformed book of saints equivalent to Villegas's or Ribadeneira's Spanish compilations, this does not mean that there were not similar efforts to update and revise hagiographic materials with the standards demanded by the Catholic Church. On the contrary, the application of Trent's decrees was done quickly by Catalan bishops, and this promoted a climate favorable to extolling the most deeply-rooted devotions. In fact, before the publication of reformed Spanish books of saints, a new edition of the Catalan *flos sanctorum* was published in Barcelona in 1575, copy-edited by a prestigious Dominican theologian, but this edition did not solve the textual problems of a medieval compilation which in fact would not be published again.

In particular the overwhelming success throughout the Peninsula of Villegas's *Flos sanctorum*, in the last two decades of the sixteenth century, and the relative ease with which a well-educated Catalan reader could read it, made it unnecessary, at least at first, to write other reformed books of saints in Catalan. However, the need to preserve, revise and legitimize the wealth of existing devotions that had not been part of these reformed compilations was soon perceived. And even Villegas himself had to publish additional volumes to enlarge the initial material and thus reflect the multiplicity of venerations that existed.

---

[83] "Ancient writers have been so negligent putting them in writing that maybe they wanted us to know about them on Judgement Day and not now", DOMÈNEC, *Historia general de los santos, op. cit.*, "Libro segundo", fol. 93ᵛ.
[84] DOMÈNEC, *Historia general de los santos, op. cit.*, "Libro segundo", fol. 2ʳ.

The efforts of Catalan compilers of the end of the sixteenth century focused mostly on hagiographic stories close to them that had received not much attention. In a markedly confessional context, local hagiography was understood as an exceptional heritage of the local sacred history, a sign of distinction among the different Catholic territories. This local sacred history, construed on the blood spilled by the first Christian martyrs, was an essential part of the historical heritage of people, as were their beliefs and devotions, and the richer this was the prouder the citizens were, for it was proof that God had favored that territory in a particular manner with his grace as a bastion of Christendom, and now it could be understood as evidence (as it had been in the past) that the land was free of heretics.

The first post-Tridentine hagiographic productions were characterized by the debates between Catholics and Protestants regarding the cult of saints, and were produced under the urgency to refute them. Precisely Gil's and Domènec's works begin underlining the need to revise hagiographic material to refute Protestants, who had insulted and mocked the lives of saints, pointing to the little quality and *veracity* of many pious writings. This intention is also what lies behind the books by Pere Gil and Antoni Vicenç Domènec, although their respective purposes are slightly different. In Gil's notes there are no geographical limits for his revision of material—the main goal of his task—and for this reason he also includes a section devoted to lives of saints from other Spanish kingdoms. In Domènec's work, on the other hand, the goal was to preserve comprehensively as many facts as possible about Catalan saints, relics and devotions. The Jesuit's work is based primarily in using sources, such as hagiographers and historians. The Dominican's is reinforced with a comprehensive archival research throughout the Principality. Both faced similar problems: contradictory information, scarce and incomplete facts, absence of written documents about some devote traditions, etc., but these inconveniences do not reduce the interest these compilations have for us. On the contrary, they allow us to observe the effort of the first post-Tridentine hagiographers to legitimize their own devout material and to endow the already-known information with the discursive strategies that could substantiate their authenticity.

The goal of this first generation of Catalan hagiographers working under the post-Tridentine directives is not really very different from other Catholic hagiographers: they wanted to preserve the tradition of the cult of saints, secure the worship of relics and, as a result, contribute to refute with their effort Protestant criticism.

Nota, pio leitor…

The Hagiographical Critical Discourse in 1567

Cristina SOBRAL
(Universidade de Lisboa, Portugal)

Robert Birely defines the historical significance of the Council of Trent as twofold: "First, it clarified Catholic teaching on most doctrines contested by the Protestants, and secondly, it put forth a series of reforms that aimed not only at the elimination of abuses but at a renewed pastoral programme that placed the Bishop and the parish Priest at the centre of the church's mission".[1] This pastoral program counts on the proper formation of the bishop and his clergy, who are responsible for training the faithful. To this end, diocesan seminaries are created and the bishops are obliged to reside in their diocese, constituting an example of frugal and poor life. Thus formed, virtuous and properly indoctrinated, the prelate and the parish priest will ensure pastoral effectiveness and will be able to show the faithful other models of behavior that the Christian tradition offers and whose Lutheran contestation Trento refutes. In fact, the Council decisively clarified the controversy about the cult of saints, recognizing its pedagogical potential, following medieval tradition. It was established that the invocation of the saints is good and useful to achieve the benefits of God[2] and the clergy, who is in charge of teaching,

---

[1] Robert BIRELEY, "Redefining Catholicism: Trent and beyond", in *The Cambridge History of Christianity. 6. Reform and Expansion 1500–1660*, ed. by R. Po-Chia Hsia, Cambridge: Cambridge University Press, 2008, pp. 145–61 (p. 148).
[2] *O Sacrosanto, e Ecumenico Concilio de Trento em Latim, e Portuguez*, 2 vols, Lisboa: Francisco Luiz Ameno, 1781, II, p. 149.

Hispanic Hagiography in the Critical Context of the Reformation, ed. by Fernando Baños Vallejo, Hagiologia, 19 (Turnhout, 2022), pp. 215–250.
© BREPOLS PUBLISHERS   DOI 10.1484/M.HAG-EB.5.131996

must diligently instruct the faithful about the intercession of the saints, their invocation, veneration of relics and legitimate use of images.[3] The examples of the saints therefore continue to offer material for preaching, because they inspire a desire to emulate them.[4] But their legitimacy depends on the authenticity of the cults, which must be monitored, prohibiting the exhibition of unusual images and rejecting new miracles or new relics that have not been validated by the bishop.

The Portuguese Dominican Bartolomeu dos Mártires (1514–1590), Archbishop of Braga, participated in the third period of the Tridentine reunions (1562–1563), advocating that certain virtues should be required of bishops,[5] whose ideal portrait he drew in his *Stimulus Pastorum*,[6] which deserved the acceptance of Saint Carlos Borromeu and the Council Fathers and inspired the approval of concrete measures on the reduction of ecclesiastical benefits, the obligation to reside in the diocese and the creation of diocesan seminaries. Back in his diocese, Fr. Bartolomeu carried out a program of reform in all areas of Christian life[7] which had as visible lines the creation of the first diocesan seminary in 1572[8] and a series of publications almost immediately upon his arrival in Portugal: a new *Cathecismo ou doutrina christãa & praticas spirituaes* (Braga, António de Mariz, 1564),[9] a *Summa caietana tresladada em portugues*, (Braga, António de Mariz, 1565) and the legendary *Historia das vidas & feitos heroicos & obras insignes dos sanctos* (Braga, António de Mariz, 1567). For the last two publications he had the collaboration of Diogo do

---

[3] *O Sacrosanto, e Ecumenico Concilio, op. cit.*, II, p. 347; Hubert JEDIN, *História del Concílio de Trento. 4. Tercer periodo: conclusion, vol. 2: Superación de la crisis. Conclusión y ratificación*, Pamplona: Universidad de Navarra, 1981, p. 280.

[4] *O Sacrosanto, e Ecumenico Concilio, op. cit.*, II, p. 353; JEDIN, *História del Concílio, op. cit.*, pp. 279-80.

[5] JEDIN, *História del Concílio, op. cit.*, pp. 64–65, 74, 107, 130–31, 220, 235, 261, 272, 274, 292; David Sampaio BARBOSA, "Portugal em Trento: uma presença discreta", *Lusitania Sacra*, 3 (1991), 11–38 (pp. 33–38).

[6] Bartolomeu dos Mártires, *Estímulo de Pastores*, Braga: Edição do Movimento Bartolomeano, 1981. About this work see David Sampaio BARBOSA, "*Stimulus Pastorum*: texto e contexto de uma proposta de renovação", *Lusitania Sacra*, 2ª série, 15 (2003), 15–41 (p. 41); David Sampaio BARBOSA, "Arquétipo de pároco na vida e na obra de D. Frei Bartolomeu dos Mártires, arcebispo de Braga (1559–1582): uma aproximação histórica", *Lusitania Sacra*, 23 (Janeiro-Junho 2011), 59–76.

[7] Giuseppe MARCOCCI, "O arcebispo de Braga, D. Frei Bartolomeu dos Mártires (1559–1582): um caso de inquisição pastoral?", *Revista de História da Sociedade e da Cultura*, 9 (2009), 119–46; Raúl Almeida ROLO, *Formação e vida intelectual de D. Frei Bartolomeu dos Mártires*, Porto: Edição do Movimento Bartolomeano, 1977.

[8] BARBOSA, "Arquétipo de pároco", *art. cit.*, p. 72.

[9] See José Augusto FERREIRA, *Estudos histórico-litúrgicos. Os ritos particulares das Igrejas de Braga e Toledo*, 2 vols, Coimbra: Coimbra Editora, 1924, II, p. 191.

Rosário, a Dominican co-friar to whom he handed over the preparation of these works.

The *History of the lives of the saints* is, therefore, the first Portuguese book legendary compiled after the Council of Trent and directly under its inspiration, designed within the framework of a reform program that intended to have the lives of saints read as examples of a new moral and historical accuracy, purging them of the taint of falsehood that Protestantism had thrown at them. Diogo do Rosário states his objectives in the *Proemio*:

> Nas historias das vidas de sanctos que andam impressas em vulgar, ha y muitas falhas: e hũa he, que trazem escriptas algũas cousas muy incertas e apocriphas. Polo que pareceo bem ao senhor Arcebispo que ja que se auia de imprimir este liuro, fosse reuisto e emendado, como zeloso de todo bem e proueito as almas.[10]

Diogo do Rosário is known to us for his collaborations with the Archbishop of Braga. We know little else more about him. He was born in Évora and was Prior of the Dominican Convent of Guimarães, where he died in 1580.[11] Besides the *Summa caietana* and *Historia das vidas dos santos*, Silva also attributed to him, in 1578, a *Tractado de avisos de confessores, ordenado por mandado do Arcebispo Primaz*, unknown. Silva describes him as "much accepted by the venerable archbishop".

A natural bond between the Dominican family and hagiography was to be expected in an order that, since the thirteenth century, had been generating authors and hagiographic works of greater diffusion and influence. The Preachers are responsible for the invention of the *legendae novae*,[12] whose authors are well known: Jean de Mailly (*Abbreviatio in gestis et miraculis sanctorum*, 1243), Bartholomew of Trent (*Epilogus in gesta sanctorum*, 1240–1245), Vincent of Beauvais (*Speculum Historiale*, 1254), Jacobus de Voragine (*Legenda Aurea*, 1265) and, from the beginning of the fourteenth century, Bernard Gui (*Speculum Sanctorale*, 1312–1316).[13] All of them obeyed a hagiographic

---

[10] Unnumbered page. "In the stories of the lives of saints that are printed in vernacular, there are many flaws and one is that they have included some very uncertain and apocryphal things. That is why it seemed right to the archbishop that since this book was to be printed, it should be revised and amended, as he is zealous about the good and profit of the souls".

[11] Inocêncio Francisco da SILVA, *Dicionário Bibliográfico Português*, 23 vols, Lisboa: Imprensa Nacional, 1859, II, pp. 173–74.

[12] Guy PHILIPPART, *Les Légendiers latins et autres manuscrits hagiographiques*, Turnhout: Brepols, 1977, pp. 45 and following.

[13] Thomas KAEPPELI, *Scriptores Ordinis Praedicatorum Medii Aevi*, 4 vols, Romae ad S. Sabinae: Typis Polyglottis Vaticanis, 1970–1993, I, pp. 172–74 (B. Trento), pp. 205–26 (B. Gui); II, pp. 348–69 (J. Voragine), pp. 473–74 (J. Mailly); IV, pp. 435–58 (V. Beauvais).

program subordinated to the same objective, which was the pastoral functionality of hagiography. To this end, they strive to produce short and true legends. As A. Dubreil-Arcin points out, "des le milieu du XIIIe siècle c'est sous l'influence d'Humbert de Romanis, cinquième maître de l'ordre, que les Prêcheurs s'emploient à construire et à diffuser un discours marquant son attachement à dire le vraie".[14] The fact that the later dissemination of this hagiography, particularly that transmitted by Jacobus de Voragine, has lost its functional link with preaching and has become a pedagogical reading for the entire clergy and also, through various vernacular translations and rewritten versions, one of the most frequent readings of lay people, cannot be obviated in this analysis.[15] How did medieval Dominican hagiographers fulfill their commitment to truth? The study by A. Dubreil-Arcin gives us a clear answer to this question and reflects on a peculiar concept of truth we are dealing with. First, the aforementioned authors increasingly reject apocryphal texts, from Jean de Mailly, who warns readers that a text he is using is apocryphal, to Bernard Gui who simply does not use it, following the statement he makes in this regard in his prologue.[16] Second, they conform to the texts fixed for the liturgy of the Order, for they had been approved (in three successive general chapters) as true and authorized. This was the case of the lectionary of the office compiled by Humberto of Romanis, in which he includes 44 critical notes, introduced by the formula "Nota quod..." and in which he discusses topics such as the identity of the author of the text used, the disagreement between sources, or the analytical list of available documentation.[17]

Jacobus de Voragine is one of the authors who was strongly influenced by the lectionary by Humberto of Romanis, especially in the second recension of *Legenda Aurea*.[18] In addition, he uses his predecessors, Jean de Mailly, Bartholomew of Trent and Vincent of Beauvais as a source, which results in an

---

[14] Agnès DUBREIL-ARCIN, "La critique dans l'écriture hagiographique dominicaine (1250–1325 environ)", in *La méthode critique au Moyen Âge*, ed. by M. Chazan, G. Dahan, Turnhout: Brepols, 2006, pp. 269–88 (p. 271).

[15] Note that soon the second version of the *Legenda Aurea* (1270) was intended for reading as a book and not just for use by preachers (Giovanni Paolo MAGGIONI, "La littérature apocryphe dans la *Légende dorée* et dans ses sources immédiates", *Apocrypha*, 19 (2008), 146–81 (p. 173), although the audience that benefited from it was relatively restricted, since it would have to know Latin. It was the vernacular translations of the legendary which really spread it throughout Christendom.

[16] DUBREIL-ARCIN, "Un hagiographe à l'œuvre", *art. cit.*, pp. 272–73, 277–78.

[17] DUBREIL-ARCIN, "Un hagiographe à l'œuvre", *art. cit.*, p. 274.

[18] For his part, Bernard Gui even reproduces the structure of the Master: name of the saint's feast, information about the sources used, critical news. In addition to using the same sources, it reproduces some of its critical news and closely follows the narrative content of his texts (DUBREIL-ARCIN, "Un hagiographe à l'œuvre", *art. cit.*, pp. 275–76).

attitude towards the apocrypha that does not always seem uniform. In general, Voragine considers that the quotation of apocryphal texts is legitimate when its agreement with the canonical texts can be defended, deserving, therefore, discussion.[19] Despite the differences between the Dominican compilers, it is certain that their works constitute "une chaîne de transmission interne à l'ordre dominicain", so that "le véritable auteur est l'Ordre dominicain même, désireux d'améliorer les instruments nécessaires à la prédication".[20] The analysis carried out by A. Dubreil-Arcin reveals that this Order took on a hagiographic program according to which since the thirteenth century principles and methods were developed that would allow the examples of the saints to be transmitted to the faithful. It is no wonder, then, that Bartolomeu dos Mártires chose a co-friar for the task of adapting the lives of the saints to the principles of Trent. In fact, these principles impose nothing more than what the Dominicans had already assumed programmatically since Humbert of Romans: purging the legendary from apocryphal narrative material, choosing authorized sources that guarantee the authenticity of the texts.

Assuming this same program, can Diogo do Rosário be a link in the "chaîne de transmission" that Maggioni talks about? Does the way in which he put the program into practice and the conceptualization that involved his choices regarding sources and narrative matter prove the existence of this chain?

Let us begin by saying that this Portuguese Dominican chooses, as his hagiological model, Luigi Lippomano (1500–1559), a promoter of the Council of Trent well known to the Portuguese.[21] He offers a first criterion for the selection of sources: in order to defend the authenticity of the cult of saints against Lutheran accusations, it is necessary to look for the oldest sources, which will be, *mutatis mutandis*, the most authentic and, therefore, legitimate. The *Historiae Aloysii Lipomani* are, therefore, mediators between ancient and medieval sources — such as Symeon Metaphrast, Adam of Vienna and Bernard of Claraval —[22] and the legendary of 1567. Rosário is, therefore, essentially, just like his model, a compiler and, in this sense, his hagiological

---

[19] MAGGIONI, "La littérature apocryphe", *art. cit.*, p. 173.
[20] MAGGIONI, "La littérature apocryphe", *art. cit.*, p. 150.
[21] Lippomano was in Portugal in 1542 as an apostolic nuncio, to invite the Portuguese bishops to participate in the council. The third volume of his *Sanctorum priscorum patrum vitae* was dedicated to King João III of Portugal. In 1565, a synthesis of his hagiographic work (*Historiae Aloysii Lipomani, episcopi veronensis de vitis sanctorum*) was published in Louvain, which was the model of Rosário.
[22] About Lipponamo's hagiographic work and its reception see Sophia BOESCH-GAJANO, "La raccolta di vite di santi di Luigi Lippomano: storia, struttura, finalità di una costruzione agiografica", in *Raccolte di vite di santi dal XIII al XVIII secolo. Messaggi, strutture, fruizioni*, ed. by S. Boesch-Gajano, Fasano di Brindisi: Schena, 1990, pp. 110-30 (pp. 119-22).

thinking must be evaluated by the way he selected sources and the method used in treating them.

If we count only the alleged sources that appear at the beginning of each text, and are presented by the author in the introduction as an innovation of his book and a guarantee of its credibility, we have in the first place the Dominicans Antoninus of Florence and Claudius of Rota. The former, with 112 assignments, is a transitional author between medieval and Renaissance historiography and in his work[23] we can find, in a typically medieval structure, several elements of critical discourse.[24] Formed in the Dominican convents since he was 17, he claims Vincent of Beauvais, Jacobus de Voragine and Bernard Gui[25] as authorities, thus constituting another link in the Dominican hagiographic transmission chain and also a defender of the "truth".

We don't know much about Claudius of Rota, with 23 assignments, other than he was a professor of Theology at the Dominican convent in Lyon. His contribution is admittedly a reedition of the *Legend Aurea*.[26] The cover page indicates:

> Nunc demum summa cura diligentiáque Fr. Claudij à Rota, sacrae Theologiae professoris, ordinis Praedicatorum, recognita, infinitisque mendis repurgata; adiectis denuò, praeter historiariam Lombardicam, aliquot Sanctorum Sanctarumque uitis, antehac non excusis.

Even without an exhaustive collation of this version with the text of the *Legenda Aurea*, a comparison of versions in the texts already analyzed[27] reveals

---

[23] The *Historiarum sive Chronicon partibus tribus distincta ab initio mundi ad MCCCLX* were first published in Venice in 1474–1479, with eight more reprints until 1587. I used the 1527 Lyon edition.

[24] For a comparative view between the history of Antoninus and that of his medieval predecessors, on the one hand and, on the other, that of Leonardo Bruni, considered the first humanist historian who actually practiced criticism of sources, see Brian Nathaniel BECKER, *The Sense of the Past in Saint Antoninus of Florence's* Summa Historialis, unpublished Master Thesis, Western Michigan University, 2002.

[25] BECKER, *The Sense of the Past, op. cit.*, pp. 36–37, 40–41.

[26] *Opus aureum et legende insignes sanctorum sanctarumque cum Hystoria lombardica*, with editions since 1519 (Lyon) up to 1554 (Lyon), mediated by impressions in 1521, 1524, 1526, 1531, with adition of new texts. I used the 1554 edition.

[27] Cristina SOBRAL, "Um legendário à saída de Trento (Frei Diogo do Rosário, 1567)", *Studia Aurea*, 11 (2017), 253–72; Cristina SOBRAL, "*Eu preegador e apostola fuy*: pregação feminina num legendário pós-tridentino português (Fr. Diogo do Rosário 1567)", *Rilce*, 36, 2 (2020), 477–98; Cristina SOBRAL, "O mar na hagiografia pós-tridentina (Fr. Diogo do Rosário, 1567)", *Lusitania Sacra*, 40 (2019), 151–67: https://revistas.ucp.pt/index.php/lusitaniasacra/article/view/9757; Cristina SOBRAL, "Baptists and baptisms in post-Tridentine hagiography (1567)", *eHumanista* 48 (2021), 172–90: https://www.ehumanista.ucsb.edu/sites/default/files/sitefiles/ehumanista/volume48/ehum48.f.sobral.pdf.

that Claudius of Rota does nothing more than edit Voragine's text with small textual variants that do not affect the narrative content, about which he does not exercise any critical judgment. Apparently, Claudius of Rota acted as a philologist, and the "infinite" errors he corrects are copyists' transmission errors, which he believed to misrepresent Voragine's genuine text. Thus, through the edition of Claudius of Rota, the *Legenda Aurea* constitutes one of the main sources of the new legendary by Rosário. Vincent of Beauvais is also important in this chain of transmission, as he is not only present in the legendary of 1567 through his followers Jacobus de Voragine and Antoninus of Florence, but he has also six direct attributions.

Thirdly, among the most quoted sources are, with 18 mentions each, the *Catalogus sanctorum et gestorum eorum ex diversis voluminibus collectus* by Peter of Natali, Bishop of Equilio, (c. 1330–1406),[28] and the *Breviary of Évora*, reformed in 1548 by the Portuguese humanist André de Resende.[29] The latter, although he soon sought innovative knowledge in several European cities, where he contacted the humanist movement, obtained his basic training in the convent of St Dominic of Évora. In his most important historiographical work, *De Antiquitatibus Lusitaniae*, published posthumously (Évora, 1593), the application of a method based on archaeological, epigraphic and documentary sources is notorious.[30] However, the correctness of the method did not always guarantee the correctness of the results, sometimes due to insufficient knowledge at the time and often due to Resende's excessive effort to exalt his nation, which led him, both in this work and in the *Breviary of Évora*, to accept apocryphal texts, forging narrative versions unauthorized by sources and even forging epigraphic sources.[31] His prestige and the novelty of his method, learned from European humanists, as well as his Dominican affiliation, were the factors that made him credible in the eyes of his co-friar Diogo do Rosário. In addition to these factors, the breviary genre also gives authority to the narratives it conveys, because since the first centuries of Christianity there has been a

---

[28] We know editions since 1493 (Vicenza, Henricus de Sancto Ursio) up to 1545 (Lyon, Jacques Giunta). I used the 1506 Venice edition.

[29] *Breuiarium Eborense*, Lisboa: Luís Rodrigues, 1548; see Miguel de OLIVEIRA, "Livros Litúrgicos de Évora", *Lusitania Sacra*, 6 (1962/63), 263–74 (p. 270).

[30] R. M. Rosado FERNANDES, "Introdução", in André de RESENDE, *As Antiguidades da Lusitânia*, Lisboa: Fundação Calouste Gulbenkian, 1996, pp. 2–38.

[31] Baudouin DE GAIFFIER, "Le bréviaire d'Évora de 1548 et l'hagiographie ibérique", *Analecta Bollandiana*, 60 (1942), 131–39; FERNANDES, "Introdução", *op. cit.*, pp. 14, 28; José D'ENCARNAÇÃO, "André de Resende, epigrafista", in *Cataldo e André de Resende – Congresso Internacional do Humanismo Português*, Lisboa: Centro de Estudos Clássicos, 2002, pp. 305–10; SOBRAL, "Um legendário", *art. cit.*, pp. 264, 267.

special care paid to the authenticity of the historical texts that were used in the liturgy, as evidenced by the Pseudo-Gelasian Decree, where they are condemned and excluded some lives of saints considered apocryphal.[32] Diogo do Rosário often cites it to legitimize his *corpus* selection.[33] Thus, other breviaries were consulted by Diogo do Rosário, adding 16 more attributions to his book (8 to Braga, 3 to Santa Cruz de Coimbra, 2 to Roman, 2 to Dominican and one to Benedictine) for a total of 34. This preference given to liturgical books is in agreement with the revision and updating policy promoted by Humbert of Romans for the lectionary and reinforces the Dominican strategy that was apparently followed by Diogo do Rosário in the selection of sources.

Peter of Natali seems to be the first author who deviates from the criteria mentioned above: he had no connection with the Order of Preachers and his ecclesiastical career has always been within the secular Venetian clergy. However, he frequented the prehumanist environment of the court of Andrea Dandolo (1306–1354), a cultured ruler, a jurist and friend of Francesco Petrarca, with whom Peter of Natali had contact.[34] His *Catalogus* benefited from several editions[35] that express its acceptance in the fifteenth and sixteenth centuries and only came to be seriously questioned by the Bollandists, in the seventeenth century.

What has been said shows that Diogo do Rosário adopted a clear criterion for the selection of sources: all of them benefit from a status of certified authenticity and credibility, both by the Dominican hagiographic program and by the critical selection process that liturgical books are supposed to have undergone throughout its history, or because of the "modernity" of the authors who were part of the pioneering circles of humanist culture. This is an ambivalent criterion: on the one hand, it reveals a critical spirit in the external selection of sources, recognizing modern and relevant factors in their classification as reference works, and on the other hand, it does not escape

---

[32] Ernst von DOBSCHÜTZ, *Das Decretum Gelasianum de libris recipiendis et non recipiendis in kritischem Texte herausgegeben und untersuchut*, Leipzig: J. C. Hinrichs, 1912, p. 13; Baudouin DE GAIFFIER, "Un prologue hagiographique hostile au Décret de Gélase?", *Analecta Bollandiana*, 82 (1964), 341–53; S. Claude MIMOUNI, *Les traditions anciennes sur la Dormition et l'Assomption de Marie. Études littéraires, historiques et doctrinales*, Leiden-Boston: Brill, 2011, pp. 247–56.

[33] SOBRAL, "Um legendário", *art. cit*, pp. 259, 261; SOBRAL, "Eu preegador e apostola fuy", *art. cit.*, pp. 492, 494.

[34] Emore di PAOLI, "NATALI, Pietro de", *Dizionario Biografico degli Italiani*, vol. 77, 2012, on line: https://www.treccani.it/enciclopedia/pietro-de-natali_(Dizionario-Biografico)/.

[35] *Catalogus sanctorum et gestorum eorum ex diversis voluminibus collectus*. We know editions since 1493 (Vicenza) up to 1545 (Lyon).

the medieval criterion of *auctoritas* regarding the uncritical acceptance of the content of these works, which is not questioned.

I recently studied the work of the Portuguese author focusing in lives such as Gonçalo of Amarante, Manços of Évora, Apollony, Ildefonse of Toledo, Peter of Rates,[36] Mary Magdalene, Martha,[37] Thecla, Barbara and Christina.[38] Furthermore, I analyzed the image of the sea in the legendary, comparing it to medieval hagiography.[39] The following are some of the main conclusions. First, the claim to have utilized sources does not always correspond to their actual use. Comparing the texts of 1567 with those of the sources, it is clear, for example, that Antoninus is cited even when he contributes only a short narrative sequence and his status as *auctoritas* often overlaps other more widely used sources. The compilation of sources is always done with a preference for the abundance of details and miracles, which are not questioned when validated by an *auctoritas*. Thus, it is acceptable the dragon of the legend of St Martha, endorsed by Jacobus de Voragine through Claudius of Rota, but not that of St George, condemned by the Pseudo-Gelasian Decree.[40] Internal inconsistencies in the texts, the result of putting together sections from different versions, not only do not arouse repudiation but are even accentuated with the claim about new sources.[41] The purging of elements that could be condemned by Trent as "abuses" was sought in vain: the image of holy women invested with priestly prerogatives, such as preaching and the power to baptize (Mary Magdalene, Martha, Thecla, Barbara and Christina) was preserved in the texts as in the Middle Ages.

The novelty of this legendary when compared to medieval Iberian descendants of the *Legenda Aurea*, the *Leyenda de los Santos* (Burgos, 1497?) and the *Flos Sanctorum em linguagem português* (Lisbon, 1513),[42] is the rewriting of some narratives according to the new pastoral orientations of Trent. That is the case of the fusion of sources in the Life of Saint Ildephonsus of Toledo, which highlights the description of the saint's customs and virtues

---

[36] SOBRAL, "Um legendário", *art. cit.*
[37] SOBRAL, "Eu preegador e apostola fuy", *art. cit.*
[38] SOBRAL, "Baptists and baptisms", *art. cit.*
[39] SOBRAL, "O mar na hagiografia", *art. cit.*
[40] SOBRAL, "Eu preegador e apostola fuy", *art. cit.*, p. 492.
[41] SOBRAL, "Um legendário", *art. cit.*, p. 264.
[42] British Library IB.53312; BETA manid 2243; Biblioteca Nacional de Portugal Res. 157 A; BITAGAP manid 1021. About these two Iberians legendaries and their relation see José ARAGÜÉS ALDAZ, "La Leyenda de los Santos: orígenes medievales e itinerario renacentista", *Memorabilia*, 18 (2016), 133–87. The BITAGAP references come from *PhiloBiblon*, dir. Charles B. FAULHABER, Berkeley, 1997–2020: https://bancroft.berkeley.edu/philobiblon/citation_ga.html: [20-11-2020].

as a student, abbot and finally as archbishop. Rosário avoids the theme of the divinely inspired election to the people — Trento approved a close scrutiny of the eligible candidates — and instead emphasizes Ildephonsus's qualities as a holder of previously acquired science (chapter 2, of the 22nd session of the Council) and for that reason competent pastor, thus tracing a model of a religious man, precocious in childhood, but above all exemplary as a prelate.[43] The second example is the Life of Mary Magdalene: the hagiographer rewrites the narrative of the scriptural period of the sinner's life, highlighting her conversion, in order to make her a current and acute example of moralizing the laity's customs.[44]

From a historical point of view, Rosário's discourse, as I have shown, can only be considered critical insofar as it transmits narratives from sources that have been subjected to a criterion of seniority or external credibility, without critical analysis of the contents transmitted in order to assess their historicity with respect to a conception of empirical factuality. We still need to analyze the moments when Rosário addresses the reader ("Nota pio leitor...") in order to clarify or discuss some points of the narrative using an expository discourse.

1. Discordant Sources

In a work that compiles several sources about the same character, it is inevitable that divergences will emerge, but they do not have to be made visible to the reader. On the contrary, by citing, at the beginning of a text, different sources but not differentiating, in the course of the narrative, what belongs to each one, it generates not an image of discord, even if it exists, but an image of unanimity that only reinforces the credibility of the narrative. We have an example in the heading of the Life of Saint Barbara, "segūdo a escreue sam antonino na primeira parte e outros".[45] The "others" are essentially Claudius of Rota, who provided almost the entire narrative, and Antoninus, from whom only a brief sentence is taken.[46] The two sources report very different contents but the reader will not be aware of it, forming, on the contrary, the idea that all sources agree on the facts narrated.

This example, which could be multiplied by many more, shows that Rosário does not feel obliged to show the differences between his sources. Therefore, when doing so, there will be reasons. Let us look at the cases.

---

[43] SOBRAL, "Um legendário", *art. cit.*, p. 265.
[44] SOBRAL, "Eu preegador e apostola fuy", *art. cit.*, p. 495.
[45] ROSÁRIO, *Historia, op. cit.*, I, 9d. "as Saint Antoninus writes it in the first part, and others".
[46] SOBRAL, "Baptists and baptisms", *art. cit.*

1.1 Birth and Burial Places

In hagiography, places of birth and burial are important identity elements, insofar as they ensure feeling of belonging to a territory, support cultural claims and have consequences for history, culture and the collective imaginary. St Andrew is the subject of a critical excursus aimed at identifying his burial place:

> E contam que do sepulchro de sam Andre emanaua manna como farinha e oleo muy suaue, em que conheciam os moradores daquella terra a fertilidade do anno (Peruentura que foy isto verdade antigamente, mas agora, segundo se diz, seu corpo estaa na cidade de Constatinopla: aa qual cidade foy trasladado no tempo do emperador Constantino).[47]

The parenthesis is intended to locate the martyr's grave in Constantinople and not in Patras, where he had suffered martyrdom at the hands of the proconsul of Achaia (Greece), Egeas: "Andando sam andre em Achaya prouincia de Grecia... enformou na fee a molher do Proconsul Egeas... Ouuindo isto Egeas, partio se pera a cidade de Patras, e começou a perseguir os Christãos... ".[48] The narrative of martyrdom follows the apocryphal *Acts of Andrew*[49] that is among the texts condemned in the Pseudo-Gelasian Decree.[50] Considering the authority that Rosário grants to this text, it would be surprising that he would not have recognized it in this case if we did not know that all the information he uses is mediated by his usual sources, that is, Rosário did not consult directly the Decree. For the Life of St Andrew, there are two sources invoked: Antoninus and the anonymous "Filateto Eusebiano".[51] The second source is a collection of apocryphal acts of the apostles published in 1531 by Friedrich Nausea[52] and which, apparently, Rosário used. Here, the narrative tells us of Andrew's martyrdom in Patras and his burial by Maximila, wife of

---

[47] Rosário, *Historia, op. cit.*, I, 8d. "And they say that from the sepulcher of Saint Andrew distilled manna like flour and very soft oil, with which the inhabitants of that land recognized the fertility of the year (Perhaps this was true in the past, but now, it is said, his body is in the city of Constantinople, whereto he was transferred during the time of Emperor Constantine)".
[48] Rosário, *Historia, op. cit.*, I, 7c. "Saint Andrew being in Achaia, in the province of Greece... informed in faith the wife of the proconsul Egeas... Hearing this Egeas, he left for the city of Patras, and began to persecute the Christians".
[49] *Acta apostolorum apocrypha*, ed. by R. A. Lipsius and M. Bonnet, 3 vols, Darmstadt: Wissenschaftliche Buchgesellschaft, 1959, I, pp. 38–45.
[50] Dobschütz, *Das Decretum Gelasianum, op. cit.*, p. 49.
[51] Rosário, *Historia, op. cit.*, I, 6c.
[52] Friedrich Nausea, *Anonymi Philalethi Eusebiani in uitas, miracula, passionesque Apostolorum Rhapsodiae*, Cologne, 1531, see *Acta apostolorum apocripha, op. cit.*, pp. i–lvii.

the pro-consul Egeas, in his own tomb, but nothing is said about the wonderful signs observed there. This information belongs to Antoninus although the miracle does not take place in Patras, but in Amalfi (Italy), whereto the body was later transferred:

> Postea translatum est corpus eius, et nunc requiescit in ciuitate Malfitana in partibus regni, et adhuc manna ad modum olei fluit de sepulchro eius, de quo omnibus datur petentibus, nec deficit.[53]

Rosário attributes the miracle to Patras and reports a transfer to Constantinople; Antoninus reports a transfer to Amalfi and attributes the miracle to this city. This means that he was not the source used by Rosário to identify the grave. None of the sources he claims were actually the source used. If we search for it among the other usual sources, we can easily find in Claudius of Rota the information translated by Rosário:

> de sepulchro sancti Andree mana in modum farine et oleum cum odore suauissimo emanare, a quo que sit anni futuri fertilitas incolis regionis ostenditur. Nam si exiguum profluit, exiguum terra exhibet fructum si copiose copiosum. Hoc forte antiquit verum fuit: sed modo eius corpus apud Constantinopolim translatum esse perhibetur.[54]

Faced with two sources, one that attributes Andrew's grave to Amalfi and the other to Constantinople, what was the selection criteria? And why was the unused source, Antoninus, explicitly included? Rosário's choice is so much stranger as it is certain that the most correct information is in Antoninus. In fact, St Jerome tells in *De viris Illustribus*, that Andrew's relics were transferred from Patras to Constantinople, a city of which Andrew was the patron saint, in 357.[55] However, in 1208, following the Fourth Crusade, the relics were brought to Amalfi by Cardinal Peter of Capua, a native of this city, to protect them from the Turks.[56] Apparently the French Vincent of Beauvais was unaware of this fact[57] and that is why neither the Genoese Jacobus de

---

[53] ANTONINUS, *Historiarum, op. cit.*, I, p. 408.
[54] ROTA, *Opus aurem, op. cit.*, 3ᵛ.
[55] Saint Jerome, *De Viris Illustribus Liber Ad Dextrum*, chapter 7: "Sepultus est Constantinopoli, ad quam urbem vicesimo Constantii anno ossa ejus cum reliquiis Andreae apostoli translata sunt" (Jean-Paul MIGNE, *Patrologiae... Latina*, Turnholti: Brepols, 1958–1974, XXIII, col. 661).
[56] There are two variants of the translation narrative; see *BHL* 0434 and *BHL* 0434b (*Bibliotheca Hagiographica Latina antiquae et mediae aetatis*, Bruxelles: Société des Bollandistes, 1898–1899).
[57] Beauvais' source for the miracle at Andrew's grave in Patras is probably Gregory of Tours, *De Gloria martyrum*, chapter 31, MIGNE, *Patrologiae... Latina, op. cit.*, LXXI, col. 731: "Andreas apostolus [...] magnum miraculum in die solemnitatis suae profert, hoc est manna in

Voragine, who used him as a source, nor Claudius of Rota, who "amended" Voragine, reported it.

But the Florentine Antoninus knew it and that is why his information is the most correct and should have been followed by Rosário. The selection of Claudius, even without mentioning it, can only be due to the discursive mode ("Hoc forte antiquit verum fuit: sed..."), which suggests updating and correcting previous information. Thus, the disagreement of the sources is not really attributable to Rosário, who inherited it from one of the sources he selected. What should be attributed to him is the preference for a discourse that assumes a critical modality (Claudius) vs. the source he cites (Antoninus), without having done any effort of his own to ascertain the truth. This reveals a taste, already revealed at other times by the Portuguese hagiographer, for an *apparently* critical discourse.

This was not the case of the legend about the martyr St Vincent. Here Rosário, we can say, felt at home, since the martyr was the patron saint of Lisbon, in whose cathedral his body allegedly rested after a miraculous transfer from Valencia to the St Vincent Cape in the Algarve, which took its name from the saint, and from there, as commanded by Afonso Henriques, to Lisbon, the city recently conquered from the Moors. In the heading, the declared sources are Antoninus and Prudentius: "Escreue tābē este martyrio elegātemēte em metro Prudēcio".[58]

The martyrdom of Saint Vincent was early divulged in a non-liturgical form through the well-known hymn dedicated to him by Prudentius (348– c. 410),[59] a prestigious source to which many later authors refer. The fact that the poem depends directly on the oldest *passio*[60] makes it an acceptable source

---

modum farinae, vel oleum cum odore nectareo, quod de tumulo ejus exundat. Per id enim quae sit fertilitas anni sequentis ostenditur. Si exiguum profluxerit, exiguum terra profert fructum; si vero fuerit copiosum, magnum arva proventum fructum habere significat. [...] Haec autem aguntur apud provinciam Achaiam, in civitate Patras".

[58] ROSÁRIO, *História, op. cit.*, I, 85a. "Prudentius also writes elegantly about this martyrdom in meter".

[59] Prudentius, a contemporary of the martyr, narrates his martyrdom in the hymn V of his *Peristhephanon* (hymn V, MIGNE, *Patrologiae... Latina, op. cit.*, LX, cols 378–411). The primitive *passio* dates back to the end of the fourth century and inspired both the poet and Saint Augustine (Sermons 274, 275, 276, 277, MIGNE, *Patrologiae... Latina, op. cit.*, XXXVIII, cols 1252–58; MIGNE, *Patrologiae... Latina, op. cit.*, Suppl. II, cols 417–19), who read it in Hippo and comments it in five sermons. See Angel FÁBREGA GRAU, *Pasionario Hispánico (siglos VII–XI)*, 2 vols, Madrid-Barcelona: Consejo Superior de Investigaciones Cientificas, 1953, pp. 92–107 (p. 102); Carmen GARCÍA RODRÍGUEZ, *El culto de los santos en la España Romana y visigoda*, Madrid: Consejo Superior de Investigaciones Cientificas—Instituto Enrique Flórez, 1966, pp. 257–64; Victor SAXER, *Saint Vincent diacre et martyr: culte et légendes avant l'An Mil*, Bruxelles: Société des Bollandistes, 2002.

[60] FÁBREGA GRAU, *Pasionario Hispánico, op. cit.*, p. 102.

for the martyr's legend. However, on this particular occasion the declared source, Antoninus, was in fact used, and although he indicates that Beauvais is his source, who was also the source of Jacobus de Voragine, in turn edited by Claudius of Rota, and although all tell essentially the same story, there are small wording details in Antoninus that show a direct ancestry:

Antoninus, *Historiarum*, I, 540	Rota, *Opus aureum*, 22ᵛ	Rosário, *Historia*, I, 86a
Cumque iussa implessent ministri, corpus sancti, quod altiotis sali profundo teneri credebatur, prius venit ad portum quam nuntiari posset expositum. Denique commonita in sommis quaedam vidua sancta vera signa quiescentis corporis accepit, et cum pluribus Christianis quibus clam visiones intimauit, ad locum accendens littoris, ad qud vnda Deo operante iactauerat, honorifice sepulchro mandarunt. Et persecutione cessante honorabilius inde leuatum extra muros ciuitatis Valentiae sub altari cuiusdam Ecclesiae condiderunt.	Naute igitur corpus in pelagus deferentes submergunt, sed ipsis nautis velocius littora corpus petijt, quod à quadam matrona & quibusdam alijs ipso reuelante inuenitur, et eis honorifice sepelitur.	E tomarão o sagrado corpo os marinheiros e leuaramno dentro ao mar: e creendo eles que ficaua no profundo pego do mar, primeiro veo ele ao porto ou aa ribeira, do que eles pudessem dar nouas donde o tinha lançado. E finalmente a hũa sancta viuua per diuina reuelaçam em sonhos foy denunciado onde acharia o santo corpo: e indo ela com outros christãos, aos quaes descobrio a reuelaçam, achou o corpo sācto, e o enterraram secretamente. E cessando depois a perseguiçam foy enterrado muy honradamente, debaixo do altar da ygreja que lhe fizeram fora dos muros da cidade de Ualença.[61]

---

[61] "And the sailors took the sacred body and brought it inside the sea, and when they believed it was at the bottom of the sea, before they could tell where they left it, it had already arrived to the port or the shore. And finally a holy widow by divine revelation, in dreams, was told where she would find the holy body. And she went with other Christians, to whom she discovered the revelation, found the holy body and buried it secretly. And after the persecution ceased he was buried very honorably, under the altar of the church that was made outside the walls of the city of Valencia".

Antoninus was the main source but not the only one, since Rosário also literally translates the final quotations by St Augustinus, St Ambrosius and Prudentius, which Jacobus de Voragine adds to the *passio*,[62] also transmitted by Claudius of Rota. Thus, once again, the Rotensian is used without due credit. However, two critical notes do not belong to any of the sources declared, nor even to any of Rosário's usual sources:

> S. Vicẽte foy natural de Espanha da cidade de çaragoça, como claramẽte diz Prudẽcio, e nã de Huesca como algũs dizem.[63]

> agora dizem que seu corpo estaa enterrado na cidade de Lixboa na ygreja de nossa senhora a virgem Maria.[64]

Both notes report information from discordant sources. The martyr's naturalization in Huesca is certainly the result of contamination with his mother's birthplace, as it is provided in a *passio* from after the fifth century.[65] It is not possible to know in which sources he may have found the incorrect information, since he does not declare them, but we emphasize the critical exercise of correction using an ancient source close in time to the narrated facts, thus obeying the Tridentine indications and the Lippomanian model to find out the historical truth from the oldest texts.

As for the second note, which locates the relics in the Lisbon Cathedral, it is easy to know which sources he read. The transfer to Lisbon, where the relics gave rise to an important pilgrimage center and, from there, also to Porto and Braga, was an important historical fact and had a significant impact on Portuguese liturgy, literature and art since the twelfth century. It could not be ignored, especially since his cult intensified in the fifteenth century. The *Flos Sanctorum* of 1513 included, among the added extravagant, the translation's narrative.[66] However, the fact that a trip was undertaken in 1173 to recover the relics, which were believed to have been kept since the Arab invasion of Valencia on the Sacred Promontory (Cape of St Vincent), does not mean that the remains transported to Lisbon really belong to the Aragonese martyr.

---

[62] Iacopo da VARAZZE, *Legenda Aurea*, ed. by G. P. Maggioni, Firenze: Sismel, 2000 (2nd ed.), pp. 178–79, clauses 68–82.

[63] ROSÁRIO, *Historia*, *op. cit.*, I, 85a. "Saint Vincent was originally from Spain in the city of Zaragoza, as Prudentius clearly says, and not from Huesca as some say".

[64] ROSÁRIO, *Historia*, *op. cit.*, I, 86a. "Now it is said that his body is buried in the city of Lisbon in the church of Our Lady the Virgin Mary".

[65] *BHL* 8629: "Extitit enim patre Euticio progenitus, qui fuit Agresti nobilissimi consulis filius: matre vero eius, Enola, ex Osca urbe noscitur procreata"; FÁBREGA GRAU, *Pasionario Hispánico*, *op. cit.*, p. 103; SAXER, *Saint Vincent*, *op. cit.*, pp. 269–79.

[66] Cristina SOBRAL, *Adições Portuguesas no* Flos Sanctorum *de 1513*, unpublished doctoral thesis, University of Lisbon, 2000, pp. 548–63.

Other claims are well known: there are reports of the relocation of the relics to France and Italy.[67] Antoninus transmits the account that attributes the relics to Metz, whose Bishop Teodoricus, during the reign of Emperor Otho, collected them, brought from Spain by two monks,[68] a narrative that is irreconcilable with the translation of the relics to Lisbon. Rosário, who knew well the Portuguese tradition, could have found this narrative in his most authoritative source, the one he trusts the most and always quotes when he wants to give credibility to his *History*. His was a difficult position, we must recognize, as he is an agent of a cultural environment where St Vincent and his patronage in the capital of the kingdom have an unavoidable weight, expressed intensely in the Portuguese collective identity, in religious institutions and in forms of religiosity, toponymy, history and art since the twelfth century.[69] All this cultural weight rested entirely on the preservation of his relics in the Lisbon Cathedral and the memory of its translation to Lisbon. Saint Antoninus says nothing about this transfer and, on the contrary, questions it when reporting a competitor. What should Rosário do? The dilemma is solved with a compromise solution: despite accepting all the extravagant saints added by the *Flos Sanctorum* of 1513[70] and still adding a few more Portuguese saints on his own, he rejects the narrative of Saint Vincent's translation that was in the previous legendary but admits the existence of relics in Lisbon, registering in St Vincent's legend the location of the relics, but distancing himself with a "It is said that...", which exempts him from endorsing it himself.

If a critical spirit is, first of all, aware of the diversity of sources and is intent on solving problems, then we can say that, regarding the legend of St Vincent, Rosário revealed some critical spirit.

A parallel case concerns Saint James the Greater, where there is also a divergence of sources:

> e depois veo a preegar a Hespanha antes da geral diuisam dos apostolos polo mundo. E vendo que aquela gente era muy ruda e grosseira, e que nam fazia aly algum fruyto (porque nam conuerteo em Hespanha mais de noue discipolos) deyxou ahy hos dous pera preegarem a fee do senhor, e tomou consigo os sete e tornou se a Judea. E inda que mestre Joam Beleth diga que nam conuerteo Santiago em Hespanha mais de hum soo, mais de creer he

---

[67] García Rodríguez, *El culto de los santos, op. cit.*, p. 261.
[68] Antoninus, *Historiarum, op. cit.*, II, p. 611. See *Vita sancti Deoderici episcopi Mettensis auctore Sigiberto Gemblacensi*, Migne, *Patrologiae... Latina, op. cit.*, CLX, cols 690–726.
[69] Aires do Nascimento, Saúl António Gomes, *S. Vicente de Lisboa e seus milagres medievais*, Lisboa: Didaskalia, 1988.
[70] The exception is Saint Goldofre, a more or less obscure saint and whose cult was practically extinct in the sixteenth century (Sobral, *Adições Portuguesas, op. cit.*, p. 481).

o que dissemos dos noue: o qual affirma ho papa Calixto segundo, no liuro que escreueo da vida e milagres e tresladaçam de Santiago, dizendo. Teue ho bemauenturado apostolo Santiago muitos discipolos mas doze foram os principaes [...] E os noue escolheo na prouincia de Hespanha, cujos nomes sam estes, Torquato, Segundo, Indalecio, Thesifon, Cecilio, Eufrasio, Isicio, Athanasio e Theodoro.[71]

João (John) Beleth, who attributes to St James only one Hispanic disciple, disagrees with Pope Callixtus, who states that there were nine and this is the source endorsed by our hagiographer. He refers to the very prestigious *Liber Sancti Jacobi*, or *Codex Calixtinus*, a set of texts on the cult of Saint James in Galicia gathered in the twelfth century (1130–1160) under the name of Pope Callixtus II and in whose third book there is a narrative of the evangelization of Hispania by Saint James and the translation of his relics to Galicia. Although this text was well known in Portugal and the Monastery of Santa Maria de Alcobaça (the most important in the country) kept one of the three known witnesses,[72] it is not necessary to assume that Rosário would have consulted it for this small critical note. In fact, in this passage he translates Claudius of Rota, the origin of the reference to João Beleth:

> Iacobus apostolus filius Zebedaei post ascensionem domini dum per Iudeam et Samariam predicaret, in Hispaniam tandem iuit, vt ibi verbum domini seminaret, sed dum ibi se proficere nil videret, et solummodo ibidem .ix. discipulos acquisiuisset, duos ex illis causa praedicandi reliquit, et alios .vij. secum assumens iterum in Iudaem redijt. Magister autem Iohannes Beleth dicit quod tantun ibi vnum conuertit.[73]

Antoninus (the only source declared in the heading: "segundo a escreue sãcto Antoninus primeira parte e outros")[74] also reports divergences regarding the

---

[71] ROSÁRIO, *Historia, op. cit.*, II, 62b-c. "and then came to preach to Spain before the general division of the apostles into the world. And seeing that those people were very rude and that there was no fruit to be had there (because he did not convert more than nine disciples in Spain) he left two to preach the faith of the Lord and took the seven with him and returned to Judea. And although Master John Beleth says that Saint James did not convert in Spain more than one, it is more to believe what we said of the nine, which Pope Callixtus the second says in the book he wrote of the life and miracles and transfer of Saint James, saying: The blessed apostle Saint James had many disciples but twelve were the main ones [...] And the nine he chose in the province of Spain, whose names are these, Torquatus, Secundus, Indalecius, Thesifon, Cecilius, Eufrasius, Isicius, Athanasius and Theodorus".

[72] Manuel C. DÍAZ Y DÍAZ, "Liber Sancti Jacobi", *Dicionário da Literatura Medieval Galega e Portuguesa*, ed. by G. Tavani e G. Lanciani, Lisboa: Caminho, 1993, pp. 393–94.

[73] ROTA, *Opus aurem, op. cit.*, 77.

[74] ROSÁRIO, *Historia, op. cit.*, II, 61d. "according to Saint Antoninus writes first part and others".

number of Saint James' disciples, although he does so more vaguely: "nam tantum nouem vel secundum alios tantum duos ad fidem conuertit...".[75] The *Codex Calixtinus* version imposes itself on the authority of the usual sources (Antoninus and Claudius of Rota) with a firm affirmation of the nine Hispanic disciples. At stake is one of the most solid traditions of the Iberian Peninsula, with clear expressions in the history and culture of the Hispanic kingdoms, that is the evangelization of Hispania by Saint James the Great, and also the legend of the so-called "Varões Apostólicos",[76] which took root in the sixteenth century and which Rosário had already credited by including in his legendary the lives of those nine disciples, Saint Torquatus and his companions, "segundo Calisto Papa, na epistola da trasladação de Santiago apostolo",[77] that is, according to the third book of the *Codex Calixtinus*, a source he used with the mediation of the readings of the Office of Saint Torquatus from the *Breviary of Évora*:

Breviary of Évora, 1548, 1162–1163	Rosário, *Historia*, I,145
Sciendum quid beatus Iacobus plures habuit discipulos: sed duodecim speciales habuit [...] Nouem vero in Gallaecia dum adhuc viueret apostolis elegisse dicitur, quorum septem alijs duobus in Callaecia predicandi causa remanentibus cum eo Hierosolymam perrexerunt...	Ho bēauenturado apostolo Santiago teue muytos discipolos, mas doze forão os especiaes [...] E segundo se diz aiuntou e elegeo em Galiza o apostolo Sãctiago noue discipolos, dos quaes dous ficaram em Galiza pera pregarem o euangelho, e os outros sete se foram com ele a Hierusalem...[78]

Thus, it is evident that the account of the sources' divergence, which was found in the *Legenda Aurea* and, therefore, could be read by many, is reported so that it can be refuted and serves as a clear statement about the Portuguese compiler's position, in favor of the peninsular foundational narratives. Once again, his position is defended by alleging a source whose authority is imposed on the rest, not only because it is older but also because it is credited by a Pope.

---

[75] ANTONINUS, *Historiarum, op. cit.*, I, p. 405.
[76] The Apostolic Holy Men. About them see Miguel de OLIVEIRA, *Lenda e História-Estudos Hagiográficos*, Lisboa: União Gráfica, 1964, pp. 88–110.
[77] ROSÁRIO, *Historia, op. cit.*, I, p. 145. "according to Callixtus the Pope, in the epistle of the apostle Saint James' translation".
[78] "The blessed apostle Saint James had many disciples, but twelve were the special ones [...] And, it is said that the apostle Saint James gathered and chose nine disciples in Galicia, of whom two stayed in Galicia to preach the Gospel, and the other seven went with him to Jerusalem".

1.2. Identification of Ambiguous Characters

Saint Cyriacus,—whose alleged sources are Saint Antoninus and "others"—is the subject of a critical note that discusses the identity of Emperor Maximian:

> Nota pio leitor, que como diz Uicente no speculo historial, nam se lee de tal Maximiano filho de Diocleciano, inda que se lee de Maximiano companheiro no imperio com Diocleciano. Outros dizem que este Maximiano que atormentou a sam Ciriaco, era gẽro de Diocleciano e nã filho, que casou cõ hũa sua filha chamada Ualeriana.[79]

A comparison of the sources shows that Antoninus was, in fact, consulted and that the "others" refer to Claudius of Rota, since the two elements that make up the critical note come from these two authors. The allegation of Vincent of Beauvais belongs to Antoninus and is found at the end of the narrative of Cyriacus's martyrdom ("De hoc tamen Maximiano filio Diocletiani dicit Vincẽ. vbi supra, quod non meminit se alibi legisse: sed quod fuit socius Diocletiani in imperio quidam Maximianus bene legitur").[80] Information about Valeriana can be found in the Jacobus de Voragine edition by the Rotensian Priest ("Iste Maximianus pro tanto potest dici filius Diocletiani, quod sibi successit: et eius filiam habuit in vxorem quae Valeriana nuncupata est").[81] Rosário's work consisted of gathering disparate information from his sources, deciding the best location for the note, when the ambiguous character is mentioned for the first time and not at the end of the text, and calling the reader's attention to the controversial identification ("Nota pio leitor..."), without intending to solve it.

Saint Lawrence has a similar problem, giving rise to a longer critical note:

> Deue aduertir ho pio leitor, que desta historia em que se diz que sam Sixto e sam Lourenço padeceram debaixo de Decio e Ualeriano, ha y muita duuida entre os historiadores, porque nas chronicas dos papas se acha que muyto tempo depois do imperio de Decio, foy sam Sixto papa, cujo arcediago foy sam Lourenço. E assi diz sancto Antonino que nam foy aquele o Decio que martyrizou sam Lourenço, senam outro Decio, cujo nome mais asitado era

---

[79] ROSÁRIO, *Historia, op. cit.*, II, 88b. "Note, pious reader, that, as Vincent says in the *Speculum Historiale*, one does not read of such Maximian son of Diocletian, although one reads of a companion Maximian during the time of Diocletian. Others say that this Maximian who tormented Saint Cyriacus was Diocletian's son-in-law and not his son, who married his daughter named Valeriana".
[80] ANTONINUS, *Historiarum, op. cit.*, I, p. 547.
[81] ROTA, *Opus aurem, op. cit.*, 89ᵛ, see VARAZZE, *Legenda Aurea, op. cit.*, p. 752, clause 38.

Galieno, e tambem se chamaua Decio, ho qual se conta no numero dos emperadores por filho de Ualeriano...[82]

The heading is the same as in the previous legend: the sources were "sancto Antonino [...] e outros".[83] As in other cases, the critical discussion is not prompted by an analysis of the sources by Rosário himself. It was already widely argued in Jacobus de Voragine,[84] who noted the anachronism evident in the meeting, under Decius, of the two young martyrs Lawrence and Vincent, the last of whom perished under Diocletian, more than 40 years later. It is the Genoese who solves the problem, explaining, with historical arguments, that the emperor is Gallienus, also called Decius. Historically acceptable or not the conclusion, the fact is that it is the medieval hagiographer who does the work of criticizing sources, something that arrived to Rosário via Claudius of Rota.[85] Again, the latter is not mentioned, giving credit to Antoninus who, in fact, assumes and summarizes Voragine's conclusions, not in the legend of Saint Lawrence that, surprisingly, he did not compile, but in a section of the Chronicle (I, 498) that tells the story of the Roman emperors.

Another example is the year of the martyrdom of the Eleven Thousand Virgins, under the Huns, in Cologne, the city where they are buried:

> Diz sancto Antonino primeira parte titolo septimo capitolo septimo .§ . segundo que inda que a ygreja catholica celebre solennemente ho martyrio de sancta Ursula e de suas companheiras, e que em Colonia se acham muitos corpos delas, não se acha claro em que tempo padecerão e quem era Emperador: porque hũs dizem que foy no anno do senhor de duzentos e trinta e sete, outros dizem que no anno do senhor de duzentos e setenta, pouco mais ou menos. Os primeiros se mouem, porque Anthero papa, que se diz que soccedeo a sam Ciriaco, que se foy com as sanctas virgẽs, e martyrizado com elas em Colonia, foy naquele tempo. Os outros mouem se a isso, porque os Hũnos que as martyrizarão forão naqueles tempos grãdes perseguidores dos christãos: em fim que padecerão no anno do senhor de duzentos e trinta

---

[82] ROSÁRIO, *Historia, op. cit.*, II, 90b. "The pious reader must be warned that historians have many doubts about this story, in which it is said that Saint Sixtus and Saint Lawrence suffered under Decius and Valerian, because in the chronicles of the popes it is said that Saint Sixtus Pope came long after the empire of Decius, whose archdeacon was Saint Lawrence. And so Saint Antoninus says that it was not that Decius who martyred Saint Lawrence, but another Decius, whose most famous name was Gallienus, and was also called Decius, which is counted in the number of emperors by the son of Valerian".
[83] ROSÁRIO, *Historia, op. cit.*, II, 88c.
[84] VARAZZE, *Legenda Aurea, op. cit.*, pp. 755, 760–62, clauses 15–16, 138–55.
[85] ROTA, *Opus aurem, op. cit.*, 90ᵛ.

e sete, no tempo do papa Anthe[r]o, e de Maximiano Emperador. E inda que aja duuida do tempo em que padecerão estas sanctas, de seu martyrio nã duuida a ygreja.[86]

Rosário does not hide that this divergence was already addressed by Antoninus and he gives him all the credit for the solution. This, however, although translated literally from the Florentine chronicler ("Passae sunt autem secundum alios anno Domini 237, tempore Antheri papae et Maximiani imperatoris. Et si dubium sit de tempore passionis, nullo modo dubitat Ecclesia de martyrio earum"),[87] does not shed light on the issue, since it overlooks the fact that neither 237 nor 270 are compatible years with the looting of Cologne by the Huns, which occurred in the year 451, during the Attila campaign in Gaul. The truly critical note was that of Jacobus de Voragine, transmitted by Claudius of Rota and which Rosário did not take into account:

> Passi sunt autem anno domini ccxxxviij. Ratio autem temporis vt quibusdam placet non sustinet, quod haec tali tempore sint peracta. Sicilia enim tunc non erat regnum nec Constantinopolis, cum hic fyuisse dicatur, cum virginibus harum reginas. Verius creditur, quod diu post Constantinum imperatorem cum Hūni et Gothi seuiebant, tale sit martyrium celebratum tempore scilicet Martiani imperatoris, vt in quadam chronica legitur qui regnauit anno domini ccccli.[88]

What were the reasons for choosing Antoninus, who had the worst solution? There is no answer besides the prestige of this source over all others. Less important than the correctness of the solution seems to be the acceptance of critical discourse from sources, which gives the legendary the appearance of credibility. This is probably why, in the legend of Justina and Cyprian,

---

[86] ROSÁRIO, *Historia, op. cit.*, II, 167c. "Saint Antoninus says —first part, title seventh, chapter seventh .§. second— although the catholic church solemnly celebrates the martyrdom of Saint Ursula and her companions, and that in Cologne many bodies of them are placed, it is not clear at what time they suffered and who was emperor. Some say it was in the year of the Lord of two hundred and thirty-seven, others say that it was in the year of the Lord of two hundred and seventy, little more or less. The first move because Pope Anterus, who is said to have succeeded Saint Cyriacus, who left with the holy virgins, and was martyred with them in Cologne, was at that time. The others move to this, because the Huns who martyred them were in those times great persecutors of Christians. Finally they suffered in the year of the Lord of two hundred and thirty-seven, in the time of Pope Anterus, and Maximian Emperor. And although there is doubt about the time when these saints suffered, the church does not doubt their martyrdom".
[87] ANTONINUS, *Historiarum, op. cit.*, II, p. 171.
[88] ROTA, *Opus aurem, op. cit.*, 129ᵛ.

Antoninus is also credited with the disambiguation between this saint and the Bishop of Carthage:

> Nota aqui pio leytor (segundo diz sancto Antonino) que este sam Cipriano que padeceo martyrio com sancta Justina nam he aquele de que falamos atraz que foy bispo de Carthago, porque este foy no tempo de Diocleciano, e o outro como dissemos foy no tempo de Decio ou Galieno. Nota tam bem que hum liuro que se intitula da penitencia de Cipriano se conta entre os apocriphos no cap. sancta Romana ecclesia disti. xv. E outras philaterias que se chama a oraçam de sam Cipriano que tem muytas supestições, deue se reprouar e asy estaa pola sancta inquisiçam defesa.[89]

Contrary to what the note suggests, Antoninus says nothing about the saint's identity, nor does he attribute it to the time of Diocletian (the persecutor of the martyrs is Count Eutolmius), limiting himself to alerting about the apocryphal nature of their works:

> Libellus autem qui intitulatur de poenitentia Cypriani inter apocryphos ponitur distinctione 15, sancta Romana. Et quaedam phylacteria quae dicitur oratio Cypriani in qua de poenitentia eius sit mentio, quae continet hoc cum multis characteribus et nominus daemonum, vt superstitiosa reprobanda sunt.[90]

Claudius of Rota also contributed little to this note, no more than the name of Diocletian, and says nothing about the homonymy with the Bishop of Carthage. Therefore, it must be deduced that the ambiguity of the characters was noted by Rosário himself and that the attribution to Antoninus is a strategy for crediting the discourse.

There is also one note on the identification of Saint Simon which is literally translated from Saint Antoninus[91] and, in the legend of Saint Clement, another one on the sequence of the first popes, which place Saint Clement should have in it (second or fourth pope) and the status of Linus and Cletus (popes or simple auxiliaries of Peter), which literally translates Chapter 2 of the *Book of Supreme Pontiffs* transmitted by Antoninus.[92]

---

[89] ROSÁRIO, *Historia, op. cit.*, II, 140a. "Note here, pious reader (as Saint Antoninus says) that this Saint Cyprian who suffered martyrdom with Saint Justina is not the one we talked about earlier, who was Bishop of Carthage, because this was in the time of Diocletian and the other, as we said, was in the time of Decius or Gallienus. Also note that a book entitled *Cyprian's Penance* is among the apocryphal in ch. *sancta Romana ecclesia disti.* xv. and there are other philaterias called *Prayer for Saint Cyprian*, which has many superstitions, must be disapproved and it is thus prohibited by the holy Inquisition".
[90] ANTONINUS, *Historiarum, op. cit.*, I, p. 540.
[91] ROSÁRIO, *Historia, op. cit.*, II, 174c-d; ANTONINUS, *Historiarum, op. cit.*, I, p. 412.
[92] ROSÁRIO, *Historia, op. cit.*, II, 193a; "De summis pontificibus illorum temporum, videlicet Lino, Cleto, et Clemente", ANTONINUS, *Historiarum, op. cit.*, I, p. 457.

1.3. Establishment of Facts

In some cases, reference to the divergence of sources is essential to justify the compiler's choice, which reports facts that diverge the common version of a text. This is the case of the Life of Saint Bartholomew, who was known in the cultural and iconographic tradition as a skinned martyr and commonly represented holding his skin. None of this can be found in the legend recorded by Rosário, which recounts the death of the crucified martyr upside down, contradicting the widespread knowledge about the saint, which gives rise to the following note:

> Nam te faça duuida pio leitor dizer este author que s Bartholomeu acabou esta vida com morte de cruz, affirmando se cõmummente que foy esfolado viuo e depois degolado: muito bem podia ser que depois de posto na cruz fosse esfolado e por derradeiro descabeçado. Porque como sabemos os barbaros e infieis enuentauam mil milhares de modos de tormentos. ¶ Sācto Antonino na .j. parte diz estas palauras. Sam Dorotheo affirma que o bēauenturado apostolo Bartholomeu foy crucificado com a cabeça pera baixo na grande cidade de Albano de Armenia. Sā Theodoro diz que foy esfolado: outros afirmā que foy degolado, as quaes cousas se podē facilmente concordar dizēdo que primeiramēte foy esfolado viuo, e depois disso crucificado, e por derradeiro descabeçado. Isto sancto Antonino.[93]

The quote from St Antoninus is accurate and is, moreover, common to Claudius of Rota, that is to say Jacobus de Voragine. However, these three authors of the Dominican "chain of transmission" report the divergence of sources after choosing the more traditional version of the facts, reporting the skinning of Bartholomew. Rosário, on the other hand, only mentions this torment in his critical note, which implies its subordination in the hierarchy of established facts. Why did he depart from what both the cultural tradition and the sources indicated? It is not possible to say it. However, there is a

---

[93] ROSÁRIO, *Historia, op. cit.*, I, 106d–107a. "Do not doubt, pious reader, because this author says that Saint Bartholomew ended this life with a death on the cross, being commonly stated that he was skinned alive and then beheaded. It could very well be that, after being put on the cross, he was skinned and finally beheaded. Because, as we know, barbarians and infidels invented a thousand ways of torments. Saint Antoninus in the first part says these words: Saint Dorotheus claims that the blessed apostle Bartholomew was crucified upside down in the great city of Albano in Armenia. Saint Theodorus says he was skinned, others say he was beheaded, which things can be easily reconciled by saying that he was first skinned alive and after that he was crucified and finally beheaded. This Saint Antoninus". See ANTONINUS, *Historiarum, op. cit.*, I, p. 411; ROTA, *Opus aureum, op. cit.*, 100; VARAZZE, *Legenda Aurea, op. cit.*, p. 838, clauses 139–40.

Figure 1: Saint Bartholomew in Rosário, *Historia*, II, 106a

contradictory fact: the woodcut chosen to head the legend of Saint Bartholomew represents him traditionally holding the skin (Figure 1).

We do not know if the compiler participated in the choice of woodcuts or if it was due only to the printer, but it is to be assumed that, if it were a slip of the printer, it would have been corrected in the second edition of the legendary,[94] made during the compiler's lifetime, but that did not happen. It seems, therefore, that the possibility of reconciling the versions still preserved the traditional iconography of the martyr for the hagiography reader. This type of solution, typically medieval and widely used by exegetes who were faced with differences in Scripture, is the one offered by Jacobus de Voragine.

2. *The Certification Discourse*

We already know that miracles are not questioned by Rosário when attested by his *auctoritates*.[95] However, sometimes they give rise to a certification discourse that we can interpret as a refutation of the doubts eventually raised in the reader's mind in face of reports that hurt the natural recognition of the empirical world. I have already analyzed one of these cases,[96] which resulted in the confirmation of Saint Christina's baptism by Jesus Christ, who especially descended from heaven for this purpose. But there are at least three more cases. The first can be found in the legend about the Dominican Pero Gonçalves, for which Rosário used the chronicle of the Order.[97] This, in

---

[94] *Historia das vidas e feitos heroicos, e obras insignes dos Sanctos*, Coimbra: António de Mariz, 1577, 110d.
[95] See the articles previously published in the scope of this project on Rosário's legendary.
[96] SOBRAL, "Baptists and baptisms", *art. cit.*
[97] António de SÃO DOMINGOS, *Compêndio de religiosos insignes da ordem dos pregadores* (Compendium of distinguished religious of the order of preachers), Coimbra, João de Barreira and João Álvares, 1552, I, 194c.

turn, derives—though not directly—from the only known medieval Latin legend,[98] which means that the font used by Rosário was considerably reliable. Even so, for the series of posthumous miracles, he found it useful to quote his favorite authority, Antoninus, introduced by a brief certification discourse:

> Mas por que nam pareça tudo o que dissemos sem fũdamēto, direy o que diz s. Antonino dele .iij. parte titolo xxiij, capitolo x. § .v. o qual diz assi. Ouue na prouincia de Hespanha hum sancto chamado frey Pero gonçaluez, frade da ordem de s. Domingos, digno de toda honra, o qual passando desta vida pera a gloria eterna, foy enterrado muy hōradamente por sua grande sanctidade, e fez muites [sic] milagres depois de sua morte, polo qual o Bispo daquela cidade mādou mais de cento e oitenta milagres a hum capitolo geral que se celebrou em Tolosa, na era de mil e duzentos e cincoenta e oito os quais foram approuados per muitos homens de authoridade que o affirmaram com juramento, e hiam todos assignados e sellados com seu signal.[99]

This statement by Antoninus, which corresponds exactly to the truth, may have been the only case in which Rosário had the opportunity to present, for a group of miracles, a legally-validated certification, an opportunity that he would not have wanted to miss, since it responds perfectly to the Tridentine desire to write only about facts and cults of confirmed authenticity. What better confirmation of authenticity than a document signed and sealed by a bishop and accepted in a general chapter? In addition to the confirmation of that concrete set of miracles attributed to Saint Pedro Gonçalves, there is another that can be obtained by an argument from *minori ad maius*: if the miracles performed by this saint are confirmed, there is no reason to doubt those of all the others. Thus it is assumed in Saint Nicholas' legend, where the topic of precocity is fulfilled with two miracles that the reader—especially

---

[98] The *Legenda B. Petri Confessoris*, written shortly after the saint's death in 1246, was published by Enrique FLÓREZ, *España Sagrada*, XXIII, Madrid: Antonio Marín, 1767, pp. 131–76, 245–89. The legend compiled by Rosário is a copy of the *Compêndio* by António de São Domingos (103–09, see SOBRAL, *Adições Portuguesas, op. cit.*, pp. 465–66). See also Lorenzo GALMÉS, *San Telmo*, Tui-Salamanca: Editorial San Esteban-Cofradía de San Telmo, 1991.

[99] ROSÁRIO, *Historia, op. cit.*, I, 197c. "But so that it doesn't look like everything we said is without foundation, I will assert what Saint Antoninus says of him, third title, 23rd part, chapter 10, § v: There was in the province of Spain a saint named Friar Peter Gonzalvez, a friar of the order of Saint Dominic, worthy of all honor, who passed from this life to eternal glory, was buried most honorably for his great holiness, and performed many miracles after his death, for which reason the bishop of that city submitted more than one hundred and eighty miracles to a general chapter that was celebrated in Tolosa, in the age of 1258, which were approved by many men of authority who affirmed it under oath, and they were all signed and sealed with their seal".

the female reader—would not fail to admire and whose certification is presented in a syntactically ingenious way:

> E segundo dizem algūs, no dia da sua nacença, estãdo o lauando, esteue em pee na bacia per algum espaço. Nam ha duuida ser este minino logo do principio de sua nacença cheo do diuino spirito e sanctificado: pois que nam soube primeiro viuer que honrar a Deos, nem soube primeiro comer que jejuar. Por certo sabemos que tomando este sancto minino o leite dos peitos de sua may nos outros dias e noytes muytas vezes, com tudo a quarta e sexta feira nam queria mais de hūa soo vez e a tarde gostar o dito manjar.[100]

In this discourse, the doubt eventually raised by the first miracle leads to the certifying expression ("There is no doubt [...]") and to a pedagogical speech that teaches that one must first fast and honor God and only eat afterwards. Then comes the narrative of the second miracle. There is no evidence to justify the miracle but, on the contrary, the evidence is the miracle itself, which is not questioned and serves a traditional function: to demonstrate the character's holiness, that is, to justify that the saint was touched by the Holy Spirit at birth. The sources indicated are Claudius of Rota and Peter of Natali,[101] but there is no certifying discourse in them ("There is no doubt [...] fast"), so we must therefore attribute it to Rosário's pedagogical concerns.

The third case is found in the Saint John Chrysostom's legend. Relating an episode in which he and Epiphanius make a prophecy to each other ("E dizem que Epiphanio lhe respondeo. Eu espero que nam has de morrer Bispo. E que sam Joam lhe respondeo. Eu espero que nam chegaras viuo a tua terra"),[102] there is a speech in the first person, which presupposes the compiler's intervention: "Eu nam sey de certo se elles isto disseram, porem assi conteceo, que ambos ouueram o fim que hum ao outro denunciou, porque Epiphanio morreo antes que chegasse aa sua ygreja e a Chrisostomo soccedeo o que contaremos".[103] It is, however, a speech copied from the source, in this

---

[100] ROSÁRIO, *Historia, op. cit.*, I, 16b–17a. "And some say, on the day of his birth, when he was being washed, he stood in the basin for a while. There is no doubt that this child was, from the beginning of his birth, filled with the divine spirit and sanctified, since he did not know how to live first to honor God, nor did he know how to eat first to fast. We certainly know that, taking this holy child milk from his mother's breasts on other days and nights many times, on Wednesday and Friday he did not want more than once and in the afternoon to enjoy the said delicacy".

[101] ROSÁRIO, *Historia, op. cit.* I, 4ᵛ, 6a-b.

[102] ROSÁRIO, *Historia, op. cit.* I, 98d–99a. "And they say that Epiphanius answered him: I hope you will not die a bishop. And that Saint John answered him: I hope you will not reach your land alive".

[103] ROSÁRIO, *Historia, op. cit.*, I, 99a "I don't know for sure if they said that. But so it happened, that both had the end that each other denounced: because Epiphanius died before he arrived at his church and to Chrysostom happened what we will tell".

case Cassiodorus' *Historia Tripartita*: "Haec utrum vere dicta sint, nescio; ambo tamen hunc habuere finem [...]".[104]

This declaration of ignorance works argumentatively like the certifying discourse in the case of Nicholas. The effects—here the death of Epiphanius and the dismissal of Chrysostom—prove the causes (the prophecies), just as the effects in Saint Nicholas—the miracles—prove the cause (the sanctity of the character). In both cases, the marvelous is closely interwoven with the empirical world and both create a worldview that is little different from the medieval one, even if the certifying discourse wants to provide these specific cases with an appearance of modernity.

3. *The Classification as Apocryphal Material*

In the legend of Saint Thomas, Jacobus de Voragine tells[105] an episode that took place at the wedding of the daughter of the king of India, in which the saint takes revenge for a slap received from a butler prophesying that his hand will appear in front of him in a dog's mouth. The bloody and terrible prophecy is fulfilled, which gives rise to the discussion of the authenticity of the episode—apocryphal according to Saint Augustine—, all of which appear in Claudius of Rota.[106] Peter of Natali, who certainly takes the Genoese archbishop as his source, tells the entire episode without raising critical doubts, including the prophecy.[107] Antoninus, on the other hand, makes abridges the episode: he omits the prophecy of the saint, which prevents reading the butler's punishment as a vengeance from Thomas and portrays only as a divine punishment.

Rosário, this time without a critical note, also omits the prophecy, although he accepts, like his source, Antoninus, the remaining episode.[108] This omission and the exclusion of the *passio* of Cyricus and Julitta, present in the medieval legendaries,[109] from his own *corpus*, seems to place the author within the branch of the Dominican "chain of transmission" intolerant to

---

[104] CASSIODORUS, *Historia Ecclesiastica Tripartita*, ed. by W. Jacob and R. Hanslik, Viena: Hoelder-Pichler-Tempsky, 1952, p. 602. This is the source declared in the legend's heading and the one that, in fact, was consulted directly: the usual sources tell the episode of mutual prophecy but without the certifying discourse (see ANTONINUS, *Historiarum, op. cit.*, II, p. 112, ROTA, *Opus aureum, op. cit.*, 113), or don't even include the episode (see NATALI, *Catalogus, op. cit.*, 39ᵛ–40).
[105] VARAZZE, *Legenda Aurea, op. cit.*, pp. 54–55, clauses 23–46.
[106] ROTA, *Opus aureum, op. cit.*, 6ᵛ.
[107] NATALI, *Catalogus, op. cit.*, 12c.
[108] ROSÁRIO, *Historia, op. cit.*, I, 32c.
[109] *Legenda Aurea* and its Castilian and Portuguese translations, see SOBRAL, "Um legendário", *art. cit.*, p. 259.

Figure 2: Saint George, Rosário, *Historia*, 212c

the apocrypha. This is confirmed with a critical note on Saint George, whose passion is present in the book as taken from Symeon Metaphrast (mediated by Lippomano) instead of the novelistic version with the dragon and the princess (Figure 2):

> segundo a escreue Simeõ Metaphrastes. A qual he autentica e nam apocripha, nem he aquela que por apocripha julgou o papa Gelasio, dist .xv. sancta Romana ecclesia, como manifesta Aloisio Lipomogno bispo de Uerona.[110]

Also very significant is the case of Saint Christopher. The main responsible for the dissemination of this legend in European art and literature is Jacobus de Voragine, who presents a narrative in two macro-sequences: conversion and martyrdom. The second one follows the usual model of epic passions and portrays the character as a Christian martyr. The first one is novelistic and narrated according to the literary model of the sacred search: a pagan, "de statura muy grande .s. de doze pees em comprido. e tinha a face muy terriuel e espãtosa",[111] who wants to serve the most powerful king in the world, is taken from the secular power (a king) to the Devil and, from there, to a hermit who orders him to serve men who need to cross a dangerous river. Here he is called at night to carry a boy who wants to cross the river and who becomes heavier and heavier during the crossing, until finally he reveals himself as Jesus Christ, the one who carries all the weight of the world. Once converted, Christopher goes on to evangelize in the Lycia region, where he suffers martyrdom. The narrative structure is parallel to that of the traditional legend of Saint George: first a novelistic narrative macro-sequence (the victory over

---

[110] ROSÁRIO, *Historia, op. cit.*, I, 212ᵛ. "as Symeon Metaphrast writes it. Which is authentic and not apocryphal, nor is it the one that Pope Gelasius judged as apocryphal, *dist.* xv. *sancta Romana ecclesia*, as expressed by Louis Lippomano, bishop of Verona".

[111] ROSÁRIO, *Historia, op. cit.*, II, 66c. "of very large stature, *scilicet* twelve feet long, and had a very terrible and amazing face".

Figure 3: Saint George and the dragon in *Flos Sanctorum*, 1513, 60c

the dragon and the rescue of the princess), construed with a more or less stereotyped narrative of martyrdom. In both cases it was the novelistic narrative that seduced medieval readers and audiences, which fueled the cult and determined the patronage (military, in the case of George; of travelers, in the case of Christopher) and the iconography (Figure 3).

In Christopher's case, the close relationship between the novelistic narrative and the name of the saint (*Christophorus* < *Christus ferens*; the one who carries Christ), which Voragine did not fail to underline,[112] even suggests an etiological function for this narrative.

Medieval sources reproduced this narrative uncritically, as seen in Peter of Natali.[113] Antoninus, on the other hand, adopts a critical attitude. He begins by claiming Vincent of Beauvais as a source, although there is no mention of Christopher in the *Speculum Historiale*.[114] Then he reverses the order of the two macro-sequences. He first presents the passion in Lycia and then the conversion, attributing it explicitly to Voragine and devaluing it as inauthentic because it cannot be found in Beauvais.[115]

André de Resende also opts for rejecting the conversion narrative, so that the *Breviary of Évora* (1548) only registers the martyrdom. As might be expected, Diogo do Rosário, who could access the full legend of Voragine through Claudius of Rota[116] or Peter of Natali,[117] positions himself as follower of the two

---

[112] VARAZZE, *Legenda Aurea, op. cit.*, p. 663, clause 1.
[113] NATALI, *Catalogus, op. cit.*, 142ᵛ–143ʳ.
[114] ANTONINUS, *Historiarum, op. cit.*, I, p. 556; I used the 1494 Venice edition of *Speculum Historiale*.
[115] "Exinde processit ad praedicandum, vt dictum est: haec tamen non scripsit Vincen. vbi supra vel quia abbreuiare voluit, vel quia forte non reputauit ista authentica, licet martyrium cuius celebret Ecclesia" (ANTONINUS, *Historiarum, op. cit.*, I, p. 557).
[116] ROTA, *Opus aureum, op. cit.*, 78ᵛ–79ᵛ.
[117] NATALI, *Catalogus, op. cit.*, 142ᵛ–143.

Figure 4: Saint Christopher in Rosário, *Historia*, 66b

critical authors: "Historia do martyrio do bemauenturado sam Christouão segundo a refere s. Antonino na j. parte de Uicente no specu. histo. e o breuiario Deuora".[118] Between Antoninus and the Breviary, Rosário chooses to omit the conversion, like the second, but he introduces a critical note that results from reading the first: "Outras muitas cousas se escreuem deste bemauenturado sancto martyr, mas porque parecem apocriphas se deixaram".[119] From the point of view of the user of the legendary, however, some perplexity emerges. If the woodcuts are intended to have an illustrative and not merely decorative function, the reader would be surprised by the fact that the representation shown (Figure 4) does not find any correspondence in the text. We have already seen, in the legend of Saint Bartholomew, a similar case (Figure 1) but then the martyrdom by skinning is admitted in the text, although secondarily. On the other hand, in George's legend, the omission of the novelistic narrative is consistent with the representation of a stereotyped martyr (Figure 2) and quite different from that found in the *Flos Sanctorum* of 1513 (Figure 3). Only in the case of Christopher there is an inconsistency between text and image. The explanation is probably of a practical nature and alien to the compiler of the texts. António de Mariz, the printer, will have used xylographic resources whose analysis deserves a detailed study but which seem to conform to a traditional iconography, unconcerned with the Tridentine requirements.[120]

---

[118] ROSÁRIO, *Historia, op. cit.*, II, 66b. "History of the martyrdom of the blessed Saint Christopher according to Saint Antoninus in the i. part of Vincent's *Speculum historiale* and the *Breviary of Évora*". Belovacense's claim intermediated by Antoninus must be considered.

[119] ROSÁRIO, *Historia, op. cit.*, II, 67b "Many other things are written on this blessed holy martyr but, because they seem apocryphal, they were left behind".

[120] The inconsistency between image and text is not new in the practices of hagiography printers; see other cases, pre-Tridentine, in Fernando BAÑOS VALLEJO, "La transformación del flos sanctorum castellano en la imprenta", *Vides medievals de sants: difusió, tradició i llegenda*, ed. by Marinela Garcia Sempere and M. Àngels Llorca Tonda, Alacant: Institut Interuniversitari de Filologia Valenciana, 2012, pp. 65–97 (pp. 84–85, 87).

Two other cases of classification of the narrative material as apocryphal are also worth noting, both registered in the Pseudo-Gelasian Decree. They give rise to a critical note that justifies the omission of the texts and in both cases the critical note is translated from Antoninus:

> A historia ecclesiastica diz que foy ele mandado a sarar a el rey Abagaro, e acha se hũa epistola d'el rey Agabaro, a Jesu mandada antes de sua paixam, e a reposta de Jesu pera ele mas como quer que estas epistolas sam apocriphas polo capitolo sancta Romana ecclesia, distinçam quinze, por tanto as deixamos de referir.[121]

> Muitas outras cousas insignes se contam do glorioso sam Clemente no liuro que se chama Itinerario de Pedro, mas como quer que aquele liuro se poem entre os apocrifos no capitolo sancta Romana ecclesia, as nam pus aqui.[122]

> Et vt dicitur in histo. eccle. hic missus fuit as Abgarum regem Edessenae ciuitatis sanandum, cuius epistola scilicet Abgari missa ad Christum ante passionem reperitur. Et responsio Iesu ad eum. Sed quia inter apocripha huiusmodi epistolae connumerantur . distinct. 15. sancta Romana, ideo eas referre omittimus.[123]

> Sed ad Clementis gesta redeundo de conuersione eius et parentibus ac fratribus recognitis multa nobilia referentur in lib. qui dicitur Itinerarium Petri, qui liber quia inter apocriphas scripturas connumeratur distin. 15. sancta romana...[124]

Thus, it seems that Rosário fulfilled the Tridentine program regarding the expurgation of apocryphal material[125] and for that he counted on the work previously done by Antoninus, where he also found critical notes ready to be translated. Although his position seems to be more rigorous, as in the case of Saint Christopher, in which he omits the macro-sequence that Antoninus accepts despite considering it apocryphal, such rigor is not systematic, as we can see in the legend of Saint Margaret of Antioch, where the critical note

---

[121] Life of Simon and Jude, ROSÁRIO, *Historia, op. cit.*, II, 174d. "Ecclesiastical history says that he was ordered to heal King Abgar and an epistle of King Abgar to Jesus was found, sent before his passion, and Jesus' response to him, but as these epistles are apocryphal according to the chapter *sancta Romana ecclesia*, distinction fifteen, so we stop mentioning them".

[122] Life of pope Clement, ROSÁRIO, *Historia, op. cit.*, II, 193b. "Many other remarkable things are told of the glorious Saint Clement in the book called Itinerary of Peter, but as that book is considered apocryphal in the chapter *sancta Romana ecclesia*, I did not put them here".

[123] ANTONINUS, *Historiarum, op. cit.*, I, p. 414.

[124] ANTONINUS, *Historiarum, op. cit.*, I, p. 458.

[125] This behaviour is coherent with other post-tridentine Iberian hagiographers, such as Villegas and Ribadeneira (see Fernando BAÑOS Vallejo, "Lanzarían grandes carcajadas': lo apócrifo del "flos sanctorum" y la burla de los protestantes", *Rilce*, 36. 2 (2020), 428–52).

translated from Antoninus did not prevent accepting in the narrative the element considered apocryphal, the martyr's victory over the devilish dragon: "Mas nota pio leitor que isto que se diz do drago, diz Jacobo de Boragine ser apochripho.[126]

It should be highlighted something I have already pointed out: Rosário's critical discourse is mediated by sources considered credible, which he reproduces in general, with few exceptions. Among them, Antoninus stands out, but Jacobus de Voragine is also worth mentioning. There is no doubt that Rosário carefully consulted his sources and collected from them everything that could give credibility to his own legendary. Does this mean that in the *Historia das vidas dos santos* there are no apocryphal texts? Not at all. We have already seen that in the Life of Saint Andrew the apocryphal Acts were used indirectly. The same could be said for other apostles. There we also find the Life of Saint Anne,[127] as it appears in the apocryphal *Book of the Nativity of Mary*,[128] an abridgement and rewriting of the also apocryphal *Gospel of Pseudo-Matthew*,[129] prefaced by the apocryphal letters exchanged between the bishops Chromatius and Heliodorus and Saint Jerome, where the first two ask the latter to translate from the Hebrew an authentic book on the life of Mary that can restore the truth versus what is found in the apocrypha. In fact, these two letters are nothing more than a credibility strategy for *Pseudo-Matthew*, necessary after the use of the apocryphal text of the second century by Manicheans and Priscillians and the consequent ban by the Pope. For this reason, the *Pseudo-Matthew*'s translator writes the two preface letters to protect his text from this discredit.[130] Anne is not in the *corpus* of Jacobus de Voragine but her life, preceded by the description of the so-called *"sancta parentela"* (the three marriages of Saint Anne and her descendants), is included in chapter 122, on the birth of the Virgin. Antoninus follows him closely and provides the same information.[131] But none of these sources has the letters from Chromatius and Heliodorus, so Rosário must have used directly the apocryphal *Book of the Nativity of Mary*, attributed to Saint Jerome.

---

[126] ROSÁRIO, *Historia, op. cit.*, II, 49a. "But note, pious reader, that what is said about the dragon, Jacobo de Boragine says it is apocryphal". See ANTONINUS, *Historiarum, op. cit.*, I, p. 556: "Hoc tamen de dracone Iacobus de Voragine dicit apocryphum".
[127] ROSÁRIO, *Historia, op. cit.*, II, 64c–66b.
[128] Aurelio de SANTOS OTERO, *Los Evangelios Apócrifos*, Madrid: La Editorial Catolica, 1991, pp. 237–52.
[129] SANTOS OTERO, *Los Evangelios Apócrifos, op. cit.*, pp. 173–236.
[130] Kathleen ASHLEY, Pamela SHEINGORN, "Introduction", in *Interpreting Cultural Symbols. Saint Anne in Late Medieval Society*, Athens and London: The University of Georgia Press, 1990, pp. 1–68 (p. 10).
[131] ANTONINUS, *Historiarum, op. cit.*, I, pp. 193–95.

He had no source to classify it as apocryphal and, on the contrary, found in it some paragraphs critical of the apocrypha, which he had no reason to suspect and which was very much in line with his Tridentine guidelines.

4. *The Pastoral Discourse*

As part of the certifying discourse present in the Life of Bishop Saint Nicholas, analyzed above, we found Rosário's original discourse, directed to the pedagogical orientation of readers. We had already seen it in the treatment of the sources of the Life of Saint Ildefonsus and in the rewriting of the Life of Saint Mary Magdalene mentioned above. There are few times when the Dominican compiler moves away from his sources: he always seems to do so in order to assume a pastoral discourse about the customs and the correct religious experience of the faithful and also to legitimize traditional narrative elements that may conflict with issues of ecclesiastical discipline that were under discussion at Trent. This is also the case with the episcopal election of Saint Nicholas.

This election constitutes a problem. It did choose the bishop by revelation (of one of the suffragan bishops) and also elected a layman as Nicholas, what was contrary to one of the most important concerns of the council fathers, for whom the education and scrutiny of the bishops was one of their basic aspects of Catholic reform. The canonical question is solved by Rosário reproducing a critical note that he found in Antoninus:

> Ser de leygo subitamente electo em Bispo (defendendo o o direito) foy por especial instincto e reuelação do Spirito sancto (como se diz dist. 61.§. huius omnibus in gloss.).[132]

As for the problem of election by revelation, it could not be concealed, not least because it constitutes the justification for the election of a layman given in the critical excursus. The solution was to balance the traditional data with an original narrative element, which is not found in any of the sources, all directly or indirectly dependent on Beauvais:[133]

> E assi no mesmo dia que foy collocado na cathedra Episcopal, disse a sy mesmo, Este dia Nicolau, e este lugar outros costumes demanda: ja nam

---

[132] Rosário, *Historia, op. cit.*, I, 17b. "Being a layman suddenly elected to be a bishop (when the law forbids it) was done by special instinct and revelation of the Holy Spirit (as said in dist. 61.§. Huius omnibus in gloss)". See Antoninus, *Historiarum, op. cit.*, II, p. 16: "Quod autem ex laico fuerit subito electus in episcopum, cum hoc iure prohibeatur, fuit ex speciali instinctu et reuelatione spiritus sancti, vt dicitur dist. 61.§. his omnibus. in gloss".

[133] Beauvais, *Speculum, op. cit.*, liv. 13, chap. 69, p. 168; see Natali, *Catalogus, op. cit.*, 6b, Rota, *Opus aureum, op. cit.*, 4ᵛ, Antoninus, *Historiarum, op. cit.*, II, p. 16.

pera ti, mas pera os outros has de viuer. Uerdade he que viuer pera os outros, he muito mais [que] viver pera ti.[134]

Although he had not been subject to the training required for the function, in this monologue it is revealed that Nicholas was aware of the importance and the demand of what was required of him and that at this moment an interior conversion took place that was symbolically comparable to canonical ordering. In this way, Rosário reshapes one of the most widespread legends in Western Christianity, reinterpreting the traditional data without questioning it but orienting it towards the instruction of the faithful, as Trent required.

5. Conclusions

The analysis of these critical excursus present in the legendary of Diogo do Rosário confirmed the conclusions that had already been found in previous analyses. There are some rhetorical strategies utilized to offer credibility to this legendary, clearly distinguishing it from the "stories of the lives of saints" that were printed in vernacular, that contained "some very uncertain and apocryphal things written in them", and that Rosário proposes to amend in the light of the guidelines issued by the Council of Trent.

The first of these strategies is the declaration of the sources used, which can be seen as a sign of his desire for critical analysis. The promise is, however, disappointing, since the simple declaration of the sources does not hide the insufficiency of good criteria in their selection or of rigor in the rightly attributing the texts to the sources mentioned. The second strategy is the use of excursus to analyze concrete cases of something that could be the subject of larger discussions and, by resolving these doubts, to imply that, where problems are not pointed out, it is because there are no problems, that is, the absence of critical excursus means unanimity, factuality and genuineness of the narratives. Thus, the register of divergences between the sources and the resolution of those divergences, the certification discourse and the classification as apocryphal of the narrative material that is omitted and also, although less frequently, of some accepted narrative elements, all have an eminently rhetorical value.

As we have seen, the content of these excursus almost always comes from the sources, mostly from the *Historiarum* by Saint Antoninus, which is by far the source that offers them most abundantly. But Jacobus de Voragine already introduced them frequently, as is well known. This means that there

---

[134] Rosário, *Historia, op. cit.*, I, 17b. "And on the same day that he was placed in the episcopal chair, he said to himself: This day, Nicholas, and this place demand other customs, you will live no longer for you but for others. It is true that living for others is much more than living for you".

is, truly, nothing new in Diogo do Rosário's method and that he can be just considered another link in the Dominican hagiographic "chaîne de transmission" mentioned by Maggioni.

To be fair to the collaborator of Friar Bartolomeu dos Mártires, however, we must emphasize the difference between the medieval Dominican hagiographers who wrote in Latin, such as those that Rosário used as sources, and what he called "histories of the lives of saints that are printed in vernacular", referring, without a doubt, to the *Flos Sanctorum* of 1513, which belongs to the group of translations into vernacular languages of the *Legenda Aurea* that progressively moved away from its Latin model, eliminating many references to sources and a good part of the critical notes of the Genoese. Rosário's task, therefore, was not to amend the medieval Dominican sources, which since the thirteenth century had sought good methods for ascertaining the truth, but to amend the works that had in the meantime distorted these sources.

We should however offer this remark: more than a hundred years after Lorenzo Valla demonstrated, with linguistic and philological arguments, the forgery of the *Donatio Constantini*, more than a hundred years after Leonardo Bruni's *History of the Florentine People*, the same year that, in Portugal, the humanist Damião de Góis[135] published, with a critical spirit, his *Chronicles*,[136] could we not expect, in 1567, a little more from Diogo do Rosário?

For a work that includes 988 printed pages and 223 hagiographic narratives, the compiler cannot be required to undertake his own research, based on archival or material documentation (as André de Resende did for some saints), especially for such a short work period (this legendary was printed only three years after the end of the Council of Trent). It remained for him to rely on carefully chosen sources. On the other hand, for the small set of 14 texts on Portuguese saints (Anthony of Lisbon, Pope Damasus,[137] Fructuo-

---

[135] Damião de Góis (1502–1574) was a Portuguese humanist who acquired his training at the universities of Padua and Louvain and who corresponded with leading figures of his time, especially Erasmus of Rotterdam (Justino Mendes de ALMEIDA, "Projecção europeia de Damião de Góis", in *Damião de Góis na Europa do Renascimento*, Braga: Universidade Católica Portuguesa, 2003, pp. 525–31).

[136] In *Crónica do Príncipe D. João* (Lisboa: Francisco Correa, 1567), he discusses the demands of historiographical work and maintains a permanent critical rigor, relying on documentation, seriously discussing divergences between sources and calling into question, with realistic reasons, divine inspiration as a motivation for the action of kings. See Manuela MENDONÇA, "Crónica do Príncipe D. João", in *Damião de Góis e o seu tempo (1502–1574)*, Lisboa: Academia das Ciências, 2002, pp. 161–93 (pp. 162, 164, 168, 170, 175–76).

[137] Portuguese naturalness is attributed to Pope Damasus I by André de Resende in the *Breviary of Évora* of 1548 ("natione hispano patria Vimaranensis ex Bracarensi prouincia", col. 837), from where the Breviary of Braga of 1549 took it, that is the "breuiario Bracarense" pointed out as source by Rosário (*Historia, op. cit.*, I, 27).

sus of Braga, Gerald of Braga, Gonçalo of Amarante, Iria, Isabel of Portugal, Martyrs of Morocco, Martin of Braga, Peter of Rates, Theotonius, Verissimus and his sisters Maxima and Julia, Vincent and his sisters Sabina and Christeta, Victor of Braga), he could be expected to undertake more research. It should be said, in defense of Rosário, that the temporal distance from the events narrated made it very difficult to quickly access sources that could serve to clarify the lives of martyrs of late Antiquity or medieval times. Finally, we could pay attention to the closing of the critical note on the life of Saint Lawrence, where the identity of Emperor Decius was discussed:

> Outras opiniões ha y acerca de quem foy este Decio que por breuidade deixo, e por nam releuar a deuaçam que ao sancto martyr se deue.[138]

The new hagiographic compilation intends to be a *History*, that is to say a true story, but it is not a scholastic or academic work, nor even a book of profane history. It is, first of all, a book of devotion for the laity, for all those who read in Portuguese and not in Latin, a book where excessive critical discussions would introduce noise into effective communication with the faithful, in the presentation of the saints as genuine models of behavior that should ignite the faith and stir up devotion. This is, after all, the main Tridentine concern: the proper direction of the pastoral discourse towards the salvation of souls. And it is in the fulfillment of this objective that we must judge the action of Diogo do Rosário, since it is also within the scope of this pastoral discourse that his contribution proved to be original, rewriting in this sense, more extensively or paying attention to some concrete facts, some lives of saints. Thus, the legendary of 1567 contributes to the two main achievements of the post-Tridentine Reformation mentioned by Bireley, that is confirming and clarifying knowledge about the saints, using them in the service of the "renewed pastoral program that placed the Bishop and the parish Priest at the center of the church's mission".

---

[138] ROSÁRIO, *Historia, op. cit.*, II, 90b. "There are other opinions about who this Decius was that I omit for brevity and in order to not diminish the devotion that is due to the holy martyr".

Abstracts

María José VEGA, "*Mediator Unus*: The Intercession of Saints in the Expurgated Bibles of the *Censura Generalis* (1554)"

María José Vega discusses the controversy surrounding the intercession of the saints in the first half of the sixteenth century (1517–1554) and, above all, its impact on the interpretation of the Bible. She thus deals with the theological bases of worship, which sustain and legitimise both Catholic social practices and hagiographic discourse, and examines the paradoxes and contradictions found in treatises in defence of the saints. Catholic polemicists and heresiologists shared the common purpose of building a repository of biblical places in relation to the saints to counter the Reformers' powerful *ex silentio Scriptura* argument, and to manage the possible interpretations given to a series of New Testament passages that explicitly identified Christ as the only mediator between God and men. The article first examines the cumulative construction of this new (Catholic) pathway for reading the Bible, and describes the coincidences and nuances between European and Spanish Catholic theologians, notably Alfonso de Castro. Vega then analyses censorship by the Inquisition of printed Bibles (*Censura generalis*, 1554) to eliminate any dissident or Lutheran interpretations regarding saintly mediation that can be found in summaries and margins. The analysis highlights both the parallels and the differences in the censorship decreed by the Universities of Louvain, Paris, Salamanca and Alcalá.

Fernando BAÑOS VALLEJO, "Villegas' Deviation in the Compositional Criteria of his *Flos sanctorum*"

Fernando Baños examines the consistency of the criteria adopted by the most representative "counter-reformist" hagiographer in the Spanish language, Alonso de Villegas. In 1578 he published the first part of his *Flos sanctorum*, which he describes as "reformed", that is, carried out 'according to the Catholic reform', and "conformed to the Roman Breviary". From the outset, the first volume showed certain contradictions, but to fully illustrate the extent of Villegas' deviation from his own initial criteria, Baños compares his preliminary statements in the First part of the *Flos sanctorum* to those in the Third part (1588), and examines the main section of the latter, which features saints not present in the Roman Breviary. What is truly shocking is that the Third part contains an extra section listing characters who were not canonized, but who, according to Villegas, are "illustrious in virtue". The most striking case is that Villegas presents the assassin of the Prince of Orange as a new martyr. Baños also considers seven other lay characters who were not canonised at that time. Despite Villegas' deviation from his initial criteria, he maintains the basic Catholic principle and opposed to the Protestant position: all these lives are examples that salvation is earned through good works and constant struggle.

José ARAGÜÉS ALDAZ, "Holy Folly and *Simplicitas* during the Counter-Reformation. A Context for Lope de Vega's *El rústico del cielo*"

The play studied is Lope de Vega's *El rústico del cielo*, whose protagonist is the discalced Carmelite Fr. Francisco del Niño Jesús. Aragüés analyses this work in the context of other similar writings by the playwright and the general context of the theme of holy folly and sacred simplicity in the Counter-Reformation, during which the concepts of humility and obedience acquired new connotations due to the religious controversies. After reviewing the texts that the playwright dedicates to holy fools and holy simpletons, Aragüés delves into the most significant features of *El rústico del cielo*, which concern the plot and the characterisation of the protagonist, whom Lope met personally. Lope accentuates the rusticity of the character and opposes it to the vanity of wisdom, represented by the university students of Alcalá and the allegorical characters of Pride and the Demon. The reading that Aragüés offers us, and its connection with other works on the same subject, shows that such texts are a counter-reformist promotion of the virtues of obedience, self-denial and self-humiliation, and the acceptance of the mysteries of faith, that is, a reaffirmation of a tradition that goes back to the story of the Passion and Paul's own reflections on the "folly of the cross".

Natalia FERNÁNDEZ RODRÍGUEZ, "Hagiographical Theater and Counter-Reformation: Between Baroque Aesthetics and *Arte Nuevo*"

The study by Natalia Fernández analyses the combination of components in the *comedia nueva* with elements that are in line with the counter-reformist ideology. She uses a comparative method whereby in order to assess the presence of post-Tridentine religious ideas in Castilian hagiographic theater, she compares three works dedicated to Saint Jerome, Saint Augustine and Saint Anthony of Padua from the last third of the sixteenth century with six more works from the following century which were also dedicated to these saints, and which by then formed part of the *comedia nueva* sub-genre, the *comedia de santos*. One of the aspects common to the works from both centuries is the iconic representation of the saints. The cult of the saints, reaffirmed at Trent, had acquired during the Middle Ages a sensory dimension, in particular through images, whose veneration is also reaffirmed at the council. The other issue that Fernández studies comparatively is the addition of profane elements that do not come from hagiographic sources, but which are added to satisfy the tastes of the spectators, namely plots involving gallantry and love, humour, conflicts of jealousy and honour, etc., which created the mixture of the sacred and the profane that is so characteristic of hagiographic theater.

Alicia MAYER, "*Delendus est Lutherus*: The Triumph of the Saints and the Virgin Mary over Heresy in New Spain's Imagery"

Mayer pays her attention here to the Mexico of the Modern Age and the connections between the popular devotions and the configuration of an image of Luther that represents heresy, error and evil. Mayer takes texts from the sixteenth to eighteenth centuries that allude to Luther and in opposition to the saints and the Virgin, and relates these texts to paintings and sculptures on the same theme and the so-called "Triumphs of the Church", which follow European models. In some of these paintings Luther's image is used as a representation of the defeat of evil and heresy. Other iconographies of the power of Catholicism over its enemies are related to some medieval saints or to the Society of Jesus and the Carmelite Order. All of these follow European models, but are adapted to the American context; in contrast, a synthesis of attributes from Mary and the woman of the Apocalypse combined with native American elements led to the image of the Virgin of Guadalupe, who also came to be praised in sermons as the guardian of Mexico against Protestant infection, and whose images, quite deliberately, associate her with the protector Archangel Michael.

Marcos CORTÉS GUADARRAMA, "The Evolution of the Figure of St Michael the Archangel: From Medieval *Flos sanctorum* to New Spain's Hagiography (ca. 1480–1692)"

Taking as a starting point Archangel Michael's depiction as a warrior, which symbolises the struggle between good and evil, and, specifically, the triumph over the devil, Cortés's article shows that in America the primary purpose behind the defence of Catholicism was to do away with and replace the pre-Hispanic religions. A significant example is the official nature given to the local cult of Saint Miguel del Milagro, the most complete account of whom can be found in the *Narración de la maravillosa aparición que hizo el arcángel san Miguel a Diego Lázaro de San Francisco* (Seville, 1692), by the Creole Jesuit Francisco de Florencia. According to this account, Archangel Michael appeared before a virtuous indigenous person, a fact that connects this narrative with the apparitions of the Virgen de Guadalupe and the Virgen de los Remedios, the most important Marian invocations in Mexico. In conclusion, if in Europe the times of the Counter-Reformation led to Archangel Michael to be seen as a defender against the Protestants, in New Spain, a place largely free from such a threat, his role is increasingly diluted and he is instead appropriated through local miracles, just like the Virgin Mary.

Carme ARRONIS LLOPIS, "Catalan Lives of Saints after Trent (1575–1602)"

Carme Arronis examines the first hagiographic samples to emerge in Catalan after the closure of Trent and tries to elucidate what specific changes were applied to the stories, and what were the intentions of the compilers of the new books of saints. She reviews three texts: the latest edition of the *Flos sanctorum romançat* (1575), which is a translation of the medieval *Legenda aurea* of Jacobus de Voragine, and the first two compilations of reformed hagiography, namely the handwritten notes of the Jesuit Pere Gil, known as *Vides de sants de Catalunya*; and the compilation by the Dominican Antoni Vicenç Domènec, *Historia general de los santos y varones ilustres en santidad del Principado de Cataluña* (1602). These three texts show strategies aimed at adapting the book of saints to post-Tridentine sensitivities, and the two new compilations allow us to appreciate the discursive efforts of the first post-Tridentine hagiographers to legitimise local devotions, trying to fit them in with the demands of authority and historicity that characterized the Church of the Counter-Reformation, in such a way that these works would help to refute Protestant criticism.

Cristina SOBRAL, "*Nota, pio leitor...*: The Hagiographical Critical Discourse in 1567"

Cristina Sobral devotes her study to the main example of post-Tridentine Portuguese hagiography, the *Historia das vidas e feitos heróicos e obras insignes dos sanctos* (1567), by the Dominican Diogo do Rosário. It is the first Iberian reformed book of saints, that is to say, derived from Tridentine stipulations and thus ruled by a new moral and historical accuracy and purged of any kind of falsehood such as those denounced by Protestantism. On this occasion Sobral analyses the points at which the author suspends the narrative to address the reader with critical considerations about the apocryphal nature of the subject matter, or to discuss the divergence of sources that sometimes leads the author to justify his choices, or to use a form of certification to support the authenticity of certain miracles that could be considered fabulous. When compared to medieval Iberian books of saints, Rosário's is characterised by the rewriting of some narratives to emphasise the saints' pastoral qualities and exemplary virtues for the faithful. His work is a balance, on one hand, between rhetorical strategies that seek credibility and imply erudition and, on the other, an accessible text in the vernacular that serves the pastoral objective of presenting models of holiness to the faithful.

INDEX

Index of Saints, Persons and Places

Abgar (king): 245 (n. 121)
Achaia (Greece): 225
Acosta, José de: 173-175, 179, 199 (n. 27)
Adam: 76, 85, 86, 194
Adam of Vienna: 219
Afonso Henriques (king of Portugal): 227
Ajofrín, María de: 71
Albano (Armenia): 237 (n. 93)
Alcalá de Henares: 10, 13, 24, 41, 48, 90-92, 98
Alciati, Andrea: 143
Alcobaça: 231
Alexandria: 58 (n. 22)
Alexis, St: 168
Algarve: 227
Alicante: 129
Amalfi (Italy): 226
Ambrose, St: 85, 149, 229
America: 8, 9, 15, 23, 133, 134, 138, 139, 141-143, 153, 157, 160, 161
Anastasius of Lleida, St: 208 (n. 65)
Andrew of Constantinople: 78
Andrew, St: 225, 226, 246
Anne, St: 246
Anterus (Pope): 235 (n. 86)
Anthony of Padua, or of Lisbon, St: 13, 94, 104, 105 (n. 10), 106, 109, 110 (n. 24), 113, 116, 117, 118, 119 (n. 54), 121, 122, 249
Anthony or Antoninus of Florence, St: 18, 210, 211, 220, 221, 223-239, 241, 243-248
Anthony, St: 94
Antichrist: 164
Antonio de Córdoba: 46, 48
Antwerp: 35, 38 (n. 39), 41
Anunciación, María de la: 71
Apocalypse, Woman of the: 153, 154, 158
Apollonia, St: 223

Aquinas, Thomas, St: 15, 35, 83, 150, 151, 194, 241
Aragon: 199 (n. 24)
Arca, Giovanni: 198, 199 (n. 27)
Archangel Michael: see Michael, Archangel
Argüello, Manuel: 157 (n. 87)
Aristotle: 150
Arius: 145, 148, 149, 151
Arlegui, José: 157 (n. 90)
Armenia: 237 (n. 93)
Asturias: 201 (n. 34)
Athanasius, St: 231 (n. 71)
Attila: 235
Augsburg: 81
Augustine, St: 13, 63, 104, 108, 109, 111, 115, 120, 124, 227 (n. 59), 229, 241
Ávila: 90

Bagès, Damià: 196 (n. 16)
Balli, Pedro: 128 (n. 3)
Barbara, St: 223, 224
Barcelona: 17, 190 (n.3), 191-193, 196, 197 (n. 18), 198-200, 203 (n. 43), 205, 206-208, 210, 211, 213
Baronio, Cesare: 60, 191, 210, 211
Bartholomew of Trent: 18, 217, 218
Bartholomew, St: 237, 238, 244
Baruch: 76 (n. 2)
Basel: 38 (n. 39), 41
Basil of Moscow: 78
Basil, St: 102 (n. 3), 193 (n. 10)
Beatriz, princess: 63
Beauvais, Vincent of: 18, 210, 211, 217, 218, 220, 221, 226, 228, 233, 243, 247
Beirut: 55
Benavente, Toribio de ("Motolinía"): 163, 173

INDEX OF SAINTS, PERSONS AND PLACES

Benedict of Palermo: 89
Benno (bishop of Meissen): 25 (n. 9)
Bernard of Clairvaux: 79, 219
Bernard of Luxemburg: 35
Bertonio, Ludovico: 174
Bertrand, St: 193 (n. 10)
Beza, Theodore: 148-149
Bolena, Ana: 183
Bonaventure, St: 194
Bora, Katherine von: 146
Borja, Francis of, St: 141, 199 (n. 24)
Borromeu, Carlos: 216
Botero, Giovanni: 200 (n. 28)
Bourg-en-Bresse, Simon de: 84 (n. 30)
Brabant: 38
Braga: 193 (n. 11), 216, 222, 229
Brittany: 83
Bruni, Leonardo: 220 (note 24), 249
Brutus: 87
Bucer, Martin: 27, 157
Bullinger, Heinrich: 28 (n. 21), 30 (n. 24)
Buñuel, Luis: 58 (n. 23)
Burgos: 166 (n. 15)
Burgundy: 65
Byzantium: 78, 81

Cabrera, Miguel: 143, 144, 145
Caçador, Guillem: 191
Cajetan, Tommaso de Vio: 30, 34 (n. 32), 36
Calaf: 210
Calamanda, Virgin, St: 210
Calderón de la Barca, Pedro: 119 (n. 55)
Calderón, Bernardo: 164, 178
Callixtus II (Pope): 231, 232 (n. 77)
Calpulalpan: 151
Calvin, John: 26, 27, 28 (n. 20), 134, 147-149, 155-157, 159, 183
Canary Islands: 90
Canfield, Benoît de: 84 (n. 30)
Cano, Melchor: 35
Carducho, Vicente: 138
Carmel (Mount): 146
Cassiodorus: 241
Castellion, Sebastian: 42 (n. 47)
Castile: 36, 39 (n. 42), 146, 152, 201 (n. 34)

Castorena y Ursúa, Juan de: 157, 158
Castro, Alfonso de: 10, 35-37, 45, 46 (n. 49), 48
Catalonia, Principality of: 191, 197 (n. 18), 200, 201 (n. 34), 204, 205, 209 (n. 67), 210, 213
Catarino, Ambrogio: 30
Catholic Monarchs (Isabella and Ferdinand): 133
Cecilius, St: 231 (n. 71)
Celano, Thomas of: 86
Celaya: 147
Cendrat, Jaume: 190, 192, 196
Cervantes, Gaspar de: 192
Cervantes, Miguel de: 80, 82, 93 (n. 57)
Charlemagne: 212
Charles V (King of Spain / Emperor of Germany): 36, 38, 133, 144
Christ: see Jesus Christ
Christeta, St: see Vincent, Sabina and Christeta, Saints
Christina or Christine, St: 165, 223, 238
Christopher, St: 242-245
Chromatius (bishop): 246
Clavijo: 177
Clement (Pope), St: 203, 236, 245 (n. 122)
Cletus (Pope): 236
Clichtove or Clichtoveus, Jodocus: 10, 29-32, 34, 37, 46 (n. 49)
Climacus, John: 81, 86, 87
Cochlaeus, Johannes: 10, 29, 30, 32, 36, 158
Coimbra: 222
Coll, Pere: 17, 193, 195, 207
Cologne: 198, 234, 235
Colombini, Giovanni: 79-80
Constantine (Emperor): 225 (n. 47), 226 (n. 55)
Constantinople: 58 (n. 22), 225, 226
Cortés, Hernán: 133
Cotlliure: 204
Cruz, Marina de la: 183
Cruz, Sor Juana Inés de la: 144, 145
Cruz, Sor Philotea de la: 145
Cucuphas, St: 208 (n. 65)
Cuéllar, Ana de: 63
Cuenca: 143

INDEX OF SAINTS, PERSONS AND PLACES

Cyprian (bishop of Carthage), St: 67, 69, 236
Cyprian, St: see Justina and Cyprian, Saints
Cyriacus (Pope): 235 (n. 86)
Cyriacus, St: 233
Cyricus and Julitta, Saints: 55, 56, 241

Damascene, John: 102 (n. 3)
Damasus (Pope), St: 107, 249
Damian, Peter: 86
Dandolo, Andrea: 222
Daniel of Alexandria: 78
Daniel: 76 (n. 2), 86
David: 84, 87, 92, 99
Decius (emperor): 234, 236 (n. 89)
Delft: 68
Diego de Alcalá, St: 90, 92
Diego Lázaro de San Francisco: 16
Dietenberger, Johannes: 29 (n. 23)
Dimes Lloris, Joan: 192 (n. 8), 198, 199 (n. 24), 205
Diocletian (Emperor): 233 (n. 79), 234, 236
Domènec, Antoni Vicenç: 17, 196, 201 (n. 34), 206-210, 211 (n. 75), 212-214
Domna and Indes: 88, 89
Dorotheus, St: 237 (n. 93)
Drucbicki, Gaspar: 83
Dürer, Albrecht: 155, 158

Echave Rioja, Baltasar de: 141, 148
Eck or Eckius, Johannes: 10, 29, 30, 32-34, 35 (n. 34), 36, 37
Egeas (proconsul of Achaia): 225
Egypt: 77, 80, 95, 97
Eiximenis, Francesc: 166
Eleazar: 66, 68, 69
Eleven Thousand Virgins: 234
Elijah (prophet): 146
Elmo, St: 193 (n. 10)
Emesa: 78
Empúries: 204
Encarnación, Isabel de la: 180
England: 202, 209
Enríquez de Ribera, Payo: 182
Epiphanius: 35 (n. 34), 240, 241
Equilio: 221

Erasmus of Rotterdam: 8, 26, 28 (n. 20), 57, 80-82, 249 (n. 135)
Ermengol of Urgell, St: 208 (n. 65)
Escotus: 194
Escudero, Francisco: 63
Estienne, Robert: 10, 38 (n. 39), 41, 47-48
Eufrasius, St: 232 (n. 71)
Eugenio, father of María, Marina, Marinus: 58
Eulalia of Barcelona, St: 197, 208 (n. 65)
Euphrosyne: 57, 58
Europe: 7, 8, 16, 21, 23, 35, 133, 134, 137-139, 141, 143, 153, 156-158, 160, 161, 191, 196-198
Eustache, St: 168
Eutolmius: 236
Évora: 217, 221

Fajardo y Acevedo, Antonio: 13, 104, 105 (n. 10), 117, 122, 123 (n. 62-66), 124 (n. 67)
Felipe (friar): 79
Felix of Girona, St: 208 (n. 65)
Felix, St.: 107
Fernández de Uribe, Patricio: 151, 152 (n. 67), 157, 159
Ferrer, Juan: 119 (n. 57)
Filateo Eusebiano: 225
Fitzsimon, Henry: 198-199
Flanders: 15, 23 (n. 6), 38, 65, 70, 139
Florencia, Francisco de: 16, 127, 132, 153 (n. 75), 164, 178, 179 (n.67), 180-182
Flores, Rodrigo de: 91 (n. 51)
France: 200 (n. 28), 202, 209, 230
Francis of Paola, St: 193 (n. 10)
Francis Xavier, St: 82, 134, 141
Francis, St: 79, 86, 88-91, 97, 116
Freud, Sigmund: 151
Fructuosus of Braga, St: 249-250
Fructuosus of Tarragona, St: 208 (n. 65)

Gabriel, Archangel: 163, 165
Galicia: 201 (n. 34), 231, 232 (n. 78)
Gallienus (Emperor): 234, 236 (n. 89)
Gargano (mount): 166, 175
Gaul: 235
Gelasius I (Pope): 55

261

Geneva: 47
Genovés, Jeroni: 196 (n. 16)
George, St: 55, 223, 242-244
Gerald of Braga, St: 250
Gérard, Balthasar: 11, 65, 66, 68-70
Germany: 15, 23, 29 (n. 23), 30, 134, 139, 141, 161, 202, 209
Gil (friar): 79, 89
Gil, Pere: 17, 196, 198, 199, 201-206, 208-211
Gilberti, Maturino: 15, 164, 167, 168, 174
Girona: 196, 204, 207, 212
God: 10, 16, 22, 25, 28, 29, 31, 33, 34, 45, 46, 48, 50, 55, 58, 59, 61, 63-67, 70, 140 (n. 40), 142 (n. 43), 144, 146, 152, 156, 157
Góis, Damião de: 249
Goldofre, St: 230 (n. 70)
Gómara, Francisco López de: 134
Gonçalo of Amarante, St: 223, 250
Gonçalves, Pero, St: 238, 239
Gonzaga, Francisco: 205
Gonzalez de Bustos, Francisco: 13, 104, 105 (n. 10), 109 (n. 20), 112 (n. 32), 125 (n. 70-72)
Gotard, Hubert: 196 (n. 16)
Granada, Luis de: 72
Great Britain: 157
Greco, El: 11, 63
Greece: 225
Gregory of Tours, St: 210, 211, 226 (n. 57)
Gregory XIII (Pope): 60, 71, 72, 127
Guadalupe, Virgin of: 15, 16
Guanajuato: 144
Guerra y Ribera, Manuel: 103
Guevara, Miguel Tadeo de: 150
Gui, Bernard: 18, 217, 218, 220
Guilloré, François: 83
Guimarães: 217

Habsburgs: 133, 153
Heidelberg: 150
Heisterbach, Caesarius of: 86
Heliodorus (bishop): 246
Henry VIII (King): 64
Herod: 95, 97
Heyden, Sebald: 26 (n. 10)

Hippo: 112
Hispania: 232
Holland: 65, 157
Holy Spirit: 148, 150
Honoratus, St: 193 (n. 10)
Huesca: 229
Huss, Jan: 46 (n. 49), 147
Hydra : 157-159

Iberian Peninsula: 8, 16, 49, 196, 200, 213
Ignatius of Loyola, St: 15, 83, 132, 134, 141, 142, 143, 144, 199 (n. 24)
Ildefonse of Toledo, St: 223, 224, 247
Immaculate Conception: 135, 144, 147, 152, 153
Indalecius, St: 231 (n. 71)
Indes: see Domna and Indes
India: 241
Ireland: 79
Iria, St: 250
Isabel of Portugal, St: 193 (n. 11), 250
Isaiah (prophet): 76 (n. 2)
Isicius, St: 231 (n.71)
Isidore (Tabennesiot nun): 78, 82, 83, 88
Isidore of Rostov: 78
Isidore the Farmer: 89, 92
Italy: 23, 202, 209 (n. 67), 226, 230
Ivo, St: 193 (n. 10)

Jacob: 84
Jacopone da Todi: 79, 82, 88
James the Grater, St: 230-232
Jauregay, Jean: 65
Jehova: 146
Jeremiah (prophet): 76 (n. 2)
Jerome, St: 13, 46 (n. 49), 57, 81, 84, 104, 109, 113, 114, 166, 211, 226, 246
Jerusalem: 76, 149, 232 (n. 78)
Jesus Christ: 10, 11, 12, 22, 25, 26-29, 32 (n. 30), 33 (n. 31), 34, 37, 46, 50, 62, 65, 66, 67, 70-72, 76, 77, 79, 81, 83-88, 90, 94-100, 131, 138, 143, 147-150, 152, 238, 242, 243, 245 (n. 121)
Joan of Arc, St: 11, 61, 63
João (John) Beleth: 231
Job: 59, 76 (n. 2), 84
John Chrysostom, St: 240, 241

INDEX OF SAINTS, PERSONS AND PLACES

John of the Cross, St: 15, 82 (n. 19), 85, 99 (n. 74), 146, 147
John the Simpleton (friar): 79
John, St: 76 (n. 5), 85, 153, 158
Jorba, Dionís Jeroni: 197, 198
José de Jesús María: 91, 95 (n. 64), 96 (n. 66), 98 (n. 70-72)
Juan de Dios, St: 11, 12, 64, 70, 88
Juan Diego, St: 154, 155
Judea: 231 (n.71)
Julia, St: see Verissimus, Maxima and Julia, Saints
Julián de Alcalá, St: 89, 100
Julian the Apostate: 147
Julitta, St: see Cyricus and Julitta, Saints
Juniper (friar): 79, 88, 89
Justina and Cyprian, Saints: 235, 236 (n. 89)
Justus of Urgell, St: 208 (n. 65)
Justus, St (and St Pastor): 94, 95 (n. 64), 193 (n. 10)

Karlstadt or Carsltadt, Andreas Bodenstein von: 26 (n. 11)

Laínez, Diego: 31 (n. 28)
Lallemant, Louis: 83
Lanini Sagredo, Pedro: 13, 104, 105 (n. 10), 109 (n. 20), 112 (n. 32), 125 (n. 70-72)
Lara, Gregorio José de: 158
Lawrence, St: 233, 234, 250
Le Nobletz, Michel: 83
Lefèvre d'Étaples, Jacques: 31 (n. 27)
Leipzig: 32 (n. 30)
León: 201 (n. 34)
Leviathan: 158
Linus (Pope): 236
Lippomano, Luigi: 11, 19, 49, 53, 55, 57, 58, 62, 69, 70, 81, 172, 191, 196, 202, 210, 219, 241, 242 (n. 110)
Lisbon: 12, 71, 227, 229, 230
Lobo, Álvaro: 198
Lonicer, John: 27
López de Haro, Thomás: 164 (n. 4), 181
López de Montoya, Pedro: 72
López, Teresa: 62
Lorenzana y Butrón, Francisco: 157, 158

Louvain: 10, 24, 37, 38-40, 42, 47, 249 (n. 135)
Low Countries: 66
Lucifer: 165, 169
Luke, St: 65, 76 (n 5.), 77 (n. 7-8)
Luther, Martin: 7, 8, 14, 15, 21, 24, 25 (n. 9), 26, 29 (n. 22-23), 30 (n. 26), 31 (n. 27), 32 (n. 30), 36 (n. 35), 46 (n. 49), 48, 49 (n. 1), 54 (n. 12), 57-59, 101, 109, 127-131, 133-139, 141-152, 155, 157-161, 183
Lycia: 242, 243
Lyon: 35, 38 (n. 39), 41, 81 (n. 17), 220

Mabbug, Philoxenus of: 85
Madrid: 97, 98, 141
Maginus of Tarragona, St: 193 (n. 10), 204, 205, 211
Mailly, Jean de: 18, 217, 218
Major, Georg: 57
Manços of Évora, St: 223
Manescal, Onofre: 197 (n. 18), 208
Manresa: 199 (n. 24)
Marcos de Lisboa: 90 (n. 49)
Margaret of Antioch, St: 151 (n. 66), 245
Margarita of Austria: 91, 92, 98
María, Marina, Marinus, daughter of Eugenio: 58
Marieta, Juan de: 206-208
Marina, Marinus: 57, 58
Mariz, António de: 216, 244
Mark of Alexandria: 78, 88
Mark, St: 76 (n. 5)
Martha, St: 223
Martin of Braga, St: 250
Martín, Antón: 64
Mártires, Bartolomeu dos: 18, 193 (n. 11), 216, 217, 219, 249
Martyrs of Morocco, Saints: 250
Mary Magdalene, St: 31 (n. 27), 223, 224
Mary, Virgin: 7, 14-16, 26 (n. 10), 46, 62, 77, 88, 98, 130, 132, 135, 136, 138, 140, 147-149, 151-157, 160, 165, 166, 167 (n. 20), 246
Matrona, St: 193 (n. 10), 197, 208 (n. 65)
Matthew, St: 33, 48, 76 (n. 5), 77 (n. 7), 84 (n. 28), 85 (n. 35)
Maunoir, Julien: 83

INDEX OF SAINTS, PERSONS AND PLACES

Maxima, St: see Verissimus, Maxima and Julia, Saints
Maximian (Emperor): 233, 235 (n. 86)
Maximila (wife of Egeas): 225
Maximilian I (Emperor of Germany): 145
Medusa: 143
Memmi, Lipo: 150
Mendieta, Jerónimo de: 164, 166-167
Mesoamerica: 128, 133, 135, 154, 161
Metaphrast, Symeon: 55 (n. 14), 219, 241, 242 (n. 110)
Metz: 230
Mexico City: 127, 128, 133, 146, 147, 154
Mexico: 14-16, 131, 136, 139, 141, 144, 147, 148, 154, 156, 157, 161
Michael, Archangel: 15, 16, 148, 158, 159, 163-169, 171, 174-177, 180-182
Millán de Poblete, Juan: 156
Molanus, Johannes: 138, 191, 197, 198
Molina, Tirso de: 110 (n. 27)
Montpezada, Eulàlia: 190, 192
Montpezat, Pere de: 190
Mont-Saint-Michel: 166
Montserrat: 199 (n. 24)
Morales, Ambrosio de: 53, 204
More, Thomas, St: 11, 61, 64, 83
Moreno, Alonso: 156
Moschus Eviratus: 81
Muhammad: 149 (n. 56)
Mülhberg: 36
Munich: 81 (n. 17)
Murillo, Bartolomé Esteban: 115 (n. 40)
Myra (Asia Minor): 151

Nacchianti, Jacopo: 30 (n. 25)
Narcissus of Girona, St: 208 (n. 65)
Natali, Peter of, or Natalibus, Petrus de: 211, 221, 222, 240, 241, 243
Nava, José de: 150
Navarra: 201 (n. 34)
Nazarius, St: 210
Néant, Louise de: 83
Neri, Felipe: 83
New Spain: 9, 14-16, 127-134, 137, 141-144, 146 (n. 51), 149, 153-156, 158-160, 163-167, 169, 170, 173, 174, 178, 179, 181-183

Nicholas of Bari, St: 15, 151, 239, 241, 247, 248
Nicolas, Armelle: 83
Nieremberg, Juan Eusebio: 16, 164, 176, 177, 179, 181, 182
Niño Jesús, Francisco del: 12, 90-100
Nycholas of Pskov: 78

Oaxaca: 158
Odile, St: 193 (n. 10)
Oecolampadius, Johannes: 46 (n. 49)
Olegarius, St: 198, 205
Orgaz: 11, 63
Osona: 203 (n. 44)
Ot of Urgell, St: 208 (n. 65)
Otho (Emperor): 230

Pacheco, Francisco: 138, 159
Pacian, St: 197, 198, 205, 208 (n. 65)
Padua: 119 (n. 54), 249 (n. 135)
Palafox y Mendoza, Juan de: 142, 149, 159, 178, 179
Paleoti, Gabriel: 138
Palladius: 81
Palma de Mallorca: 199 (n. 24)
Paris: 10, 31 (n. 27), 35, 38 (n. 39), 41, 46-48
Paschal III, Antipope: 212
Pastor, St: see Justus, St
Patmos Isle (Greece): 153
Patras: 225, 226
Paul (monk): 86, 94
Paul, St.: 12, 13, 25, 27, 28, 34, 42, 45, 47, 77, 79, 80, 82 (n. 19), 86, 100, 109 (n. 21), 200 (n. 30)
Paul, Vincent de, St: 85
Pelagius (heresiarch): 145, 148
Penyafort, Raymond of, St: 198
Pérez de Montalbán, Juan: 13, 104, 105 (n. 10), 106, 110 (n. 25), 116, 117 (n. 47), 121, 122 (n. 60)
Perú: 173
Peter of Capua (Cardinal): 226
Peter of Rates, St: 223, 250
Peter, St: 85, 147-149, 200 (n. 30), 236
Petrarca, Francesco: 222
Philip II: 11, 15, 50, 51, 52, 65, 66, 97, 98, 119, 128, 129, 132-134, 140 (n. 39)

INDEX OF SAINTS, PERSONS AND PLACES

Philip III: 91, 98
Pigghe, Albert: 30, 31 (n. 28), 36
Pilate: 67
Pius V (Pope): 51, 55, 58, 65
Politi, Ambrogio Catarino: see Catarino
Porres, Gaspar de: 90
Porto: 229
Portugal: 23 (n. 6), 198, 201 (n. 34), 216, 231, 249
Prierias, Sylvester: 31 (n. 28)
Procopius of Ustyug: 78
Proculus of Bologna, St: 68-70 (n. 50)
Prudentius: 227, 229
Pseudo-Gelasius: 222, 223, 242 (n. 110), 245
Puebla: 141, 150

Quevedo, Francisco de: 93 (n. 57)
Quiroga, Gaspar de: 72

Rader, Mattäus: 81, 87, 88, 97
Ramon Berenguer IV: 212
Raphael, Archangel: 165
Rebollosa, Jaume: 200 (n. 28)
Regensburg: 36
Remedios, Virgen de los: 16
Resende, André de: 221, 243, 249
Ribadeneira, Pedro de: 15, 50 (n. 1), 54 (n. 13), 55, 57, 81, 90 (n. 49), 117, 142, 164, 175, 176, 182, 196, 203, 206, 245 (n. 125)
Ribera Flores, Dionisio: 128, 132
Ribera, Francisco de: 145
Ripa, Cesare: 143
Roch, St: 198 (n. 19)
Rodríguez Juárez, Nicolás: 147, 148
Romans, Humbert of: 218, 219, 222
Rome: 107, 109, 127, 143, 202
Romuald, St: 79
Rosário, Diogo do: 18, 19, 193 (n. 11), 216-217, 219, 221, 222, 224, 225, 229, 230-240, 243-250
Roses: 204
Rosweyd, Heribert: 81
Rota, Claudius of: 220, 221, 223, 224, 226, 227-229, 231-237, 240, 241, 243
Rubens, Peter Paul: 141, 148

Ruffino (friar): 79
Ruiz de Toledo, Gonzalo: 11, 63, 69
Russia: 78

Sabellius (heresiarch): 149
Sabina, St: see Vincent, Sabina and Christeta, Saints
Saint Peter Basilica (Rome): 143
Saint Vincent Cape: 227
Saint-Samson, Jean de: 84 (n. 30), 85
Saint-Thierry, Guillaume de: 86
Salamanca: 10, 24, 34, 35, 37, 40, 41, 47, 48, 90
Salaunus: 88, 92
Sales, Francis de, St: 84 (n. 30)
Salmerón, Pedro: 164, 180
Samson: 86, 99
San José, Jerónimo de: 99 (n. 74)
Sánchez de la Torre, Juan: 91 (n. 51)
Sandoval, Bernardo de: 72, 194
Santiago, Bárbara de: 62, 63
Santoro, Juan Basilio: 62
Satan (devil: Lucifer): 131, 133, 135, 139, 140, 144, 149, 156
Sattlers, Balthasar: 27 (n. 18)
Schatzgeger, Caspar: 29 (n. 23)
Schmalkald: 28, 36
Sebastian, St: 198 (n. 19)
Secundus, St: 231 (n. 71)
Severus of Barcelona, St: 193 (n. 10), 197, 204 (n. 45), 208 (n. 65)
Severus of Ravenna, St: 204 (n. 45)
Seville: 37 (n. 37), 39, 181
Shakespeare, William: 80
Shepherd of Hermas: 85
Sigismund of Burgundy, St: 192 (n. 8), 193 (n. 10), 211
Sigüenza y Góngora, Carlos de: 182, 183
Simeon of Emesa: 78, 82, 88, 100
Simeon Stylites: 57, 58
Simon and Jude, Saints: 245 (n.121)
Simon, St: 236
Sixtus II (Pope): 234 (n. 82)
Sixtus V (Pope): 23 (n.4), 90
Solon: 87
Soranzo, Vittore: 30 (n. 25)

Spain: 15, 22 (n. 1), 23 (n. 6), 24, 29 (n. 22), 37, 40 (n. 44), 42, 130, 131, 133-135, 138, 139, 140 (n. 39), 143, 146, 149 (n. 56), 153, 156, 157, 161, 177, 200 (n. 30), 202, 204, 206, 211, 229, 230, 231, 239 (n. 99)
Spanish Indies: 129
Stephen, St: 63
Strasbourg: 41
Suárez, Francisco: 159
Surin, Jean: 83
Surius, Laurentius: 11, 19, 49, 53, 54 (n. 13), 55, 57, 58, 62, 68-70, 81, 172, 182, 191, 196, 198, 202, 210, 211,
Syria: 77

Tabennisi: 83
Tarragona: 191, 192, 205
Tenochtitlan: 133, 158
Teodoricus (bishop of Metz): 230
Tepeyac: 154
Teresa, St (of Ávila or de Jesús): 15, 134, 141, 144, 146, 147
Tezcatlipoca: 16, 175, 179
Thanner, Matthias: 82, 87
Thecla of Tarragona, St: 208 (n. 65), 223
Theodoret of Cyrrhus: 35, (n. 34)
Theodorus, St: 231 (n. 71), 237 (n. 93)
Theotonius, St: 250
Thesifon, St: 231 (n. 71)
Thomas, St: see Aquinas
Tianguismanalco (Puebla): 179
Tlatelulco: 166, 167 (n. 17)
Tlaxcala: 178, 180, 181-183
Toledo, Hernando de: 190
Toledo: 37 (n. 37), 38 (n. 40), 62, 196
Tolosa: 239 (n. 99)
Tommaso de Vio: see Cajetan
Torquatus, St: 231 (n. 71), 232
Trent: 10, 13, 14, 16-18, 22, 23 (n. 6), 30, 34, 54, 101, 102, 104, 106, 108, 113 (n. 36), 116, 124, 126, 130, 132-136, 138, 140, 143, 150, 153, 155, 160, 161, 189-192, 213
Trinxer, Francesc: 196 (n. 16)

Ulysses: 87
Uriel, Archangel: 165
Ursula, St: 235 (n. 86)

Usuard: 191, 197

Valadés, Diego: 134
Valderas, Ignacio: 149
Valdés, Fernando de (General Inquisitor): 26 (n. 10), 37 (n. 37), 40 (n. 43)
Valdivielso, José de: 100
Valencia, Martín de: 134
Valencia: 37 (n. 37), 98, 99, 227, 228 (n. 61), 229
Valeriana: 233
Valla, Lorenzo: 249
Valladolid: 37, 39, 40, 105 (n. 11)
Van Dyck, Anton: 115 (n. 40)
Vatican, The: 134, 143
Vega, Lope de: 12, 13, 64, 88-100, 104, 106, 113 (n. 35), 115, 116 (n. 44)
Vega, Pedro de la: 169, 172
Vélez de Guevara, Luis: 100
Venice: 35, 41, 222
Vergerio, Pier Paolo: 30 (n. 25)
Verissimus, Maxima and Julia, Saints: 250
Verona: 191
Verónica: 62
Vic: 203, 205, 212
Victor of Braga, St: 250
Vigilantius: 46 (n. 49)
Viladrau: 212
Villalpando, Cristóbal de: 141, 147, 148
Villegas, Alonso de: 11, 12, 15, 49-66, 68-73, 81, 107, 108, 110 (n. 24), 119 (n. 54), 164, 172, 175, 182, 196, 201 (n. 34), 202, 203, 205-209, 213, 245 (n. 125)
Vincent, Sabina and Christeta, Saints: 250
Vincent, St: 227-230, 234
Vió, Gaspar de: 210 (n. 70)
Virgin Mary: see Mary, Virgin
Virgin of Guadalupe (Extremadura): 152
Virgin of Guadalupe (of Tepeyac: or Tonantzin): 136, 150 (n. 6), 153 (n. 75), 154-159
Virgin of Remedios: 154
Viscay: 65
Visitación, María de la: 11, 62 (n. 30), 71
Vitalis, St: 197

Voragine, Jacobus de: 17, 18, 49, 164, 169, 190, 193, 217-221, 223, 226-229, 233, 234, 235, 237, 241-243, 246, 248
Vos, Martin de: 181

Waldo, Peter: 147
Werboldo (canon): 86
Wesaliensis, Arnoldus: 30
Wierix: 181
William of Nassau, William the Silent, Prince of Orange: 65, 66
Wittenberg: 26 (n. 12), 27 (n. 18)

Worms: 133
Wycliff or Wycliffe, John: 31 (n. 27), 46, 147

Zacatecas: 171
Zachary: 211
Zaragoza: 229 (n. 63)
Zeeland: 65
Zumárraga, Juan de: 155
Zúñiga, Diego de: 34
Zuri-Calday, Santiago de: 182
Zurich: 38 (n. 39)
Zwingli, Ulrich or Huldrych: 26, 27